Immigrant Pupils Learn English

A CEFR-related empirical study of L2 development

Immigrant Pupils Learn English

A CEFR-related empirical study of L2 development

Bronagh Ćatibušić
Research Associate, Centre for Language and Communication Studies,
Trinity College Dublin, Ireland

and

David Little
Associate Professor of Applied Linguistics Emeritus, Trinity College
Dublin, Ireland

CAMBRIDGE
UNIVERSITY PRESS

CAMBRIDGE
UNIVERSITY PRESS

University Printing House, Cambridge CB2 8BS, United Kingdom

Cambridge University Press is part of the University of Cambridge.

It furthers the University's mission by disseminating knowledge in the pursuit of education, learning and research at the highest international levels of excellence.

www.cambridge.org
Information on this title: www.cambridge.org/9781107414563

© Cambridge University Press 2014

First published 2014

Printed in the United Kingdom by Hobbs the Printers Ltd

A catalogue record for this publication is available from the British Library

Library of Congress Cataloguing in Publication data
Catibušic, Bronagh'.
 Immigrant pupils learn English : a CEFR-related empirical study of L2 development / Bronagh' Catibušic, Research Associate, Centre for Language and Communication Studies, Trinity College Dublin, Ireland ; David Little, Associate Professor of Applied Linguistics Emeritus, Trinity College Dublin, Ireland.
  pages cm. -- (English profile studies ; 3)
 Summary: "The Common European Framework of Reference (CEFR) was used to develop guidelines for the provision of English L2 support for newcomer children in Irish primary schools. The guidelines present age-appropriate and domain-specific 'can do' descriptors for the first three levels of the CEFR (A1-B1). This book reports on an in-depth empirical investigation of the English L2 development of 18 primary pupils over the course of one school year. It presents case studies which illustrate the often uncertain progress of pupils' language development, and examines the wide range of variance across the sample. It also provides an analysis of the data as a whole, which reveals a number of regular patterns. The findings confirm that pupils' communicative capacity developed according to the functional trajectory proposed by the guidelines and derived from the CEFR; they also allow us to attach a great deal of linguistic detail to descriptors of underlying linguistic competence"-- Provided by publisher.
 Includes bibliographical references and indexes.
 ISBN 978-1-107-41456-3 (pbk.)
 1. English language--Ireland. 2. English language--Study and teaching. 3. Immigrant children--Education--Ireland. 4. English language--Dialects--Ireland. 5. English language--Variation--Ireland. 6. Ireland--Languages. I. Little, D. G. II. Title.

 PE2401.C56 2014
 372.652'109417--dc23
          2013048158

Contents

Acknowledgements

We are grateful to the principals and English language support teachers of the three schools that provided the data on which this book is based. We would also like to thank the 18 English as an Additional Language pupils who participated in the research and their parents for consenting to their participation.

Bronagh Ćatibušić thanks her husband Mirza and daughters Ayumi, Selma and Leyla for their love and support not only during the writing of this book but through the years of her PhD research.

David Little gratefully acknowledges Barbara Lazenby Simpson's indispensable contribution to the development of support for teachers of English as an Additional Language in Ireland during her years as deputy director of Integrate Ireland Language and Training. He also thanks his wife Jean for her unfailing love and support.

Series Editors' note

We are pleased to introduce the third volume in the *English Profile Studies* series by Bronagh Ćatibušić and David Little: *Immigrant Pupils Learn English: A CEFR-related empirical study of L2 development.*

In keeping with the series in general, this volume reports on an application of the Common European Framework of Reference for Languages (CEFR; Council of Europe 2001) to the teaching and learning of English as an additional language (EAL). In this case the focus is on the Irish educational context and specifically on the developing English language proficiency of immigrant children in primary school. For the first time in this series the empirical research being reported was originally conducted as part of a PhD programme and written up as a doctoral thesis.

Following the publication of the CEFR in 2001, the Council of Europe promoted the development of Reference Level Descriptions (RLDs) for national and regional languages. RLDs represent a new generation of descriptions that identify the specific forms (grammatical and lexical) of a given language at each of the six CEFR reference levels. These language-specific descriptions are designed to be used in setting objectives for learning or to establish whether a user has attained the level of proficiency in question. Since 2005 a team in Cambridge, together with a growing network of collaborators around the world, has been working on the long-term English Profile Programme (EPP) with the goal of developing RLDs for English.

The EPP has placed particular emphasis on empirical research rooted in data (such as learner corpora) and on the study of learner language to explore language development across the reference levels. The publication of the research findings has therefore been a central goal for the EPP and the EP Studies series was in part launched in order to achieve this.

In the first EP Studies volume Hawkins and Filipović (2012) focus on *Criterial Features in L2 English,* bringing together contributions from the EP research teams in a concise and accessible way. The criterial features in the title are: 'the properties of learner English that are characteristic and indicative of L2 proficiency at each of the levels and that distinguish the higher levels from lower levels' (Hawkins and Filipović 2012:11). In other words, the main objective was to report which words and phrases are mastered by learners as they progress in their learning "up the CEFR ladder". The authors also reflected on the reasons why some learners progress more rapidly than others as a result of their individual characteristics, such as their first language and socio-cultural context. This is a point covered in some detail by Ćatibušić and Little in the Irish schools context.

In the second volume, Green (2012) discusses the CEFR's functional approach and its theoretical and empirical origins. He also provides guidance on adapting the 'Can Do' functions in order to set English-specific language learning goals for local contexts and purposes. In compulsory schooling it is the lower levels of the Framework which are of most relevance in setting learning objectives, and it is usually the case that the 'Can Do' approach provided by the CEFR needs to be amended or supplemented in various ways to meet local needs. Again, the current volume provides an interesting example of how this was done for the teaching/learning context in question.

More broadly, the EP Studies series is designed to support and promote work in the field of English language learning, teaching and assessment where the CEFR is being used as the frame of reference, and also to enable the language teaching and testing communities to access research which makes a contribution to these fields but which otherwise might not reach publication. We are particularly pleased therefore to be publishing a volume based on a doctoral research programme and a completed PhD thesis. In this respect we are following the editorial policy for the *Studies in Language Testing* (SiLT) series – also published jointly by Cambridge English and Cambridge University Press.

Since its inception (1995), the SiLT series has published high quality PhDs in accordance with certain criteria which include the following:

- being a contribution to knowledge
- being previously unpublished
- having a sound theoretical basis
- being well-referenced to the literature
- being research-based
- being executed with care and rigour
- demonstrating analysis and interpretation
- having the style of an academic monograph.

As Series Editors we were pleased to receive the manuscript of Bronagh Ćatibušić's PhD thesis, with the full support of her supervisor Professor David Little, and to have the opportunity to review it with these criteria in mind. It became clear that this study did indeed meet the criteria well, but in addition provided the potential for a third volume in the series that would extend the research themes from the earlier volumes in an original way – as noted above.

However, we also felt that a jointly-authored volume, drawing on Little's wide experience as an advisor for the Council of Europe, especially in the development of the European Language Portfolio (ELP), combined with Ćatibušić's micro-level classroom observations would not only make a unique contribution, but would also broaden the relevance of the volume for the readership of this series.

The writing of the volume has been aptly managed by the two authors and shared so that the resulting book is broadly in two parts. Little has mainly contributed to the first two chapters and Ćatibušić to the rest. In the first chapter, the macro-context within the Irish educational system is set out and the impact of large-scale immigration from the mid-1990s on primary schools is discussed. In the second chapter, the use of the CEFR is explored and in particular how it was used to develop the *English Language Proficiency Benchmarks* for the provision of English L2 support for the newcomer children in the Irish primary system. These *Benchmarks* make reference to the CEFR levels – A1 to B1 – and aim to provide age-appropriate and domain specific 'Can Do' descriptors – thus extending the CEFR functional framework for English in line with the general EP objectives.

Against this policy context in Ireland, the authors argue for the desirability of plurilingualism, as intended within the original CEFR (Council of Europe 2001:4–5), and for the benefits of enhanced language awareness that the approach can bring. The authors highlight the importance of recognising and supporting the home languages of the children while simultaneously developing their English language skills for use in school and within the wider English-speaking community.

The authors contend that the CEFR's 'descriptive apparatus' enables a dual focus: a focus on the *communicative activities* needed for functional communication, and a focus on the development of the *underlying competences* in English needed for steady progression in proficiency.

The *Benchmarks* are important in that they enable teachers to track progress and provide a staged description of the EAL pupils' functional development over time. The authors use the metaphor of 'a map' which details the overarching curriculum goals sets out 'the ground to be covered' for the target learners. They explain why the CEFR was an obvious source and model to be used for this purpose giving three main reasons:

a) it provides an articulated system of *levels* which are quite detailed but are not language-specific;

b) it provides an action-oriented, *Can Do approach* focusing on the immediate communicative needs of the target learners;

c) it enables 'Can Do' descriptors to be adapted for relevant *curriculum goals* that imply well-specified learning activities and 'invite the definition of assessment criteria'.

This means that there can be a close relationship in the learning context between curriculum, pedagogy and assessment, and the fostering of an "assessment culture" that recognises the importance of formative uses of assessment, including learner self-assessment.

Chapters 3 to 5 are largely based on Ćatibušić's doctoral work and the in-depth investigation that she carried out of the English second language (L2) development of a sample of primary pupils in three different schools over the course of a school year (2007–08). The pupils were from various national backgrounds and age groups and the case studies illustrated individual differences in the pupils' language development. However, the analysis of the data set as a whole also revealed a number of potentially generalisable patterns and confirmed the positive influence of the *English Language Proficiency Benchmarks*.

This unique empirical study is described at length in Chapter 3 and the research questions which were used to explore the relation between the *Benchmarks* and classroom realities in the schools are set out clearly. A case study approach was adopted to provide in-depth insights at the micro-level in three primary schools that agreed to take part in the study. There were repeated visits to the schools throughout the year (up to 28 in one case) to ensure close observation of the learning contexts, including extensive audio recordings of the classrooms.

The children in the study were typically between 5 and 8 years old and were from 11 national backgrounds and at least 12 home languages. As the main focus of the research was on their developing *oral skills in English* over the 10-month period, 154 English support lessons were recorded and broadly transcribed. This allowed for an impressive number of over 7,000 spoken turns produced by the children to be analysed. Some writing samples were also collected to allow for a much more limited focus on developing literacy in L2.

The findings are discussed in Chapter 4 and in order to capture the diversity of the children's backgrounds, the chapter is broken down into a series of 18 'pupil profiles'. Of particular relevance to the EPP is the detailed analysis of the actual language samples produced by these learners and the search in the analysis for *linguistic indicators of developing proficiency*; these include grammatical indicators (both morphological and syntactic) and lexical indicators.

Chapter 5 summaries the results from the case studies and examines the extent to which the development in the children's English communicative ability reflected the progression described in the *Benchmarks* (from A1 to B1 in CEFR terms). In this chapter other possible influences on L2 English development are also considered, including individual *learner characteristics* (referred to as 'internal factors'), such as age, home language, learning style and personality, and also *interaction-related factors* in the context of learning. Not surprisingly the internal factors all played a role to some extent; for example there was some evidence that oral skills developed slightly faster among the older pupils (aged over seven years) and the home language (L1) influenced phonological features and some aspects of syntax. This latter point supports findings reported in the first volume of this series and in other projects being conducted in the EP Network (e.g. Barker, Post and Schmidt in press). Patterns of classroom interaction also appeared to affect both the *quality and quantity* of English used by the learners, and again for the older children, previous educational experiences and L1 literacy appeared to be relevant.

In concluding in Chapter 6, the authors confirm the usefulness of the *Benchmarks* in the Irish context and more generally they suggest that their research endorses the CEFR, especially the close relation between 'the CEFR's functional progression and the growth of learners' linguistic resources'.

Finally they consider future avenues of research to address some limitations in their study and express the wish for the *Benchmarks* to be 'refined, expanded on and applied beyond the Irish context to enable L2 learners to learn more effectively *through* their second language in the context of L2-dominant education'.

It is to be hoped that such research goes ahead to inform the development of RLDs for English and we look forward to more studies of this kind that help us to understand how English is taught and learned in specific contexts such as those described in this book.

Nick Saville and Michael Milanovic
Cambridge
March 2014

Abbreviations

BICS	Basic Interpersonal Communication Skills
CA	Conversation Analysis
CALP	Cognitive Academic Language Proficiency
CEFR	Common European Framework of Reference for Languages
CLC	Cambridge Learner Corpus
DES	Department of Education and Skills (formerly Department of Education and Science)
EAL	English as an Additional Language
EFL	English as a Foreign Language
ELP	European Language Portfolio
EPP	English Profile Programme
EU	European Union
IILT	Integrate Ireland Language and Training
IRF	Initiation, Response, Feedback
L1	First Language
L2	Second Language
NCCA	National Council for Curriculum and Assessment
OECD	Organisation for Economic Co-operation and Development
PISA	Programme for International Student Assessment
RLD	Reference Level Description
RLSU	Refugee Language Support Unit
SPSS	Statistical Product and Service Solutions

Introduction

This book reports on a longitudinal study of the acquisition of English L2 by 18 children from immigrant families attending primary schools in the north-east of Ireland. The purpose of the research was to explore the extent (if any) to which these pupils' L2 development confirmed the learning trajectory hypothesised in the *English Language Proficiency Benchmarks* (Integrate Ireland Language and Training 2003a), the officially sanctioned framework designed to guide the delivery of English language support in primary schools. The *Benchmarks* are a domain-specific and age-appropriate adaptation of the first three levels of the Common European Framework of Reference for Languages (CEFR) (Council of Europe 2001); hence the inclusion of this book in the *English Profile Studies* series.

Because the CEFR is non-language-specific it provides only the most general description of the linguistic resources learners need in order to function effectively at its successive proficiency levels. Those resources must be described separately and in detail for each language in what the Council of Europe terms Reference Level Descriptions (RLDs) – 'inventories of the linguistic material necessary to implement the competences [defined in the CEFR]' (Council of Europe 2005:5). The English Profile Programme (EPP) is the most ambitious set of RLDs to be developed so far. Its aim is 'to investigate what learner English is really like at each level of the Common European Framework of Reference (CEFR)' (Cambridge Assessment 2007). The first volume in the *English Profile Studies* series, by John A Hawkins and Luna Filipović (Hawkins and Filipović 2012), focuses on 'criterial features' of the six CEFR levels: 'properties of learner English that are characteristic and indicative of L2 proficiency at each of the [CEFR] levels and that distinguish higher levels from lower levels' (Hawkins and Filipović 2012:11). The second volume, by Anthony Green (Green 2012), explores the theoretical and empirical bases for a functional approach to the definition of language learning level and provides guidance to users of the CEFR on adapting the framework to local needs. Our own research addresses both these themes. It reports on empirical research that set out to validate an adaptation of the CEFR's first three proficiency levels and in doing so collected data that enabled us to describe proficiency at each level in functional, linguistic and interactional terms. But whereas the EPP is based on computational analysis of an extensive and continuously expanding corpus of learner English (the Cambridge Learner Corpus (CLC), which currently contains over 55 million words of written data, and the Cambridge English Profile Corpus, which aims to collect 10 million words of spoken and written data), our own insights derive from analysis of the language produced by 18 pupils attending English language support classes over the course of a school year. Despite this enormous difference in scale, our findings constitute a first step towards transforming the *English Language Proficiency Benchmarks* from a framework into domain-specific and age-appropriate RLDs.

We expect our research methods, data analysis and findings to be of interest to students of L2 acquisition generally, but especially to those who wish to explore the descriptive approach and levels of the CEFR from the perspective of empirical enquiry. To the best of our knowledge, the *Benchmarks* are the first and so far the only attempt to adapt the levels of the CEFR and key elements of its descriptive scheme to the specific needs of immigrant pupils. For this reason the book should also be of interest to those responsible for the linguistic and educational integration of immigrant children and adolescents in other countries, especially since our findings validate the framework approach exemplified in the *Benchmarks*.

Ireland experienced immigration on an unprecedented scale from the mid-1990s until the economic collapse of 2008. Relatively small numbers of refugees were admitted under a European Union (EU) quota system established with the United Nations High Commission for Refugees; the beginnings of the economic boom led to the targeted recruitment of economic migrants; the country attracted large numbers of asylum seekers; and no limit was put on immigration from the eastern European and Baltic states that joined the EU in 2004. Other countries, in particular other EU member states, experienced similar flows of immigration during this period. What made Ireland's experience different was its lack of a history of immigration. Having been a colony rather than a colonial power, Ireland had no established non-English-speaking immigrant communities, and it did not act as a magnet for immigrants from particular countries – compare with this immigration to the United Kingdom from Commonwealth countries, to France from North Africa, and to Spain from South America. Immigrants to Ireland came from many different countries, and until the EU enlargement of 2004 new immigrant communities were mostly small and often scattered. Indeed, it was official policy to disperse refugees and asylum seekers to centres around the country, some of them in rural areas. But as the flow increased immigrants tended to converge on cities and towns, where they could find work and relatively cheap accommodation.

Educational underachievement among children and adolescents from immigrant backgrounds is a well-documented phenomenon that has assumed greater prominence for policy-makers under the impact of the Programme for International Student Assessment (PISA) studies conducted by the Organisation for Economic Co-operation and Development (OECD) (see especially Organisation for Economic Co-operation and Development 2004, 2006, 2010). In PISA 2006, for example, first-generation immigrant students lagged significantly behind their native peers in all the participating countries except Australia and Israel, while second-generation immigrants lagged behind their native peers in all participating countries except Australia, Canada, Israel, New Zealand and the United Kingdom. A particularly worrying trend emerged in Austria and Germany, where second-generation migrant students performed worse than first-generation migrants (for a detailed discussion, see Christensen and Segeritz 2008, Cummins 2013). The causes of this underachievement are many, and generalisations across countries are difficult to sustain; though it is probably fair to say that each new wave of immigration into a country brings new complexity to the challenges already faced by its education system. Lacking a history of immigration, Ireland also had no history of integrating immigrant children and adolescents into its education system; and with the exception of small groups of economic immigrants, Ireland did not seek immigrants: they simply came.

Research into the linguistic challenges faced by immigrant pupils and students and the effectiveness of various responses at the levels of policy and pedagogy has failed to produce a consensus (for a summary, see Little 2010). To take just one example, Cummins's 'interdependence hypothesis' (see e.g. Cummins 2000), for which there is significant empirical support, argues that immigrants' L1 plays an essential role in their acquisition of the language of schooling. Yet in many countries schools forbid the use of any language in school apart from the language of schooling. The pedagogical measures taken by education systems and individual schools to support the integration of pupils and students from migrant backgrounds are almost infinitely variable (for an overview of different approaches, see Sierens and Van Avermaet 2013). In Ireland official policy was formulated reactively rather than proactively, and its implementation was seen, at least in the early stages, in deceptively simple terms: immigrant children and adolescents would be a problem for schools and teachers as long as they lacked proficiency in English.

The book is organised as follows. Chapter 1 describes the context in which the research was conducted, providing a statistical overview of recent immigration into Ireland, summarising the policy response of the Department of Education and Science (subsequently Department of Education and Skills) and the pedagogical response co-ordinated by Integrate Ireland Language and Training (IILT), and concluding with the three questions that our research was designed to answer. Chapter 2 explains why and how the *English Language Proficiency Benchmarks* were developed, describes their structure and content, and shows how they are related to the CEFR. Chapter 3 provides a detailed description of our research methodology: how classroom data was collected through the 10 months of the school year 2007–08; how it was transcribed, analysed and interpreted; and what methods were used to construct individual case studies of the 18 participating pupils and then bring those case studies together in a unified account of English L2 development across the cohort. Chapter 4 presents the case studies, no two of which are identical; while Chapter 5 re-analyses the case study data to provide an overall representation of immigrant pupils' acquisition of English – the first step in transforming the *Benchmarks* into a set of RLDs. Finally, Chapter 6 summarises our findings and explores the implications of our study for further research, the revision and possible expansion of the *English Language Proficiency Benchmarks*, and the application of the CEFR's descriptive apparatus and proficiency levels to other domains of language learning.

1 The context: Large-scale immigration to Ireland from the mid-1990s and its impact on primary schools

From the late 1990s into the 2000s Ireland experienced a sustained wave of immigration that transformed the country's demographic profile. The population grew by 8% between 1996 and 2002, by 8.2% between 2002 and 2006, and – despite the country's economic decline, which began in 2008 – by 8.2% between 2006 and 2011 (Central Statistics Office 2012:9). In 2002, non-Irish EU residents totalled 133,436; by 2006 this figure had risen to 275,775, which included 120,534 citizens of states that acceded to the EU in 2004 – the largest groups came from Poland, Lithuania and Latvia (Smyth, Darmody, McGinnity and Byrne 2009:4). In the four years to April 2006, total net migration was 192,000, whereas in the five years to April 2011 it dropped to 125,000 (Central Statistics Office 2012:10). This latter figure reflects the impact of the economic crisis, but it is nevertheless significant for a country with a total population of just over four and a half million. In their Intercultural Education Strategy 2010–15, the Department of Education and Skills (DES) and the Office of the Minister for Integration noted that 'the recent profile of migrants is changing, with an increasing proportion in the 0–15 year old age category', acknowledging that 'immigrants will remain a definite feature of Irish society and education into the future' (Department of Education and Skills and Office of the Minister for Integration 2010:5).

These changes in Ireland's demographic profile have had a major impact on the education sector. Many schools have enrolled children and adolescents from immigrant backgrounds for the first time, and many of those children and adolescents have home languages other than English or Irish. While the highest numbers of immigrants are concentrated in urban areas, especially parts of greater Dublin, where in some schools more than 50% of the pupils come from immigrant backgrounds (McGorman and Sugrue 2007:51), the enrolment of non-English/Irish-speaking pupils has also extended unpredictably to small schools in rural areas. The Irish education system has thus been confronted with the challenge of enabling pupils from immigrant backgrounds to integrate socially and achieve their full academic potential. An essential part of this response is to ensure that all such pupils can access and develop fluency in the language of education, which in most primary schools in Ireland is English.

To begin with, the official designation for children and adolescents from immigrant backgrounds was 'non-national', but this was gradually replaced by 'newcomer'. Both terms are unsatisfactory, however, because they evidently exclude the significant numbers of children born in Ireland to immigrant parents. Such children are Irish nationals and certainly not 'newcomers', but they may grow up with a home language other than Irish or English. 'Non-English-speaking' was avoided by officialdom lest it be wrongly applied to children who spoke only Irish when they started school. More recently the term 'English as an additional language' has gained currency, and throughout this book we refer to EAL pupils (primary) and students (post-primary).

The official policy response: Provision of two years of English language support for each EAL pupil-student

In the late 1990s the DES introduced measures to support the integration of immigrant pupils in primary and immigrant students in post-primary schools. Pupils and students are assigned to a mainstream class on the basis of their age, but they are provided with two years of specially funded English language support. Schools are free to organise this support in whatever way they wish, though there is a general expectation that it will be delivered to small groups of pupils separately from their mainstream class. In practice, most primary schools provide EAL pupils with one English language lesson a day, of between 35 and 45 minutes, organised to harmonise thematically with whatever part of the primary curriculum is in focus in the pupils' mainstream class. This means that most immigrant pupils spend at least 80% of their time in an immersion situation without special English language assistance.

In 2007 a ministerial decision allowed English language support to continue beyond the two-year limit in the case of pupils who after two years were still not ready for full integration in the mainstream. In 2009, however, deteriorating economic circumstances caused the two-year limit on English language support to be reimposed, and extended language support was allowed only in the most strenuously appealed cases. Subsequent cuts in public spending have led to a significant reduction in the number of English language support teachers and thus in the amount of English language teaching that schools are able to provide.

The pedagogical response

The role of Integrate Ireland Language and Training

When the DES introduced the policy of two years' English language support for all EAL pupils and students, it allocated funding to allow schools to provide additional teaching but took no further measures. The official line seemed to be that as fully trained professionals, teachers should know how to deal with the situation. This was, however, unrealistic. Although primary teachers in Ireland are required to teach Irish, which is a compulsory subject from the beginning to the end of schooling, they are not trained specifically as language teachers; and post-primary teachers whose subject is not Irish or a foreign language can be guided only by memories of the language teaching they themselves received at school. Not surprisingly, the DES came under pressure from the teachers' unions and various professional bodies to do more to facilitate the provision of English language support. It turned to the Refugee Language Support Unit (RLSU) for help.

The DES had established the RLSU in March 1999 as a two-year pilot project under the aegis of the Centre for Language and Communication Studies, Trinity College Dublin. The RLSU's primary function was to co-ordinate the provision of intensive English language programmes for adult refugees admitted to Ireland. In September 2001, the RLSU became Integrate Ireland Language and Training (IILT), a not-for-profit campus company of Trinity College Dublin that was wholly funded by the Irish government until funding was withdrawn in the summer of 2008. In the summer of 2000 the DES had already extended the RLSU's function to include the provision of various kinds of support for primary and post-primary schools. The terms of reference laid down by the DES were as follows:

1. To analyse the linguistic demands of the primary and post-primary curricula and identify the language needed by non-English-speaking 'non-national' pupils in order to participate fully in the educational process.
2. To develop materials designed to support the teaching and learning of EAL in primary and post-primary schools.
3. To mediate materials, teaching approaches and supplementary aids to English language support teachers via an ongoing in-service training programme.

Work undertaken in fulfilment of the first of these terms of reference yielded two sets of *English Language Proficiency Benchmarks*, one for primary pupils and one for post-primary students. Chapter 2 explains in some detail how the primary *Benchmarks* were developed. The first versions of the *Benchmarks* were published in 2000 and substantially revised in 2003

(Integrate Ireland Language and Training 2003a, 2003b); the present study refers to the revised versions.

In fulfilment of the second term of reference, IILT developed versions of the Council of Europe's European Language Portfolio (ELP) for primary and post-primary learners of EAL. These were validated and accredited by the ELP Validation Committee in 2001, revised to bring them into line with the revised *Benchmarks*, and re-accredited in 2004 – accreditation nos. 11.2001 rev. 2004 (Integrate Ireland Language and Training 2004a) and 12.2001 rev. 2004 (Integrate Ireland Language and Training 2004b). The ELP has three obligatory components: a language passport that summarises the owner's language profile and experience of learning and using second languages; a language biography that supports goal setting and self-assessment and encourages learners to reflect on different dimensions of the language learning process; and a dossier in which learners collect work in progress and/or samples of work that support their self-assessment. In the ELP for primary learners of EAL, goal setting and teacher-supported self-assessment are based on checklists of 'I can' descriptors derived from the Can Do descriptors of the *Benchmarks* and arranged according to 13 recurrent curriculum themes called 'units of work'. Altogether 211 descriptors capture the gradually developing repertoire that EAL pupils need to acquire in order to participate in mainstream education. Whereas the dossier in most ELPs is empty, providing instructions for use and perhaps a blank table of contents, in the model for EAL pupils it includes various worksheets designed to link the themes of the checklists to classroom activities. This ELP is available from the website of the National Council for Curriculum and Assessment (www.ncca.ie/iilt); for more general information on the ELP, go to the Council of Europe's ELP website (www.coe.int/portfolio).

Besides supporting the development of the individual pupil's proficiency in English, the primary ELP provided teachers, school principals, inspectors and parents with a dynamic record of progress. It also coincided with key principles that underpin the Irish primary curriculum: learning how to learn; accommodating individual difference; basing learning on what is already known and on the immediate social and educational environment; integrating the development of new knowledge and skills; and, by making learners active agents in their learning, fostering the development of the individual learner's full potential. The primary ELP is also designed to validate pupils' home languages. Both the language passport and the language biography contain pages that focus on languages that the pupil knows in addition to English as the language of schooling, and teachers were encouraged to get parents to translate key headings into their home language.

Between 2000 and 2006 IILT developed a range of materials that support the action-oriented, communicative approach to language teaching and learning derived from the Common European Framework of Reference for Languages (CEFR) (Council of Europe 2001) and implied by the *Benchmarks*. In 2006 these were brought together in a single publication, *Up and Away* (Integrate Ireland Language and Training 2006b). All materials remain freely available online.

In fulfilment of the third term of reference IILT organised a series of twice-yearly in-service seminars for English language support teachers. Post-primary English language support was usually provided by teachers with spare capacity. This tended to result in haphazard provision (Lyons and Little 2009); it also meant that few English language support teachers could be spared to attend in-service seminars. For this reason each post-primary seminar was given just once, in Dublin, and attended by an average of 70 English language support teachers. There were more EAL pupils at primary level than EAL students at post-primary level, and thus more English language support teachers. At primary level, moreover, English language support funding was used to create additional teaching posts. This meant that schools could assign teachers to specialise in English language support, which made it easier for them to attend in-service seminars since the only consequence of their absence from school was a one-day suspension of English language classes. Thus from an early stage, significantly more primary than post-primary English language support teachers attended in-service seminars, which made it necessary to hold seminars in different centres around the country. In the autumn term of 2005, for example, seven seminars were held (four in Dublin and one each in Dundalk, Mallow and Galway), with a total attendance of 548 teachers from 411 schools (Integrate Ireland Language and Training 2006a). IILT used the seminars to disseminate the *Benchmarks*, the ELP and other teaching materials, but also to give teachers an opportunity to discuss the challenges they faced in common and to share experiences, methods and materials. IILT also depended on the seminars to provide critical feedback on its materials; the revision of the *Benchmarks*, for example, was informed by detailed discussions with teachers at in-service seminars.

From a very early stage, teachers attending in-service seminars began to ask for instruments that would enable them to gauge newly arrived pupils' proficiency in English (if any) and assess their progress through the two years of English language support. IILT responded by developing and piloting simple communicative tests of listening, speaking, reading and writing, between 2003 and 2006. As far as possible, assessment tasks were communicative activities typical of primary classrooms: in effect, realisations of *Benchmarks* descriptors. For speaking and writing, rating scales and scoring grids were designed on the basis of *Benchmarks* descriptors of underlying linguistic competence (for further discussion, see Chapter 2). Each suite of tests was introduced at in-service seminars and teachers were recruited to pilot them and provide critical feedback to inform the revision of the tests.[1] In 2007 the assessment kit was published by the DES and copies were distributed to every primary school in the country (Little, Lazenby Simpson and Finnegan Ćatibušić 2007). The DES intended that arguments for additional English language support should be based on a pupil's performance on the tests. The validity and reliability of this procedure were undermined, however, when, following the closure of IILT in 2008, the DES made the assessment kit freely available online as the least expensive way of responding to the demand for more copies.

Three research questions

By 2006 IILT had fulfilled the terms of reference that it was given in 2000. The *English Language Proficiency Benchmarks* were widely accepted as a map of the ground that English language support pupils had to cover in order to gain full access to mainstream education; a majority of schools were using the ELP as a key teaching and learning tool;[2] and a new impetus was given to IILT's teaching and learning supports when they were brought together in a single publication, *Up and Away* (Integrate Ireland Language and Training 2006b), which the DES distributed free of charge to all primary schools in the state. A great deal had been achieved in a relatively short period; it was now time to undertake the empirical research whose results are reported in this book.

The research sought to answer three questions:

1. *To what extent does the development of EAL pupils' L2 communicative proficiency – their capacity to participate in classroom discourse – correspond to the trajectory hypothesised in the* English Language Proficiency Benchmarks?
   From the beginning teachers welcomed the *Benchmarks*, which they could use to plan their teaching and gauge the progress of their pupils. At a functional level the progression implied by the *Benchmarks* is perhaps a matter of common sense, but it lacked empirical support. Also, the thematic scope of the *Benchmarks*, intended to reflect the

---

[1] In the autumn of 2004 tests of speaking and writing were sent to 50 teachers in 41 primary schools around the country; 287 language support pupils were assessed, and 252 rated recordings of the speaking tests and 186 rated writing tests were returned to IILT. In the spring of 2005 tests of reading were sent to 56 teachers in 48 primary schools; 266 language support pupils were assessed and 52 assessment packs were returned. And in the autumn of 2005 listening tests were sent to 49 teachers in 39 primary schools; 311 language support pupils were assessed and 45 assessment packs were returned.

[2] In each of IILT's last two years of operation it sold some 5,000 copies of the primary ELP. Given that language support is provided for two years and at that time there were estimated to be some 12,000 EAL pupils attending primary schools, these sales figures imply a take-up rate in the region of 80%.

thematic scope of the primary curriculum, was based on consultation with teachers' focus groups and reflected their understanding of the primary curriculum, but we had no confirmation that this scope was adequate to the daily reality of English language support.

2. *How do individual pupils develop underlying L2 linguistic competence – the linguistic resources on which their capacity to communicate depends – and to what degree is this development marked by back-sliding, variance, etc.?*
   Although it seemed unlikely that pupils would be able to perform, for example, A2 level speaking tasks before first developing the capacity to perform A1 tasks, we had no information concerning the development of the linguistic competence that underpins learners' functional capacity.

3. *What does analysis of data obtained from a group of pupils allow us to say about the overall relation between L2 communicative capacity and underlying linguistic competence?*
   Progress in the provision of English language support clearly depends, among other things, on knowing a great deal more about this relation, not just in individual case studies but in the immigrant population as a whole.

In Chapter 2 we explain why and how the *English Language Proficiency Benchmarks for Non-English-speaking Pupils at Primary Level* (Integrate Ireland Language and Training 2003a) were developed, describe their structure, summarise their content, and show how they are related to the CEFR.

The English Language Proficiency Benchmarks

In Chapter 1 we briefly introduced the challenge that large-scale immigration poses to Ireland's schools, explained the official policy response (two years of focused English language support for each EAL pupil or student), and described the various actions undertaken by IILT in support of that policy. Those actions were essentially of three kinds: the development of the *English Language Proficiency Benchmarks* that provide a map of the journey EAL students must make from zero proficiency in the language of schooling to the ability to participate with a degree of independence in mainstream classroom activities; a version of the ELP and various other teaching/learning materials; and a suite of simple communicative tests that schools could use to assess the English language proficiency of EAL pupils/students and the extent of their progress at the end of their first and second years of English language support. *Benchmarks*, pedagogical materials, and successive components of the assessment kit were introduced to teachers via a programme of in-service seminars, which ensured that their ongoing development was informed by interaction with classroom reality.

In this chapter we introduce the *English Language Proficiency Benchmarks* for EAL pupils at primary level, which provided the focus for the empirical research reported in this book. We begin by briefly explaining why the *Benchmarks* were developed, what we hoped they would achieve, and why we modelled them on the CEFR (Council of Europe 2001). Next we consider the CEFR's action-oriented approach to the description of language proficiency and its pedagogical implications. After that we describe the sources of information on which we drew in order to develop the *Benchmarks* and the design considerations that determined their content and structure. Finally we present samples of the *Benchmarks* themselves, and conclude the chapter by briefly restating the three focuses of our research.

Why English Language Proficiency Benchmarks?

The first reason for developing the *Benchmarks* was that the DES asked for them. DES officials who visited Canada to find out how that country manages the linguistic integration of immigrants had been introduced to the *Canadian Language Benchmarks* (www.language.ca). These are designed with the language needs of adult immigrants in mind; they seek to capture the skills that immigrants must develop in English or French in order to perform effectively in the workplace. What the DES seemed to have in mind when it commissioned IILT to develop the *English Language Proficiency Benchmarks* was a series of thresholds that EAL pupils and students must cross in order gradually to become fully integrated in mainstream education.

In response to this requirement, we set out to develop instruments that would be at once simpler and more complex than the *Canadian Language Benchmarks*: simpler in the sense that they would be relatively short and easy for teachers to use on a daily basis; more complex in the sense that they would describe progression in learning, thus providing teachers with a 'map' of the ground to be covered by their EAL pupils and students. From the beginning we were clear that what was needed was not a separate EAL curriculum, but some sort of prism through which English language support teachers could view the different components of the mainstream curriculum and the linguistic demands that they imposed on EAL pupils and students.

The metaphor of a map is a way of acknowledging that the *Benchmarks* would not perform their intended function if they simply provided a more or less detailed description of the repertoire that EAL pupils should possess after two years of English language support. Only if we identified stages in the development of that repertoire could we expect the *Benchmarks* to exert a direct influence on EAL teaching. A staged description of EAL pupils' functional development would, we believed, help teachers to select appropriate learning activities and materials; it would also provide them with a simple metric against which they could gauge their pupils' progress.

The CEFR (Council of Europe 2001) offered itself as an obvious source and model, for three reasons. First, it has a clearly articulated system of proficiency levels whose components are described in great though non-language-specific detail; secondly, its action-oriented ('Can Do') approach to the description of proficiency encourages teachers to focus on communicative outcomes, which we believed was imperative in the case of immigrant pupils and students; and thirdly, the fact that each 'Can Do' descriptor can simultaneously specify a curriculum goal, imply a learning activity, and invite the definition of assessment criteria emphasises the close relation between curriculum pedagogy and assessment. This last consideration implies an assessment culture in which learner self-assessment is an important part of formative assessment, which in turn is guided by the same criteria that shape summative assessment (see Little 2006, 2009, 2011 for further discussion). Such an assessment culture was already on the educational agenda in Ireland at the end of the 1990s, thanks in part to the introduction of a new primary curriculum in 1999 (National Council for Curriculum and Assessment 1999).

The CEFR's description of second language proficiency

Scales and levels

The CEFR describes language learning targets and outcomes in terms of language use, which it divides into four kinds: reception (listening and reading), production (speaking and writing), interaction (spoken and written), and mediation (translating and interpreting). For the activities of listening and reading, spoken and written interaction, and oral and written production it provides illustrative scales comprising six levels of proficiency arranged in three bands: A1 and A2 (basic user), B1 and B2 (independent user), and C1 and C2 (proficient user). These bands are roughly equivalent to the traditional categories of beginner, intermediate and advanced, which no doubt helps to explain the speed with which they have been adopted internationally. The CEFR's illustrative scales focus on different dimensions of each activity. For example, there are nine scales for spoken interaction: overall spoken interaction; understanding a native speaker interlocutor; conversation; informal discussion (with friends); formal discussion and meetings; goal-oriented co-operation; transactions to obtain goods and services; information exchange; and interviewing and being interviewed. The illustrative scales lie behind the 'global scale' (Council of Europe 2001:24), which gives a holistic summary of each of the six levels; they also lie behind the 'self-assessment grid' (Council of Europe 2001:26–27), which gives a summary descriptor of proficiency at each of the six levels for five communicative activities: listening, reading, spoken interaction, spoken production and writing (see Appendix 1). The two-dimensional character of the self-assessment grid (communicative activities on the vertical axis, proficiency levels on the horizontal) reminds us of the often uneven nature of L2 proficiency development: receptive skills ahead of productive skills, reading more advanced than listening, spoken interaction better developed than writing, and so on.

Two complementary dimensions of the CEFR's descriptive apparatus

The CEFR's 'Can Do' approach to the description of communicative proficiency has two complementary dimensions: communicative activities and the competences on which we draw when we engage in those activities. Chapter 4 of the CEFR is concerned with communicative activities. Altogether it provides 40 illustrative scales: five for spoken production, three for written production, five for listening, five for reading, one for audio-visual reception, nine for spoken interaction, three for written interaction, three for production strategies, one for reception strategies, three for spoken interaction strategies, and one each for note-taking and processing text. The second volume of *English Profile Studies* (Green 2012) provides a detailed theoretical and empirical exploration of this functional dimension of the CEFR.

In order to engage in language activities, we need to draw on linguistic and other cognitive resources. Thus Chapter 5 of the CEFR is concerned with the competences that underpin communicative behaviour. It divides the user/learner's general competences into four categories: declarative knowledge; practical and intercultural skills and know-how; existential competence (attitudes, motivations, values, beliefs, cognitive style, and personality factors); and ability to learn. These general competences interact with and contribute to the development of the user/learner's communicative language competences, which are divided into three categories: linguistic (lexical, grammatical, semantic, phonological, orthographic, and orthoepic), sociolinguistic (the ability to handle linguistic markers of social relations, politeness conventions, expressions of folk wisdom, register differences, dialect and accent), and pragmatic (discourse and functional competences). Altogether Chapter 5 provides 13 illustrative scales: six for linguistic competences, one for sociolinguistic competence, four for pragmatic competences, and two for qualitative aspects of language use (fluency and propositional precision). The first volume of *English Profile Studies* (Hawkins and Filipović 2012) explores the linguistic resources that learners of English L2 need to command in order to act effectively at each of the CEFR's proficiency levels.

These two dimensions of the CEFR's descriptive apparatus are mutually supporting: our understanding of the descriptors of communicative activities should always be informed by our understanding of the descriptors of communicative language competence and vice versa.

Implications for pedagogy

The authors of the CEFR insist at various junctures that it is not their role to tell readers of the framework what to do but rather to present them with options. At the same time, however, the CEFR's approach to the description of language proficiency has clear pedagogical implications, starting with its comprehensive summary of that approach at the beginning of Chapter 2:

> Language use, embracing language learning, comprises the actions performed by persons who as individuals and as social agents develop a range of **competences**, both **general** and in particular **communicative language competences**. They draw on the competences at their disposal in various contexts under various **conditions** and under various **constraints** to engage in **language activities** involving **language processes** to produce and/or receive **texts** in relation to **themes** in specific **domains**, activating those **strategies** which seem most appropriate for carrying out the **tasks**

to be accomplished. The monitoring of these actions by the participants leads to the reinforcement or modification of their competences (Council of Europe 2001:9 [emphases in original]).

According to this paragraph, communicative proficiency develops when the user/learner's existing competences are brought to bear on a communicative agenda within a particular context or set of contexts (the words and phrases printed in bold refer to the different components of the CEFR's descriptive apparatus). In other words, according to the CEFR's socio-cognitive view, language learning is inseparable from language use, underlying competence is ultimately inseparable from behavioural repertoire, and communicative language proficiency is infinitely variable and always uniquely personal. The last sentence of the paragraph draws attention to the role played by the user/learner's metacognitive as well as communicative agency. In short, the CEFR's action-oriented approach to the description of language proficiency implies a communicative approach to teaching and learning in which learner initiative and reflection play an essential role. This pedagogical orientation seemed to us entirely appropriate to the needs of EAL pupils immersed in primary schooling.

An important policy dimension

The CEFR was developed to further the Council of Europe's language education agenda, which in turn supports the broader political, social and cultural policies that flow from the European Convention on Human Rights (1950) and the European Cultural Convention (1954). One item on this agenda was of great background importance when we developed the *Benchmarks*: the promotion of plurilingualism. As the CEFR explains:

> . . . the plurilingual approach emphasises the fact that as an individual person's experience of language in its cultural contexts expands, from the language of the home to that of society at large and then to the languages of other peoples (whether learnt at school or college, or by direct experience), he or she does not keep these languages and cultures in strictly separated mental compartments, but rather builds up a communicative competence to which all knowledge and experience of language contributes and in which languages interrelate and interact (Council of Europe 2001:4).

Although the *Benchmarks* are concerned exclusively with the development of EAL pupils' proficiency in English as the language of schooling, it was essential to bear in mind that those pupils already possessed a proficiency appropriate to their age in at least one other language, and that their home language had personal, communicative, social and cultural value. When EAL pupils come to school with zero proficiency in English, that is not a sign of deficit or handicap; and the proficiency they have already developed in their home language should be seen as an asset, especially if they are able to use it to access parts of the culture expressed in and through that language. As we explained in Chapter 1, the version of the ELP that was developed to mediate the *Benchmarks* to pupils takes account of pupils' home languages, and our in-service seminars repeatedly emphasised the desirability of plurilingualism. Before long some schools were finding ways of using EAL pupils' home languages to provide enriched language awareness for all pupils (Kirwan 2013).

How the English Language Proficiency Benchmarks were developed

Sources of information

When we set about developing the *Benchmarks*, our first source of information was the newly published multi-volume primary curriculum (National Council for Curriculum and Assessment 1999). This provided us with essential insights into the intended ethos, nature and purpose of primary education in Ireland as well as detailed information about curriculum content. It also confirmed that the pedagogical approach we wanted the *Benchmarks* to imply was fully harmonious with officially sanctioned approaches to teaching and learning.

The size and scope of the curriculum documents meant, however, that teachers were mostly familiar with them only at second hand. To take account of this we established two focus groups of primary teachers already engaged in English language support. They informed us about teachers' understanding of the curriculum, their sense of the challenge posed by EAL pupils, and their classroom practice. Our study of the curriculum had already suggested a number of recurrent themes that we could use to structure the *Benchmarks*, making them easy to relate to curriculum content on the one hand and classroom activities on the other. Discussion with the focus groups yielded the 14 themes that we included in the first version of the *Benchmarks*: myself; our school; food and clothes; colours, shapes and opposites; people who help us; weather; transport and travel; seasons, holidays and festivals; the local and wider community; time; people and places in other areas; animals and plants; caring for my locality; and water (the last of these themes was dropped from the 2003 revision of the *Benchmarks* on the ground that it was already present in several other themes).

Finally, we observed a number of primary classrooms in order to add substance to the descriptions of practice that our focus groups had provided us with. This enabled us to be reasonably confident that the descriptors we formulated for listening, reading, spoken interaction, spoken production and writing were harmonious with the realities of language use in the primary classroom.

Design considerations

We wanted the *Benchmarks* to be a tool that teachers could use on a daily basis. This meant that they must not contain a lot of discursive prose but present information schematically. Clearly, we would have to be highly selective in the use we made of the CEFR and its descriptive apparatus.

In this regard our task was made easier by two considerations. The first had to do with the extent of proficiency development the *Benchmarks* were intended to support. The trajectory of learning described by the CEFR's six proficiency levels begins with self-identification and survival, progresses through an expanding capacity to engage in transactional and interactional communication, and is then increasingly implicated in academic and/or professional/vocational use of the target language (see Appendix 1). This prompts the question: To what extent can the successive levels of the CEFR be adapted to the needs of very young learners? At risk of over-simplification, one might say that Levels A1-B1 are largely concerned with 'general' language learning: developing a capacity to use the target language in relatively predictable everyday situations. This is something that all language users need to be able to do, children as well as adolescents and adults, so it should be possible to create age-appropriate descriptors for the CEFR's first three levels. Thereafter it becomes increasingly difficult to adapt the levels to the needs and capacities of young learners. The B2 descriptor for overall written production, for example, coincides with the writing skills that Irish school-leavers are expected to possess in their first language: 'Can write clear, detailed texts on a variety of subjects related to his/her field of interest, synthesising and evaluating information and arguments from a number of sources' (Council of Europe 2001:61). However, we needed to 'map' the development of pupils' English language proficiency only to the point at which they would be capable of participating as relatively independent agents in mainstream classroom activity; in other words, we identified our exit point as falling within the B1 range of the CEFR.

The second feature of the *Benchmarks* that made their development relatively straightforward is their domain-specificity. Their structure and content are determined by just one of the four domains of language use that the CEFR sets out to describe: education. Pupils have identities that are shaped to a large extent outside school; and most of the themes treated by the curriculum refer to the wider world. But all of the themes treated in the *Benchmarks* are part of a curriculum that is mediated, discussed, digested and reproduced via the various modes of classroom discourse. In the CEFR, descriptors at Level A1 have to do with physical and social survival; when adapted to the primary classroom they have to do first and foremost with communicative survival. In the CEFR, descriptors at Level A2 include the highly predictable transactional and interactional routines that account for a high percentage of everyday communication; when adapted to the primary classroom they have to do first and foremost with the predictable interactive routines that are enacted in classroom discourse. In the CEFR, descriptors at Level B1 mark a significant increase in the learner's capacity for flexible and independent communicative behaviour; when adapted to the primary classroom they focus first and foremost on the EAL learner's capacity to participate in the educational process as an increasingly independent agent. As we noted above, the successive levels of the CEFR describe a learning trajectory that moves from everyday communication in which listening and speaking predominate to ever more specialised language use in which reading and writing are progressively more central (again, see Appendix 1). In the *Benchmarks*, on the other hand, oral and literacy skills are equally important from the beginning because they are of equal importance in primary education.

By adopting the CEFR's action-oriented, 'Can Do' approach we intended to emphasise the crucial role that language use plays in language learning and to encourage teachers to support the emergence of EAL pupils' proficiency in English by engaging them in appropriate communicative activity. More specifically, we wanted to discourage 'grammar teaching', which had dominated most teachers' own experience of language learning; and by making the *Benchmarks* strongly domain-specific and context-bound we hoped to discourage the use of English as a Foreign Language (EFL) textbooks. This relatively widespread practice arose from the mistaken assumption that language learning is a 'general' matter rather than one that is always context-bound, and in this particular case strongly domain-specific. EFL textbooks inevitably lack the curriculum focus that is essential for effective English language support.

The structure and content of the English Language Proficiency Benchmarks

In the 2003 version, the *Benchmarks* begin with a brief general introduction that explains where they come from, describes how they are intended to be used, and introduces the ELP as a support for *Benchmarks*-related teaching and learning. Part I of the *Benchmarks* proper comprises two grids, the 'global benchmarks of communicative proficiency', organised in the same way as the CEFR's self-assessment grid, but with just three levels (A1–B1), and 'global scales of underlying linguistic competence'. We developed the global benchmarks by first reformulating the descriptors of the self-assessment grid to make them age-appropriate and domain-specific, then checking our reformulations against the illustrative scales in Chapter 4 of the CEFR and the results of our classroom observations. Bearing in mind that we wanted to discourage 'grammar teaching' and most teachers providing English language support had no training as language teachers, far less as linguists, we limited the scales of underlying linguistic competence to just four categories: vocabulary, grammar, phonology and orthography. We based our descriptors on the relevant illustrative scales in Chapter 5 of the CEFR, again doing our best to ensure that our reformulations were age-appropriate. The introduction to Part I summarised the trajectory of proficiency development that the *Benchmarks* were designed to capture as follows:

> Level A1 *Breakthrough* focuses on the very basic communication necessary in order to familiarise pupils with the daily routines and general environment of the school and thus launch the educational process. As its name implies, A2 *Waystage* defines an intermediate level at which the pupil is able increasingly to benefit linguistically and educationally from his/her presence in the mainstream classroom. And level B1 *Threshold* defines the communicative proficiency that pupils must achieve in order to be fully integrated in the mainstream (Integrate Ireland Language and Training 2003a:5).

The need to use the global benchmarks in interaction with the scales of underlying linguistic competence was explained with particular reference to the development of literacy skills:

> The successive levels defined in the benchmarks involve cognitive and educational as well as linguistic development. Reading, for example, progresses from familiarity with the alphabet and simple acts of comprehension based on word recognition (A1), through the ability to read simple texts that make frequent use of familiar vocabulary (A2), to the development of basic study skills, e.g. using diagrams and illustrations to support reading comprehension (B1). Similarly, writing begins as a matter of copying or writing individual words and copying simple sentences from the board (A1); the pupil then moves on to writing his/her own sentences (A2); and from there he/she progresses to the composition of short texts (B1). These are essentially the same developmental paths as are followed by native speaker pupils, and for that reason it is necessary to supplement the benchmarks with a global scale of underlying linguistic competence. This defines the quality of language appropriate to each of the three levels in terms of vocabulary, grammar, phonology and orthography. These scales should be used in conjunction not only with the global benchmarks but also with the units of work (Integrate Ireland Language and Training 2003a:5).

Part II of the *Benchmarks* comprises 13 grids ('units of work') that restate the global benchmarks in terms of recurrent curriculum themes. The introduction contains the following suggestions for use:

> The order in which the units of work are presented is dictated by the need to draw pupils as quickly as possible into full participation in the life of the school: the first two units are necessarily *Myself* and *Our school*. Pupils' confidence will grow as they develop the ability to communicate about themselves at a basic level and as they begin to understand the routine cycle of school activities. Note that *Our school* includes the identification of the different physical areas of the school as well as classroom behaviour, routines and commonly used requests.
>
> It is important to remember that the tasks described in the units of work are by no means exhaustive; all of them can be adapted to other themes. For this reason it is important always to interpret the units of work in the light of the *Global benchmarks of communicative proficiency* and the *Global scales of underlying linguistic competence* (Integrate Ireland Language and Training 2003a:9).

Finally, the self-assessment grid from the CEFR is reproduced in an appendix (Integrate Ireland Language and Training 2003a:24) in order to remind users where the approach adopted in the *Benchmarks* came from.

In Tables 2.1 and 2.2, sample descriptors from the global benchmarks and the global scales of underlying linguistic competence are set beside the CEFR descriptors from which they derive; while Table 2.3 shows how some of the descriptors in the global benchmarks are reformulated in five of the units of work. All the grids from the *Benchmarks* are given in Appendix 2.

Table 2.1 Sample descriptors from the global benchmarks of communicative proficiency and the CEFR descriptors from which they were derived

	Global benchmarks of communicative proficiency (Integrate Ireland Language and Training 2003a:6–7)	Common European Framework of Reference for Languages, self-assessment grid (Council of Europe 2001:26–27)
A1 **Listening**	Can recognize and understand basic words and phrases concerning him/herself, family and school. Can understand simple questions and instructions when teachers and other pupils speak very slowly and clearly.	I can understand familiar words and very basic phrases concerning myself, my family and immediate concrete surroundings when people speak slowly and clearly.
A2 **Reading**	Can read and understand very short and simple texts that contain a high proportion of previously learnt vocabulary on familiar subjects (e.g., class texts, familiar stories). Can use the alphabet to find particular items in lists (e.g., a name in a telephone book).	I can read very short, simple texts. I can find specific, predictable information in simple everyday material such as advertisements, prospectuses, menus and timetables and I can understand short simple personal letters.

Table 2.1 (continued)

	Global benchmarks of communicative proficiency (Integrate Ireland Language and Training 2003a:6–7)	Common European Framework of Reference for Languages, self-assessment grid (Council of Europe 2001:26–27)
B1 Spoken Interaction	Can speak with fluency about familiar topics such as school, family, daily routine, likes and dislikes. Can engage with other pupils in discussing a topic of common interest (songs, football, pop stars, etc.) or in preparing a collaborative classroom activity. Can keep a conversation going, though he/she may have some difficulty making him/herself understood from time to time. Can repeat what has been said and convey the information to another person.	I can deal with most situations likely to arise whilst travelling in an area where the language is spoken. I can enter unprepared into conversation on topics that are familiar, of personal interest or pertinent to everyday life (e.g. family, hobbies, work, travel and current events).
A2 Spoken Production	Can use a series of phrases and sentences to describe in simple terms his/her family, daily routines and activities, and plans for the immediate or more distant future (e.g. out-of-school activities, holiday plans).	I can use a series of phrases and sentences to describe in simple terms my family and other people, living conditions, my educational background and my present or most recent job.
B1 Writing	Can write a diary or news account with accuracy and coherence. Can write a short letter describing an event or a situation. Can write a brief summary of a book or film. Can write an account of his/her feelings or reactions to an event or situation. Can write a short dialogue to be performed by puppets.	I can write simple connected text on topics which are familiar or of personal interest. I can write personal letters describing experiences and impressions.

Table 2.2 Sample descriptors from the global scales of underlying linguistic competence and the CEFR descriptors from which they were derived

	Global scales of underlying linguistic competence (Integrate Ireland Language and Training 2003a:8)	Common European Framework of Reference for Languages, Chapter 5: The user/learner's competences (Council of Europe 2001:112–118)
B1 Vocabulary Control	Can recognize, understand and use a range of vocabulary related to familiar classroom themes, school routines and activities. Errors still occur when the pupil attempts to express more complex ideas or handle unfamiliar topics.	Shows good control of elementary vocabulary but major errors still occur when expressing more complex thoughts or handling unfamiliar topics and situations.
A2 Grammatical Accuracy	Can use simple grammatical structures that have been learnt and practised in class. Makes frequent basic mistakes with tenses, prepositions and personal pronouns, though when he/she is speaking or writing about a familiar topic the meaning is generally clear.	Uses some simple structures correctly, but still systematically makes basic mistakes – for example, tends to mix up tenses and forget to mark agreement; nevertheless, it is usually clear what he/she is trying to say.
B1 Phonological Control	Can pronounce words with confidence in a clearly intelligible way. Some mispronunciations still occur, but in general he/she is closely familiar with the sounds of English.	Pronunciation is clearly intelligible even if a foreign accent is sometimes evident and occasional mispronunciations occur.
A2 Orthographic Control	Can copy or write short sentences or phrases related to what is being studied in class. Sentence breaks are generally accurate. Words that he/she uses orally may be written with phonetic accuracy but inaccurate spelling.	Can copy short sentences on everyday subjects – e.g. directions, how to get somewhere. Can write with reasonable phonetic accuracy (but not necessarily fully standard spelling) short words that are in his/her oral vocabulary.

Table 2.3 Sample descriptors from the global benchmarks of communicative proficiency and the units of work (Integrate Ireland Language and Training 2003a)

	Global benchmarks of communicative proficiency	Units of work
A2 Listening	Can recognize and understand frequently used words relating to him/herself and family, classroom activities and routines, school instructions and procedures, friends and play. Can understand a routine instruction given outside school (e.g. by a traffic warden). Can understand what is said in a familiar context such as buying something in a shop (e.g. price). Can follow at a general level topics covered in the mainstream class provided key concepts and vocabulary have been studied in advance and there is appropriate visual support. Can follow and understand a story if it is read slowly and clearly with visual support such as facial expression, gesture and pictures.	*Unit 2: Our school* Can understand instructions given in the classroom, gym, playground, etc. Can understand basic information about half days, school closures, doctor's visits, etc. Can understand at a general level topics dealt with in the mainstream class when they are introduced and explained clearly.
A1 Reading	Can recognize the letters of the alphabet. Can recognize and understand basic signs and simple notices in the school and on the way to school. Can recognize and understand basic words on labels or posters in the classroom. Can identify basic words and phrases in a new piece of text.	*Unit 3: Food and clothes* Can recognize and understand the names of basic foods. Can recognize and understand the names of the principal items of clothing.
A2 Spoken Interaction	Can ask for attention in class. Can greet, take leave, request and thank appropriately. Can respond with confidence to familiar questions clearly expressed about family, friends, school work, hobbies, holidays, etc., but is not always able to keep the conversation going. Can generally sustain a conversational exchange with a peer in the classroom when carrying out a collaborative learning activity (making or drawing something, preparing a role-play, presenting a puppet show, etc.). Can express personal feelings in a simple way.	*Unit 5: People who help us* Can ask and answer questions about what people in familiar roles do in their jobs. Can talk with the teacher or another pupil about personal experiences with people in roles of responsibility (e.g. visit to doctor, parent is a nurse/doctor, school traffic warden, postman).

Table 2.3 (continued)

	Global benchmarks of communicative proficiency	Units of work
B1 **Spoken** **Production**	Can retell a story that has been read in class. Can retell the plot of a film he/she has seen or a book he/she has read and describe his/her reactions. Can describe a special event/celebration in the family (religious festival, birthday, new baby, etc.). Can give an account of an experience or event (travel, an accident, an incident that occurred, etc.). Can briefly give explanations and reasons for opinions and plans.	*Unit 7: Transport and travel* Can give a short talk about the types of transport seen outside the school. Can talk in an age-appropriate way about his/her experiences when travelling a long distance.
A1 **Writing**	Can copy or write his/her name. Can copy or write words and short phrases that are being learnt in class. Can copy or write labels on a picture. Can copy short sentences from the board. Can spell his/her name and address, and the name of the school.	*Unit 11: People and places in other areas* Can copy from a poster or map the names of countries and other places relevant to the class (e.g., countries of origin of other pupils). Can copy or write the name of his/her country of origin. Can draw a map of another country and copy or write the names of the country and its principal cities, etc.

Conclusion

As we explained in Chapter 1, the primary *Benchmarks* quickly established themselves as the officially supported framework for planning and delivering English language support. But when IILT had fulfilled the various tasks it had been assigned relative to the school sector, it was clear that we needed to undertake empirical research in order to (i) determine the extent to which the development of EAL pupils' communicative proficiency in English corresponded to the trajectory hypothesised in the *Benchmarks*; (ii) explore the development of individual pupils' underlying linguistic competence in English and the degree to which that development was marked by backsliding, variance, etc.; and (iii) consider what the analysis of data obtained from a selection of individual pupils allowed us to say about the overall relation between communicative capacity in English and underlying linguistic competence. Chapter 3 explains how we went about these research tasks, provides an overview of the data we collected, and describes in detail the analytical techniques we employed.

3 Exploring the relation between the English Language Proficiency Benchmarks and classroom reality: Data collection and analysis

In order to answer the three research questions with which we concluded Chapter 1 it was necessary to undertake a longitudinal study of a diverse group of EAL pupils. In the school year 2007–08 a substantial bank of data was collected from English language support classrooms in three primary schools. In this chapter we describe the participating schools and pupils and explain the procedures we adopted to collect, transcribe, code and analyse the data.

Collecting the data

Participating schools

The three primary schools that participated in the project were all located in the north-east of Ireland. School 1 was a large boys' school in an urban area, School 2 was a small mixed-gender school in a semi-rural area, and School 3 was a medium-sized girls' school in another urban area. Schools 1 and 3 were under the patronage of the Catholic Church, while School 2 was multi-denominational; all three were in the non-fee-paying state sector. School 3 was included in the DES's Delivering Equality of Opportunity in Schools scheme that addresses the educational needs of children and young people from disadvantaged communities. Neither of the other schools had this status, though both were in economically challenged areas. The inclusion of different school types in different locations increased the chances that the EAL pupils involved would be appropriately diverse in terms of linguistic and cultural background, age, gender, duration of English language support, and school experience. It is important to note, however, that it was impossible to obtain analysable data on participating pupils' socio-economic status, a potentially significant variable in the study of EAL pupils' language development and educational achievement.

Arrangements were made with each school to visit English language support lessons regularly, at times appropriate to the school schedule. The extent of the three schools' participation in the project is shown in Table 3.1.

The goal was to visit each school once a week, though this was not always possible because of school holidays, in-service training days and visits from advisors working with the DES's Primary Curriculum Support Programme. The early termination of data collection in School 3 was due to the fact that the English language support teacher was on sick leave from March 2008 onwards. Regular weekly visits to School 1 were easier to manage because it was a large school with two full-time English language support posts, whereas Schools 2 and 3 had only one English language support teacher each.

Table 3.1 Extent of schools' participation in project

	Dates of first and last visits	Total number of visits
School 1	25 September 2007–10 June 2008	28
School 2	26 November 2007–26 May 2008	13
School 3	3 October 2007–27 February 2008	17

Participating pupils

The research was carried out under the aegis of the School of Linguistic, Speech and Communication Sciences, Trinity College Dublin, and thus subject to the School's research ethics regulations. Besides securing the formal consent of school principals and teachers it was also necessary to secure parental consent to the participation of EAL pupils. A letter addressed to parents explained the purpose of the research and requested the participation of their child, emphasising that pupils' involvement in the study was entirely voluntary, data would be stored confidentially, and the anonymity of individual pupils was guaranteed (they are all referred to by pseudonyms). The letter was professionally translated into the home languages of potential participants, insofar as these were known to the teachers involved (in cases of doubt, official languages of the parents' countries of origin were used). Altogether parental consent was secured for 29 pupils to participate in the study. Inevitably the recordings of English language support lessons included contributions from pupils for whom parental consent had not been received, but they were never transcribed.

Table 3.2 provides an overview of the participating pupils. Of the 29 participants, 15 were boys and 14 were girls; 15 were in their first and 14 in their second year of English language support. Almost all the pupils belonged to junior primary classes (from Junior Infants to Third Class). This was not surprising considering both demographic factors and the way in which the English language support programme is delivered. In Ireland, while education is not compulsory until the age of 6 years, most children start school

Table 3.2 Overview of participating pupils

	Pupil (pseudonym)	Gender	School class[1]	Age at end of study[2]	National/cultural background	Home language[3]	English language support from
School 1	Andrei	M	First Class	8	Romanian	Romanian	June 2007
	Stefan	M	First Class	8	Polish	Polish	Sept. 2007
	Tomasz	M	Junior Infants	5	Polish	Polish	Oct. 2007
	Patryk	M	Junior Infants	5	Polish	Polish	Oct. 2007
	Yemi	M	Senior Infants	5	Nigerian	English used at home (?)	Oct. 2006
	Ivan	M	Senior Infants	6	Croatian	Croatian	Sept. 2006
	Ravi	M	Second Class	8	Indian	Malayalam	Jan. 2008
	Lukas	M	First Class	8	Lithuanian	Lithuanian	March 2008
	Constantin	M	Senior Infants	6	Romanian	Romanian	Oct. 2006
	Obinze	M	Senior Infants	6	Nigerian	English used at home (?)	Oct. 2006
	Benjamin	M	Senior Infants	6	Nigerian	English used at home (?)	Oct. 2006
School 2	Marko	M	Junior Infants	5	Serbian	Serbian	Sept. 2007
	Dimitrie	M	Junior Infants	5	Romanian	Romanian	Sept. 2007
	Jin	M	Junior Infants	6	Chinese	Cantonese (?)	Sept. 2007
	Vladimir	M	Junior Infants	6	Serbian	Serbian	Sept. 2007
	Edyta	F	Junior Infants	5	Polish	Polish	Sept. 2007

School 3	Karina	F	Junior Infants	5	Latvian	Latvian	Oct. 2007
	Faith	F	Junior Infants	5	Nigerian	English used at home (?)	Oct. 2007
	Tina	F	Junior Infants	5	Nigerian	English used at home (?)	Oct. 2007
	Zofia	F	Junior Infants	5	Polish	Polish	Oct. 2007
	Ifemelu	F	Senior Infants	6	Nigerian	English used at home (?)	Sept. 2006
	Ginika	F	Senior Infants	6	Nigerian	English used at home (?)	Sept. 2006
	Doris	F	Senior Infants	6	Nigerian	English used at home (?)	Sept. 2006
	Linda	F	Senior Infants	6	Nigerian	English used at home (?)	Sept. 2006
	Beatriz	F	First Class	8	Portuguese	Portuguese	Sept. 2006
	Chimamanda	F	First Class	7	Nigerian	English used at home (?)	Sept. 2006
	Nasreen	F	First Class	8	Pakistani	Urdu/Punjabi (?)	Feb. 2006
	Fatima	F	Third Class	10	Pakistani	Urdu/Punjabi (?)	Feb. 2006
	Eniola	F	Fifth Class	15	Nigerian	Igbo/Yoruba /English (?)	Sept. 2006[4]

1 *School class among participating pupils ranges from Junior Infants to Fifth Class. The Irish system of primary education comprises eight years of schooling: two Infant Classes (Junior and Senior) followed by First to Sixth Class.*

2 *Age in years relates to pupil age at the end of data collection in each school: June 2008 in School 1, May 2008 in School 2, and February 2008 in School 3. In the case of Ivan, this represents the pupil's age when he left School 1 in February 2008.*

3 *Home language refers to the home language of the pupils insofar as this was known to the teacher; (?) indicates lack of precise information.*

4 *Eniola received English language support at another school in Ireland in September 2006 and enrolled in School 3 in September 2007.*

between the ages of 4 and 5. The first two preliminary years – known respectively as Junior and Senior Infants – are followed by six years of primary education proper (First to Sixth Class). It is clear from Table 3.2 that children in the Infant years were particularly well represented in the participant group, with 11 pupils in Junior Infants and nine in Senior Infants. A further six pupils were in First Class, while the remaining three pupils belonged to Second, Third and Fifth Class respectively. This distribution reflects national demographic patterns associated with pupils from immigrant backgrounds at the time of the data collection. By 2007 many of the children termed 'newcomers' were not themselves first-generation immigrants but had been born in Ireland to 'newcomer' parents. As a result, many children from immigrant backgrounds, like the majority of the participants in our study, were enrolling at primary school at entry level (Junior Infants). This meant that they received their two-year entitlement to English language support during the Infant years. Nevertheless, as Table 3.2 shows, our research also included some slightly older pupils who arrived in Ireland and entered primary school at a later stage.

Since age can influence L2 acquisition (see, e.g. Hyltenstam and Abrahamsson 2003, Johnson and Newport 1989, Muñoz 2006, Singleton and Ryan 2004), it is a factor which we will consider in discussing the results obtained from this study. In view of the context of English language support in Irish primary schools, the range of communicative language use among older pupils is likely to be more extensive than among younger pupils, particularly as regards the development of L2 literacy skills. From Table 3.2, it is evident that most of the pupils participating in our project could be classified as belonging to the 'early childhood' period (2–7 years) identified by Philp, Mackey and Oliver (2008). Inevitably, this means that our findings will be more reflective of the experience of younger than of older pupils. Accordingly, further research into the L2 development of pupils receiving English language support in the senior primary years is necessary to confirm, supplement or qualify the conclusions drawn in this study.

The participating pupils came from 11 different national backgrounds spanning three continents and were broadly representative of immigration patterns at the time of the data collection. There was evidence of at least 12 different home languages in use among them. However, determining pupils' language background was not always easy. In some cases teachers had to deduce home languages from pupils' national background, contact with parents, and any references that pupils themselves made to home languages in the classroom. When pupils or their parents came from countries with several national (and often numerous regional) languages, it was often impossible to determine L1 background with absolute certainty. For instance, in the case of the one Chinese pupil, the teacher was unsure whether the child's first language was Mandarin or Cantonese; though because the child came from

Hong Kong, Cantonese seems more likely. Likewise, there is no certainty that the two Pakistani pupils (sisters) were native speakers of either Urdu or Punjabi. However, the older of the two had attended school in Pakistan and on one occasion presented some examples of home-language writing. This suggests that she had some familiarity with Urdu, although her home language could have been either Punjabi or some other regional language.

For a considerable number of the participating pupils, English was almost certainly used as a means of communication at home as well as at school. Based on the pupils' classroom performance and communication with parents, the teachers involved believed that for 10 of the 11 Nigerian pupils included in the sample, Nigerian English was (at least one of) the language(s) of the home. These pupils' contributions to the research data support this view: some aspects of their language production (specific phonological features, as well as some distinctive but readily comprehensible use of lexis or grammatical structures) suggested difference in dialect rather than L2 learning. The eleventh Nigerian pupil, an older child who had spent her formative years in Nigeria and began to attend school in Ireland in 2006, exhibited some characteristics of language use more identifiable with L2 learning (lexical deficit, some systematic non-native-like structures). The teacher concerned was not entirely sure of this pupil's home language(s), though cultural clues pointed towards Igbo or Yoruba. But given the use of English as an official language in Nigeria, the possibility that she had experienced sustained exposure to English beyond that associated with her primary education in Ireland could not be disregarded.

The inclusion of data from pupils whose L1 was another dialect of English would have seriously distorted our investigation of the relation between the acquisition of English L2 and the learning outcomes described in the *Benchmarks*. Accordingly, our analysis focuses exclusively on the English language development of the 18 pupils who were unambiguously L2 learners. At the same time, the language samples obtained from Nigerian pupils who may have had English as (one of) their home language(s) provided a useful point of comparison with the production of the 18 'definite' English L2 learners.

It is appropriate to conclude this section with a closer look at the linguistic origins of the 18 EAL pupils central to our study. Among the 10 L1s other than English in Table 3.2, seven are European: Slavic languages (Polish, Serbian, Croatian) were spoken by eight pupils, Romance languages (Romanian and Portuguese) by four pupils, and Baltic languages (Latvian and Lithuanian) by two pupils. In addition, three Asian languages were represented, two from the Indian sub-continent and one from China. One of the Indian languages, probably Urdu or Punjabi (both Indo-European languages), was spoken by two pupils; the other, Malayalam (a Dravidian language), was spoken by one pupil. The remaining pupil was a native speaker of a Sino-Tibetan language, probably Cantonese. The diversity of the participants' home languages meant that the data collected should provide linguistically balanced evidence of English L2 acquisition for comparison with the *Benchmarks*. L1 impacts on L2 acquisition in a variety of ways (see, for example, Gass and Selinker 2008, Odlin 2003, Lakshmanan 2009, Pienemann 2005, Romaine 2003), and to some extent it was possible to explore the influence of cross-linguistic transfer on pupils' English L2 development (see the individual case studies presented in Chapter 4).

Finally, it is important to point out that the L1s recorded for individual pupils may not fully reflect their plurilingual competence. During the recorded lessons, some pupils mentioned activities that involved other languages; for example, a Lithuanian-speaking pupil talked about watching a film in Russian and having a Russian-speaking relative, while a Pakistani pupil mentioned learning Arabic for religious reasons. Also, in addition to learning English L2 since starting primary school in Ireland, the participants had been simultaneously learning Irish in the mainstream classroom, and there was some production of Irish in several of the recorded lessons.

The composition of the group of 18 EAL pupils shared the characteristics of the original group of 29 participants in terms of age, gender and school class. However, a greater proportion of these pupils (11 of 18) were in their first year of English language support than had been the case among the entire sample.

Recording and transcribing English language support lessons

Lessons were recorded with 11 groups of pupils, though due to practical constraints the number of recordings made of each group varied significantly. The composition of groups also fluctuated as a result of pupil mobility and, in School 1, the organisational flexibility allowed by the presence of two English language support teachers. Table 3.3 gives an overview of the groups visited in the three participating schools, the home languages present in each group, and the number of recordings made. The lesson groups were generally small; on average they comprised between two and four pupils, although groups in School 2 tended to be slightly larger (five to eight pupils). Lesson groups were generally arranged according to school class, although L2 proficiency was also taken into account. The organisation of English language support lessons within each school was in line with the typical model of delivery outlined in Chapter 1: daily withdrawal classes of 35–45 minutes' duration. Some pupils received additional support lessons (due to scheduling issues, these were not recorded), particularly if they faced significant challenges with mainstream literacy activities.

The format of English language support lessons was roughly similar from school to school. Classroom activities tended to focus on oral L2 use, but L2 literacy activities were often included, as appropriate to the age and the

Table 3.3 Overview of lesson groups and recording schedule

	Group	Participating pupils	National/cultural background	Lessons recorded
School 1	Junior Infants	Tomasz	Polish	19
		Patryk	Polish	
		(with 2 non-participating pupils)		
	Senior Infants (A)	Yemi	Nigerian	12
		Ivan	Croatian	
		(occasionally with Stefan or Ravi)		
	Senior Infants (B)	Constantin	Romanian	5
		Obinze	Nigerian	
		Benjamin	Nigerian	
	First Class (A)	Andrei	Romanian	24*
		Stefan	Polish	
	First Class (B) & Second Class	Ravi	Indian	9
		Lukas	Lithuanian	
School 2	Junior Infants (A)	Marko	Serbian	12
		Dimitrie	Romanian	
		Jin	Chinese	
		(with up to 5 non-participating pupils)		
	Junior Infants (B)	Vladimir	Serbian	11
		Edyta	Polish	
		(with 3 non-participating pupils)		
School 3	Junior Infants	Karina	Latvian	16
		Faith	Nigerian	
		Tina	Nigerian	
		Zofia	Polish	
		(occasionally with non-participating pupil)		
	Senior Infants	Ifemelu	Nigerian	15
		Ginika	Nigerian	
		Doris	Nigerian	
		Linda	Nigerian	
	First Class	Beatriz	Portuguese	16
		Chimamanda	Nigerian	
		Nasreen	Pakistani	
	Third Class & Fifth Class	Fatima	Pakistani	15
		Eniola	Nigerian	

** This group was affected by the staff changes mentioned on page 46 and recorded in Table 3.4 on page 47.*

English language proficiency of the children. The extent to which teachers used the *Benchmarks* in their lesson planning varied. In Schools 1 and 2, teachers often (but not always) structured their lessons loosely around themes presented in the *Benchmarks* units of work. They also used materials (worksheets, flashcards etc.) included in the *Benchmarks*-based resource book *Up and Away* (Integrate Ireland Language and Training 2006b). However, other materials – typically resources used in the mainstream classroom (readers, workbooks etc.) – also featured prominently in English language support lessons in these two schools. In School 3, the teacher made no direct use of the *Benchmarks* and only very occasionally used accompanying resources, usually *My First English Book* (Integrate Ireland Language and Training 2005), as the basis for classroom activities.

It can thus be said that, while the *Benchmarks* provided some guide to the delivery of English language support in the participating schools, their use was in no way systematic. For instance, none of the teachers explicitly based their lesson objectives on *Benchmarks* descriptors, even if they planned their teaching around the units of work and included resources derived from the *Benchmarks* (see Appendix 2 for a complete set of *Benchmarks* descriptors). This rather light application of the *Benchmarks* meant that they had some impact on the semantic fields emerging in the recorded lessons. However, the topics covered would also be typical of pupils' mainstream classroom learning since the units of work were derived from recurring themes in the primary curriculum (as explained in Chapter 2). While some of the activities organised by teachers (e.g. shopping role-plays) corresponded closely to particular descriptors, this was the exception rather than the rule. Such activities were often typical of those used in the mainstream classroom context (e.g. when teaching strands of the maths curriculum which introduce the concept of money, 'play shop' activities are a frequent means of demonstrating transactions). Generally, however, there was little targeted elicitation of specific forms suggested by the functions inherent in the *Benchmarks* descriptors, apart from occasional activities (e.g. the discussion of preferences) which, by their nature, necessitated the use of particular structures. Teaching approaches promoting a more conscious 'focus on form' were not the norm.

With regard to pedagogical practice, it should also be pointed out that most of the teachers who took part in this study had received little or no training in the delivery of English language support. The IILT seminars had ceased in 2006 and during the school year 2007–08 there was no in-service training available for teachers in this field. As well as influencing the degree to which teachers applied the *Benchmarks*, this may also have affected their pedagogical practice. Although the English language support lesson groups were small, most teachers simply replicated practices typical of mainstream teaching, in which teacher-led discourse still tends to predominate. The opportunity which this small-group context offered for extensive peer-to-peer inaction was significantly under-exploited. Overall, little evidence emerged that the more autonomous approaches to second language learning supported by the *Benchmarks* and their associated resources were widely adopted.

Clearly, this may have had implications for the study, particularly in relation to the interactional characteristics of the recorded lessons. Consequently, in our derivation of individual and overall results, we will consider the issue of interaction-related influences on L2 acquisition. However, as this study was primarily an investigation of whether the *Benchmarks* reflect English L2 acquisition among primary school pupils, it was actually better for research purposes that the application of the *Benchmarks* in all three schools was not very meticulous. Rigorous adherence to the *Benchmarks* (i.e. exclusive and careful use of the descriptors as goals for learning activities) could have impacted on the validity of our results. Instead, the recorded lessons simply offered a representative sample of how English language support is delivered in Irish primary schools. They thus served as an appropriate data source for the comparison of the independent variables: empirical evidence of English L2 acquisition and the trajectory of English language proficiency development described in the *Benchmarks*. Using this data, we could respond to the research questions outlined in Chapter 1.

Altogether 154 English language support lessons were recorded over a 10-month period using an mp3 digital recorder (which meant that the recording process was unobtrusive, and secure storage of the data was easy to manage). Detailed field notes were made for each lesson to augment the information contained in the audio recordings. The notes were an essential reference when recordings proved unclear or ambiguous. They also made it easy to distinguish between pupils when transcribing and to ensure that the utterances of non-participating pupils were excluded from the transcription.

The principal focus of the research was on the development of English L2 oral skills, for three reasons: spontaneous speech is a key indicator of L2 acquisition; spoken interaction is in any case the dominant communicative mode in English language support lessons; and given the age of the participating pupils, most of them were likely to be at a very early stage of literacy development. Samples of written production were nevertheless collected, generally from pupils from First Class upwards in Schools 1 and 3; some examples of emergent literacy activities were also collected from Junior Infants in School 1. As far as possible, the written work collected was directly related to activities in the recorded lessons. More substantial data related to English L2 literacy skills was provided by the recordings themselves, which often included reading or writing activities and produced both direct evidence (reading aloud) and indirect evidence (talk about literacy-related activities) of English L2 literacy development.

Because the ultimate goal of the research was to arrive at an impression of overall English L2 development among a group of EAL pupils over time, it was decided that broad transcription would be sufficiently informative. It could effectively capture the L2 lexis and L2 grammatical structures used by pupils in the recorded lessons and offer some, albeit very limited information as to their L2 phonological development. Broad transcription could thus provide considerable evidence as to the pupils' development of English L2 oral skills. Also, for practical reasons, it was the most feasible approach given the time constraints of the study and the fact that over 80 hours of lessons were recorded. The system of transcription used was adapted from Schiffrin (1994) (see Appendix 3). Repeated playback and reference to detailed field notes were used in order to capture pupil utterances as precisely as possible. Where any ambiguity remained, parentheses were used to indicate lack of clarity, while indecipherable utterances were designated as such. In order to achieve maximum accuracy, the transcription of recorded lessons was carried out as soon as possible after recording and was generally completed within one week of the school visit in question. All activities that involved spoken interaction and spoken production were fully transcribed, as was the reading aloud of worksheet questions or cues in relation to a topic under discussion. Activities that involved listening, reading and writing were transcribed as far as possible; this included most of pupils' extended reading aloud from graded readers (short books read at home and re-read the following day to the teacher). But in some cases listening or literacy-focused activities were not transcribed but described in depth, using the audio recordings, field notes and (where relevant and obtainable) any written work produced by the pupils. Typically, these activities involved more proficient pupils engaging with exercises (usually taken from mainstream workbooks) designed to develop English orthographic skills. Activities of this kind tended not to generate much oral output from pupils – the emphasis was on their written production. As the recordings of such exercises were often mostly of teachers' explanations, they were not always transcribed.

Regarding listening-focused activities, again these predominantly featured teacher discourse – generally the reading of a prepared script. Pupils responded non-verbally, apart from occasional comments, typically repetition of instructions for clarification. Evidence of listening comprehension was usually visual (a picture or colouring) or kinaesthetic (movement following instructions). Activities specifically aimed at the development of L2 listening skills were, however, not very numerous in the recorded lessons. The recordings of activities requiring L2 spoken interaction offered a much more extensive source of evidence relating to pupils' L2 listening abilities, as apparent from their understanding of their teachers and peers. Admittedly, this can give only a rough indication of their receptive oral skills since receptive and productive skills often develop at different rates. Nevertheless, pupils' ability to engage in any instance of spoken interaction suggests they have acquired sufficient L2 listening skills to do so. Therefore, evidence of skills in L2 spoken interaction may provide secondary evidence of L2 listening ability.

In relation to the development of L2 reading skills, oral comprehension questions, which were almost always interspersed in the recorded 'reading aloud' activities, offered evidence of pupils' receptive skills based on their engagement with L2 written text. Samples of pupils' L2 writing often served this purpose too, for example, written responses to questions based on the reading of a short text. Again, this evidence was inevitably influenced by the extent of pupils' L2 productive skills and its impact on their ability to demonstrate comprehension. In order to ensure that the transcripts preserved their anonymity, pupils were assigned numbers, which were later changed to pseudonyms.

Data Analysis Phase I

Preliminary considerations

Once the recordings had been transcribed, it was necessary to decide how to compare pupils' English L2 development with the learning outcomes described in the *Benchmarks*; this was the central concern of the first phase of data analysis. Before describing the approach adopted, it is worth reiterating that the *Benchmarks* are not intended to be prescriptive and schools are not obliged to apply them in any uniform manner. In all three participating schools the *Benchmarks* appeared to be used for overall lesson planning rather than as a basis for learning activities linked to specific descriptors (they were referred to much less frequently in School 3 than in Schools 1 and 2). Also, as pointed out earlier, when IILT materials developed from the *Benchmarks* were used, it was always together with mainstream classroom activities and resources. The fact that the *Benchmarks* were applied so loosely and to varying extents in each school and lesson group was, as we have stressed, an advantage: it meant that more objective results could be obtained as regards the *Benchmarks*' relation to empirical evidence of English L2 acquisition.

All the transcribed data for 10 of the 11 recorded lesson groups was included in the first phase of data analysis. As we have already explained, one group (School 3, Group 2) was excluded because it consisted entirely of pupils of Nigerian background whose L1 appeared to be Nigerian English. Otherwise, the transcribed oral production of all participating pupils was analysed, including that of the remaining Nigerian children, which had the potential to serve as a 'native-speaker reference' and provide further information regarding the classroom talk in which the discourse produced by EAL pupils was situated. Altogether 135 transcribed lessons were included in this phase of analysis, which comprised three strands.

First strand of analysis: Acquisition of English grammar

As Ellis and Barkhuizen (2005) point out, 'L2 use' cannot be equated with 'L2 acquisition', and the extent to which the former can serve as an indicator of the latter is controversial. They nevertheless argue that naturally occurring samples of L2 use provide the best evidence of L2 acquisition (2005:364). In principle, therefore, transcriptions of extensively recorded L2 use that occurred in the normal course of regular English language support lessons offered substantial evidence of pupils' L2 acquisition over time. When children are educated through an L2 it is particularly difficult to differentiate between 'natural' and 'instructed' language learning (Watson-Gegeo and Nielsen 2003). EAL pupils' English L2 use at school spans a range of different contexts – from informal communication with friends to the more academic language associated with classroom activities – all of which form part of their everyday experience. By extension, as our pupils' use of English L2 in the recorded lessons was directly linked to their use of the language for socialisation and mainstream curriculum learning, it may likewise be considered typical of their daily English L2 use (rather than distinctly 'instructed' L2 learning). Also, because their use of English in these lessons was not predetermined in any way – the lessons were just recordings of normal classroom activities without, for example, any experimental procedures – it may be viewed as 'natural' data. Of course, written transcription can yield only a limited representation of oral language use; in particular, the ability of broad transcription to capture phonological detail is severely restricted. Nevertheless, our transcripts could tell us much about pupils' L2 grammatical and lexical development, and that was sufficient for them to serve as analysable evidence of L2 acquisition.

Since grammar is a major indicator of L2 development, a comprehensive analysis of the formal features of each transcribed pupil turn was both an appropriate and a sufficiently rigorous means of determining the characteristics of pupils' English L2 acquisition over the course of the study. Accordingly, the first strand of this phase was a formal analysis of each decipherable pupil turn in the 135 recorded lessons under consideration. This entailed breaking down each transcribed turn into its constituent linguistic elements and coding each element. The system of coding used was derived from syntactic and lexico-grammatical accounts of English grammar, including Baker (1997), Klammer, Schultz and Della Volpe (2006), and Morley (2004). It covers all linguistic elements produced by participating pupils, generally with a one-to-one mapping between word and code (e.g. /N/: noun, /A/: adjective, /PREP/: preposition), although occasional multi-word elements received a single code (e.g. 'thank you' – coded /INTsoc/: social interactive, or 'Santa Claus' – coded /PN/: proper noun). Additional codes were included to mark, for example, pauses (/-/) and non-verbal utterances (/nv/), while prominent instances of interruption or hesitation leading to repetition were marked by adding (~) to coded elements. Two examples of the linguistic coding of pupil turns are provided in the next paragraph and the full coding scheme can be found in Appendix 4.

Because many of the participating pupils were very young, the standard of accuracy applied to the data was the one typically associated with native English-speaking children of a similar age. The pupils of Nigerian origin and

Bronagh Ćatibušić's own school-going children (aged 5–6 and 8–9 years) were used as a reference. Linguistic elements that were clearly at variance with these native speaker norms were marked with an asterisk as shown in the second of these examples produced by Stefan:

> *Stefan*: yeah I like milk.
> Coded for linguistic analysis as LA: /INTmin/PROpers/V/N// – minimal interactive (agreement marker)/personal pronoun/verb (present tense)/ noun (singular)
> *Stefan*: I like banana. LA: /PROpers/V/N*//
> Coded for linguistic analysis as LA: /PROpers/V/N*// – personal pronoun/verb (present tense)/noun (singular – incorrect form)

Further investigation of the specific nature of these incorrect forms was carried out in Phase II of our analysis. Finally, whether due to context or the often highly creative and idiosyncratic nature of children's talk, elements that were best considered ambiguous were marked with a hash symbol. This formal analysis remained focused on grammatical development, and the limitations of broad transcription were recognised and accepted. However, any phonological issues that had been highlighted in the transcribed data were indicated by adding (#) to their linguistic coding, since they were potential sources of (albeit phonologically related) ambiguity. Occasionally, particularly in relation to decontextualised reading activities, the categorisation of certain words was indefinite. Such words were coded to include all options, unless the context suggested otherwise (e.g. the word 'tug' read in a list of words ending in an '-ug' sound was coded as /NorV/).

Second strand of analysis: Communicative purpose linked to Benchmarks

In order to explore possible links between the pupils' production of English L2 and the learning outcomes described in the *Benchmarks*, it was necessary to investigate the communicative purpose of pupils' utterances. By regarding them as evidence of communicative activity in progress, transcribed pupil turns could be linked to individual *Benchmarks* descriptors, principally those presented in the 13 theme-based units of work. A direct link was coded using a shorthand reference to the descriptor in question, for example: BM: U1/ A1/SpInt/1// = *Benchmarks*: Unit 1 (Myself)/proficiency level A1/spoken interaction/descriptor 1 (of 4): 'Can answer basic questions about his/her name, age, family when supported by prompts' (Integrate Ireland Language and Training 2003a:10). Some examples of pupil turns associated with *Benchmarks* descriptors (Integrate Ireland Language and Training 2003a:14–15, 21) for the three proficiency levels A1, A2 and B1 are provided below.

Level A1:

> *Marko*: it's a sunny day.
> Functionally coded as: BM: U6/A1/SpInt/1// to show that it relates to
> Unit 6 (Weather)/level A1, spoken interaction/descriptor 1 (of 1): 'Can
> respond non-verbally (e.g. with a nod or shake of the head) or with
> single-word or very brief answers to basic questions about the weather
> (e.g., *Is it cold outside?*) and the kind of weather he/she likes and dislikes.'

Level A2:

> *Andrei*: and my brother talk my dog she say she 'ave to talk in Romania.
> Functionally coded as: BM: U12/A2/SpInt/2// to show that it relates to
> Unit 12 (Animals and plants)/level A2/spoken interaction/descriptor 2
> (of 2): 'Can ask and answer questions about keeping a pet.'

Level B1:

> *Nasreen*: because if somebody drinks lots of em whiskey and beer and-
> and- em then- then they em the eyes start to close and em they start going
> in the road and then they fell down and eh and that's why the- the police
> is there.
> Functionally coded as BM: U5/B1/SpProd/1// to show that it relates to
> Unit 5 (People who help us)/level B1/spoken production/descriptor 1 (of
> 1): 'Can talk about the responsibilities of people who help, using an age-
> appropriate range of descriptive vocabulary.'

When the link was approximate, this was coded by adding a percentage
symbol to the relevant descriptor code – BM: U1/A1/SpInt/1%//. In cases
of approximation, it was sometimes possible to suggest ways in which the
descriptor in question might be edited or extended in order to correspond
more closely to actual pupil production. For example:

> *Karina*: this is hat. *(referring to a picture of different items of clothing)*
> This turn was coded as BM: U3/A1/SpInt/3%//: an approximation to
> Unit 3 (Food and clothes)/level A1, spoken interaction/descriptor 3 (of
> 3): 'Can respond non-verbally (e.g. with a nod or a shake of the head) or
> with single word or very brief answers to questions about the food/drink
> and clothes he/she likes or dislikes.'

The link to the *Benchmarks* made here was an approximation as, while the
turn fulfilled the thematic and linguistic criteria associated with this descriptor, it was a statement identifying an item of clothing rather than an expression of personal preference. In contrast, the examples given in the section on
linguistic coding regarding food or drink preferences (e.g. 'yeah I like milk')

fulfilled all the requisite criteria and thus were linked directly to this descriptor. A suggestion was made in this case to widen the scope of the descriptor slightly, revising the second part of it to: '. . . answers to questions about food/ drink and clothes, for example about his/her likes and dislikes'. A full list of proposed revisions to individual *Benchmarks* descriptors (most of which were, as in the example above, minor) together with suggestions for possible additions or adjustments to existing units of work is provided in Appendix 5.

Pupil turns were generally linked to one *Benchmarks* descriptor only. However, if a turn involved more than one communicative skill, it could be linked to two descriptors. This was often the case with regard to literacy-related talk. Transcription of a lesson that was focused on writing necessarily captured the oral interaction associated with engagement in the written task. In such cases it seemed appropriate to code pupils' turns with reference to descriptors for both spoken interaction and writing. For example, BM: U1/ A1/SpInt/1(>U1/A1/Write/1)// could be used to indicate that the A1 descriptor for spoken interaction quoted above was activated (e.g. by asking a question about spelling) during a writing activity related to Unit 1 (Myself)/level A1/writing/descriptor 1 (of 2): 'Can copy or write his/her name, address, name of school' (Integrate Ireland Language and Training 2003a:10). Links to more than one unit of work could also be captured. For example, BM: U8/ A2/SpInt/1(>U11) could be used to indicate that a pupil turn associated with the first A2 descriptor for spoken interaction in Unit 8 (Seasons, holidays and festivals) – 'Can respond in simple terms to questions about a festival or occasion that is important to his/her family or community' (Integrate Ireland Language and Training 2003a:17) – was also related to Unit 11 (People and places in other areas), possibly due to the child's reference to experience of that celebration in another country. Ambiguous turns were accounted for in two ways. If the turn was partial (typically a turn interrupted by another speaker) but still exhibited functional characteristics linking it to a specific descriptor, this was indicated by according it the relevant *Benchmarks* link but noting, with a hash sign, its potential for ambiguity as a fragmented turn. For example, BM: U1/A2/SpInt/1#// was used to code an unfinished turn showing features associated with the first A2 descriptor for spoken interaction in Unit 1 (Myself): 'Can reply with confidence to familiar questions about his/her name, age, number of brothers and sisters, etc.' (Integrate Ireland Language and Training 2003a:10). If a turn was impossible to interpret from its discourse context, it was marked as such using the code BM: X//. Non-ambiguous turns that could not be linked to *Benchmarks* descriptors, i.e. cases of communicative activities or language themes not included in the *Benchmarks* (e.g. the recitation of nursery rhymes), were accounted for by coding them with a dollar symbol, followed by a thematically appropriate label, for example: BM: $(*nursery rhymes*)//. This aspect of the coding captured information that could be used if the *Benchmarks* were to be revised.

This second strand of data analysis is functional in orientation. It offers a detailed overview of the direct and indirect links that can be made between the *Benchmarks* and the language produced by pupils in the classroom. It also matches the action-oriented approach to language use that the *Benchmarks* inherited from the CEFR.

Third strand of analysis: The interactive dimension

As Ellis and Barkhuizen point out, formal/functional analyses can be 'powerful tools for examining both how learners make use of their linguistic resources to meet their communicative needs and also how communicative needs drive the process of L2 acquisition forward' (2005:137). For this reason, either a 'function-form' analysis or, as in the present study, a 'form-function' analysis (seeking formal evidence of L2 acquisition for subsequent comparison with a functionally oriented L2 curriculum) seems an appropriate analytical choice. However, L2 acquisition does not occur in a vacuum, neither are the communicative activities from which evidence of language learning may emerge context-free. The range of internal and external factors possibly influencing L2 acquisition must therefore be considered in any analysis of learners' L2 production.

In the present study potentially influential internal factors such as age, L1 background and duration of L2 learning could be determined with reasonable certainty, though the problems encountered in ascertaining some pupils' home languages show that this was not always the case. The way in which data was collected made other internal influences – for example, learning styles and affective factors – more difficult to assess. However, observational notes made about each pupil, based on aspects of their participation in the recorded lessons (e.g. personality traits, such as introvert or extravert tendencies, and any evident learning preferences) offered some useful information. As regards external factors, wider social issues – for example, pupils' experience in the mainstream classroom and in the host society at large – could only be considered anecdotally since the study was carried out exclusively in the micro-environment of the English language support classroom. However, research suggests that the impact of interaction on L2 acquisition may be significant (Gass 2003, Swain 2000), and the transcribed data offers concrete and objective information regarding the impact of the interactive dynamic on pupils' immediate L2 production and possibly, over time, on their L2 acquisition.

There were two further reasons for considering interactive factors in conjunction with the form-function analysis outlined above. First, by taking account of the possible effects of interaction on pupils' L2 production, we hoped to reduce the risk of distorting, in a discourse-related way, the results obtained from form-function analysis. Investigating interactive patterns raised questions such as: 'Can a directly repeated form be accorded the same analytical weight as the same form spontaneously produced by the learner?' And answering these questions made it easier to isolate and focus on pupils' spontaneous L2 speech. Secondly, analysis of the interactive features of pupil discourse had the potential to enhance whatever conclusions emerged from the form-function analysis. For example, it could reveal information regarding how features of interaction might vary with increasing proficiency, and how classroom conditions might facilitate or inhibit the development of certain formal structures or communicative abilities. An analysis of the data from this perspective also promised to provide a starting point for any future efforts to optimise the pedagogical impact of classroom interaction.

The decision to investigate interaction-related factors added a third strand to the first phase of data analysis. As with the first and second strands, it was necessary to choose an analytical method that would be feasible, maximally informative, and appropriate to both the data and the aims of the study; a method that would allow the data to be explored as 'talk in progress' while according all participants equal status. Many approaches to the analysis of classroom interaction focus on specific interactional features such as recasts, or particular interactive conditions like those thought to promote 'negotiation of meaning' (see Ellis and Barkhuizen 2005:166). In other words, the researcher decides in advance what aspects of interaction to examine in order to assess their possible impact on learners' L2 acquisition. When this kind of analysis is applied to discourse that involves teachers and learners in an institutional L2 learning environment, it may be coloured by role-related expectations; for example, learners may be regarded as in some sense 'deficient'. 'Critical' discourse analysis may seek to challenge the power relations implied by these roles, but again the researcher's aim is to highlight certain pre-selected interactional features in order to propose change. By contrast, the aims of the present study required a method that would try to 'get inside' classroom talk in order to examine it from the different perspectives of its participants, even if some of them had very limited proficiency in English. This did not mean that the potential implications of the individual acting in the role of 'pupil' could be ignored; rather that each pupil's production would be analysed in terms of its contribution to the classroom talk in progress before considering any apparent effects of the classroom dynamic.

Conversation analysis (CA) offered an approach that could supplement the form-function analysis by providing information about the interactional context of pupils' recorded turns. The purpose of CA is to investigate the workings of 'talk-in-interaction' (Schegloff 2007:1) by focusing on the interactive dynamic rather than the content of the talk or the social identities of the parties involved. Based on the idea that talk is a 'deeply ordered and structurally organised phenomenon' (Ellis and Barkhuizen 2005:198), CA explores the structure of interaction by focusing on the characteristics of turn-taking and sequence organisation that hold it together, and by looking at the repair strategies which prevent communication from breaking down (Ellis and Barkhuizen 2005:203–204). This interactional structure is an essential aspect of any instance of spoken language use because, as Schegloff stresses, in organising sequences of talk, the speakers' focus is 'not, in general, on convergence on the same *topic* being talked about but on the contingent development of *courses of action*' (2007:251 [emphasis in the original]). Speakers may, for example, disagree or misunderstand each other, but their interaction is ultimately shaped not by the content of their talk but by the nature of the turns they take within it. The concept of interaction sequences as 'courses of action' accords well, of course, with the 'action-oriented' approach to language learning that the *Benchmarks* inherit from the CEFR.

CA tends not to make overt reference to the social context of the interaction or the relationship between the speakers, but this does not mean that the social context is ignored. Instead of treating attributes that constitute the social identities of participants in the interaction as 'external variables', CA regards them as factors that may have 'procedural consequentiality or demonstrable relevance for the participants themselves in terms of the specific ways in which the interaction is organised' (Sidnell 2009:9). Obviously the organisation of classroom talk cannot be immune to the social influences and power relationships associated with the socially created context of 'school', and more specifically, 'the English language support classroom'. However, since CA seeks to uncover the sequential characteristics of any instance of interaction, it has the potential to offer an 'insider' view of how EAL pupils use English in this interactive context, rather than how they act as a 'pupil' being 'taught' English within roles presupposed by the researcher. CA cannot be used to account for L2 acquisition, of course, but it can offer valuable descriptive detail at the 'micro-level' (Hellerman 2008:28) in relation to learners' L2 use. This information may then be used to determine the possible influence of the interactional environment on learners' L2 development since, as Hellerman stresses, the focus of CA 'highlights the individual's microgenesis of language development and can also describe the sociogenesis of language practices for the entire classroom community of practice' (2008:28).

For the purposes of the present study, it was necessary to distinguish between 'pure' and 'applied' CA. Pure CA is highly detailed, usually based on very narrow transcriptions of interaction that are made with repeated recourse to original recordings; it often involves collaboration between analysts working on selected, manageable chunks of data (see ten Have 2007:8 for definition and discussion). As its name suggests, applied CA is more flexible and can be used in a wider range of situations, typically related to medicine, business or education (see Richards and Seedhouse 2005, also ten Have 2007:8). Detail of transcription and depth of analysis tend to be reduced in order to transcend the limitations imposed by strict adherence to pure

CA procedures. In view of the quantity of data to be analysed, applied CA offered a realistic but informative means of analysing classroom interaction in the present study.

In order to code the data a very simple template was devised, based on the principles outlined by Schegloff, who views the organisation of turn-taking as 'one of the most fundamental organisations of practice for talk-in-interaction' (2007:1). The 'adjacency pair', comprising consecutive turns by two participants in the interaction, constitutes the 'basic unit of sequence construction' (Schegloff 2007:13). Coding was informed by the work of experienced practitioners such as ten Have (2007) and Liddicoat (2007), and guided by CA studies that focus on L2 learning, particularly those reported by Richards and Seedhouse (2005). Essentially, it was a matter of determining the role played by each pupil turn in the underlying adjacency pair structure: whether it was a 'first pair part' (Fb) or a 'second pair part' (Sb) (Schegloff 2007:13). Then the overall sequence was examined in order to determine the sequential nature of any preliminary turns (PRE) or subsequent expansions (POST) on the core adjacency pair, including any repair turns (REP) which the participants produced in cases of misunderstanding and interaction breakdown (on repair sequences in the L2 classroom, see Young 2007). Extended sequences in which speakers appeared to 'suspend the normal operations of turn-taking' (Liddicoat 2007:302) for a particular interactional purpose such as story-telling were also accounted for (EXT).

Besides indicating the position of each transcribed turn in its interactional sequence, the CA codes identified participating speakers in terms of their classroom role; for example, turns were coded p-p (pupil to pupil), p-t (pupil to teacher), or t-p (teacher to pupil). Here is an example of how we coded a turn produced by Beatriz in response to her teacher's question as to which game she had played in the mainstream classroom the previous day:

> *Beatriz:* mine was bingo and the same like hers.
> Coded for conversation analysis as CA: p-t:Sb:Ans(Iprov)// – pupil to teacher interaction/second part of an adjacency pair/answer providing information (as opposed to opinion).

In order to analyse the transcribed talk-in-interaction in as much detail as possible, teacher turns as well as pupil turns were coded. The only breaks in analysis were those caused by the input of non-participating pupils, which was not transcribed. Turns were also coded to show the speech act they performed; they were identified as questions, answers, requests, offers, etc. The coding system also took account of further details, for example, the presence of hesitation, pauses, repetition or recasts. Although it was very much a working document, continuously adapted and refined in response to the demands of the data, the coding scheme (Appendix 4) served to indicate the interactional characteristics of each transcribed turn not only in the immediate context of the lesson transcript but when extracted from this context for further analysis. An excerpt from the transcripts showing the three-way coding applied in Data Analysis Phase I can be found in Figure 3.2 (pages 63–64).

Data Analysis Phase II

Extent of analysis

When the three-strand coding of the data – formal, functional and interactional – had been completed, it was necessary to decide how to proceed with the analysis in order to obtain results that would answer the research questions. It was not possible to include all 135 recorded lessons in the second phase of analysis: there was simply too much data. In order to arrive at a representative sample for each of the 18 participating pupils, two criteria were applied. First, for each pupil at least 50% of the recorded lessons would be included. As we have noted, pupils occasionally changed groups because of scheduling difficulties (this particularly affected Andrei and Stefan). Observation suggested that inclusion in an unfamiliar group tended to have an adverse effect on pupils' language production, so these lessons were excluded from the analysis. Secondly, in order to ensure that each pupil's production was adequately represented, a minimum of six recorded lessons would be included, even for pupils who participated in fewer than 12 lessons overall. This criterion was met for 17 of the 18 participating pupils. The exception was Constantin, for whom there were only four recorded lessons. His English language support group (School 1, Group 3) met at the same time as another group (School 1, Group 1) and was visited only when the latter group was unavailable. But because he was in his second year of English language support, Constantin was at a level of proficiency that was under-represented in the data, and for this reason it was decided to include him. It was an advantage that he was very talkative.

As far as possible, lessons were selected at approximately two-week intervals, though for reasons of scheduling and attendance this was not always feasible. Also, priority was given to lessons with the highest levels of pupil participation in the discourse, since they had the potential to yield the most informative findings with regard to L2 acquisition. Since the lesson groups were, as noted earlier, generally small (usually 2–4 pupils, with the exception of the two groups recorded in School 2), pupil absences could significantly change the group dynamic. For this reason efforts were made to exclude one-to-one teacher-pupil lessons; in some instances (involving Lukas, Constantin, and Fatima), however, such lessons were unavoidably selected. Table 3.4 shows the extent to which each of the 18 participating pupils was represented in the second phase of data analysis.

Table 3.4 Selection of lessons for Data Analysis Phase II

Selection of lessons

Pupil	Duration of participation	Lessons recorded*	Lessons selected	% of recorded lessons covered*
Andrei	Oct 07–May 08	21	11	53%
Stefan	Oct 07–Jun 08	20	11	55%
Tomasz	Nov 07–Jun 08	17	10	59%
Patryk	Nov 07–Jun 08	19	10	53%
Ivan	Nov 07–Feb 08	8	6	75%
Ravi	Jan 08–Jun 08	12	8	67%
Lukas	Mar 08–Jun 08	9	7	78%
Constantin	Oct 07–Apr 08	4	4	100%
Marko	Dec 07–May 08	9	7	78%
Dimitrie	Dec 07–May 08	8	6	75%
Jin	Dec 07–May 08	12	8	67%
Vladimir	Dec 07–May 08	10	7	70%
Edyta	Dec 07–May 08	9	7	78%
Karina	Oct 07–Feb 08	11	8	73%
Zofia	Oct 07–Feb 08	14	8	57%
Beatriz	Oct 07–Feb 08	15	8	53%
Nasreen	Oct 07–Feb 08	15	8	53%
Fatima	Oct 07–Feb 08	13	8	62%

** Lessons recorded within pupils' familiar English language support group; does not include three lessons for Andrei and one lesson for Stefan which were recorded during their temporary participation in other groups.*

Analysing the acquisition of L2 English – methodological approach adopted

The question then arose: How would the English L2 production of the participating pupils be analysed on a pupil-by-pupil basis? It was decided that the formal analysis carried out in the first phase of data analysis would provide the principal focus; in other words, that indicators of grammatical development would serve as the main source of evidence. However, it was also decided to take account of pupils' lexical development. Up to this point in the study, the methodology employed had been entirely qualitative, in keeping with current practice in the study of child L2 acquisition, in which qualitatively focused longitudinal studies have proved significant and much-needed sources of information (see Philp, Mackey and Oliver 2008:11). Yet the consistent application of the same three coding systems to the data created the potential for analysis that extended beyond a purely descriptive snapshot of an individual pupil's production at a particular point in time. The codes were designed to facilitate cumulative description, tracking the appearance of a particular linguistic feature over time in order to describe the development of that feature in a particular pupil. Essentially, the detailed coding employed in the first phase of data analysis set firm foundations for the more mixed methods approach adopted in the second phase.

Like any methodological choice, the decision to mix methods must be justified by the aims of the research and must be compatible with the data obtained. Care must be taken not to over-quantify what is essentially qualitative data, as that could cause some of the most revealing detail, including exceptional instances, to be overlooked. As Dörnyei (2007:272) points out, such 'outliers' may offer unique insights if qualitatively analysed. Nevertheless, if it is conducted in a manner which does not involve the distortion or over-sanitisation of primarily qualitative data, some level of quantitative analysis may be highly advantageous. In particular, quantitative procedures may allow the statistical evaluation of emerging trends in L2 development. This has the potential to add weight to detailed qualitative description, but may also facilitate comparison of results obtained for different participants. In multiple-participant research like the present study, the combination of both qualitative and quantitative analysis appears both useful and appropriate.

Goals of analysis

Even the most detailed analysis of the data collected from 18 pupils in 80 selected lessons over nine months can offer no more than a limited impression of the English L2 development to be expected among EAL pupils in general. But while acknowledging that limitation, it should still be possible to construct informative profiles of the 18 pupils' individual L2 development over the study period; and taken together, those profiles should give a representative indication of what is happening in English language support classrooms. In relation to L2 acquisition, therefore, the goal of the second phase of data analysis was to identify any common features or trends across these pupil profiles, and to consider their implications as potential indicators of developing English L2 proficiency.

By the same token, a selection of lessons recorded in three schools cannot determine the relevance of the learning outcomes specified in the *Benchmarks* to the generality of EAL pupils. Nevertheless, it seemed useful to establish which *Benchmarks* descriptors were activated in the selected lessons, identifying any aspects of the descriptors that seemed to require revision and any aspects of the recorded discourse that called for new descriptors. What is more, the exploration of possible links between the proficiency levels described in the *Benchmarks* and evidence of particular stages or features of L2 acquisition could suggest how EAL learning outcomes might best be described in detail.

Finally, bringing these two goals together, comparative examination of the formal, functional and conversational features of pupils' English L2 production offered to provide evidence not only of how far their language learning needs were reflected in the *Benchmarks*, but of how interactive dynamics in the language support classroom may impact on L2 learning.

Preparation of data

In order to create accurate and sufficiently detailed profiles of individual pupils' L2 acquisition, the data required a considerable amount of preparation. First, since one of the objectives of the quantitative analysis was to examine the type (and not merely the frequency) of linguistic errors, additional sub-coding was necessary. In the first phase of data analysis errors were marked with an asterisk; now error types were specified. To illustrate this, we return to the example provided earlier:

> *Stefan*: I like banana.
> This was linguistically sub-coded as LA: /PROpers/V/N*NoPLR// – personal pronoun/verb (present tense)/noun (singular – incorrect form, error of number, plural required)

The omission of single elements was also sub-coded (e.g. /O*PROpersSubj/ = omission of a subject-form personal pronoun), whereas the omission of multiple elements (marked as /O*Mult/) was coded without detailed specification since the nature of such omissions was often ambiguous. A guide to the sub-coding of linguistic elements is included in Appendix 4 and further examples of the sub-codes used are included in Figure 3.2 on pages 63–64.

Once the linguistic sub-coding had been completed for a given lesson, the construction of individual profiles based on that lesson data could begin. A folder was created for each pupil in Microsoft Word, with a sub-folder for each selected lesson; within each sub-folder, a 'data file' was created, containing only the turns produced by the pupil in question; and each 'data file' served as the basis for the analysis of that particular pupil's L2 use in that selected lesson.

Before examining a pupil's actual English L2 use in a given lesson, consideration was given to the *Benchmarks* descriptors activated in the lesson and any suggestions made in the first phase of data analysis regarding their adjustment or expansion. For each selected lesson, this meant scanning the data file(s) for the pupil(s) involved and recording all *Benchmarks* descriptors identified in the initial functional analysis in a '*Benchmarks* record file'. Three such files (one for each school) were created to indicate which specific *Benchmarks* were activated in each selected lesson for each of the 10 English language support groups. This information was stored on a lesson-by-lesson basis, as *Benchmarks* were generally activated by the overall lesson theme (as decided by the teacher) rather than by individual pupils. In addition, all coded approximations to *Benchmarks* descriptors were recorded in a separate '*Benchmarks* adjustments' file, together with recommendations, based on evidence from the data, for the revision or expansion of specific descriptors and for the possible inclusion of new themes or sub-themes. As mentioned in relation to Data Analysis Phase I, all suggestions for the revisions to the *Benchmarks* based on this research are summarised in Appendix 5.

Once this information from the functional analysis had been logged, it was possible to concentrate on the individual pupil profiles. Each pupil data file was examined to identify which communicative skills were activated according to the functional (*Benchmarks* descriptor-linked) coding for each turn. Literacy-linked turns within each pupil-specific data file were moved to a 'literacy development' file and stored in a 'literacy' sub-folder for the pupil in question. These turns included reading and talk directly related to reading or writing activities. They did not, however, include spontaneous talk following on from a literacy activity or indirect reference to literacy activities, for instance, talking about homework tasks or retelling stories without direct reference to the relevant printed text. The latter activity was more appropriately linked to *Benchmarks* descriptors for spoken production, for example, at level B1 in Unit 12 (Animals and plants): 'Can retell a story about animals' (Integrate Ireland Language and Training 2003a:21). This segregation of literacy-related turns created an easily accessible record of pupils' development of reading and writing skills over the study period; and given that spontaneous speech is the best indicator of L2 acquisition, it also ensured that data directly linked to text that the participating pupils themselves had not produced was excluded from the analysis of their oral production. Turns that simply repeated, without recasting or elaboration, a previous turn (generally one produced by another speaker, often the teacher) were removed from the files because they were usually examples of 'parroting' rather than attempts at meaningful involvement in the discourse. On the other hand, because all naturally occurring speech, including that produced by native speakers, contains a certain amount of repetition, within-turn repetitions of the speaker's own utterances were not excluded from the analysis.

Other turn-types that were eliminated from pupils' 'analysable turn' files included minimal confirmations of previously given information, typically unelaborated 'yes' or 'no', which added no new meaning to the discourse. On the other hand, minimal statements of acceptance/agreement or rejection (involving, e.g. the use of 'yes' or 'no') were included since these constituted meaningful use of pupils' L2. Wholly ambiguous or radically incomplete turns (e.g. a partial utterance of a single word) were also removed as they could not be properly analysed.

Finally, attention was paid to the functional codes that linked each turn to one of the CEFR-derived proficiency levels defined in the *Benchmarks*. For example, if a turn was coded BM: U5/A2/SpInt/1// it was linked to a level A2 descriptor for spoken interaction in Unit 5 (People who help us) (Integrate Ireland Language and Training 2003a:14). By segregating the remaining data for each pupil on the basis of these *Benchmarks*-linked codes, it was possible to create proficiency-level-specific files of spontaneous speech per pupil per lesson.

Turns were discarded if they were impossible to link or approximate to particular descriptors or fell beyond the scope of the *Benchmarks*. The exclusion of turns in the latter category did not prejudice the analysis in favour of the existing *Benchmarks*, however, for two reasons. First, it was possible to link the great majority of turns to *Benchmarks* descriptors, either through direct correspondence or by approximation; and secondly, turns were excluded only after their implications for *Benchmarks* revision had been recorded in the '*Benchmarks* adjustment files'.

Spoken responses to listening-related activities were primarily coded using a speaking-related descriptor, since oral production was the 'hard evidence' provided by the data. These turns were then linked to an appropriate listening-related descriptor, since comprehension abilities could only be inferred from pupils' spoken output. In such cases the primary (speaking-related) code determined at what proficiency level the turn would be classified for analysis.

Once the data for a particular pupil in a given lesson had been organised according to the above procedures, a breakdown of pupil turns for that lesson was recorded in a 'skills' file that was used to give a numeric overview of each selected lesson. The overview listed the number of transcribed turns, literacy-related turns (reading turns and literacy-related talk turns), and additional references to listening, reading and writing (inferred from non-transcribed literacy-related material and non-verbal responses to listening such as drawing). The number of 'analysed spoken turns' extracted from the original pupil 'data' file was also recorded in the 'skills' file. These 'analysable turns' constituted the main focus of the second phase of data analysis.

Quantitative procedures

Quantitative procedures were used to explore participating pupils' English L2 grammatical development, focusing on six morphological indicators: nouns, verbs, personal pronouns, articles, prepositions, and auxiliaries. These were chosen for quantitative analysis on the basis of their prominence in the data. We felt that this selection – a reasonably diverse range of indicators which were widely distributed across the recorded L2 production of the 18 pupils – could offer substantial evidence of English L2 acquisition among the participant group. Each proficiency-linked 'analysable turn' file, for each pupil, for each selected lesson, was searched for instances of these six indicators and the results were logged using the Statistical Product and Service Solutions (SPSS) software package and entered in pupil-specific databases, one for each indicator. Each database recorded the relevant indicator's frequency of occurrence (token-count) across all forms of the indicator used by the pupil in question over the study period (in the case of nouns, for example, these included singular, plural, and possessive forms). Target-like and non-target-like use of the indicator was differentiated across its various forms, and total error counts for each form (e.g. inappropriate use of singular nouns) were broken down into classified sub-counts for particular error types (e.g. use of a singular noun when a plural noun is required). Omissions of the indicator were also recorded, and where appropriate classified in greater depth (e.g. omissions of personal pronouns were sub-categorised as omission of subject or object pronouns).

As each 'analysable turn' file consisted of turns associated with a specific *Benchmarks* proficiency level, the database entries for any given indicator were also, initially, linked to proficiency levels. For example, the counts for level A1 singular nouns and level A2 singular nouns were recorded in separate database columns. However, once all the entries had been made for the indicator over the series of lessons selected for a particular pupil, totals relating to the frequency and accuracy of the indicator's use could be obtained for each lesson as a whole, using the SPSS 'compute' function. Cumulatively these totals, now independent of *Benchmarks* levels, provided an overall impression of the pupil's acquisition of that particular grammatical indicator during the study period. Basic descriptive statistics such as rate of accuracy or rate of omission could also be calculated, either at a specific proficiency level or overall. Information on the frequency and accuracy with which each pupil produced the different grammatical indicators was graphically displayed for ease of comparison with the findings obtained for other pupils.

SPSS was used to apply two further statistical analyses to the data. First, pupils' verb-to-noun ratio was calculated for each lesson as a means of gauging the L2 syntactic development of pupil-produced turns over the study period, given that nominals (nouns, pronouns and proper names) tend to predominate over verbals (verb forms except for verbal adjectives and verbal nouns) in the early stages of L2 acquisition. The verb-to-noun ratio could be calculated for specific proficiency levels or for overall analysable pupil production in each lesson.

Secondly, SPSS was used to focus on three interactional features of pupils' production: 'answers' (Ans), in which the speaker responds to another participant in the interaction; 'tellings' (TEL), in which the speaker introduces new information; and 'topic elaborations' (TOPEL), in which the speaker adds information to an ongoing conversational sequence regardless of who initiated the topic. An example of an 'answer' was given earlier:

    Beatriz: mine was bingo and the same like hers.

This was an answer to a genuinely 'information seeking' question (Q(IS)) asked by the teacher about the pupil's mainstream classroom. However, most 'answers' recorded in the selected lessons were in response to 'known information' questions (Q(IK)), often in the context of short 'initiation, response, feedback' (IRF) sequences. This example in response to the teacher's question as to what is a 'mechanic' was typical:

    Answer:
    Edyta: car fixer.

'Tellings' were found at the beginning of new interactional sequences and could be followed by 'topic elaborations' in subsequent expansion (POST) sequences as the conversation developed from its initial adjacency pair. Here are two examples from classroom talk in which Jin is trying to describe a 'dragon'.

    Telling:
    Jin: I saw this dinosaur is . . . (xxx) is fire.

The teacher and other pupils respond to this initiation of information and Jin elaborates further on the topic with the following example:

    Topic elaboration:
    Jin: and and and there was smoke comin'.

These three turn-types were analysed because they were the most typical (frequently occurring) indicators of responsive (Ans) and active discourse (TEL and TOPEL) in the pupils' recorded classroom interaction. Therefore, like the choice of grammatical indicators, discussed above, the selection of turn-types for analysis was also data-driven. The number of 'answers', 'tellings' and 'topic elaborations' was calculated for each proficiency-linked pupil file and then totalled for each selected lesson.

Two further indicators of the interactive dynamic of a given lesson were included in the quantitative analysis. These were counts both for the number of pupil-to-teacher turns and for the number of pupil-to-pupil turns in each proficiency-linked file for each pupil for each lesson, from which lesson totals could then be calculated. In this way it was hoped to provide some (possibly generalisable) statistical support for any conclusions based on qualitative descriptions of the interactive dynamic in the selected lessons.

The final quantitative procedure included in the second phase of data analysis focused on the evidence of L2 lexical development displayed by each pupil in each selected lesson. Wordlist (part of the software package Wordsmith Tools) was used to create lists of lexical types produced and compute frequency of occurrence. The proficiency-linked and overall word-lists for each pupil in each selected lesson could then be used to provide not only detailed qualitative evidence, but also some basic statistical overviews of EAL pupils' L2 lexical development over the study period.

Qualitative procedures

In order to provide information on L2 syntactic development beyond the rudimentary indication of turn complexity offered by the verb-to-noun ratio, the development of three specific structural features – negative forms, questions and clause linkage – was tracked for each pupil, for each selected lesson. All unique instances of each structure were identified and stored in chronological order in structure-specific files that were drawn on qualitatively in the compilation of the pupil profiles. Summarised versions of these profiles are presented, as 18 short case studies, in Chapter 4.

Finally, for each pupil, notes were compiled to accompany each selected lesson. These summarised some of the most salient issues arising from the quantitative analysis of L2 grammatical development, highlighting particular linguistic challenges faced by a particular pupil in a given lesson, but also adding qualitative detail to the statistical analyses (e.g. which actual past tense verbs or prepositions were used by the pupil). In this way, aspects of L2 lexical and grammatical development could be brought into combined focus. The 'notes' file also included comments on features of L2 acquisition not subjected to quantitative analysis: issues related to literacy development, phonological characteristics of pupils' speech, home language and other possible internal influences on their L2 development. These points were taken into consideration in compiling the pupil profiles.

Production of pupil profiles

The combination of mixed methods and qualitative analysis carried out in this analytical phase resulted in the production of the profiles, which are summarised in Chapter 4. For each individual pupil these case studies report:

- the results of the functional analysis of the pupil's oral English L2 use, based on links between the pupil's spoken turns and the *Benchmarks* descriptors
- the results of the analysis of English L2 grammatical development, based on the pupil's oral L2 use
- the results of the analysis of English L2 lexical development, based on the pupil's oral L2 use

- an overview of the pupil's English L2 literacy development over the study period
- an overview of observable internal factors and analysable interaction-related factors which may have influenced the pupil's English L2 acquisition.

Since the same analytical procedures were applied to the data obtained for each pupil, it is apparent, merely from reading through Chapter 4, that these profiles are comparable. However, to draw conclusions as to any overall patterns of L2 acquisition among this group of 18 EAL pupils, and to examine how this may relate to the *Benchmarks'* trajectory of English L2 development, we had to analyse the results emerging from the individual case studies in greater depth.

Obtaining overall results

Theoretical considerations

Firstly, the findings for each of the 18 pupils had to be brought together in a way that facilitated cumulative analysis. To do this, we adopted a similar approach to the one we used in Data Analysis Phase II. This allowed us to compare the results obtained for individual pupils, in relation to each of the criteria which we had identified for analysis, across the participant group. By doing this, we could derive overall findings which would enable us to respond to our research questions. However, this process of comparison was not without its challenges. In this section, we outline concerns which arose and explain our responses to them.

Representativeness

As we acknowledged in Chapter 1, 18 case studies can yield only a limited amount of evidence regarding the English L2 acquisition patterns of EAL pupils at primary school in Ireland. However, it is apparent from Table 3.2 that the EAL pupils participating in our study came from a relatively wide range of linguistic and national backgrounds. The diversity of the sample was quite typical of the representation of immigrant children in education in Ireland in recent years (see Lyons and Little 2009, McGorman and Sugrue 2007). Also, the participants' age span was representative of the overall population of pupils receiving English language support when the study was conducted. As we pointed out in our description of the participant group, by 2007 an increasing proportion of children from migrant backgrounds were starting school, alongside their native English-speaking peers, at initial enrolment level. Many of them had been born in Ireland, and newly arrived older pupils were generally fewer by the time our study began. The fact that across the three schools involved, a considerable proportion of the participating pupils were aged between 4 and 6 and were members of the mainstream Infant Classes was thus in keeping with a national trend. Nevertheless, while the sample was quite large for a longitudinal study of child L2 acquisition, it would be unrealistic to claim that a detailed examination of 18 participants' L2 use over a selected series of lessons can do more than suggest some of the characteristics of English L2 development among EAL pupils in Irish primary schools generally.

Selection of L2 indicators

Another challenge was posed by the selection of linguistic features for investigation as possible indicators of L2 acquisition: to what extent did our choices allow conclusions to be drawn as to emerging patterns of L2 development? Clearly, practical limitations on the duration of the research had implications regarding the extent of the data it generated. Also, the amount of data varied from pupil to pupil. This is evident from Table 3.5, which shows differences in the number of lessons per pupil analysed in each case study. The pupil profiles in Chapter 4 reveal further variation in the total number of turns analysed for each pupil across these selected lessons. As well as access to the lesson groups involved, factors relating to L2 proficiency, personality and classroom dynamics also contributed to these differences in the volume of data available per pupil. Finally, as 11 pupils were in their first year of English language support and seven were in their second year, the quantity of data we obtained was greater for pupils in the earlier stages of English L2 acquisition than for those who were slightly more proficient.

However, for each participating EAL pupil, it was possible to examine a range of grammatical and lexical indicators of L2 acquisition in considerable depth, using both qualitative and mixed methods analysis. Furthermore, as pointed out in our discussion of Data Analysis Phase II, the selection of these indicators was data-driven. Thus, it focused on features of L2 morpho-syntax and lexis which seemed, from the transcribed recordings, to be most pertinent to participants' actual L2 development. In addition, the analysis of pupils' English L2 literacy development and consideration of evidence of possible cross-linguistic influence allowed for further investigation of linguistic aspects of L2 acquisition which lay outside the main focus of the study. For example, analysis of 'reading aloud' activities often offered useful insights into pupils' L2 phonological development.

Comparability

Given that we wished to obtain evidence that could be, to some extent, representative of English L2 development among EAL pupils at primary school in

Ireland generally, it was appropriate and advantageous that the participants in the study varied in age and came from a wide range of home language and national backgrounds. At the same time, however, as we pointed out above in relation to our choice of L2 indicators, this diversity complicated the comparison of evidence across the 18 participating pupils. That is why, in response to this challenge, we designed a replicable framework for our analysis of the case studies. By applying the same analytical procedures to the data obtained for each child, we could compare features of English L2 acquisition emerging from the individual analyses across the sample.

Nevertheless, possible individual influences on the pupils' English L2 acquisition cannot be underestimated when comparing such findings. Therefore, in both the case studies and the derivation of overall results, we had to take into account the impact of other variables, such as internal and interaction-related factors, which could affect L2 acquisition. In this regard, we sought to consider the pupil-specific influences which were observable in our research: issues relating to age, home language, personality, and learning style. We also investigated how characteristics of classroom discourse across the lesson groups in the three participating schools may have impacted on pupils' English L2 development. However, as we have already acknowledged, external factors such as pupils' socio-economic status or their level of social integration within the mainstream educational environment were beyond the scope of our study. The possible influence of these variables on EAL pupils' educational experience and English L2 development is an issue that requires further research.

Independence of analytical strands

Our study comprised two main strands of analysis: a formal (linguistic) strand and a functional (*Benchmarks*-linked) strand. Ensuring that these strands were analysed independently was one of the key concerns throughout Data Analysis Phases I and II. Certain features built into the analytical process helped in this regard. Firstly, the analysis was iterative, carried out in two distinct phases several months apart. Data Analysis Phase II was similar in approach to Phase I, but more detailed, which enhanced the accuracy and consistency of coding. This proved particularly useful in relation to the linkage of pupil turns to *Benchmarks* descriptors (essentially a subjective decision made by a single researcher). The recursive, more finely tuned cycle of analysis conducted in Phase II allowed for greater confidence in this decision-making process. This ensured that the functional coding was the best possible fit for pupils' recorded English L2 use, and that its degree of accuracy was on a par with the more objective formal coding system used to capture analysable elements of their English L2 production.

This form-function analysis, supplemented by further analysis of interactional characteristics of the recorded lessons, served as a template which could be replicated and applied to the data available for each of the 18 participating pupils. This ensured that the variables – (i) *Benchmarks*-linked English L2 proficiency and (ii) linguistic indicators of English L2 acquisition – could be analysed cumulatively and independently of one another. It also facilitated the comparison of individual results, which was carried out by applying the same combination of quantitative and qualitative procedures employed in the individual case studies to the data obtained across the entire sample of 18 EAL pupils. The overall results emerging from this process could then offer an empirical answer to the research question: whether and, if so, to what extent the *Benchmarks* reflect actual English L2 development, based on evidence of L2 acquisition obtained from a longitudinal study of a representative group of EAL pupils.

Methodological considerations

Because the data-driven approach adopted for the production of the pupil profiles was also followed in deriving overall results, the format of this final analysis was broadly similar to that of the case studies presented in Chapter 4. However, some methodological refinement was necessary in order to account for variation in the length and nature of the lessons selected for each of the participating EAL pupils. The overall impact of time on English L2 development across the study period also required consideration. In addition, procedures had to be devised to allow effective comparison of cumulative data relating to pupils' *Benchmarks*-linked L2 proficiency and evidence of their English L2 acquisition based on the analysed linguistic indicators. This final analysis involved:

- overall functional analysis based on the *Benchmarks*-linked distribution of all 18 EAL pupils' analysed spoken turns in the selected lessons, in relation to the stage they had reached in their English language support
- overall analysis of the 18 pupils' English L2 grammatical development at successive stages of their English L2 proficiency, in relation to the *Benchmarks* proficiency levels linked to pupils' oral L2 use across the selected lessons
- overall analysis of English L2 lexical development among the participants, again in relation to their oral L2 proficiency and linked to the *Benchmarks*
- a general overview of evidence relating to the 18 EAL pupils' English L2 literacy development during the study
- a general summary of observable internal and analysable interaction-related factors which may have influenced these pupils' English L2 acquisition over the study period.

It was clear in many of the case studies that factors associated with the structure of the lesson could influence the availability of data. Such factors could also affect the extent and nature of English L2 use by pupils involved in that lesson. For example, the degree to which a lesson focused on literacy skills could have consequences for the number of turns that contained information about pupils' L2 oral development. Therefore, in the cumulative analysis, steps were taken to account for the different amounts of data available for different pupils. All calculations relating to the frequency of use of specific linguistic elements were based on their mean frequency per turn (rather than on raw frequency scores). This meant that data obtained for pupils who contributed many turns (often due to classroom variables, personality factors and frequency of recording as much as to L2 proficiency) did not take precedence over that associated with pupils who were less able (or had less opportunity) to participate in the analysed lessons. As well as ensuring that the data obtained for each pupil was equally important in this final stage of analysis, using mean values also reduced the risk that the overall findings would be distorted by outlying individual results. Values for overall accuracy were similarly derived from the mean of all accuracy ratios for L2 use associated with specific stages of developing English L2 proficiency. Other aspects of the learning context which may have impacted on the overall results were also considered, both in describing evidence of pupils' English L2 acquisition and in the subsequent discussion of classroom interaction patterns and their potential impact on their L2 development.

Processing data for L2 proficiency development and evidence of L2 acquisition

To obtain overall findings, it was necessary to analyse evidence of acquisition of the English L2 grammatical indicators for the 18 participating pupils, using mean values for frequency and accuracy. This evidence then had to be compared to findings relative to pupils' development of English L2 proficiency based on the links between their analysed turns and the *Benchmarks* levels: A1, A2 and B1.

Two issues arose in this regard. First, our evidence of pupils' English L2 proficiency development was limited. It was based solely on data obtained from their English language support lessons recorded at varying intervals over an eight-month period. In addition, pupils' L2 production in these lessons seemed to be susceptible to the influence of non-linguistic factors. These included pedagogical decisions such as choice of classroom activity, but also affective factors (health, fatigue etc.) which could influence pupil participation in any given lesson. However, as pointed out in our discussion of the initial methodological considerations involved in undertaking this research, naturally occurring L2 use is arguably the best possible indicator of L2 development. The English L2 production recorded among the 18 participating pupils in their English language support lessons was typical of their everyday L2 use in the context of immersion education. This meant that it could offer a good indication of the pupils' L2 development. Relying on pupils' L2 use in their English language support lessons as our main source of data was also justifiable considering the approach to language learning adopted by the *Benchmarks*. Derived from the CEFR, this approach is one that views language learning as a variety of language use. Consequently, by analysing pupils' L2 use in the recorded lessons, we could investigate whether the *Benchmarks* describe L2 learning outcomes which reflect EAL pupils' English L2 development and thus provide appropriate guidelines for English language support.

Accepting the pupils' recorded L2 use as an adequate source of data, our next step was to derive cumulative results for *Benchmarks*-linked proficiency development across the sample. However, since the *Benchmarks* were designed to guide English language support delivered over a two-year period, we also had to consider time as a variable. This was done by linking the *Benchmarks* levels associated with each pupil's analysed turns in each of the selected lessons to the point that pupil had reached in the two-year allocation of English language support. The distribution of turns across the three proficiency levels (A1, A2 and B1) could then be calculated for each month of English language support, which allowed us to track pupils' developing L2 proficiency over time.

Secondly, to answer the research question, it was necessary to devise a robust method of comparing evidence of pupils' English L2 acquisition to their *Benchmarks*-linked English L2 proficiency levels as revealed in the selected lessons. To do this, we had to bring together data obtained for English L2 proficiency development among the 18 participating pupils, based on the *Benchmarks* levels associated with their analysed turns. Then we had to compare this proficiency-related data to evidence of English L2 acquisition derived for each pupil with regard to the grammatical and lexical indicators identified in Data Analysis Phase II and then analysed on an individual basis (see Chapter 4 for results). To facilitate such comparison across the sample, some adjustment of the raw data used in the analysis of individual pupils' English L2 development was required. This involved, as mentioned above, using mean values for frequency and accuracy to achieve maximum comparability between lessons which yielded varying quantities of analysable spoken turns.

Furthermore, in order to compare overall results related to the analysed linguistic indicators with *Benchmarks*-linked data for English L2 proficiency development, it was necessary to devise a system that could identify pupils at apparently similar stages and examine features emerging from evidence of their L2 acquisition. In order to do this, 'proficiency ratio bands' were defined as a means of grouping pupils of roughly equivalent L2 proficiency. These bands were expressed on the basis of a straightforward ratio: the number of turns at a given pupil's highest recorded proficiency level in a particular lesson as a proportion of the total number of analysable turns that pupil produced in that lesson. For example, if a pupil produced a total of 50 turns within a lesson, 42 of which were linked to level A1 *Benchmarks* descriptors, and eight of which were linked to level A2 descriptors, that pupil's proficiency proportion for that lesson would be *0.16 A2*. Separate 'bands' covered the three proficiency levels and were divided at intervals of 0.1: from *A1 only*, followed by *0.01–0.1 A2, 0.11–0.2 A2* etc., up to *0.91–1.0 B1*. It must be emphasised that these indicators of proficiency did not represent some kind of 'absolute' proficiency score (akin to a test score). They merely described the extent to which pupils used English at their apparent maximum level of proficiency in each of the selected lessons. Nevertheless, using these bands proved effective. They provided a guide to proficiency development which offered a feasible and useful means of comparing evidence of L2 acquisition – drawn from the L2 use of the 18 participating pupils – to the *Benchmarks* proficiency levels.

Following this approach, it was possible to bring together the results of the form-function analysis carried out for each pupil (and presented in Chapter 4) in order to obtain overall findings. Evidence of pupils' individual L2 literacy development, which was qualitatively analysed in the compilation of the individual profiles, could also be brought together to examine any emerging trends among the group. Finally, the apparent influence of the internal and interactional factors on each pupil's English L2 acquisition which were considered in the case studies could be investigated across the participant group to see if any overall conclusions could be drawn in relation to the impact of these variables.

Conclusion: A summary of the analytical procedures used

At this point the reader may find it helpful to consider a schematic overview of the analytical procedures on which the findings presented in Chapters 4 and 5 are based. Figure 3.1 summarises the succession of methodological decisions taken, from initial data collection to overall results; Figure 3.2 shows how the data analysis progressed, from initial broad transcription to the three-strand coding (formal, functional and interactional) of the first phase to the more detailed linguistic coding of the second; Table 3.5 shows the distribution of the 7,455 analysed turns across the 18 participating pupils; and Table 3.6 provides an overview of the methods used to derive and present the findings for each grammatical indicator, both in the pupil profiles and in the derivation of overall results.

Figure 3.1 Summary of methodological procedures

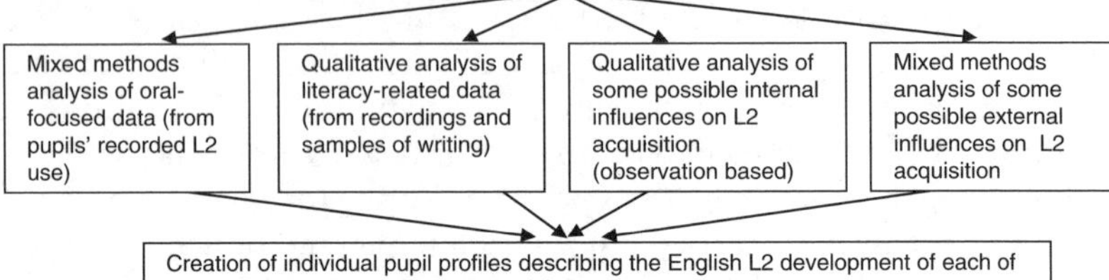

Figure 3.2 Sample of transcript and coding

Original transcription	
Ravi and Lukas, two 8-year-old boys, from India and Lithuania respectively (see Chapter 4) engage in a 'restaurant' role-play, with some correction (repair) provided by the teacher. (School 1, Group 5, Lesson 7–20 May 2008).	*Ravi:* yeah … what do you want. (*through mic.*) *Teacher:* now, instead of what do you want, do you know what's better to say, what would you like. *Ravi:* what do-do you like. (*through mic.*) *Lukas:* I'm like- I don't like- I would like em a burger. *Ravi:* what- what burger, plain burger, burger? *Lukas:* no. *Ravi:* cheeseburger? *Lukas:* yes. *Ravi:* OK.
Data Analysis Phase I coding*	

In the first section of the role-play, Ravi and Lukas make and respond to requests typical of a restaurant setting (linking/approximating to *Benchmarks* descriptor for Unit 3, level A2, spoken interaction: *Can discuss a menu and select what he/she would like* (Integrate Ireland Language and Training 2003a:5).
 	
 In the second section, the interaction becomes a simpler series of food-related suggestions (approximating to descriptor Unit 3, level A1, spoken interaction: *Can request basic items of food/drink in a shop* (Integrate Ireland Language and Training 2003a:5).
	Ravi: yeah … what do you want. (*through mic.*) **BM: U3/A2/SpInt/2%// LA: INTmin/-/Q/ AUXdo#/PROpers/V// CA: 1.p-p':SCT:Ac(EL)&NEL/Pau/} {2.p-p':Fb:Q(OS)#//(!)**
	 Teacher: now, instead of what do you want, do you know what's better to say, what would you like. **CA:t-p:REP:Rej(Q)/SUG(COR)//**
	 Ravi: what do-do you like. (*through mic.*) **BM: U3/A2/SpInt/2%// LA: Q/AUXdo*~ /AUXdo* /PROpers/V// CA: p-p':REP(Fb):Q(OS)&COR#//(!)**
	 Lukas: I'm like- I don't like- I would like em a burger. **BM: U3/A2/SpInt/2// LA: PROpers/ AUXbe* /V~/PROpers/AUXdoNeg* /V/PROpers/AUXmod/V/nv/DETart/N// CA: p'-p:Sb:REQ&CORself//**
	 Ravi: what- what burger, plain burger, burger? **BM: U3/A2/SpInt/2%// LA: Q~/Q/N/O*/A/ N~/N// CA: p-p':Post:TOPQ(OS)/SUG(1)+//(!)**
	 Lukas: no. **BM: U3/A1/SpInt/1%// LA: INTminNeg// CA: p'-p:Post:Rej(SUG)(1)//**
	 Ravi: cheeseburger? **BM: U3/A1/SpInt/1%// LA: # /N// CA: p-p':Post:SUG(2)//**
	 Lukas: yes. **BM: U3/A1/SpInt/1%// LA: INTmin// CA: p'-p:Post:Ac(SUG)(2)//**
	 Ravi: OK. **BM: U3/A1/SpInt/1%// LA: INTmin// CA: p-p':Post:Ac(REQ)//**

Figure 3.2 (continued)

Data Analysis Phase II coding*		
Linguistic sub-codes specify errors, for example, instances of incorrect auxiliary choice (modal 'would' required) or article omission.	*Ravi:*	yeah … what do you want. *(through mic.)* **BM: U3/A2/SpInt/2%// LA: /INTmin/-/Q/ AUXdo#/PROpers/V// CA: 1.p-p':SCT:Ac(EL)&NEL/Pau/} {2.p-p':Fb:Q(IS)#//(!)**
	Teacher:	now, instead of what do you want, do you know what's better to say, what would you like. **CA:t-p:REP:Rej(Q)/SUG(COR)//**
	Ravi:	what do-do you like. *(through mic.)* **BM: U3/A2/SpInt/2%// LA: /Q/AUXdo*ICmodR~/AUXdo*ICmodR/PROpers/V// CA: p-p':REP(Fb):Q(IS)&COR#//(!)**
	Lukas:	I'm like- I don't like- I would like em a burger. **BM: U3/A2/SpInt/2// LA: /PROpers/ AUXbe*ICmodR/V~/PROpers/AUXdoNeg*ICmodR/V~/ PROpers/AUXmod/V/nv/DETart/N// CA: p'-p:Sb:REQ&CORself//**
	Ravi:	what- what burger, plain burger, burger? **BM: U3/A2/SpInt/2%// LA: /Q~/Q/N/ O*DETart/A/N~/N// CA: p-p':Post:TOPQ(IS)/SUG(1)+//(!)**
	Lukas:	no. **BM: U3/A1/SpInt/1%// LA: /INTminNeg// CA: p'-p:Post:Rej(SUG)(1)//**
	Ravi:	cheeseburger? **BM: U3/A1/SpInt/1%// LA: /#nob/N// CA: p-p':Post:SUG(2)//**
	Lukas:	yes. **BM: U3/A1/SpInt/1%// LA: /INTmin// CA: p'-p:Post:Ac(SUG)(2)//**
	Ravi:	OK. **BM: U3/A1/SpInt/1%// LA: /INTmin// CA: p-p':Post:Ac(REQ)//**

** See Appendix 4 for a full list of codes used – coding based on norms for native speaker child interaction.*

Table 3.5 Total number of analysed spoken turns included in Data Analysis Phase II

Pupil	No. selected lessons	No. analysed spoken turns[1]
Andrei	11	1,188
Stefan	11	653
Tomasz	10	217
Patryk	10	385
Ivan	6	466
Ravi	8	563
Lukas	7	628
Constantin	4	434
Marko	7	227
Dimitrie	6	155
Jin	8	556
Vladimir	7	276
Edyta	7	425
Karina	8	316
Zofia	8	111
Beatriz	8	220
Nasreen	8	376
Fatima	8	259
TOTAL		7,455

1. The number of analysed spoken turns varied among pupils, due not only to the extent of their participation in this study but also to the interactional dynamics of each group and the individual characteristics of each participant.

Table 3.6 Overview of analytical methods with respect to L2 grammatical indicators

Indicator of L2 acquisition	Analytical method	
	Quantative analysis	Qualitative analysis
1 Nouns	YES	YES
2 Verbs	YES	YES
3 Pronouns	YES	YES
4 Articles	YES	YES
5 Prepositions	YES	YES
6 Auxiliaries	YES	YES
7 Verb-to-noun ratio	YES	YES
8 Negative formation	NO	YES
9 Question formation	NO	YES
10 Clause linkage	NO	YES

4 The English L2 development of 18 EAL pupils

Overview of case studies

Chapter 3 explained the methodology underpinning our investigation of the relation between the *English Language Proficiency Benchmarks* and evidence of second language acquisition derived from actual English L2 use by EAL pupils. In this chapter, we present the findings of this research for each of the 18 English L2 learners who participated in the study. As pointed out in Chapter 3, these children came from a wide range of linguistic and cultural backgrounds; they also varied considerably in their age and stage of primary education. To capture this diversity, the findings of the study are presented here as a series of 'pupil profiles'. Overall results derived from these 18 profiles will be presented and discussed in Chapter 5.

Based on an analysis of pupils' oral L2 use and samples of their L2 writing across a comprehensive selection of recorded lessons, the profiles present key aspects of their English L2 development. The relation of each pupil's L2 development to the *Benchmarks* is also outlined. For ease of comparison, the formatting of the profiles follows the same pattern for each pupil:

- a brief introduction to the pupil, summarised in a table of personal details
- a functional analysis of the pupil's oral L2 use, to determine the relation between the child's analysed turns-at-talk and the *Benchmarks* proficiency levels, with graphic presentation of the results of this analysis
- analysis of 10 grammatical indicators of L2 development, with graphic illustration of quantitative results for the frequency (token-count) and accuracy of nouns, verbs, personal pronouns, articles, prepositions and auxiliaries produced by the pupil, followed by more detailed description, based on qualitative evidence, of the child's acquisition of the analysed morphological and syntactic features
- analysis of lexical aspects of the pupil's L2 development, with supporting data presented in table form, including qualitative description of the semantic fields apparent in the child's L2 use and examples of L2 lexis, supplemented by an overview of the 18 participants' L2 lexical production provided in Appendix 6

- an overview of the pupil's L2 literacy development during the study period
- a brief consideration of factors that may have influenced the pupil's English L2 acquisition, based both on observation of the child's engagement in classroom activities and on analysis (presented graphically) of interaction patterns in the recorded lessons.

1 Zofia

Table 4.1 summarises personal details for Zofia. Figure 4.1 indicates that her analysed spoken turns were all associated with *Benchmarks* proficiency level A1. The frequency and accuracy of the quantitatively analysed grammatical indicators she produced are shown in Figure 4.2.

Table 4.1 Zofia – personal details

National/cultural background	Polish	**Age at end of study**	5 years
School attended	School 3	**School class**	Junior Infants
English language support commenced	October 2007	**Duration of participation in study**	October 2007 – February 2008
Number of lessons selected for detailed analysis	8 (of total 14)	**Number of turns-at-talk analysed**	111

Figure 4.1 Benchmarks levels recorded for analysed turns produced by Zofia in selected lessons

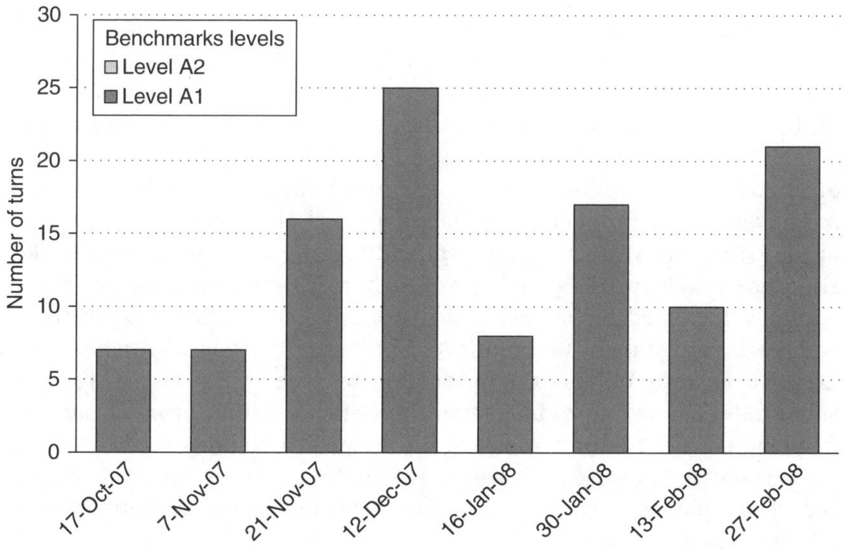

Figure 4.2 Frequency and accuracy of quantitatively analysed grammatical indicators used by Zofia

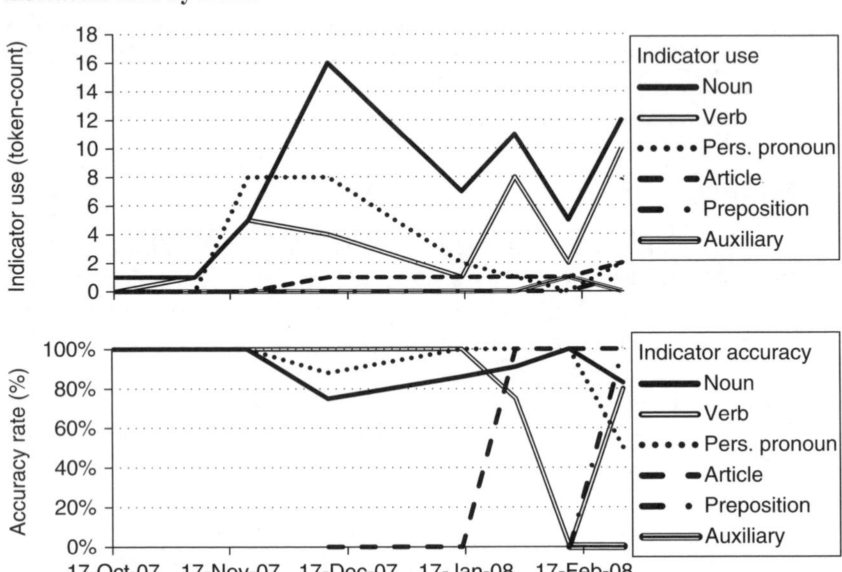

Evidence of L2 acquisition – grammatical indicators

Morphological features

Zofia was at a very early stage in her acquisition of the L2 grammatical indicators shown in Figure 4.2. Her use of these indicators was limited throughout, although there was evidence of increasing production towards the end of the study. Actual token-count was, however, affected by classroom factors, notably the extent of Zofia's participation in the selected lessons. Her use of nouns was limited but relatively accurate, although errors became more prominent as her production increased. Lexical choice accounted for 75% of the errors, but syntactic placement and her rare attempts at pluralisation also proved problematic. Zofia's use of verbs rose from a minimal level but its accuracy fluctuated; it consisted almost exclusively of uninflected stem forms and the present tense of the copula *be*. She began to produce pronouns from Lesson 6 onwards. Initially, this production involved basic personal pronouns and simple demonstratives but later included the substitute pronoun *one*. The frequency of her personal pronoun use seemed to be influenced by lesson-related factors. For instance, it rose in Lesson 6, in which a card game activity elicited the phrase: *I have it*. Her personal pronoun use was relatively accurate, with little omission.

Articles first emerged in Zofia's recorded L2 use in Lesson 9, but their use was infrequent thereafter. Her initial attempts at article production were often inaccurate. There was some evidence of improving accuracy towards the end of the study, although her overall token-count was too low to confirm a trend. Article omission was also frequent. Only one instance of preposition use was recorded; that of *at* in the final lesson (in the construction *look at*). Zofia's auxiliary use was likewise confined to a single instance. She made an incorrect attempt at using the auxiliary *is* with a stem verb in a context requiring simple rather than progressive aspect.

Syntactic features

The turns recorded for Zofia were structurally very simple (single-word or short-phrase utterances) and predominantly noun based. This was reflected in her verb-to-noun ratio which was generally much less than 0.5. For negation, she relied solely on the negative marker *no* (e.g. *mammy no ham*). Only one attempt at question formation appeared in her analysable spoken turns (*hey where is this?* – Lesson 16). No instances of clause linkage were recorded, due to the structurally limited nature of Zofia's L2 use in the selected lessons.

Evidence of L2 acquisition – lexical indicators

Regarding L2 lexical development, it appears that Zofia's English language vocabulary rose, not always consistently, from a minimal level as the study progressed. The results for 'Wordlist entries per turn', presented in Table 4.2, show that her lexical range remained limited throughout the study. The data recorded reflects Zofia's L2 proficiency during the study, which could be linked entirely to *Benchmarks* level A1 (see Figure 4.1). However, her actual L2 lexical production may also have been affected by her limited capacity to participate in the selected lessons.

Although the teacher in School 3 did not structure her programme of English language support directly around the *Benchmarks*, many of the units of work themes emerged in the semantic fields covered by Zofia. Within these

Table 4.2 Zofia – indicators of L2 lexical development

Wordlist results								
Lesson	2	4	6	9	10	12	14	16
Wordlist entries per turn per lesson	4	7	27	31	15	25	11	25
Wordlist entries per turn	0.57	1.00	1.69	1.24	1.88	1.47	1.10	1.19
Verb lexemes per lesson	0	1	2	2	1	4	1	3

themes, the lexis she used was restricted to core words such as, on the topic of 'animals', *cat*. She produced adjectives such as basic colours and size referents (e.g. *big*) and possessive determiners (e.g. *my, your*) emerged later in the study. The lexical diversity of her verb use was limited to basic verbs such as *be* and *look*. During the study period, a total of only eight distinct verb lexemes were recorded in her L2 production. In later lessons she occasionally used simple adverbs of place (e.g. *here*).

L2 literacy development

Despite being at an extremely early stage of L2 development, Zofia was capable of engaging in some simple L2 literacy-related activities, typical of the mainstream classroom for children in their first year of schooling in Ireland. By the end of the study, she could recite nursery rhymes quite fluently and accurately, although much of the lexis used in these was well beyond her spontaneous oral L2 production. From Lesson 10 onwards, she could also read short sentences based on her mainstream reader (e.g. *Sam is the robot*), initially with support from the teacher and later more independently. However, she still found some English grapho-phonic relations rather difficult and tended to guess new words rather than using their sounds as cues. An attempt at writing her name, with some assistance, was recorded in Lesson 10.

Possible influences on L2 development

Individual factors

Zofia was just 5 years of age by the end of the study. This affected the cognitive as well as the linguistic challenge of activities in the recorded lessons which, in both respects, were very simple. It was difficult to assess the influence of her home language, Polish, on her L2 acquisition, since she was at such an early stage of L2 morpho-syntactic development. Regarding phonology, her English was quite intelligible although her lengthening of vowels, her tendency to produce the front vowel /æ/ for /ʌ/ and her pronunciation of word-final /t/ sounds as /tʃ/ may have been due to cross-linguistic transfer. While it was unlikely that she had received any direct L1 literacy instruction, she was aware of some of the grapho-phonic differences between English and Polish (e.g. those associated with the written letter 'w'). Zofia seemed to be a very quiet child, even in comparison to another member of her group, Karina (see below), who was at a similarly early stage of English L2 development. However, although her L2 use was very limited it was often relatively accurate. This may indicate that she was going through a 'silent phase'; a frequent feature of L2 acquisition among young children (see Integrate Ireland Language and Training 2006b, Nicholas and Lightbown 2008). Over the course of the study, her communicative competence increased somewhat, but she remained reluctant to risk L2 use.

Interaction-related factors

The dynamics of Zofia's lesson group may also have affected her capacity to participate in classroom talk, since she was the least L2 proficient and quietest member of this group. Figure 4.3 shows the results of analysis of specific features of her L2 oral production. As explained in Chapter 3, this focuses on Zofia's use of three turn-types – 'answer', 'telling' and 'topic elaboration'. Turn-types indicating a responding role in interaction, i.e. those coded 'answers', were dominant over initiative-taking 'tellings' or 'topic elaborations'. Occasionally, when the lesson theme was very relevant and familiar, she participated more actively. However, throughout, her involvement accounted for less than 20% of this group's classroom talk and her recorded turns were almost always teacher directed.

Figure 4.3 Turn-type indicators of interaction patterns for Zofia in selected lessons

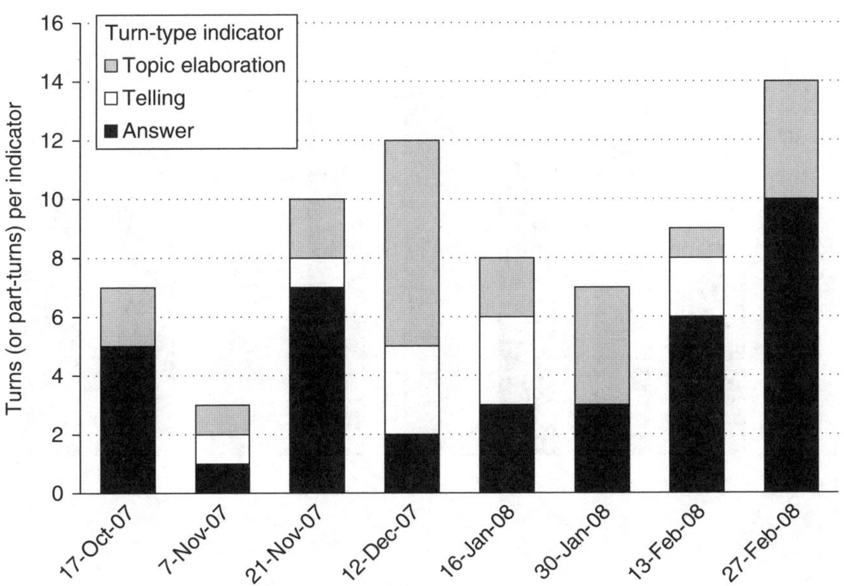

2 Karina

Karina's personal details are summarised in Table 4.3. Figure 4.4 shows that most of her analysed spoken turns were associated with *Benchmarks* proficiency level A1. Her use of the quantitatively analysed grammatical indicators is presented in Figure 4.5.

Table 4.3 Karina – personal details

National/cultural background	Latvian	Age at end of study	5 years
School attended	School 3	School class	Junior Infants
English language support commenced	October 2007	Duration of participation in study	October 2007 – February 2008
Number of lessons selected for detailed analysis	8 (of total 11)	Number of turns-at-talk analysed	316

Figure 4.4 Benchmarks levels recorded for analysed turns produced by Karina in selected lessons

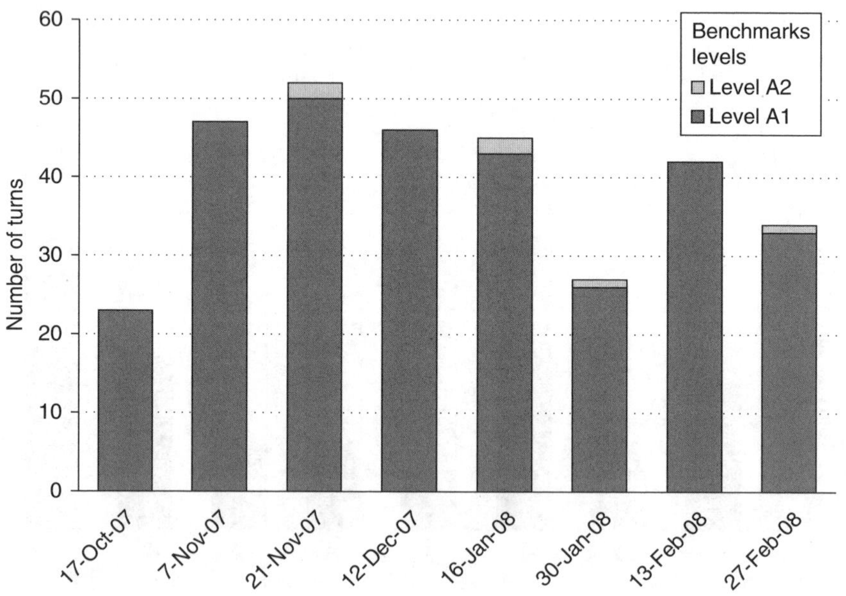

Figure 4.5 Frequency and accuracy of quantitatively analysed grammatical indicators used by Karina

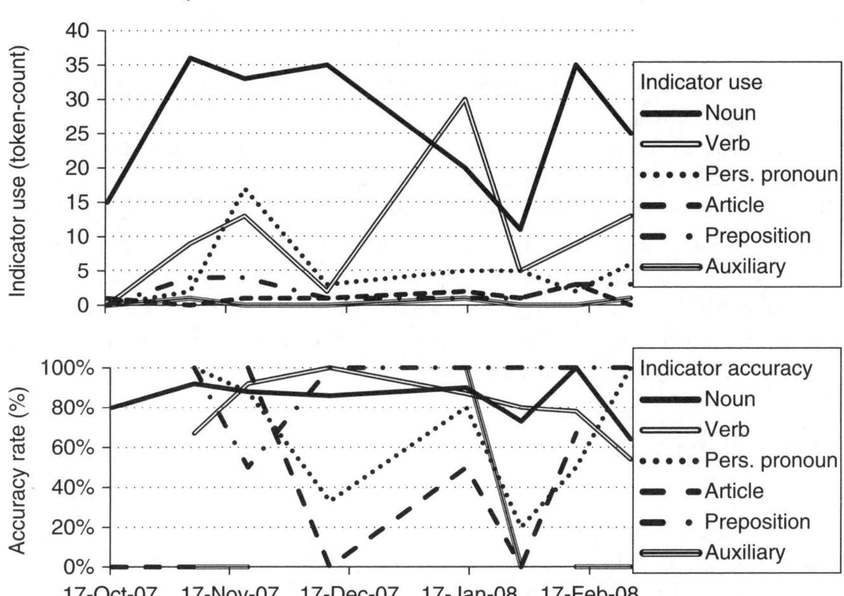

Evidence of L2 acquisition – grammatical indicators

Morphological features

The development of the L2 grammatical indicators shown in Figure 4.5 suggests that Karina was at a very early stage of English language acquisition. Her use of the analysed indicators diversified and generally rose across the study, although the accuracy of her production fluctuated considerably. Her L2 oral production was strongly noun based in the selected lessons. This may also have been influenced by features of the recorded lessons, particularly the tendency towards 'known-answer' questions eliciting short responses – generally nouns. Her noun use was usually over 80% accurate but errors of lexical choice and lack of pluralisation in required contexts were apparent. Karina's verb use was limited, but it showed some signs of increase (not always consistent) over the study period. Non-inflected verb stems and the present tense copula *be* accounted for most instances of verb production. Very occasional use of progressive (e.g. *watching*) or simple past (e.g. *made*) forms were recorded towards the end of the study. The emergence of slightly more diverse verb use was accompanied by a decline in verb accuracy in the second half of the study. Karina's pronoun use initially involved personal and demonstrative pronouns. However, during the study this diversified to include instances of the possessive marker *mine* and the substitute *one*. The frequency and accuracy of her personal pronoun production varied considerably. Confusion of case (e.g. use of *me* for *I*) was a common source of error. Omission of personal pronouns, although rather infrequent, generally involved subject rather than object pronouns.

Karina's production of articles was sparse and often inaccurate. Her rate of article omission was up to three times higher than her rate of production. Preposition use was likewise limited and confined to the isolated production of *in, out, up* and *to*. Her production of these was generally accurate, although she also omitted some prepositions. Karina rarely used auxiliaries during the study period. Her attempts were confined to very occasional use of the auxiliaries *be* and *do*. Typically, these were inaccurately used with errors, for example of syntactic placement (e.g. *understand don't*).

Syntactic features

The nominal bias of Karina's analysed spoken turns was reflected in her verb-to-noun ratio. Although it rose slightly over the study period, it was generally under 0.3. She relied almost entirely, and often incorrectly, on the marker *no* for negation. However, attempts at *not* were recorded by Lesson 14 (e.g. *not hen!* when refuting a suggestion). Her first attempts at question formation were recorded in Lesson 6, but these remained very simple (e.g. *what's this/ that?*). No instances of appropriate inversion were recorded for Karina in the selected lessons. Throughout the study, her production comprised, almost entirely, short single-clause units in which she occasionally linked items with the conjunction *and*.

Evidence of L2 acquisition – lexical indicators

Karina's results for 'Wordlist entries' and 'Wordlist entries per turn', shown in Table 4.4, were relatively constant, with some fluctuation, over the study period. Lesson-related factors which may have affected this data should, however, be noted. For instance, in Lesson 2, Karina spontaneously produced

Table 4.4 Karina – indicators of L2 lexical development

Wordlist results								
Lesson	2	4	6	9	10	12	14	16
Wordlist entries per turn per lesson	43	42	54	50	40	37	49	37
Wordlist entries per turn	1.87	0.89	1.04	1.09	0.89	1.37	1.17	1.09
Verb lexemes per lesson	0	6	5	2	5	3	7	5

extended counting sequences, which may have rendered comparatively more lexical items per turn for this lesson than for others.

In terms of semantic range, her production in the selected lessons could be readily linked to many of the units of work in the *Benchmarks* despite the fact that the teacher in School 3 did not plan her lessons specifically around these. Karina's L2 vocabulary included basic nouns, for instance, *apple* on the topic of 'food'. She also used adjectives describing familiar colours or attributes (e.g. *lovely*), as well as the possessive determiner *my*. Evidence of increasing lexical diversity emerged in her verb use, which ranged across 22 distinct lexemes, from *go* and *finish* in early lessons, to *clap* and *burst* towards the end of the study. Simple adverbs of place (e.g. *there* and *here*) also emerged.

L2 literacy development

Karina was in her first year of primary education and thus at a very early stage of literacy development. It is likely that her introduction to literacy was through her L2; no evidence of home-language literacy emerged in the data. However, she could engage quite actively with L2 literacy-related tasks, despite her limited L2 proficiency. This was apparent from Lesson 9 onwards in her identification of basic grapho-phonic relations and letter names. By Lesson 10, she could competently read words and short sentences extracted or adapted from her mainstream reader (e.g. *Molly is the ghost.*). Awareness of the L2 lexis used in these activities proved crucial to Karina's participation. Many of these activities relied on a very restricted range of vocabulary, which appeared to be within her receptive L2 competence. She could write her name, but no other evidence of L2 writing was recorded.

Possible influences on L2 development

Individual factors

Regarding age, as a very young child (5 years old by the end of the study), Karina had some advantages over older EAL pupils. The cognitive and, particularly, literacy-related requirements of her mainstream class demanded simple language use and frequent repetition. Cross-linguistic influence from her home language, Latvian, was apparent in her L2 production. Instances of home-language use in order to demonstrate cognitive ability were recorded early in the study (e.g. counting to 30 in Latvian) and these seemed to support her expression of the same concepts in English. Other cases of lexical transfer (e.g. *policija* for 'police') and some phonological influence were also evident. Karina was a confident child who occasionally recycled 'chunks' of classroom discourse to bootstrap communication. Her keen engagement with both literacy and numeracy activities suggested that she was a focused learner.

Interaction-related factors

Karina and Zofia (Profile 1) belonged to a group comprising four pupils. Karina was one of the least proficient in English in this group. However, she proved capable of taking initiatives and expanding on lesson topics, even from an early stage in the data collection. This was evident in the relative dominance of 'telling' and 'topic elaboration' turn-types over 'answers' in her analysed oral L2 use, as shown in Figure 4.6. However, despite her willingness to communicate, the classroom dynamic may have restricted her opportunity to do so. Almost all her turns were teacher directed. This may have meant that she was missing out on potential chances for L2 learning which could have been made available through increased peer interaction.

Figure 4.6 Turn-type indicators of interaction patterns for Karina in selected lessons

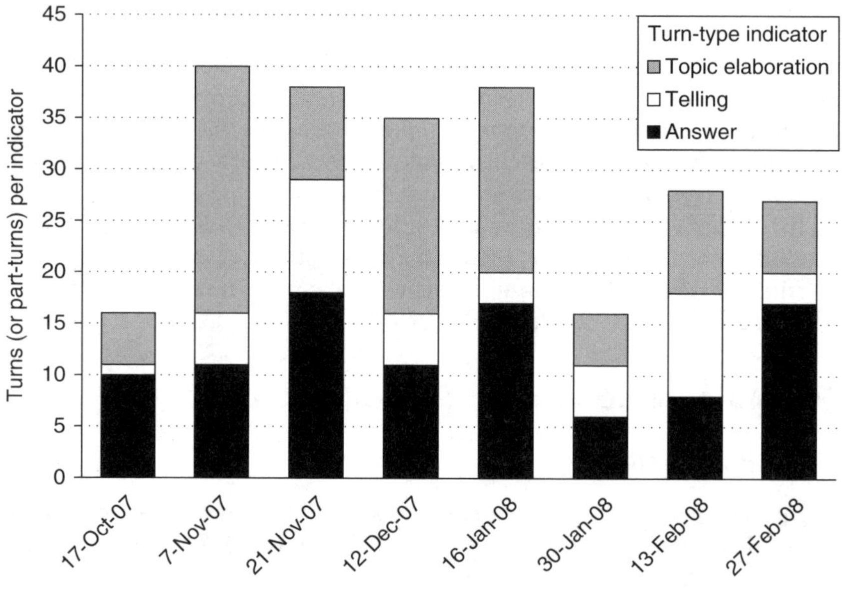

3 Dimitrie

Personal details for Dimitrie are provided in Table 4.5. Figure 4.7 shows how he initially produced few turns, most of which could be linked to *Benchmarks* proficiency level A1. However, towards the end of the study, evidence of more extensive and proficient L2 production emerged. Findings from the quantitative analysis of grammatical indicators for Dimitrie are presented in Figure 4.8.

Table 4.5 Dimitrie – personal details

National/cultural background	Romanian	**Age at end of study**	5 years
School attended	School 2	**School class**	Junior Infants
English language support commenced	September 2007	**Duration of participation in study**	December 2007 – May 2008
Number of lessons selected for detailed analysis	6 (of total 8)	**Number of turns-at-talk analysed**	155

Figure 4.7 Benchmarks levels recorded for analysed turns produced by Dimitrie in selected lessons

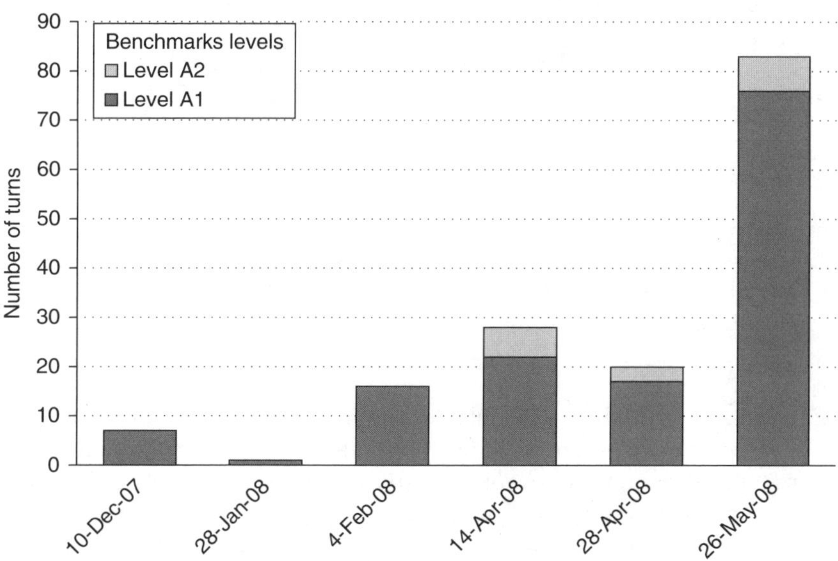

Evidence of L2 acquisition – grammatical indicators

Morphological features

Dimitrie's use of the grammatical indicators presented in Figure 4.8 rose relatively consistently from a very limited level at the start of the study to increased production by the final lesson. As his use of the indicators emerged and became more frequent, his accuracy declined somewhat. Dimitrie's production of nouns rose from Lesson 1 onwards and was generally over 80% accurate. Most errors involved incorrect lexical choice. His attempts at pluralisation were rare and confined to later lessons. His verb use likewise increased as the study progressed. Initially it was limited to stem forms and

Figure 4.8 Frequency and accuracy of quantitatively analysed grammatical indicators used by Dimitrie

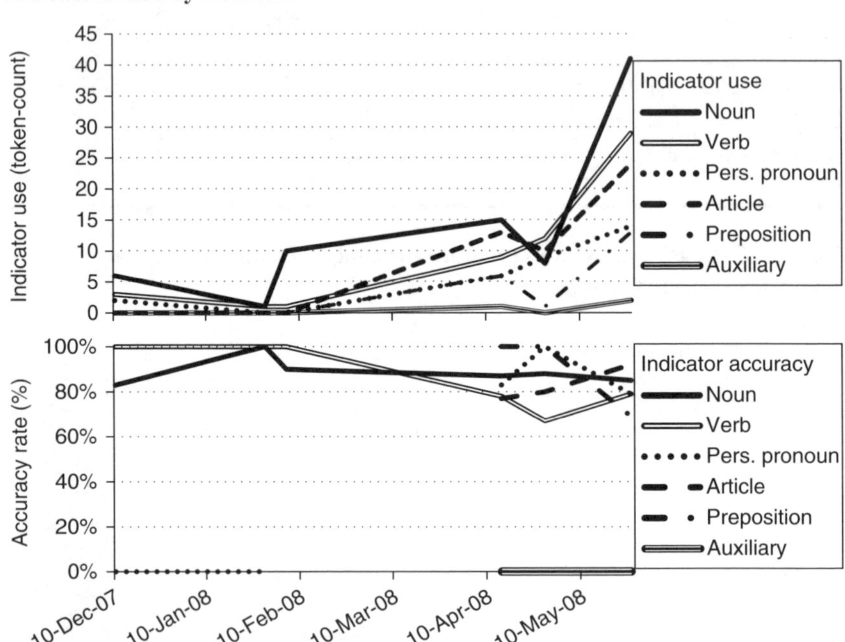

the copula *be*, although in the final lesson progressive forms and participles (e.g. *looking, broken*) were recorded. Diversification of verb production was often typified by inaccuracy, particularly the continued use of uninflected stem verbs where morphologically more complex forms were required. Dimitrie's production of pronouns increased during the study. It usually comprised only personal and demonstrative pronouns but the substitute *one* was also recorded. His use of personal pronouns was generally accurate, with omission infrequent.

Articles emerged in Dimitrie's recorded L2 use only in Lesson 7. However, his article production then increased substantially. It was relatively accurate, with non-required use his main source of error. He rarely omitted articles. Dimitrie's first instances of preposition production also occurred in Lesson 7. By Lesson 12, he could produce a range of basic prepositions; however, his accuracy appeared to decline as his preposition use increased and diversified. Most errors involved inappropriate preposition choice (e.g. *in* for *on*, *at* for *to*). Only three instances of auxiliary use by Dimitrie emerged from the recorded lessons. These attempts occurred towards the end of the study and involved the inaccurate use of *be* (e.g. *very fast are go*). Omission of auxiliaries, particularly in question forms, was also evident.

Syntactic features

The structures produced by Dimitrie tended to be short and predominantly noun based. However, towards the end of the study, his verb-to-noun ratio (which was generally under 0.5) rose slightly. For negation, he relied entirely on the inappropriate use of *no* until Lesson 12, when *not* was first recorded (e.g. *the book is not open*). Dimitrie's attempts at question formation emerged from Lesson 7 onwards. These were infrequent and often inaccurate, with inversion proving problematic (e.g. *where I have . . . ?*). Dimitrie occasionally linked clauses using simple co-ordinating conjunctions such as *and* or, later, *but*. However, he made no attempts at more complex clause linkage.

Evidence of L2 acquisition – lexical indicators

An indication of Dimitrie's L2 lexical development over the study period is provided in Table 4.6. Regarding his 'Wordlist entries per turn', the slightly higher results for Lessons 1 and 3 are probably due more to the paucity of analysable turns available for him in the first half of the study: in the early lessons he was often almost silent. However, the results for the second half of the study, in which his contribution to lessons increased, suggest some rise in his lexical diversity. Lesson-related factors may, however, have impacted on these results, as classroom interaction often elicited short turns (e.g. single-word answers).

Table 4.6 Dimitrie – indicators of L2 lexical development

Wordlist results						
Lesson	**1**	**3**	**4**	**7**	**9**	**12**
Wordlist entries per turn per lesson	10	2	14	38	27	93
Wordlist entries per turn	1.43	2	0.88	1.36	1.35	1.12
Verb lexemes per lesson	2	1	1	5	7	15

The semantic themes covered by Dimitrie reflected many of the units of work in the *Benchmarks*, which were the basis for some, but not all, of his group's lessons. While most of the nouns he used were lexically very simple, some more specific items (e.g. *dragon*, on the theme of 'animals') emerged later in the study. Adjectives such as colours and simple opposites (e.g. *hot/cold*) were also recorded, and from Lesson 4 he could express possession with the determiner *my*. Dimitrie's verb lexeme production diversified from basic verbs (e.g. *be* and *finish*), to cover a much wider range (e.g. *copy* and *smell*) in the final lesson. In total, he produced 19 distinct verb lexemes. His use of adverbs included deictic referents (e.g. *here, there*), and from Lesson 7 the modifier *very*.

L2 literacy development

The lessons recorded for Dimitrie's group were primarily concerned with the development of L2 oral skills. However, they also featured some literacy-focused activities. Dimitrie's engagement in these tasks increased as the study progressed. From Lesson 7 onwards, he could participate in emergent literacy activities such as suggesting rhyming words. In Lesson 9, with help from the teacher, he copied words labelling a picture of a bird. His unfamiliarity with the L2 vocabulary required for this task (e.g. *wings, feathers*) added to its challenge. By the final lesson, he could also write his name unassisted.

Possible influences on L2 development

Individual factors

Dimitrie was 5 years old at the end of the study and, like other participants in the Junior Infants mainstream class, he was adjusting both to the new experience of school and to immersion in an L2 environment. Like Zofia (Profile 1), Dimitrie exhibited characteristics associated with a 'silent period' of receptive L2 acquisition prior to significant production. In early lessons, L2 comprehension was evident in his ability to follow the teacher's instructions in classroom activities and to explain these in his home language, Romanian, to another pupil. Regarding the possible influence of Romanian on his acquisition of English, Dimitrie's lengthening of vowels and occasionally his pronunciation of cognate lexis (e.g. *cafea*/coffee) suggested transfer. His heavy reliance on *no* for negation may also have been home-language influenced. As regards his personality and learning style, it seemed that while Dimitrie tended towards receptive L2 learning, he could be talkative in his home language. Also, when he began to articulate more in English, he often produced quite intelligible and well-formed utterances.

Interaction-related factors

Analysis of Dimitrie's turns showed that whenever he was prepared to engage in oral L2 use, he could initiate and elaborate on topics. Although the limited number of turns recorded for him restricted this analysis, he seemed able to take an active part in classroom interaction when he felt capable of L2 production. The distribution of the turn-types 'tellings', 'topic elaborations' and 'answers' in Dimitrie's analysed L2 use is shown in Figure 4.9. Regarding interlocutor identity, almost all of his turns were teacher directed. This dynamic may have reduced his opportunities for L2 use in a large group whose members were more L2 proficient than Dimitrie.

Figure 4.9 Turn-type indicators of interaction patterns for Dimitrie in selected lessons

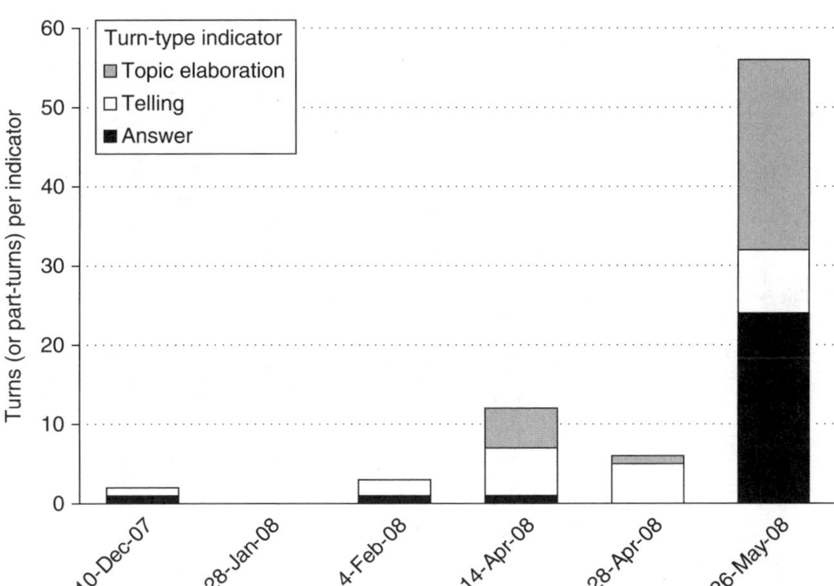

4 Patryk

Relevant personal details are provided for Patryk in Table 4.7. The distribution of his analysed spoken turns is presented in Figure 4.10. This indicates that at the start of the study, his turns were overwhelmingly associated with *Benchmarks* proficiency level A1, but that later he began to produce A2-linked turns. Figure 4.11 shows his use of the quantitatively analysed grammatical indicators and illustrates the accuracy of this use.

Table 4.7 Patryk – personal details

National/cultural background	Polish	**Age at end of study**	5 years
School attended	School 1	**School class**	Junior Infants
English language support commenced	October 2007	**Duration of participation in study**	November 2007 – June 2008
Number of lessons selected for detailed analysis	10 (of total 19)	**Number of turns-at-talk analysed**	385

Figure 4.10 Benchmarks levels recorded for analysed turns produced by Patryk in selected lessons

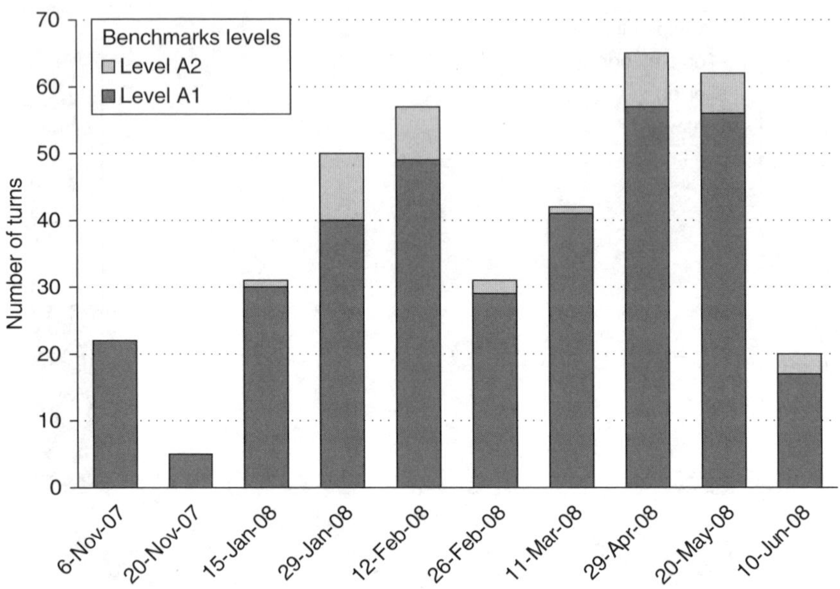

Figure 4.11 Frequency and accuracy of quantitatively analysed grammatical indicators used by Patryk

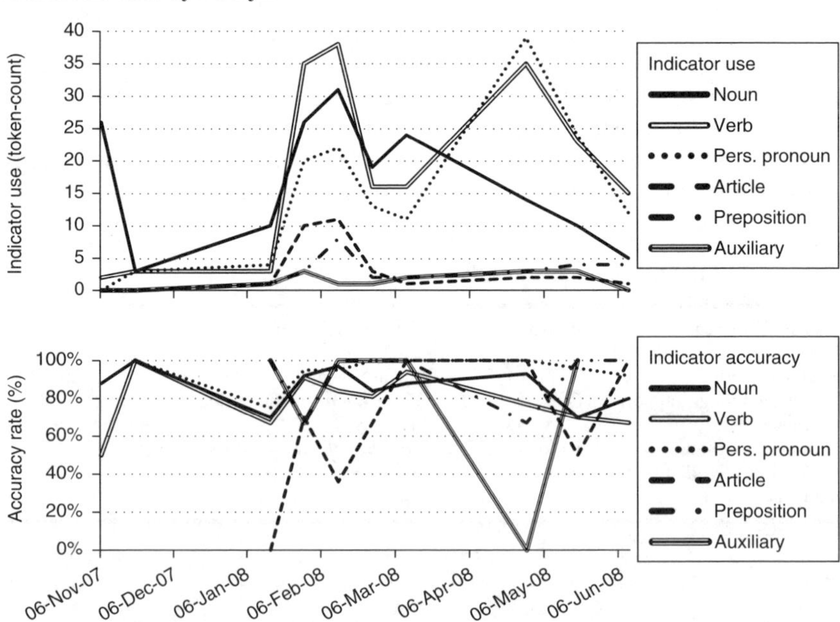

Evidence of L2 acquisition – grammatical indicators

Morphological features

Patryk's use of the grammatical indicators represented in Figure 4.11 increased over the study period. However, lesson-related factors could influence actual token-count for each of these variables. This was clear, for instance, in Lesson 19, which focused on L2 literacy skills (reading and writing in response to prepared worksheets) and thus offered fewer spontaneous L2 oral turns-at-talk for analysis. Accuracy of indicator use fluctuated as production increased and diversified. Patryk's use of nouns rose (subject to lesson-related factors) over the study period. The accuracy of his noun use was usually over 80%. Typical errors involved incorrect lexical choice or the use of singular nouns in plural contexts. Patryk's verb use also increased, although its accuracy declined somewhat as he produced a wider range of verb forms. Initially, it comprised uninflected stems and the copula *be*. However, from Lesson 7 onwards he produced some progressive and simple past forms (generally irregular, e.g. *went*). Patryk's production of pronouns diversified to include, by the end of the study, pronouns such as the substitute *one* and possessive *mine*. His personal pronoun use was usually accurate, although errors relating to case (object pronouns in place of subject pronouns) were particularly evident. Omission of personal pronouns was infrequent (generally under 10% of actual use).

Article use by Patryk was first recorded in Lesson 5 and remained limited throughout the study. It usually involved production of the definite article, often incorrectly applied to contexts requiring the indefinite article or no article. His omission of articles was, however, very prominent (up to twice or three times his rate of article production). Preposition use, albeit infrequent, emerged from Lesson 5 onwards. Patryk produced a limited range of prepositions (e.g. *in, on, to, with, for*). Although this production was generally accurate, inappropriate preposition choice also occurred. From Lesson 5, he occasionally produced auxiliaries, although their frequency and diversity were limited. Accurate use of present tense forms of the auxiliaries *be, can* and *have* was recorded, while *going to* was used for future reference. Incorrect choice and omission of auxiliaries was also apparent.

Syntactic features

Patryk's analysed turns were predominantly noun based. However, although his verb-to-noun ratio never exceeded 0.6, it rose during the study period, suggesting some increase in structural complexity. Regarding negation, Patryk initially relied on the marker *no*, often used inappropriately. By Lesson 7 he could produce negative structures using *not*. From the beginning of the study, he could form simple questions (e.g. *what is . . .?*). Inverted questions (e.g. *is it that?*) emerged from Lesson 7 and some attempt at indirect question formation was subsequently evident. However, such structures were infrequent and rarely well formed. Patryk generally linked clauses with simple co-ordinating conjunctions (typically *and*); appropriate use of the subordinating *because* was occasionally recorded from Lesson 15.

Evidence of L2 acquisition – lexical indicators

Results for 'Wordlist entries per turn', shown in Table 4.8, suggest that Patryk's lexical range widened during the study, albeit with some fluctuation from lesson to lesson.

Table 4.8 Patryk – indicators of L2 lexical development

Wordlist results										
Lesson	**1**	**3**	**5**	**7**	**9**	**11**	**13**	**15**	**17**	**19**
Wordlist entries per turn per lesson	18	8	34	72	69	40	37	76	66	34
Wordlist entries per turn	0.82	1.6	1.10	1.44	1.21	0.76	0.88	1.17	1.06	1.7
Verb lexemes per lesson	2	2	2	13	12	7	8	13	11	9

The semantic fields associated with Patryk's L2 use related closely to the units of work in the *Benchmarks*, whether or not the lesson was structured around these units. The nouns he produced tended to be basic, although on topics of interest, such as modes of transport vehicles, he used a wider range of lexis (e.g. *lorry, helicopter*). His adjective production included colours and simple size-referents, with comparatives (e.g. *higher*) occasionally recorded towards the end of the study, although generally their use was inaccurate. Diversification of L2 verb lexemes was also apparent; from *be* and *have* at the beginning of the study to more specific verbs such as *swim* and *remember* later on. In all, 33 distinct verb lexemes were recorded in his L2 production. Patryk produced basic adverbs of place and modifiers (e.g. *only, very*) in early lessons. More adverbs relating to frequency and time (e.g. *again, tomorrow*) emerged later in the study.

L2 literacy development

During the study, Patryk was in the first year of Irish primary education. Like his peers (EAL and native English-speaking pupils) he was at a very early stage of English literacy development. He proved capable of engaging in emergent literacy activities associated with his mainstream class (Junior Infants). During the first half of the study, he could recognise basic L2 grapho-phonic relations. By the final lessons, he was competently reading short words by identifying the sounds associated with their onset and ending. However, his knowledge of the L2 lexis used in these phonics-based activities affected his engagement – unfamiliar vocabulary proved more challenging to read. His L2 writing skills also developed in the second half of the study, by which time he could copy words and short sentences relating to lesson topics.

Possible influences on L2 development

Individual factors

Patryk was aged 4–5 years during the study period and this affected the cognitive challenge of the tasks in the recorded lessons. As mentioned above, many of the literacy-related activities with which Patryk engaged were typical of mainstream classroom tasks for children in their first year of schooling in Ireland. It must be noted, however, that these activities often required a limited range of L2 use. With regard to possible home-language influence, some cross-linguistic transfer was evident in relation to phonology (e.g. differences in English and Polish consonantal voicing patterns) and grammar (e.g. omission of articles). In relation to personality and learning style, Patryk appeared to be quite an extravert child. His confident nature may have supported his L2 development by enabling him to seize opportunities for L2 use/learning. From a very early stage of L2 proficiency, he was willing to ask questions, volunteer information, and even attempt jokes in English.

Interaction-related factors

Patryk proved capable of taking initiatives and actively participating in L2 interaction (e.g. 'telling' and 'elaborating' on topics), particularly from Lesson 7 onwards, as is evident from Figure 4.12. Instances of more active discourse seemed to coincide with evidence of slightly higher proficiency in his L2 use (see Figure 4.10). They also reflected personal interest in the lesson theme. Classroom talk was mostly teacher directed. Peer-to-peer interaction generally accounted for less than 5% of his analysed L2 production.

Figure 4.12 Turn-type indicators of interaction patterns for Patryk in selected lessons

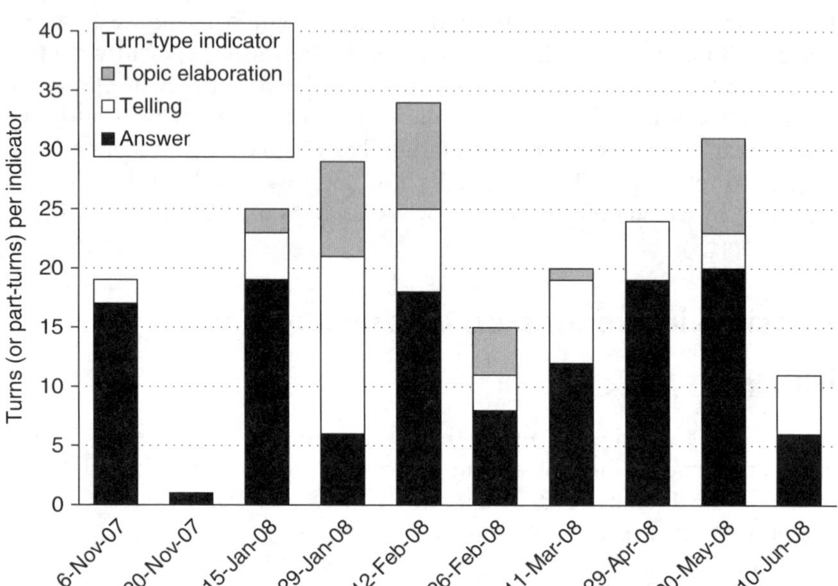

5 Tomasz

Table 4.9 provides personal details for Tomasz. Figure 4.13 shows the *Benchmarks* proficiency levels associated with his analysed spoken turns: at first predominantly A1, but with more evidence of A2 proficiency later in the study. The frequency and accuracy of his use of the quantitatively analysed grammatical indicators is shown in Figure 4.14.

Table 4.9 Tomasz – personal details

National/cultural background	Polish	**Age at end of study**	5 years
School attended	School 1	**School class**	Junior Infants
English language support commenced	October 2007	**Duration of participation in study**	November 2007 – June 2008
Number of lessons selected for detailed analysis	10 (of total 17)	**Number of turns-at-talk analysed**	217

Figure 4.13 Benchmarks levels recorded for analysed turns produced by Tomasz in selected lessons

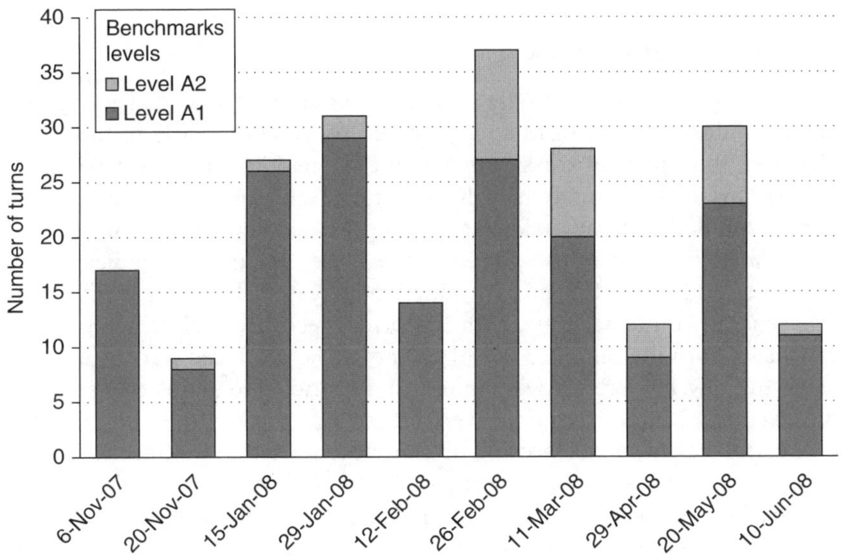

Figure 4.14 Frequency and accuracy of quantitatively analysed grammatical indicators used by Tomasz

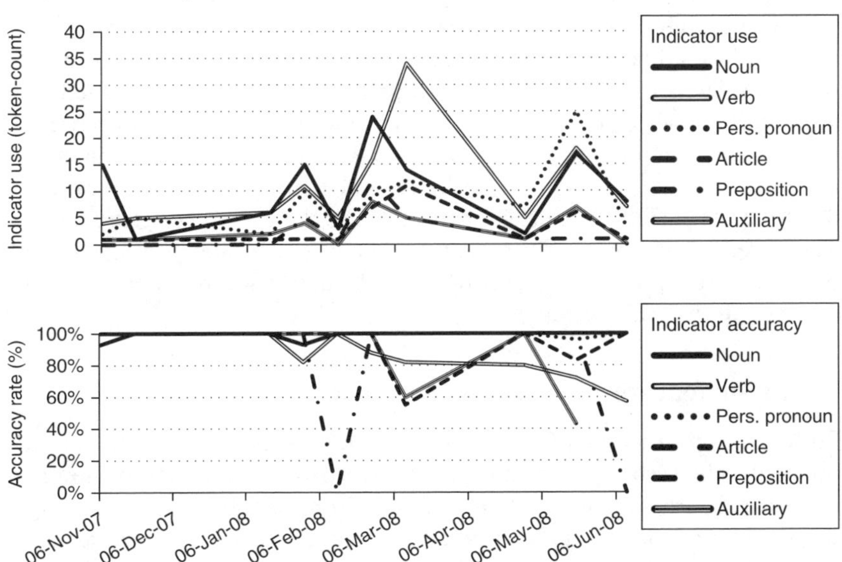

Evidence of L2 acquisition – grammatical indicators

Morphological features

Figure 4.14 shows that Tomasz's use of the quantitatively analysed grammatical indicators rose from a very limited token-count early in the study. However, the nature of classroom activities sometimes affected the number of turns available for analysis of his L2 oral development. For example, the final lesson had a literacy-related focus and yielded fewer turns which could be considered instances of spontaneous L2 use. Accuracy of indicator use fluctuated and often declined as production increased. Tomasz's use of nouns was generally quite accurate, with few errors recorded. While he appeared capable of forming plurals, most of the nouns he produced were in singular form. Initially, his verb use was limited, and restricted to uninflected stems or present tense forms of the copula verb *be*. Midway through the study, his verb production began to increase and diversify. He started to produce past tense forms, although not always accurately (e.g. *I saw him did this*). Use of progressive forms and, very occasionally, past participles also emerged. Tomasz's pronoun use was largely confined to personal and demonstrative pronouns. However, later in the study, it included the substitute pronoun *one* and the reflexive *myself*. His use of personal pronouns was generally accurate but omission, usually of subject pronouns, was equivalent to 50% of his rate of personal pronoun use.

Tomasz rarely used articles in the first half of the study, and although their production gradually increased, it remained infrequent. His rate of article omission often exceeded his rate of article use. Preposition use emerged only in the second half of the study. Tomasz produced basic prepositions (e.g. *in, on, with, at, for, to*), although incorrect preposition choice was sometimes apparent. His use of auxiliaries was recorded from Lesson 5 onwards. It diversified to include auxiliary forms of *be, do, have, will, going to* and *can*. These were generally used in present tense contexts although past forms of *be* and *did* were produced. Inaccuracies, particularly non-required use of the auxiliary *be*, were also evident.

Syntactic features

Structures produced by Tomasz were generally short and biased towards nominals. His verb-to-noun ratio rarely exceeded 0.4, although it showed a rising trend across the study. From Lesson 1, Tomasz was able to create negative structures using the marker *not*, often with auxiliaries (e.g. *my dog can't see really well* – Lesson 5). Evidence of question formation was more limited. In the second half of the study, he produced inverted questions (e.g. *do you like this?*) and attempted indirect questions, though not always successfully. Beyond the use of simple co-ordinating conjunctions, his clause linkage involved the isolated production of *because* and, in Lesson 17, an attempt at a conditional structure involving *if*.

Evidence of L2 acquisition – lexical indicators

An indication of Tomasz's L2 lexical development is offered by data obtained from the Wordlist program shown in Table 4.10. Considering the results for 'Wordlist entries per turn', increasing lexical diversity is evident across the selected lessons.

Table 4.10 Tomasz – indicators of L2 lexical development

Wordlist results										
Lesson	**1**	**3**	**5**	**7**	**9**	**11**	**13**	**15**	**17**	**19**
Wordlist entries per lesson	19	16	23	42	20	58	56	21	65	26
Wordlist entries per turn	1.11	1.77	0.85	1.35	1.43	1.57	2.00	1.75	2.17	2.17
Verb lexemes per lesson	3	3	4	5	3	9	10	4	14	7

The semantic fields which featured in Tomasz's analysed oral L2 use were clearly linked to the units of work included in the *Benchmarks*. While the *Benchmarks* formed the basis of some lessons for this group, the teacher frequently structured activities around topics (and resources) associated with pupils' mainstream classroom learning. Generally the nouns used by Tomasz across these themes were lexically simple (e.g. *hair* on the topic of 'body parts'). He used adjectives for colours and attributes such as size (e.g. *long*), while the possessive determiner *my* was produced from Lesson 11. The range of verb lexemes produced by Tomasz increased over the study period from very basic verbs (e.g. *know* and *have*) in the initial lessons, to words associated with more specific actions (e.g. *watch* and *write*). In total, his L2 production featured 27 distinct verb lexemes. Adverbs recorded early in the study included basic deictic referents and modifiers such as *really*; adverbs of time (e.g. *now, sometimes*) emerged later.

L2 literacy development

Tomasz was in his first year of primary education and, like his mainstream classroom peers, at the earliest stage of English literacy development. From lessons which focused on aspects of L2 reading or writing, it was apparent that Tomasz could engage with literacy activities typical of mainstream education at this stage of schooling. This was most evident in the second half of the study. By Lesson 13, he demonstrated considerable competence in identifying basic L2 grapho-phonic relations. He could also write his name, with help from the teacher. Towards the end of the study, he could read monosyllabic words with rhyming endings in phonics-based activities and complete worksheets involving the writing of these words. He could also copy or fill gaps in short sentences on lesson topics. Unfamiliarity with the L2 lexis used in such tasks sometimes restricted his engagement. No evidence of the acquisition of home-language literacy skills emerged during the study.

Possible influences on L2 development

Individual factors

Tomasz was a very young child (5 years old at the end of the study), and this may have enabled him to engage with greater ease in mainstream classroom activities than older EAL pupils. However, his engagement with these cognitively and linguistically simple activities depended on access to the English required to understand both the tasks and accompanying instructions. Regarding cross-linguistic influence, phonological transfer from Polish, his home language, was detectable in Tomasz's L2 use (e.g. his frequent palatalisation of the English consonant /l/). His confusion of simple and progressive forms suggested transfer in the marking of aspect (this was typical of participants in this study who came from Slavic language backgrounds). Home-language characteristics may also have contributed to his omission of articles and subject pronouns. As regards personality and learning style, Tomasz was a quiet child who could concentrate well on classroom tasks but seemed reluctant to take initiatives in interaction. However, as his L2 proficiency increased he participated more actively in classroom talk.

Interaction-related factors

Analysis of Tomasz's interaction patterns, based on the three turn-type indicators shown in Figure 4.15, indicates that 'answers' predominated in early lessons. However, in the second half of the study, he produced an increasing proportion of 'tellings' and 'topic elaborations' which suggested more active participation in classroom interaction. This corresponded to the evidence of increased L2 proficiency apparent in Figure 4.13. Almost all Tomasz's analysed turns were teacher directed. This may have limited his opportunities for L2 learning/use, particularly as there were three other children in the group and Tomasz was its quietest member.

Figure 4.15 Turn-type indicators of interaction patterns for Tomasz in selected lessons

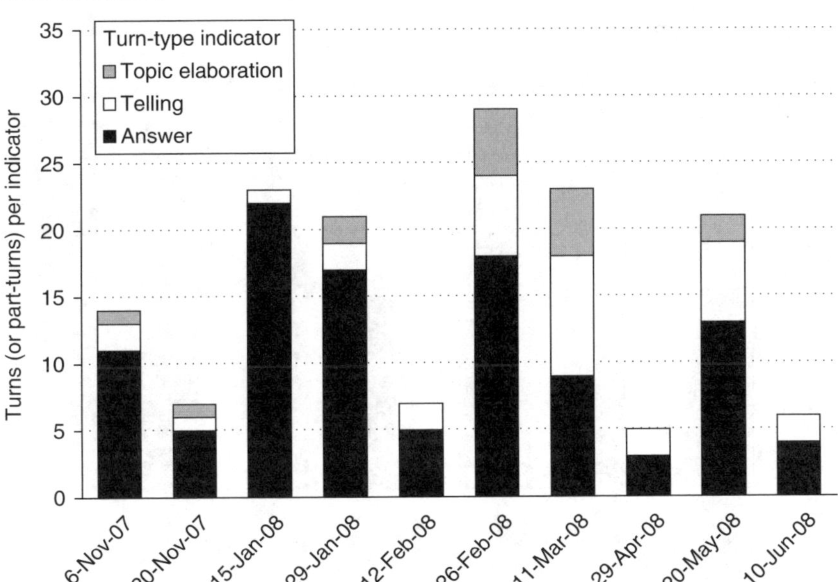

6 Marko

Marko's personal details are presented in Table 4.11. The *Benchmarks* proficiency levels associated with his analysed spoken turns are shown in Figure 4.16. While most of his L2 oral production in the selected lessons could be linked to level A1, evidence of A2 proficiency emerged as the study progressed. Figure 4.17 illustrates the frequency and accuracy of his use of the quantitatively analysed grammatical indicators.

Table 4.11 Marko – personal details

National/cultural background	Serbian	Age at end of study	5 years
School attended	School 2	School class	Junior Infants
English language support commenced	September 2007	Duration of participation in study	December 2007 – May 2008
Number of lessons selected for detailed analysis	7 (of total 9)	Number of turns-at-talk analysed	227

Figure 4.16 Benchmarks levels recorded for analysed turns produced by Marko in selected lessons

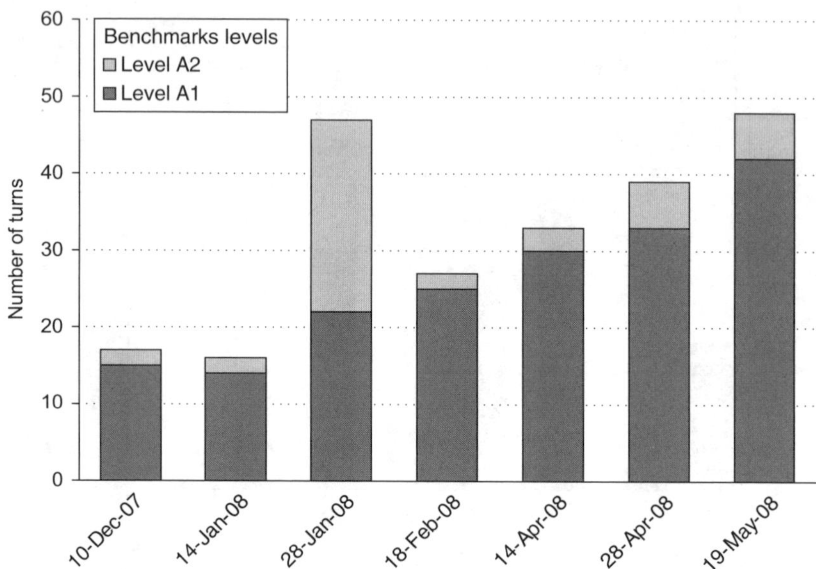

Figure 4.17 Frequency and accuracy of quantitatively analysed grammatical indicators used by Marko

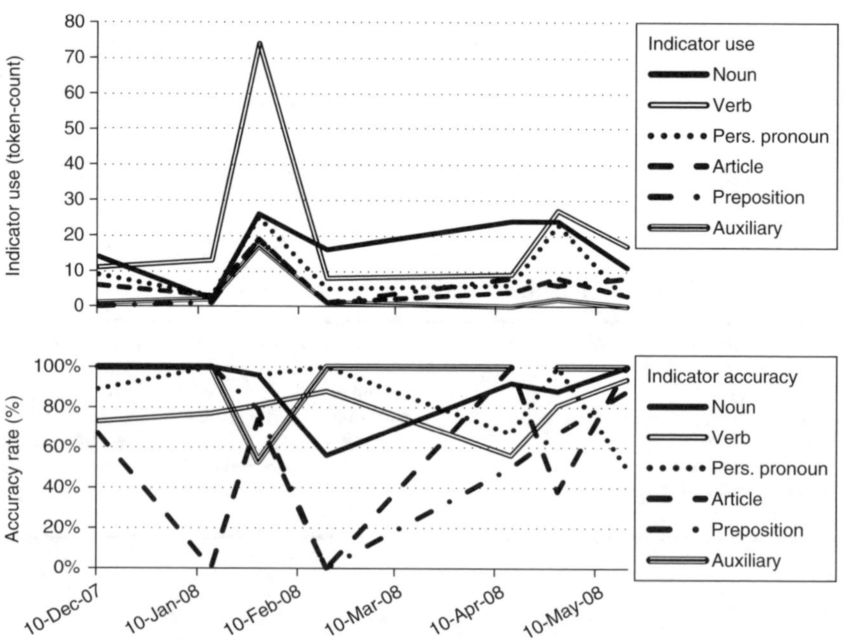

Evidence of L2 acquisition – grammatical indicators

Morphological features

Figure 4.17 shows a generally rising trend in Marko's production of the quantitatively analysed grammatical indicators, although his accuracy levels fluctuated considerably for each. The peak recorded in his production of all these indicators in Lesson 3 may be attributable to the fact that in this lesson he contributed particularly actively to classroom interaction. However, his group was rather large (up to eight children of varying L2 proficiency), so it was often difficult to secure turn-taking opportunities in classroom discourse. Regarding noun use, Marko's production appeared in general to increase. His accuracy level dipped to 56% in Lesson 5 but rose again later in the study. Most noun-related errors were lexical or due to lack of required pluralisation. Marko's verb production peaked in Lesson 3, in which he made widespread use of the verbs he knew. From Lesson 1, he used present tense stem verbs and the copula *be* and occasionally attempted progressive forms (e.g. *it's not raining*). His first recorded instance of past tense use (*found*) was in Lesson 9. Typical errors included omission of the third person present tense marker (*-s*) and use of present simple forms in contexts requiring past verbs or progressive aspect. Marko's pronoun use diversified during the study to include personal, demonstrative, substitute, quantifying and indefinite pronouns. His personal pronoun use was generally quite accurate, although case-related errors were recorded and some omission of subject pronouns occurred in early lessons.

Marko used articles rather infrequently and with considerable fluctuations in accuracy. Article confusion and non-required use featured prominently among his errors, while his rate of article omission was sometimes twice that of production. His use of prepositions gradually became more diverse, and while his accuracy rate initially fell, it rose again in the final lessons. Inappropriate use of *in* rather than *to* and *in/on* confusion were typical errors. His production of auxiliaries was relatively infrequent and generally involved present tense forms of *be* or *do*. He occasionally used *can* from Lesson 5 onwards. Incorrect auxiliary choice and non-required use of the auxiliary *be* emerged as sources of error.

Syntactic features

Structurally, Marko's production tended to be noun based. In Lessons 2 and 3, the proportion of verb use in his analysed turns was higher than in later lessons. However, this may have been due to activities on the theme of 'actions' in these lessons. From early in the study, Marko could use *not* as a negative marker, in both full and contracted form (e.g. *don't*), and his negation became more consistently accurate in later lessons. Question formation using basic question words was evident in his production from Lesson 3 onwards. However, his attempts at inverted questions were rare and generally unsuccessful. He usually linked clauses with *and*; occasional use of *because* was recorded from Lesson 2.

Evidence of L2 acquisition – lexical indicators

Results for 'Wordlist entries per turn', presented in Table 4.12, suggest that the lexical diversity of Marko's L2 use varied across the study period. This was possibly influenced by lesson-related factors which may have affected his participation.

Table 4.12 Marko – indicators of L2 lexical development

Wordlist results							
Lesson	**1**	**2**	**3**	**5**	**7**	**9**	**11**
Wordlist entries per turn per lesson	29	21	84	32	48	52	50
Wordlist entries per turn	1.71	1.31	3.36	1.19	1.45	1.33	1.05
Verb lexemes per lesson	3	8	19	5	6	12	6

His lexical production spanned a range of semantic fields. Most of these corresponded closely to the units of work in the *Benchmarks*, although the teacher in School 2 did not structure her English language support exclusively around these themes. While most of his L2 vocabulary was quite basic, evidence of more specific nouns and adjectives (e.g. *sentence* and *correct*, on the topic of 'school') also emerged. He could indicate possession using the determiner *my* (recorded from Lesson 7). Marko produced a total of 38 distinct verb lexemes across the study. The range of his L2 verb use was widest in Lesson 3, possibly due to lesson-related factors, but its lexical complexity increased across the study, from basic verbs such as *be* and *like* in Lesson 1 to *climb* and *grow* in later lessons. Adverbs used in the early lessons included basic referents to place and modifiers (e.g. *too*), with frequency referents (e.g. *again*) apparent from Lesson 7.

L2 literacy development

The lessons recorded in School 2 focused primarily on L2 oral development. However, they included some instances of literacy-related activities. These were equivalent to mainstream emergent literacy tasks for children who, like Marko, were in their first year of education in Ireland. In Lesson

1, he could identify, with visual support, words starting with the same initial sound (e.g. *panda, parrot* etc.). By Lesson 3 he could also read words which had featured in previous mainstream activities. He could also recite nursery rhymes, although some of the vocabulary used in these was probably beyond his L2 understanding. Towards the end of the study, evidence of L2 writing skills emerged in his ability to label pictures such as parts of a bird (in Lesson 9).

Possible influences on L2 development

Individual factors

Aged 5 years at the end of the study, Marko could, with support, take part in some classroom activities typical of the first year of schooling. However, he was still acquiring the L2 vocabulary necessary for full cognitive engagement with mainstream learning. His home language, Serbian, influenced his L2 development phonologically, for example in his pronunciation of /h/, which was much closer to the velarised /x/ and in his articulation of vowels and diphthongs (e.g. /æ/ as /ɛ/). Certain traits of Serbian transferred to his L2 grammar, from omission of articles and subject pronouns to confusion of prepositions (*in, on* and *to* have Serbian equivalents *u* and *na*, with case-marking to indicate movement) to problems of aspect selection. Some lexical *faux amis* also appeared (e.g. using *paket* in the sense of 'parcel'). Regarding learning style, Marko seemed a cautious child, who preferred to raise his hand and wait for attention rather than speak out in class.

Interaction-related factors

Considering his personality and his position as one of the less L2 proficient pupils in quite a large group (maximum eight children), Marko's opportunities for classroom interaction may have been somewhat restricted. Analysis of his spoken turns, presented in Figure 4.18, suggested that he often played a responding role in interaction. However, in some lessons (e.g. Lesson 3) the proportion of more active turn-types ('tellings' and 'topic elaborations') increased. This coincided with greater evidence of A2 proficiency in his L2 use (see Figure 4.16). Marko's discourse was almost entirely teacher directed. Given the classroom dynamic, increased peer interaction might have enabled him to participate more actively, possibly to the benefit of his L2 development.

Figure 4.18 Turn-type indicators of interaction patterns for Marko in selected lessons

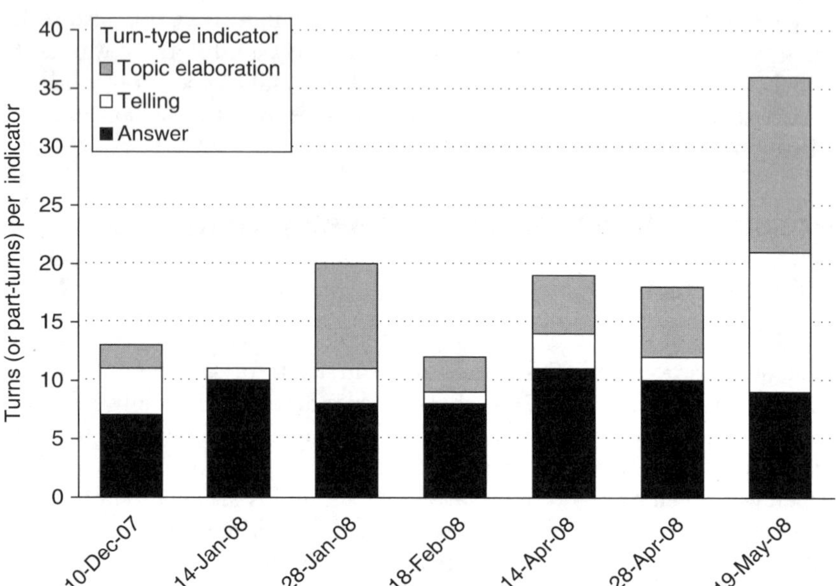

7 Jin

Personal details for Jin are presented in Table 4.13. The *Benchmarks* proficiency levels associated with his analysed spoken turns are illustrated in Figure 4.19. These turns linked predominantly to proficiency level A1. However, in the second half of the study an increasing proportion of A2-linked turns emerged. The frequency and accuracy of analysed grammatical indicators produced by Jin is shown in Figure 4.20.

Table 4.13 Jin – personal details

National/cultural background	Chinese	**Age at end of study**	6 years
School attended	School 2	**School class**	Junior Infants
English language support commenced	September 2007	**Duration of participation in study**	December 2007 – May 2008
Number of lessons selected for detailed analysis	8 (of total 12)	**Number of turns-at-talk analysed**	556

Figure 4.19 Benchmarks levels recorded for analysed turns produced by Jin in selected lessons

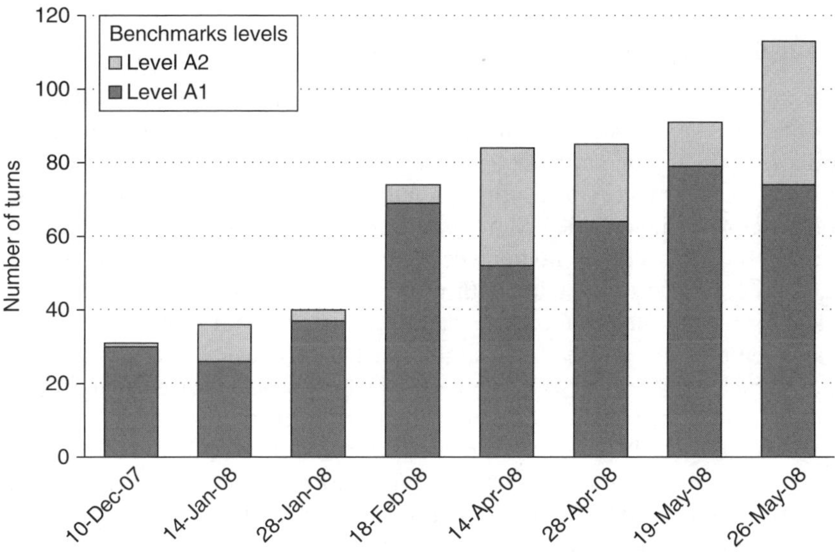

Figure 4.20 Frequency and accuracy of quantitatively analysed grammatical indicators used by Jin

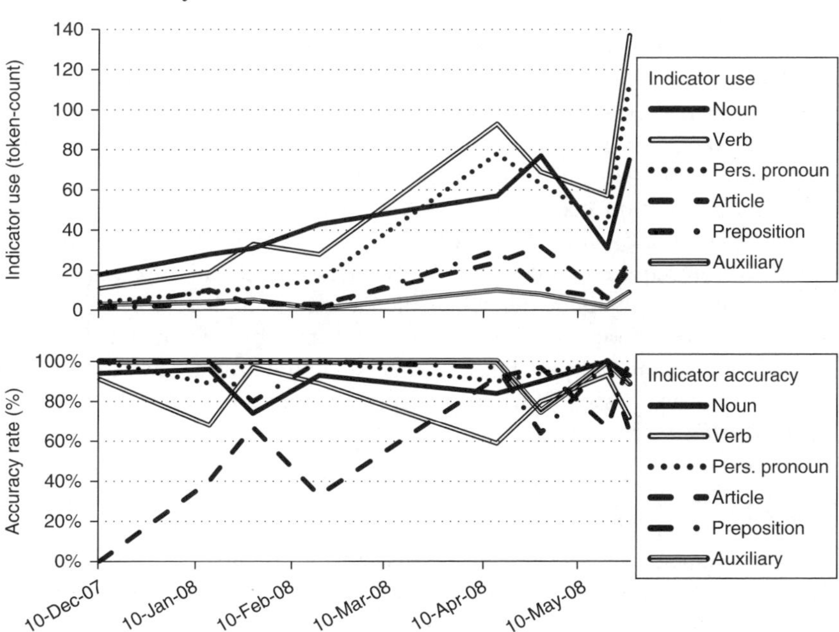

Evidence of L2 acquisition – grammatical indicators

Morphological features

Jin's use of nouns generally rose across the selected lessons; the slight dip in noun frequency recorded in Lesson 11 may have been due to a focus on opposites (hence an emphasis on adjectives) in this lesson. His noun use was usually over 80% accurate, although lack of pluralisation in required contexts was sometimes evident. Jin's verb production increased during the study period but its accuracy fluctuated, particularly in later lessons. This fluctuation appeared to coincide with more diverse use of verbs beyond basic stem forms and the present tense of the copula *be*. From Lesson 2 onwards, Jin attempted progressive and simple past forms (usually irregular verbs, but occasionally regular (e.g. *pushed*). In later lessons, past participles (e.g. *broken*) were recorded, although these were infrequently and not always appropriately used. Typical verb-related errors involved omission of the third person (*-s*) morpheme in the present simple forms and use of present verbs in past contexts. Jin's use of pronouns also increased over the study, diversifying from personal and demonstrative pronouns to substitute, indefinite and possessive pronouns. His use of personal pronouns rose and was reasonably accurate throughout, with only occasional errors (usually of gender) and little omission.

Jin produced few articles in the first half of the study. However, from Lesson 7 an increase in article production was recorded. His accuracy rate for articles also rose, although article use in non-required contexts was a common source of error. Article omission was frequent in early lessons, but its rate declined (to 0.36 of article production by the end of the study). Jin's use of prepositions also diversified, especially in later lessons, although its accuracy varied as production became more widespread. Errors often involved the inappropriate use of *in* (rather than *on, to, into* or *at*) or the use of prepositions in non-required contexts. Jin's production of auxiliaries was limited throughout the study but evidence of increasing, more diverse auxiliary use emerged in later lessons. Auxiliaries produced appropriately included *be* and *do* (both in present and past tense forms). Jin could also use *can* to indicate ability and, from Lesson 7, he could express future reference with *will* (e.g. *crocodile will eat something*).

Syntactic features

Nominal elements (nouns and pronouns) were more numerous than verbal elements in Jin's analysed turns. However, a slight rise in his verb-to-noun ratio (to 0.59 by the end of the study) reflected the production of slightly more complex structures. Attempts at negation were recorded from Lesson 2, and these became more accurate, with appropriate use of *not* prevailing as the study progressed. In early lessons Jin produced only simple questions. Inversion was recorded from Lesson 7 (e.g. *do you know my mum like eat chicken?*) and his question formation developed to include indirect forms by the end of the study. He generally linked clauses with simple co-ordinating conjunctions. An isolated and partial attempt at relativisation using *when* was recorded in Lesson 14.

Evidence of L2 acquisition – lexical indicators

Evidence of Jin's L2 lexical development is presented in Table 4.14. This shows a marked rise in the 'Wordlist entries' recorded for Jin across the study period. While the results for 'Wordlist entries per turn' remain more stable throughout, this calculation may have been affected by lesson-related factors, notably the frequent requirement for short, often one-word, answers.

Table 4.14 Jin – indicators of L2 lexical development

Wordlist results								
Lesson	1	2	3	5	7	9	11	12
Wordlist entries per turn per lesson	42	56	56	76	117	111	104	140
Wordlist entries per turn	1.35	1.55	1.40	1.03	1.39	1.31	1.14	1.24
Verb lexemes per lesson	5	11	8	13	22	20	16	25

Semantically, the themes represented in Jin's analysed spoken turns correspond with many of the units of work in the *Benchmarks*. These were used by the teacher to some extent, although not exclusively, to plan English language support in School 2. While most of Jin's lexis was basic, more specific nouns appeared during the study (e.g. *rainbow* on the topic of 'weather'). His adjective use also became more extensive (e.g. *delicious, stupid*), and he used the possessive determiners *my* and *your* from early lessons. His L2 production across the study included 52 distinct verb lexemes. It diversified from simple verbs (e.g. *look, want*) in early lessons to more complex verbs later (e.g. *taste, crack*). From the outset, Jin could use basic adverbs of place, frequency and time; modifiers such as *nearly* were recorded from Lesson 7.

L2 literacy development

The lessons recorded for Jin's group (of which Marko (Profile 6) and Dimitrie (Profile 3) were also members) focused mainly on L2 oral skills. Nevertheless, some activities offered evidence of his L2 literacy development. From Lesson 1, he could identify some basic sight vocabulary and demonstrated L2 phonetic awareness in his ability to suggest words beginning with the same sound. By Lesson 3, he could read familiar words (e.g. *water*) on flashcards and write his name. Later in the study, he could also read and copy more complex words in order to label a picture.

Possible influences on L2 development

Individual factors

Jin, who was aged 6 at the end of the study, could engage with activities typical of mainstream education in the first year at Irish primary school. However, due to his early stage of L2 development, this engagement depended on sustained support. Although the teacher was not sure of Jin's home language, it was likely from his family origins (as explained in Chapter 3) to be Cantonese. While it was impossible to gauge with any accuracy the extent of possible cross-linguistic influence on Jin's acquisition of English, some phonological evidence was apparent, for instance in his minimal distinction between particular phonemes (e.g. /ɹ/ and /l/) and potentially L1-like characteristics of his L2 prosody. Regarding personality, Jin was a confident, communicative child who could secure turn-taking slots, even in a group which included pupils with higher levels of L2 proficiency. This may have afforded him more opportunities for L2 use/learning than would have been available to a more reticent child. His learning style appeared rather holistic; he used 'chunks' of language effectively to bolster communication. He also made good use of compensation strategies, such as circumlocution.

Interaction-related factors

Perhaps due to his personality, Jin could take initiatives and elaborate on classroom topics. The analysis of selected turn-types, presented in Figure 4.21, showed the predominance of these 'active' discourse patterns in his L2 interaction from early in the study. This may have offered him richer opportunities for L2 learning than talk confined to responding roles. However, the majority of Jin's turns were teacher directed, which may have curtailed his overall contribution to classroom discourse since he had to compete with other pupils to secure his turns-at-talk.

Figure 4.21 Turn-type indicators of interaction patterns for Jin in selected lessons

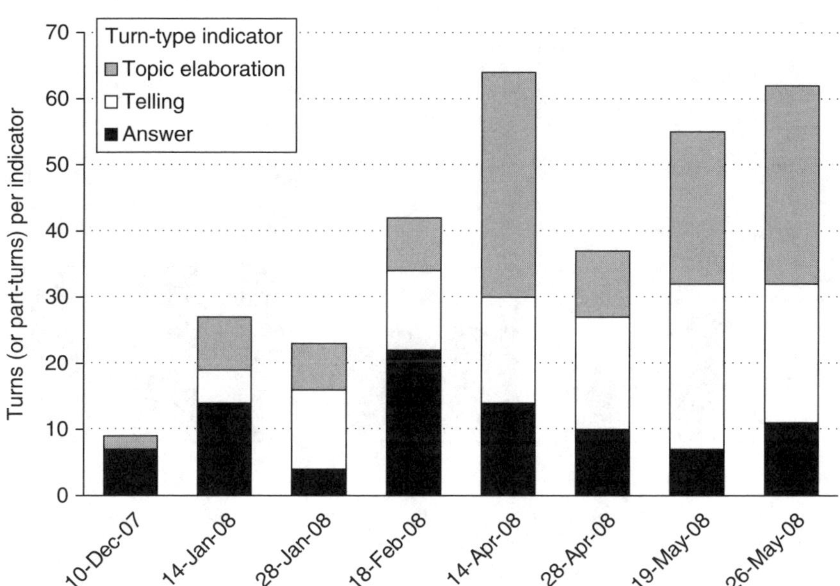

8 Edyta

Edyta's personal details are shown in Table 4.15. From the *Benchmarks* proficiency levels associated with her analysed spoken turns (indicated in Figure 4.22) it is evident that Edyta could produce level A2-linked turns in the first half of the study and that A2 production increased in the second half. Figure 4.23 illustrates the frequency and accuracy of her use of the quantitatively analysed grammatical indicators.

Table 4.15 Edyta – personal details

National/cultural background	Polish	**Age at end of study**	5 years
School attended	School 2	**School class**	Junior Infants
English language support commenced	September 2007	**Duration of participation in study**	December 2007 – May 2008
Number of lessons selected for detailed analysis	7 (of total 9)	**Number of turns-at-talk analysed**	425

Figure 4.22 Benchmarks levels recorded for analysed turns produced by Edyta in selected lessons

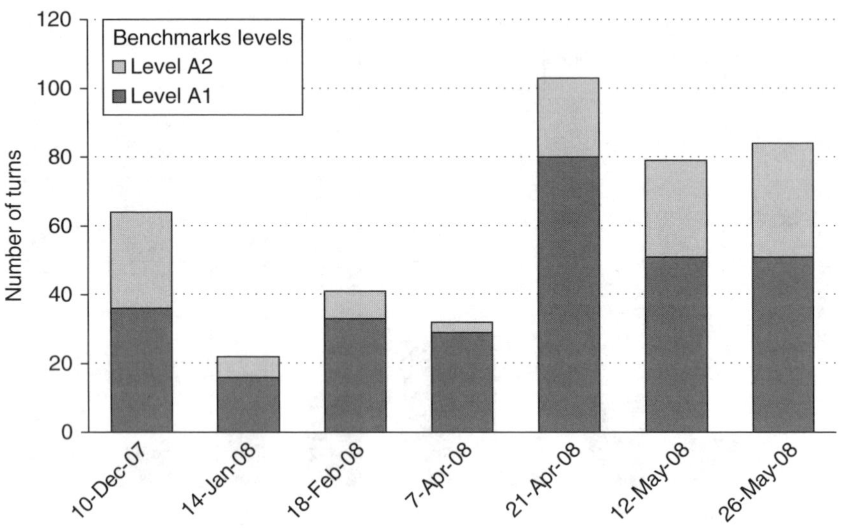

Figure 4.23 Frequency and accuracy of quantitatively analysed grammatical indicators used by Edyta

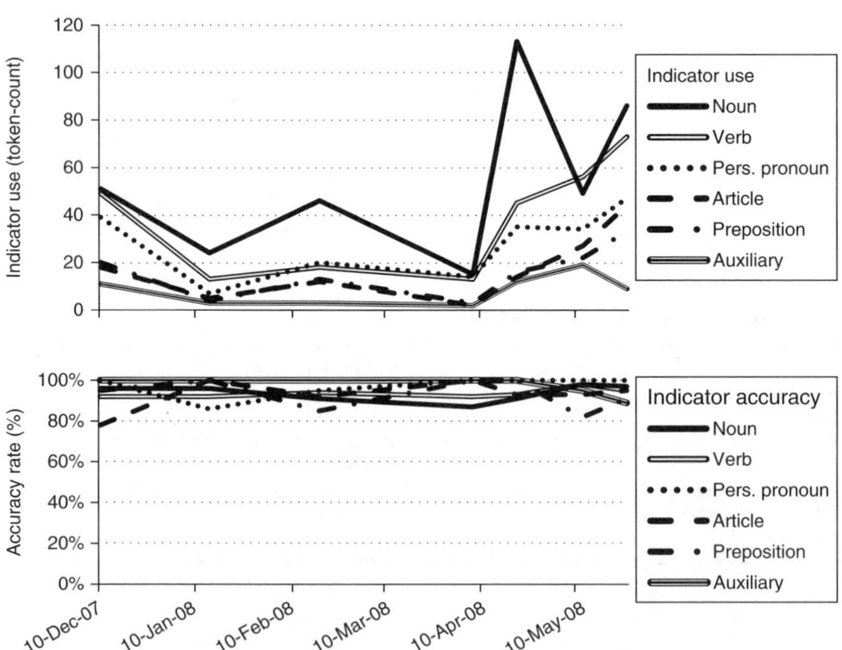

Evidence of L2 acquisition – grammatical indicators

Morphological features

Edyta's noun production generally increased during the study. However, her noun token-count in specific lessons was affected, to an extent, by factors such as the nature of classroom activities and the degree to which she engaged with these. Her noun use was usually over 90% accurate with competent pluralisation. Errors were almost always of lexical choice. Edyta's verb use also rose, relatively consistently, across the study period and was characterised by a high level of accuracy. From the outset of the study she could use past tense forms appropriately (both irregular, e.g. *ate* and regular, e.g. *washed*). Accurate use of progressive forms and, much less frequently, past participles was also recorded. Errors tended to involve the non-inflection of third-person present tense verbs or the use of present verbs in past contexts. Over-generalisation of the regular *–ed* ending to irregular past tense verbs (e.g. *catched*) also occurred. Edyta used quite a wide range of pronouns from the beginning of the study. These included indefinite, substitute and reflexive pronouns, with possessive pronouns apparent from Lesson 11. Her use of personal pronouns generally rose, with her accuracy of production increasing to 100% in the final lessons. Occasional instances of non-required personal pronoun use or single/plural confusion were recorded; her rate of omission for personal pronouns was always under 10%.

Edyta's use of articles increased across the selected lessons and became more accurate as the study progressed. Errors included article confusion or the use of *a* before a vowel. Article omission – a feature of early lessons – later became infrequent. Edyta's use of prepositions also increased and diversified during the study. Her accuracy rate was generally over 80%, though with some fluctuation. Errors usually involved incorrect preposition choice, particularly the misuse of *in* (where *on* or *into* was required). Edyta's use of auxiliaries was highest and most diverse in the last three selected lessons. It generally involved forms of auxiliaries *be* and *do* (in present and past contexts) and *can* to express ability. Occasional use of *have* and *going to* was also recorded, and she attempted to express conditionality using *could* in Lesson 7. Auxiliary production was usually accurate, although omission was also evident, particularly in early lessons.

Syntactic features

The verb-to-noun ratio calculated for Edyta in each of the selected lessons lay within the range 0.4–0.6, its value highest towards the end of the study. The apparent bias towards nominal elements in her production may, however, have been influenced by classroom activities which favoured short, noun-based responses. Edyta's formation of negative structures involved competent use of *not* from the outset of the study. From Lesson 1, she could produce inverted questions (e.g. *can I put it in here?*). Her attempts at more complex question forms were not always accurate, however, with omission of auxiliaries apparent (e.g. *how you know . . .?*). Edyta used simple co-ordinating conjunctions and the subordinating *because* for clause linkage from the start of the study. Early attempts at relativisation using *when* and forming *that* clauses became more accurate in later lessons. She also linked clauses with *if* in the final lesson (e.g. *I always swim in it if the sun too hot*).

Evidence of L2 acquisition – lexical indicators

Findings in relation to L2 lexical development, presented in Table 4.16, show a general rise in the number of 'Wordlist entries' recorded for Edyta. This trend is less apparent in her 'Wordlist entries per turn', although classroom activities may have affected this ratio. Some back-sliding, possibly a consequence of her return to Poland between Lessons 2 and 4, or of physical factors (e.g. tiredness or illness), may also have impacted on her L2 production.

Table 4.16 Edyta – indicators of L2 lexical development

Wordlist results							
Lesson	1	2	4	5	7	9	11
Wordlist entries per turn per lesson	138	55	69	50	156	132	155
Wordlist entries per turn	2.16	2.50	1.68	1.56	1.51	1.67	1.85
Verb lexemes per lesson	21	9	7	5	22	16	24

The semantic fields covered by Edyta corresponded closely to the units of work in the *Benchmarks*, which were among the resources used with her lesson group. Edyta's L2 production often went beyond prototypical vocabulary; nouns such as *decorations* (on the topic of 'Christmas') and adjectives like *cosy* were recorded. She also used the possessive determiners *my* and, later, *his*. In total, she produced 56 distinct verb lexemes. By the end of the study, verbs such as *pretend* and *sharpen* featured in her L2 use. From early lessons, she produced various adverbs of place and time (e.g. *somewhere, always*), with modifiers such as *almost* emerging subsequently.

L2 literacy development

Although not many L2 literacy activities featured in the lessons recorded for her group, Edyta demonstrated a degree of competence on a par with many of her native English-speaking peers with regard to reading and writing English. From early lessons, she recognised letters and their associated sounds and could copy short sentences. By Lesson 5 she could competently read and spell familiar words in an animal bingo game (e.g. *spider*). In later lessons she demonstrated her ability to read labels on posters and food items, to recite rhymes, and to make observations about L2 phonological features, for example noticing similarities in word endings.

Possible influences on L2 development

Individual factors

It seemed that Edyta had some experience of English prior to her enrolment in School 2. However, although her L2 proficiency exceeded that of most other participants in their first year of Irish primary education, she still needed support and scaffolding to engage in classroom activities to her full potential. Her L2 production was quite accurate and intelligible, but traces of cross-linguistic transfer were detectable. These included Polish-influenced phonological features, most notably in relation to the voicing of consonants (/z/ for /s/) and vowel lengthening. Some grammatical influence seemed to be apparent in her frequent non-inversion of questions and over-use of *in* (similar to other Slavic-language-speaking participants). An isolated case of lexical transfer was recorded (with code-mixing): *delfins* used for 'dolphins'. Edyta was generally willing to contribute to classroom discourse. She also used strategies such as circumlocution to communicate effectively. Affective issues due to readjustment after returning from Poland or to feeling ill or tired seemed, however, to impact on her participation.

Interaction-related factors

Analysis of specific turn-types evident in Edyta's L2 use (see Figure 4.24), proved she was capable of initiating discourse and elaborating on classroom topics. Comparison of the three turn-types in focus showed that the combined total of 'tellings' and 'topic elaborations' exceeded the number of 'answers' in most of the selected lessons. This was particularly evident towards the end of the study. Most turns were teacher directed but some lessons enabled greater peer interaction, such as Lesson 5, in which pupils played flashcard bingo in pairs (in this lesson, 25% of Edyta's L2 production was peer directed).

Figure 4.24 Turn-type indicators of interaction patterns for Edyta in selected lessons

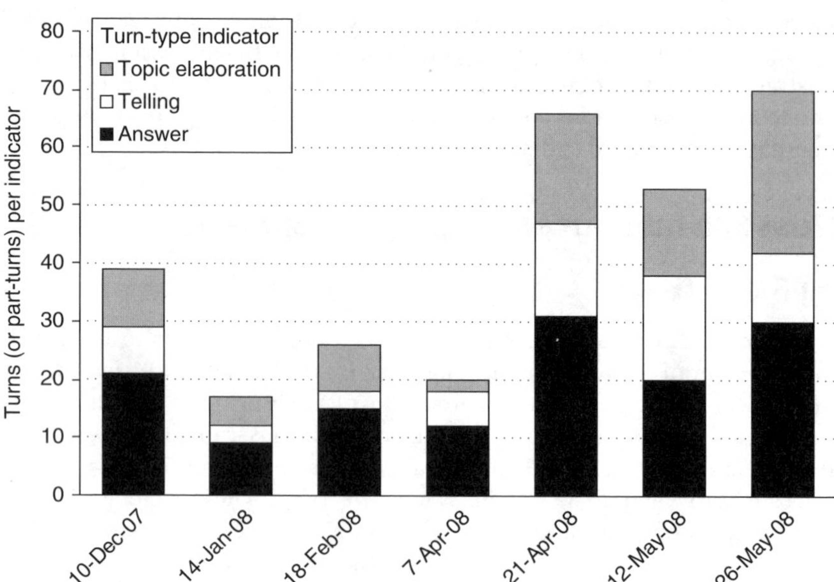

9 Vladimir

Table 4.17 provides personal details for Vladimir. In Figure 4.25, the *Benchmarks* proficiency levels associated with his analysed spoken turns indicate that he was capable of L2 oral production level A2 from the outset of the study and that the proportion of his A2-linked turns increased in later lessons. The frequency and accuracy of his use of the quantitatively analysed grammatical indicators is illustrated in Figure 4.26.

Table 4.17 Vladimir – personal details

National/cultural background	Serbian	**Age at end of study**	6 years
School attended	School 2	**School class**	Junior Infants
English language support commenced	September 2007	**Duration of participation in study**	December 2007 – May 2008
Number of lessons selected for detailed analysis	7 (of total 10)	**Number of turns-at-talk analysed**	276

Figure 4.25 Benchmarks levels recorded for analysed turns produced by Vladimir in selected lessons

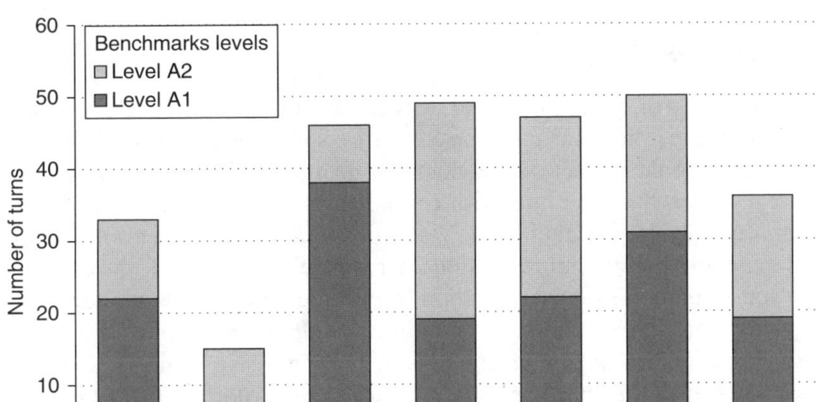

Figure 4.26 Frequency and accuracy of quantitatively analysed grammatical indicators used by Vladimir

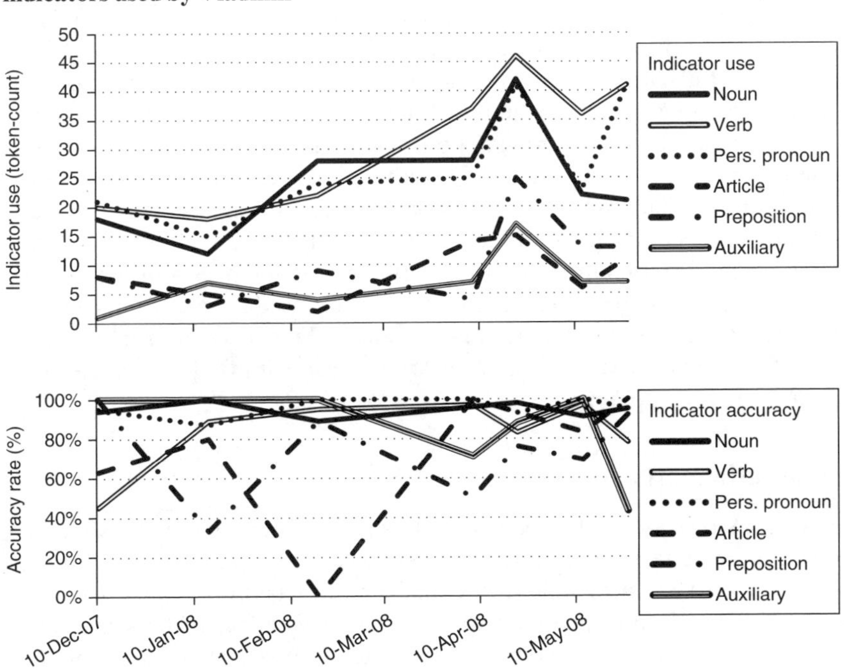

Evidence of L2 acquisition – grammatical indicators

Morphological features

Vladimir's use of nouns increased during the study, although lesson-related factors, such as the focus on opposites in Lesson 9 (which primarily elicited adjectives), could impact on the extent of his production. His noun use was generally over 90% accurate, with competent pluralisation and only minor errors (usually of lexical choice). Vladimir's verb production also increased and generally became more accurate across the study period, though there was some fluctuation. Diversification from basic stem and copula forms was apparent throughout the study. Vladimir could produce past tense verbs (usually irregular, e.g. *saw*) from Lesson 1. Progressive forms (e.g. *coming*) and occasional past participles (e.g. *called*) were recorded from Lesson 5. Vladimir's pronoun use ranged from basic demonstratives and personal pronouns to indefinite, substitute and possessive pronouns. His production of personal pronouns increased, although features of specific lessons could influence the extent of their use. His personal pronoun use was usually over 90% accurate with little omission (infrequent errors related to case or gender).

Vladimir's article production rose, somewhat erratically, over the course of the study. In early lessons his accuracy of article use fluctuated significantly, although more accurate production emerged later. Errors generally involved article use in non-required contexts. In early lessons, Vladimir often omitted articles, but his article omission rate decreased as the study progressed. His preposition use was initially limited, but it rose towards the end of the study. His accuracy rate varied, though; prominent errors involved the use of *on* in contexts requiring *in* and his use of *in* rather than *to* or *into*. He rarely omitted prepositions. Vladimir's use of auxiliaries also increased across the study period. His accuracy level was generally quite high, although it fluctuated in later lessons. He used the auxiliaries *do* (in present and past contexts), *be* and *can* with some competence. Occasionally he also used the auxiliaries *going to* and *will* for future reference (e.g. *he will melt* – Lesson 7). Non-required use of the auxiliary *be* was his main source of error, with frequent omission of auxiliaries also apparent.

Syntactic features

Vladimir's turns tended to be nominal based, although there was some evidence of an increasing proportion of verbal elements; his verb-to-noun ratio rose to a maximum of 0.56 in the final lesson. Classroom activities which favoured short noun-focused responses may have affected the structure of his turns. Vladimir could construct accurate negative statements using 'not' from early lessons, often in contraction (e.g. *I can't push my chair* – Lesson 2). His recorded questions were often very simple (e.g. *how many?*) but appropriate inversion emerged from Lesson 5 and his attempts at question formation became more complex as the study progressed (e.g. *do you know what I like?* – Lesson 7). Evidence of clause linkage beyond the use of simple co-ordinating conjunctions was apparent from early lessons. This involved the relativising use of *when* and *where*, although these attempts were not always successful. The subordinating conjunction *if* emerged from Lesson 2 (e.g. *the fireman em em maybe if it eh fire in house you can call the fireman*), and *because* was also recorded.

Evidence of L2 acquisition – lexical indicators

Vladimir's 'Wordlist entries', shown in Table 4.18, suggest increasing diversity in the L2 lexis he produced across the study. While his 'Wordlist entries per turn' ratio fluctuated somewhat, these results may have been influenced by the extent of his participation in each lesson.

Table 4.18 Vladimir – indicators of L2 lexical development

Wordlist results							
Lesson	**1**	**2**	**4**	**5**	**7**	**9**	**11**
Wordlist entries per lesson	64	50	66	80	116	99	95
Wordlist entries per turn	1.94	3.33	1.43	1.63	2.47	1.98	2.64
Verb lexemes per lesson	10	11	8	12	21	14	19

Overall, the semantic fields covered by Vladimir bore close resemblance to those suggested by the units of work in the *Benchmarks* which, as mentioned in relation to Edyta (Profile 8), served as one of the resources for planning this group's lessons. Vladimir's production included more lexically complex nouns (e.g. *coconuts*, on the topic of 'food') and adjectives (e.g. *giant*). He used the possessive adjective *my* from the start of the study, while *his* emerged in Lesson 7. Vladimir produced a total of 53 distinct verb lexemes. These diversified from basic verbs (e.g. *play*, *give*) in early lessons to more specific verbs, which often related to curriculum topics or classroom instructions, later in the study (e.g. *shine*, *match*). His range of adverbs widened to include referents for place, time, frequency (e.g. *sometimes*), and other modifiers (e.g. *so*).

L2 literacy development

Both English language support groups recorded in School 2 concentrated on oral L2 activities. However, some evidence of Vladimir's developing L2 literacy abilities emerged. In Lesson 1 he could read familiar words on flash-cards (e.g. *Monday*) and copy associated sentences from the board. By Lesson 5 he could read and spell common animal names (e.g. *dog*), when playing a bingo game. He could also engage competently with emergent literacy activities such as reciting rhymes, even if the vocabulary used in these was quite challenging.

Possible influences on L2 development

Individual factors

Aged 6 years at the end of the study, Vladimir was one of the younger participants. Like Edyta (Profile 8), he appeared to have had some experience of English, albeit limited, prior to his enrolment in School 2. Nevertheless, although he seemed slightly more proficient than some of the other participating pupils who were in their first year of education in Ireland, he was still at a relatively early stage of L2 acquisition. The influence of his home language, Serbian, was apparent in his L2 phonology in features such as vowel lengthening, velarisation of the glottal /h/ consonant to /x/, articulation of the approximant /w/ as /v/, and his pronunciation of cognate lexis (e.g. *policeman* was pronounced with phonological similarity to the Serbian *policijac*). Evidence of cross-linguistic influence in his developing L2 grammar included: uncertainty regarding aspect choice, article omission and confusion of prepositions (as discussed in Profile 6 for Marko). Non-inversion of questions (e.g. *how it's called?*) and incorrect lexical choice in interrogatives were also common. Vladimir participated eagerly in classroom talk, even if he was less L2 proficient than some members of his group.

Interaction-related factors

Vladimir was capable of initiating and sustaining communication, particularly on topics of personal interest. Figure 4.27 shows that there were usually more 'tellings' and 'topic elaborations' than 'answers' in his analysed L2 speech. While most of his recorded turns were teacher directed, the final two lessons showed a slight increase in peer interaction. Whether or how this may have affected discourse patterns is difficult to say, although evidence of active forms of interaction emerged from these lessons (in both, the combined total of 'telling' and 'topic elaboration' turn-types exceeded the number of 'answers').

Figure 4.27 Turn-type indicators of interaction patterns for Vladimir in selected lessons

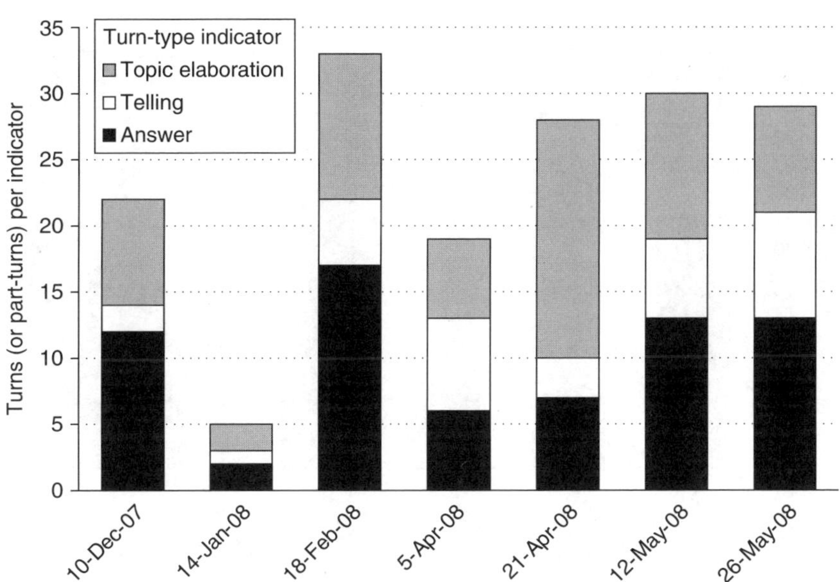

10 Ivan

Personal details for Ivan are presented in Table 4.19. The *Benchmarks* proficiency levels associated with his analysed spoken turns are shown in Figure 4.28. It is evident that he was capable of A2 level L2 use from the beginning of the study and that the proportion of A2-linked production increased towards the end of his participation (he returned to his home country in February 2008). Figure 4.29 indicates the frequency and accuracy of his use of the quantitatively analysed grammatical indicators.

Table 4.19 Ivan – personal details

National/cultural background	Croatian	**Age at end of study**	6 years
School attended	School 1	**School class**	Senior Infants
English language support commenced	September 2006	**Duration of participation in study**	November 2007 – Februrary 2008
Number of lessons selected for detailed analysis	6 (of total 8)	**Number of turns-at-talk analysed**	466

Figure 4.28 Benchmarks levels recorded for analysed turns produced by Ivan in selected lessons

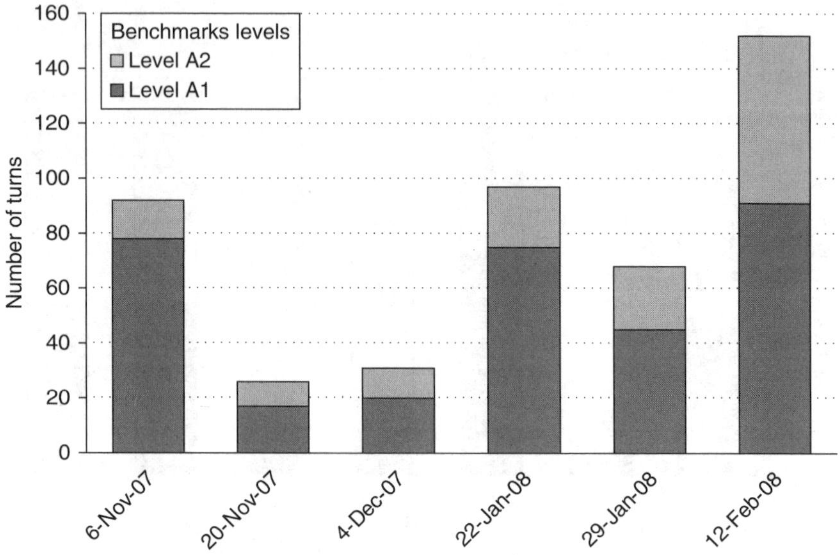

Figure 4.29 Frequency and accuracy of quantitatively analysed grammatical indicators used by Ivan

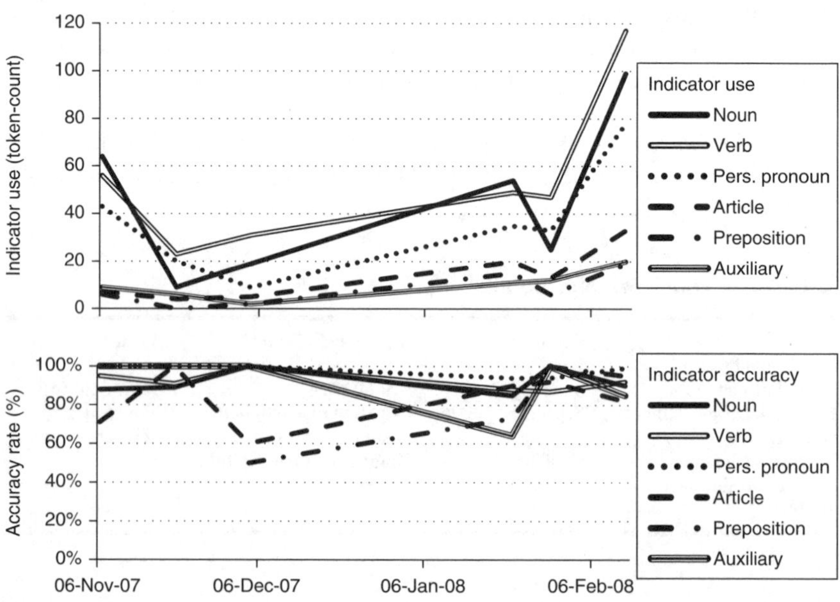

Evidence of L2 acquisition – grammatical indicators

Morphological features

Noun production by Ivan generally increased over the study period. Lower token-counts in Lessons 3 and 5 were largely due to the smaller number of turns available for analysis (these lessons were literacy focused). Ivan's noun use was usually over 90% accurate. Incorrect lexical choice was his main source of error, but problems with pluralisation and marking of possession were also recorded. Accepting lesson-related variation, Ivan's verb use followed an upward trend during the study. While his accuracy rate was generally quite high, it fluctuated slightly as production increased. Most verbs used by Ivan were uninflected stem forms, but his production also included past tense (generally irregular), progressive forms and isolated use of past participles (e.g. *been*). Typical errors included omission of the third-person morpheme (*-s*) and the use of present tense verbs for past reference. Ivan produced a range of pronouns from the outset of the study. These included personal, demonstrative, substitute, indefinite and possessive pronouns. His use of personal pronouns generally rose across the study and was over 90% accurate throughout, with little omission.

Article use by Ivan increased steadily, although his accuracy rate varied considerably. Towards the end of the study, more accurate production emerged. Errors included article confusion and non-required use; in early lessons he frequently omitted articles, but his omission rate decreased as the study progressed. Ivan's production of prepositions became more diverse during the study. Preposition accuracy improved, although over-use of *in* (rather than *on* or *into*) was a prominent error. His use of auxiliaries also increased and diversified. Initially it involved the auxiliaries *be* and *do*, but later the production of *have, can* and *going to* was recorded. However, the accuracy of Ivan's auxiliary use fluctuated and he frequently omitted auxiliaries in required contexts.

Syntactic features

Ivan's verb-to-noun ratio varied across the study, although it was usually in the range 0.4–0.6. The continued dominance of nominal elements in his L2 production may also have been influenced by classroom activities which demanded short, noun-focused responses. Regarding negation, Ivan used *not* quite competently, although he often omitted necessary auxiliaries in negative structures (e.g. *he not going up* . . . – Lesson 7). His question formation ranged from simple *wh-* questions, recorded from Lesson 1, to attempts at inversion (e.g. *did you read this book?*), apparent from Lesson 5. Non-inversion prevailed, however, particularly as he attempted more complex question forms. Although Ivan usually relied on simple co-ordinating conjunctions, by the final lesson he proved capable of using relativisers (e.g. *where*) and the subordinating conjunctions *because* and *if* for clause linkage (e.g. *and if eh you work then you get money*).

Evidence of L2 acquisition – lexical indicators

Table 4.20 shows a general rise in the number of 'Wordlist entries' recorded for Ivan; lower results for Lessons 3 and 5 are due to the fact that these lessons yielded fewer analysable turns. Lesson-related influences (the prevalence of short answers) also affected the data for 'Wordlist entries per turn', which were higher in the lessons with fewer turns.

Table 4.20 Ivan – indicators of L2 lexical development

Wordlist results						
Lesson	1	3	5	7	8	10
Wordlist entries per turn per lesson	87	43	51	110	101	180
Wordlist entries per turn	0.94	1.65	1.65	1.13	1.48	1.18
Verb lexemes per lesson	14	12	11	16	19	30

The semantic themes emerging from Ivan's recorded L2 production can be linked to many of the units of work in the *Benchmarks*. This is not unexpected as his teacher used the *Benchmarks* as a resource for lesson planning (along with mainstream educational material). Ivan's L2 vocabulary went beyond core words associated with these semantic fields and included nouns such as *skateboard* (on the topic of 'toys') and adjectives such as *stinky*. He could also produce the possessive adjectives *my* and, later, *his* and *your*. Despite the short duration of Ivan's participation in the study, 44 distinct verb lexemes were recorded in his L2 use. Early lessons featured common school-linked verbs (e.g. *draw, write*), while more specific or abstract verbs emerged towards the end (e.g. *race* and *happen*). Basic adverbs of place and time were evident throughout, and Ivan used *really* and *altogether* in the final lesson.

L2 literacy development

Most lessons selected for Ivan featured some L2 literacy-related activities. In Lesson 1, he tried to read the names of familiar food items but, relying on prompts or guessing, his attempts were inaccurate. Lessons 3 and 5 focused on phonics activities involving short words with rhyming endings (e.g. *-ug* or *-ig*). This proved difficult for Ivan, particularly when unfamiliar L2 lexis (e.g. *pug, rig*) was used. He also attempted a simple dictation exercise based on this vocabulary but needed considerable support. In Lesson 6, he tried to read aloud from an age-appropriate reader; however, recognition of basic sight vocabulary (e.g. *the, are* etc.) proved challenging and he depended on visual cues to identify content words. Although he recognised letters (e.g. on a poster), he found it difficult to use these grapho-phonic cues to read familiar words.

Possible influences on L2 development

Individual factors

Ivan was aged 6 and mid-way through his second year of education in Ireland when he returned to Croatia. Although his participation in the study was limited, the challenges he faced in meeting Irish curriculum requirements were apparent. He found the literacy-related activities typical of his Senior Infants school class very difficult, even though these were only slightly more demanding than tasks aimed at children in Junior Infants. This was despite the fact that Ivan had better L2 communication skills than many of the participants who were in their first year of primary school. The phonological influence of Ivan's home language, Croatian, was evident in his lengthening of vowels and articulation of diphthongs (e.g. /æ/ as /ɛ/), and also in his pronunciation of the consonants /w/ as /v/ and /ɹ/ as /l/ (possibly reflecting a developmental feature sometimes apparent among languages with a late-acquired trilled /r/). Grammatically, cross-linguistic transfer was suggested by expression of tense (particularly the present perfect), aspect choice, lack of inversion in *wh-* questions (e.g. *how you draw boat?*), omission of auxiliaries (especially in negative structures), preposition choice (*in/on/into/to*), and occasional double negation. Regarding personality, Ivan was an extravert pupil who contributed readily to classroom talk and used communication strategies such as compensation effectively (e.g. saying *donut bread* for bagel).

Interaction-related factors

Ivan's good communication skills were evident in his willingness to volunteer information and discuss classroom topics. Analysis of his L2 oral production, presented in Figure 4.30, showed more 'telling' and 'topic elaboration' than 'answer' turn-types in most of the selected lessons. Although he was an active participant, most of his discourse was teacher-directed; peer-to-peer interaction never accounted for more than 15% of his analysed L2 use.

Figure 4.30 Turn-type indicators of interaction patterns for Ivan in selected lessons

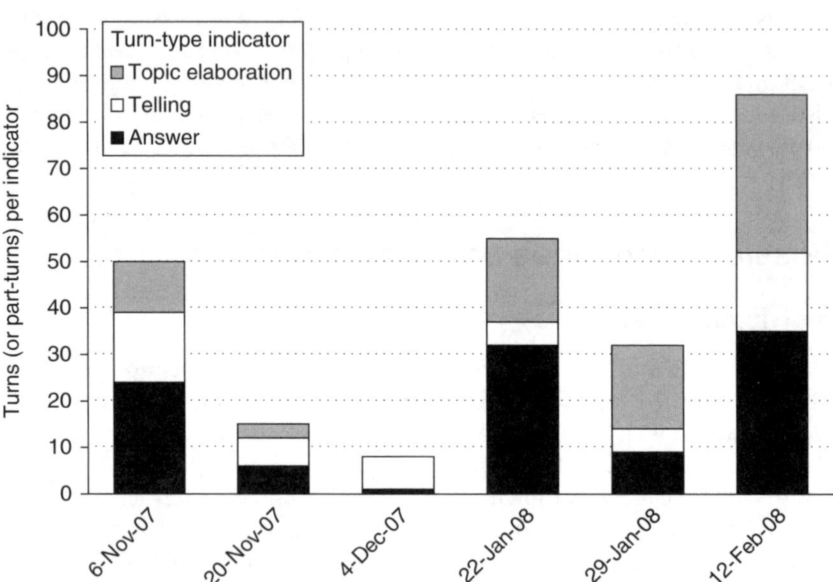

11 Constantin

Constantin's personal details are shown in Table 4.21. Although only four lessons were recorded for his English language support group (as explained in Chapter 3, the timing of its lessons generally coincided with that of another recorded group), Constantin produced a substantial number of analysable turns. From the outset, he could produce turns associated with *Benchmarks* proficiency level A2, and this proportion increased in later lessons (see Figure 4.31). The frequency and accuracy of the quantitatively analysed grammatical indicators he used is illustrated in Figure 4.32.

Table 4.21 Constantin – personal details

National/cultural background	Romanian	**Age at end of study**	6 years
School attended	School 1	**School class**	Senior Infants
English language support commenced	October 2006	**Duration of participation in study**	October 2007 – April 2008
Number of lessons selected for detailed analysis	4 (of total 4)	**Number of turns-at-talk analysed**	434

Figure 4.31 Benchmarks levels recorded for analysed turns produced by Constantin in selected lessons

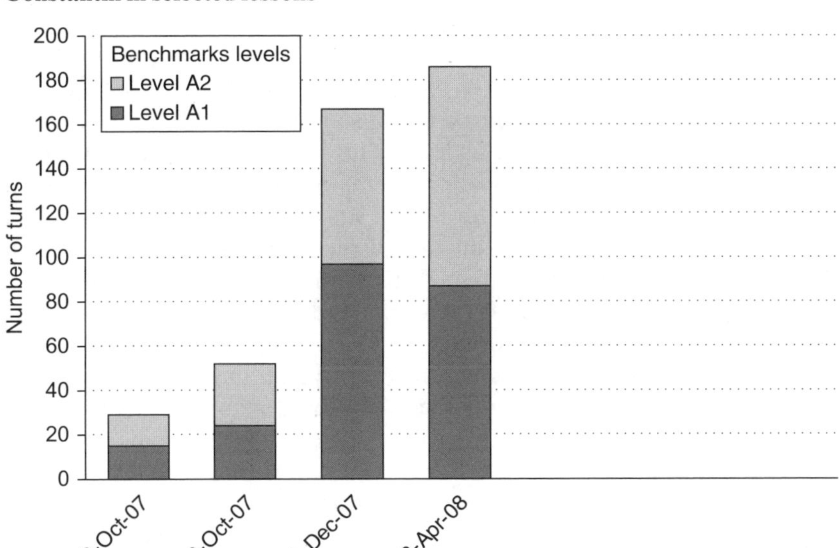

Figure 4.32 Frequency and accuracy of quantitatively analysed grammatical indicators used by Constantin

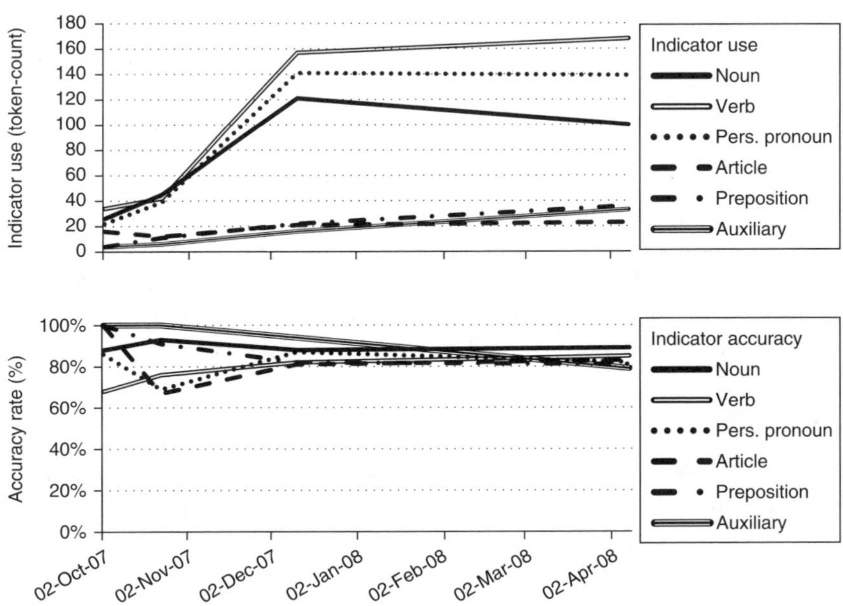

Evidence of L2 acquisition – grammatical indicators

Morphological features

Figure 4.32 shows an overall increase in Constantin's use of the analysed morphological indicators. However, as lessons for his English language support group were infrequently recorded, only tentative conclusions can be drawn regarding his L2 development during the study period. Classroom factors may also have influenced his production of these indicators. For instance, in the final lesson, Constantin was the sole participant due to the absence of the other two group members. By the end of the study, Constantin could produce nouns frequently and with around 90% accuracy. His errors generally involved lack of pluralisation or incorrect lexis. Increasing verb use and accuracy were also apparent, accepting the lesson-related factors and limitations on research already mentioned. From the outset of the study, he could use progressive and past forms (regular and irregular). He occasionally used past participles, sometimes to express passive mood (e.g. *you're not allowed . . .*). Constantin's range of pronouns widened over the study to include possessive, reflexive, quantifying and relative pronouns. His personal pronoun use increased and became more accurate later in the study. Errors, most evident in early lessons, were generally of case; omission was infrequent.

Constantin's token-count for article use was relatively consistent in the selected lessons, despite variations in their number of analysable turns. His accuracy rate fluctuated, but rose towards the end of the study; non-required article use accounted for most errors. Articles were sometimes omitted, although his rate of omission rarely exceeded 50% of actual article use. Constantin's production of prepositions diversified over the study period, although its accuracy appeared to decline in later lessons. Errors typically involved use of *to* rather than *for* and over-use of *in*; occasional omission of prepositions was also apparent. Constantin could use the auxiliaries *be* and *do* in present tense contexts, with past tense forms of *do* emerging in Lesson 4. He could also use *will* and *going to* for future reference and express ability with *can*. His auxiliary production was relatively accurate. Errors included non-inflection of auxiliaries and incorrect choice. However, auxiliary omission often occurred.

Syntactic features

Constantin's verb-to-noun ratio was quite stable over the study period, generally around 0.5. As with other participants, the predominance of nominal elements in his recorded turns may also have been influenced by noun-based classroom activities. While inappropriate use of *no* was evident in the early lessons, Constantin became more accurate at forming negative structures with *not*, often in contraction (e.g. *didn't*). Attempts to use *never* for negation also emerged from Lesson 4. Constantin could form simple *wh-* questions throughout the study, but these were not always successfully inverted. His rare attempts at indirect questions also featured inaccurate patterns of inversion (e.g. *do you know where is the cut? –* Lesson 3). Constantin generally relied on simple co-ordinating conjunctions for clause linkage, although the subordinating *because* emerged in the final lesson. Very occasionally, he attempted to link clauses using *that* or relativisers such as *when*, but these efforts were often inaccurate.

Evidence of L2 acquisition – lexical indicators

Results for indicators of L2 lexical diversity are shown in Table 4.22. It is clear that Constantin's 'Wordlist entries' increased across the study. However, classroom factors (number of turns available for analysis and features of activities) impacted on his 'Wordlist entries per turn'.

Table 4.22 Constantin – indicators of L2 lexical development

Wordlist results				
Lesson	**1**	**3**	**4**	**5**
Wordlist entries per turn per lesson	71	87	199	200
Wordlist entries per turn	2.45	1.67	1.19	1.08
Verb lexemes per lesson	14	18	38	40

The semantic range of Constantin's L2 vocabulary corresponded with many themes suggested by the units of work in the *Benchmarks*. These were used, along with mainstream resources, to structure his group's lessons. His L2 lexis in relation to these themes often went beyond core words to include, for example, *armies* (relating to the topic of 'jobs') and adjectives such as *different*. Comparative adjectives (e.g. *harder*) emerged in Lesson 3; he also produced the possessive determiners *my, your* and *his*. Constantin produced a total of 60 distinct verb lexemes, with evidence of increasing lexical diversity as the study progressed. By the final lesson, he could use specific verbs such as *stick* and *press* regarding stages of an art activity. Throughout, he produced basic adverbs of place and time, along with emerging modifiers (e.g. *very, too*) and frequency referents (e.g. *again*).

L2 literacy development

Due to Constantin's limited participation in the study, evidence of L2 literacy development could only be gleaned from the final two selected lessons.

In Lesson 4, he attempted a simple reader about familiar foods (based on the sentence structure: *I like* [name of food]) but he relied heavily on the pictorial cues provided. He also had problems reading basic sight vocabulary (e.g. *the, a* and *is*) presented on flashcards. In Lesson 5, he tried to read an age-appropriate book, although he found it difficult. He then attempted a simpler text but it appeared that, while he often used visual supports to identify content words, function words remained challenging. His decoding of L2 grapho-phonic relations was not always accurate. There was no evidence that he had any literacy skills in his home language, Romanian.

Possible influences on L2 development

Individual factors

Constantin was 6 years old and in the second year of mainstream education in Ireland (Senior Infants). Also in his second year of English language support, it was clear that his L2 oral proficiency exceeded that of participants who had just enrolled in Irish primary schools. However, the challenges he faced in relation to L2 literacy development were apparent and similar to those experienced by Ivan, another child at the same stage of schooling (see Profile 10). It was evident that, even towards the end of his English language support allocation, Constantin required substantial support with L2 literacy. Although he seemed to have no literacy experience in Romanian, his L2 oral development showed signs of cross-linguistic influence. Like his brother Andrei (see below) some phonological features of his L2 use (particularly vowel lengthening) and grammatical tendencies (e.g. the use of *no* rather than *not* in negative structures) may have been affected by transfer. Constantin was an extravert child who participated eagerly in class activities. However, his adept oral communication may have masked some of the difficulties he faced, particularly in relation to L2 literacy development.

Interaction-related factors

As an outgoing child, Constantin readily took initiatives and contributed to classroom discussion. Figure 4.33 shows that the turn-types 'telling' or 'topic elaboration' out-numbered those coded as 'answers' in all the selected lessons (the one-to-one nature of the final lesson may have inflated his otherwise low proportion of responses). The extent to which his capacity for more active discourse was attributable to developing L2 proficiency or to personality characteristics is difficult to say. Constantin's interaction patterns appeared less response based than many participants in their first year of English language support. However, like the other pupils, his classroom discourse was almost wholly teacher directed.

Figure 4.33 Turn-type indicators of interaction patterns for Constantin in selected lessons

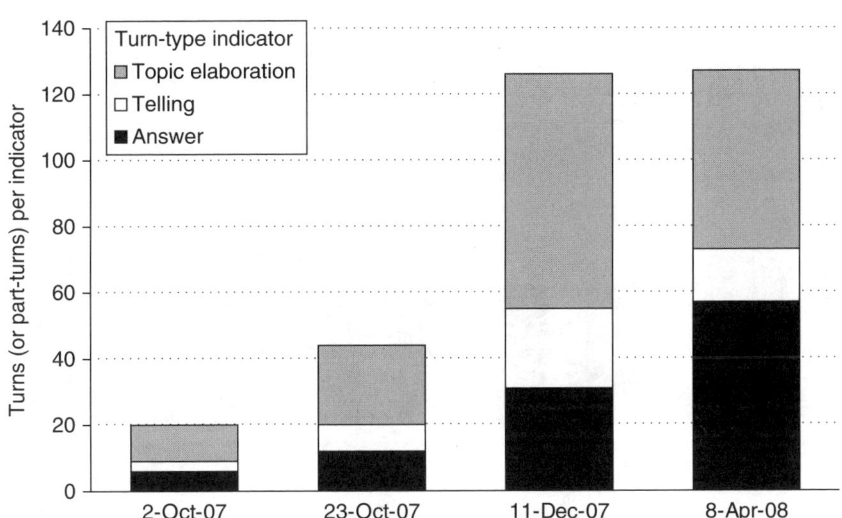

12 Ravi

Ravi was a new arrival who enrolled in School 1 during the study period. His personal details are presented in Table 4.23. The *Benchmarks* proficiency levels associated with his analysed spoken turns, shown in Figure 4.34, indicate that most of his L2 production was at level A1. However, A2-linked turns also emerged, particularly towards the end of the study. The frequency and accuracy of Ravi's use of the quantitatively analysed grammatical indicators is illustrated in Figure 4.35.

Table 4.23 Ravi – personal details

National/cultural background	Indian	**Age at end of study**	8 years
School attended	School 1	**School class**	Second Class
English language support commenced	January 2008	**Duration of participation in study**	January – June 2008
Number of lessons selected for detailed analysis	8 (of total 12)*	**Number of turns-at-talk analysed**	563

** Ravi initially joined an existing English language support group (G1), for the first three selected lessons; in March 2008, he was moved to a new group (G2), created after the arrival of Lukas.*

Figure 4.34 Benchmarks levels recorded for analysed turns produced by Ravi in selected lessons

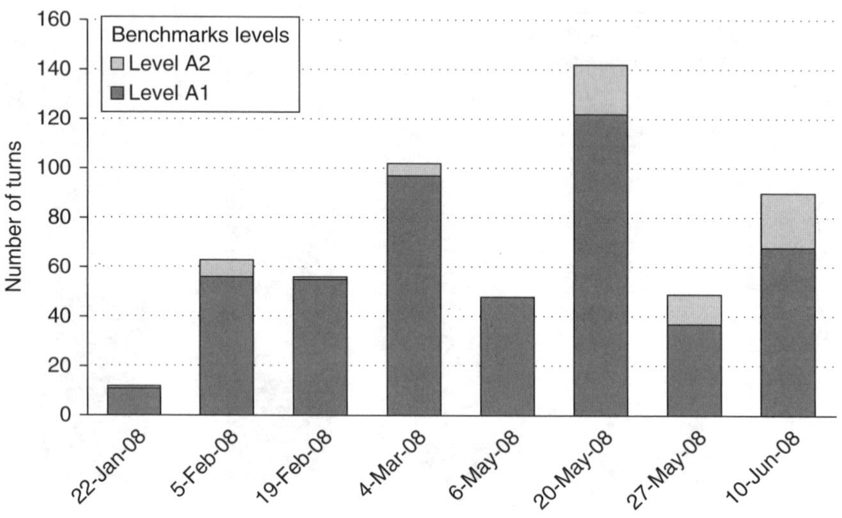

Figure 4.35 Frequency and accuracy of quantitatively analysed grammatical indicators used by Ravi

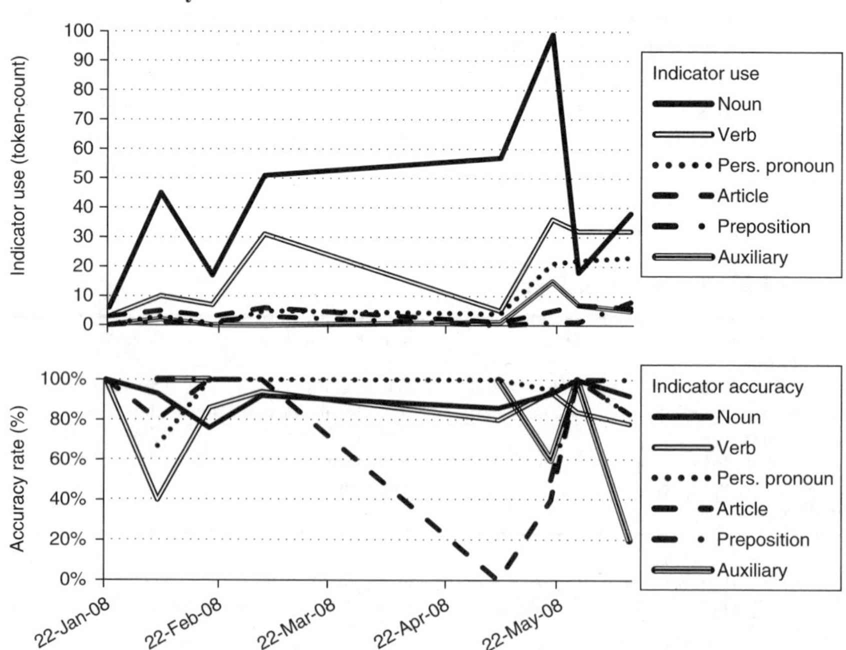

Evidence of L2 acquisition – grammatical indicators

Morphological features

Ravi's production of nouns generally rose over the course of the study, although lesson-related factors impacted on his actual token-count (e.g. the penultimate lesson focused on food names and thus yielded more nouns). His accuracy also appeared to increase (to over 90% in the three final lessons). Errors were usually of lexical choice, although pluralisation sometimes proved problematic. Ravi produced verbs with increasing frequency but some fluctuation in accuracy, especially in early lessons. Most verbs were present tense forms – uninflected stems or the copula *be* – but progressive forms emerged from the third selected lesson onwards. In the final lesson, he correctly produced a past tense verb (*got*) and made a less successful attempt at past participle use. Verb errors generally involved omission of the third person *-s* in the present tense, confusion of *is* and *are*, and use of present forms for past reference. Ravi's use of pronouns widened from basic personal and demonstrative pronouns to include substitute and indefinite pronouns and an isolated instance of the relative pronoun *who*. His personal pronoun use was initially infrequent but it increased and became more accurate in later lessons. Errors often related to case. Some omission was also apparent (usually of subject pronouns) mainly in early lessons.

Ravi's production of articles was rather limited, although it increased somewhat towards the end of the study. His accuracy varied considerably, with over-use of articles a common source of error. In early lessons he sometimes omitted articles more than twice as often as he used them, but this rate subsequently declined. Ravi produced a limited range of prepositions over the study period. Generally the few prepositions he attempted were accurately used, but he sometimes used *in* where *on* was required and also omitted prepositions. His use of auxiliaries was not extensive, although he could employ the auxiliaries *be* and *do* appropriately in present tense contexts. In later lessons, auxiliary use in questions was recorded (e.g. *are you doing . . .*). Over-use of the auxiliary *be* emerged as a prominent error, while auxiliary omission was also common.

Syntactic features

Ravi's L2 production was strongly noun based. This was reflected in his verb-to-noun ratio which, though it peaked at 0.6 in the penultimate lesson, was frequently under 0.4. In addition, classroom activities often emphasised noun use. Early negative structures produced by Ravi involved the incorrect use of *no*. Attempts at negation using *not* subsequently emerged, but this was often associated with the omission of auxiliaries (e.g. *no eh he not take it –* final lesson). Basic question words were used by Ravi from the early lessons. Later in the study some successful attempts at inversion emerged (e.g. *what do you want?*), but again, necessary auxiliaries were frequently omitted. Ravi used simple co-ordinating conjunctions to link clauses. He attempted relativisation in an incomplete turn (*people who is . . . sick*) in the third lesson and in the final lesson tried to link clauses using *that*.

Evidence of L2 acquisition – lexical indicators

Results for both 'Wordlist entries' and 'Wordlist entries per turn', shown in Table 4.24, indicate that Ravi's L2 lexical range widened over the study period. The slight drop in the fourth-last lesson may be due to the fact that he returned to India for a few weeks between this selected lesson and the previous one.

Table 4.24 Ravi – indicators of L2 lexical development

Wordlist results

Lesson	1st Group			2nd Group				
	7	9	11	1	5	7	8	9
Wordlist entries per turn per lesson	13	47	38	69	45	94	55	82
Wordlist entries per turn	1.08	0.75	0.68	0.68	0.94	0.66	1.12	0.91
Verb lexemes per lesson	3	4	5	8	3	11	18	16

The themes he covered were semantically linked to the units of work in the *Benchmarks*, around which the teacher structured many of her lessons, although mainstream classroom resources were also used. Evidence of L2 lexical diversification was apparent in the nouns (e.g. *cricket*, on the topic of 'sport') and adjectives (e.g. *plain*) produced by Ravi. The possessive determiners *my* and *your* also emerged in the second half of the study. His verb lexemes diversified from a small range of basic verbs (e.g. *be, have*) to lexically more specific verbs (e.g. *brush, understand*), recorded towards the end of the study. He produced a total of 45 distinct verb lexemes. He also used simple adverbs of place and time (e.g. *somewhere, then*).

L2 literacy development

It appeared that Ravi had some literacy experience prior to arriving in Ireland. Although his L2 proficiency was at an early stage, he attempted in the first lesson to read flashcards (showing the names of vehicles). By the next lesson, he could read simple books (aimed at native English-speakers aged 5–6 years) with some support, though the vocabulary and structures these contained were beyond his spontaneous L2 oral production at that time. From the early lessons onwards, he could spell familiar words and copy sentences from the board. Later, he could read simple storybooks with greater fluency and accuracy, although reading aloud sometimes posed phonological challenges. With help from the teacher, he could also write short sentences based on picture prompts (e.g. *The fish is swimming*).

Possible influences on L2 development

Individual factors

Aged 8 by the end of the study, Ravi was one of the older participants. As a child in mainstream Second Class, he required a deeper knowledge of English than children in Infant Classes in order to engage with the curriculum. However, it seemed that his L2 development was somewhat faster than that of younger participants, particularly regarding L2 lexis and literacy. This may have been partly due to greater cognitive knowledge, but Ravi also seemed to have had literacy experience in India which may have supported his L2 literacy development. Unfortunately, any age-related advantage was probably outweighed by higher curriculum demands on older children. It is impossible to evaluate cross-linguistic influence on Ravi's L2 development without thorough knowledge of his home language, Malayalam. However, some characteristics of his L2 phonology suggested transfer: his tendency to lengthen vowels, his articulation of the unvoiced consonants /k/ and /p/ (voiced as /g/ and /b/ respectively), his pronunciation of the fricative /v/ as /ʊ/, and his sentence prosody. Ravi was a confident child who contributed to classroom activities to the best of his L2 ability.

Interaction-related factors

Although Ravi was very new to English, he could engage in active discourse from early lessons. This was more apparent from the fourth selected lesson, when he joined a new group with Lukas, another recent arrival. Figure 4.36 shows that, while 'answers' predominated over 'tellings' or 'topic elaborations' throughout, evidence of more active discourse began to emerge as the study progressed. In most lessons, Ravi's discourse was almost entirely teacher directed. However, in the third-last lesson, peer-directed talk (in shopping role-plays) accounted for 45% of his analysed L2 use. This lesson also showed an increase in his production of turns at A2 level English proficiency (see Figure 4.34).

Figure 4.36 Turn-type indicators of interaction patterns for Ravi in selected lessons

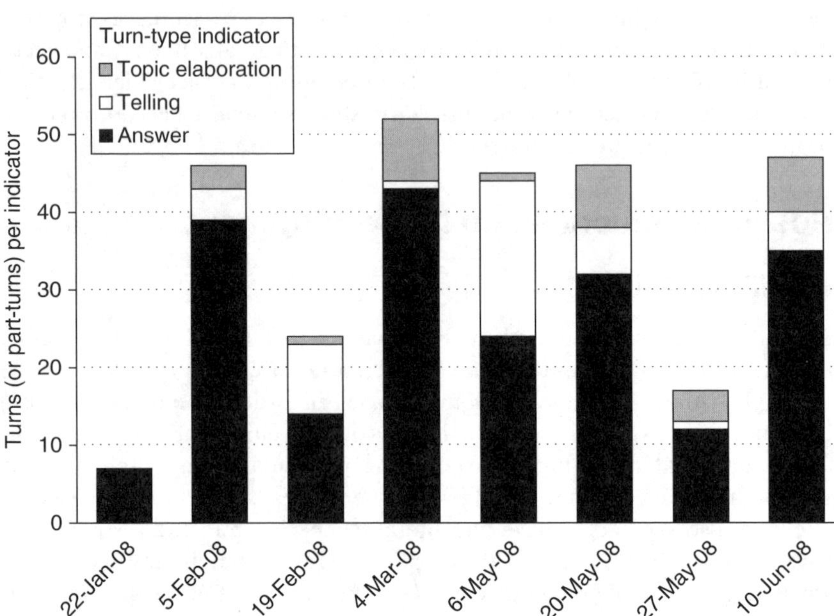

13 Lukas

Lukas enrolled in School 1 during the study period, following his arrival in Ireland. Table 4.25 shows his personal details. Figure 4.37 indicates that, while most of his analysed spoken turns were associated with *Benchmarks* proficiency level A1, he also produced A2 level turns, particularly towards the end of the study. Graphics showing the frequency and accuracy of Lukas's use of the quantitatively analysed grammatical indicators are displayed in Figure 4.38.

Table 4.25 Lukas – personal details

National/cultural background	Lithuanian	**Age at end of study**	8 years
School attended	School 1	**School class**	First Class
English language support commenced	March 2008	**Duration of participation in study**	March – June 2008
Number of lessons selected for detailed analysis	7 (of total 9)	**Number of turns-at-talk analysed**	628

Figure 4.37 Benchmarks levels recorded for analysed turns produced by Lukas in selected lessons

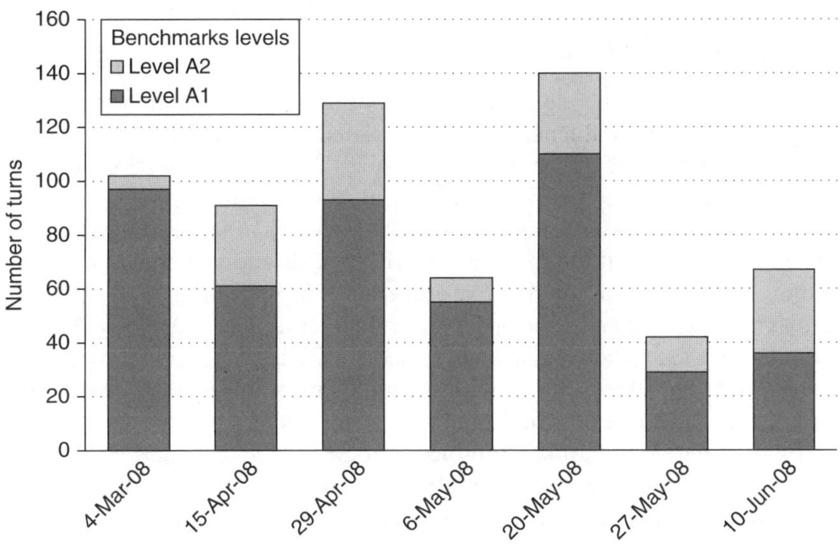

Figure 4.38 Frequency and accuracy of quantitatively analysed grammatical indicators used by Lukas

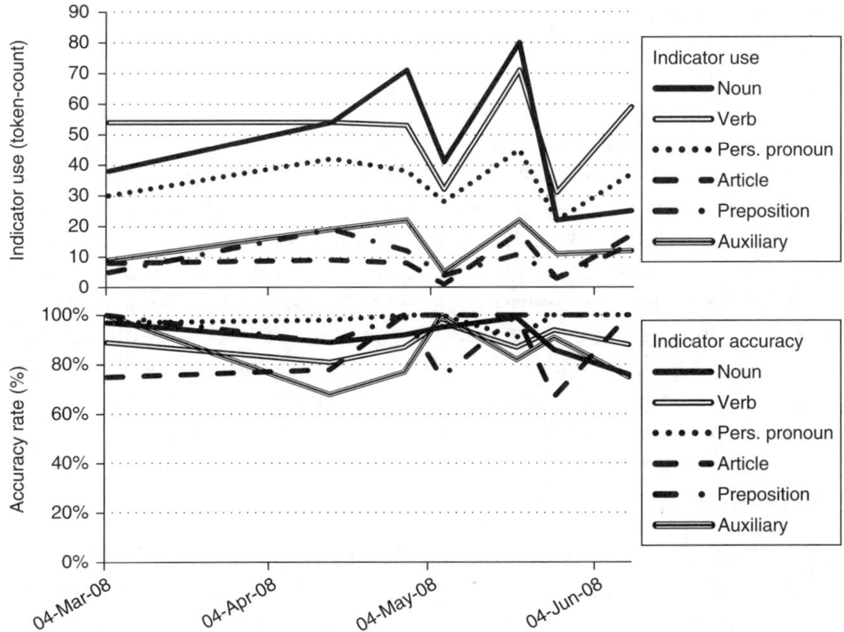

Evidence of L2 acquisition – grammatical indicators

Morphological features

Lukas's noun use generally rose over the study period, although results for frequency were also influenced by lesson-related factors. The final two lessons were literacy focused and yielded fewer turns for analysis of L2 oral development, hence the lower token-counts. Lukas was quite competent in noun production, with an accuracy rate usually higher than 90%. Most recorded errors were lexical, although problems with pluralisation emerged, including the over-generalisation of the *-s* morpheme to irregular plurals (e.g. *mens*). Lukas's use of verbs also showed a general increase, accepting some fluctuation due to the availability of analysable turns. His verb production tended to be more than 80% accurate, with a slight increase in accuracy towards the end of the study. Use of uninflected verb stems and the present tense copula *be* predominated, but Lukas produced progressive verbs (e.g. *joking*) from Lesson 3, and past forms (e.g. *went*) from Lesson 7. Isolated instances of past participle use were also recorded. Typical errors involved non-inflection of present tense verbs, aspect choice and the use of present forms for past reference. Lukas produced a widening range of pronouns during the study period, from personal and demonstrative pronouns to quantifiers, ordinals and indefinite pronouns. His use of personal pronouns increased and was over 90% accurate throughout, with only infrequent errors and a low rate of omission.

Lukas's use of articles also increased during the study. His accuracy varied, but it was generally higher in later lessons. His omission rate (sometimes more than 50% of required article use) also began to fall as the study progressed. His production of prepositions appeared to rise and diversify across the selected lessons. It was relatively accurate throughout, with occasional errors, usually involving the over-use of *in*. His omission rate for prepositions was negligible. Auxiliary use by Lukas also became more frequent and diverse. It ranged from present tense forms of *be, do* and *can*, to past tense forms (of *be* and *do*) and, from Lesson 4, future reference (using *will* and *going to*). Lukas also made isolated but appropriate attempts at *would* and *have*. The accuracy of his auxiliary use fluctuated, particularly in earlier lessons, with non-required use of the auxiliary *be* emerging as a prominent error. Omission of auxiliaries (notably *be* and *do*) was also evident, especially in the first half of the study.

Syntactic features

Lukas's verb-to-noun ratio generally lay in the range 0.4–0.7 and was highest in the second half of the study. However, this ratio was susceptible to the influence of classroom activities; for instance, a lesson on the theme of 'actions' yielded comparatively more verb use than other lessons. Lukas could use *not* for negation from the beginning of the study and his use of *never* was recorded in Lesson 3 (e.g. *I never see a red squirrel*). Omission of auxiliaries was often a feature of his negative structures. He formed basic questions effectively from Lesson 1, although his early attempts at inversion were generally inaccurate. Appropriately inverted questions emerged later (e.g. *do you need to get eggs?* – Lesson 7). Clause linkage beyond the use of simple co-ordinating conjunctions emerged in the first half of the study with the production of the subordinating *because*. In the final lesson Lukas attempted structures using *when* and *where* as relativisers, although these were not always accurate.

Evidence of L2 acquisition – lexical indicators

'Wordlist entries per turn' for Lukas, presented in Table 4.26, suggest growing lexical diversity in later lessons. Variations in the actual number of 'Wordlist entries' are, to an extent, attributable to lesson-related factors (e.g. availability of analysable turns).

Table 4.26 Lukas – indicators of L2 lexical development

Wordlist results							
Lesson	1	3	4	5	7	8	9
Wordlist entries per turn per lesson	73	113	120	68	162	69	104
Wordlist entries per turn	0.72	1.24	0.93	1.06	1.16	1.64	1.55
Verb lexemes per lesson	12	20	19	10	21	18	19

The semantic fields evident in Lukas's production were linked to the units of work in the *Benchmarks*. This was partly due to the teacher's structuring of her lessons around some of these topics, although mainstream learning resources were also used for lesson planning. Many of the nouns and adjectives produced by Lukas (e.g. *buttons*, on the topic of 'clothes', and *naughty*) went beyond basic lexis. He could also use the possessive determiners *my, your* and, later, *their*. He produced 55 distinct verb lexemes during the study. These showed evidence of increasing lexical complexity in later lessons, for instance, featuring synonyms such as *start* and *begin*. Basic deictic adverbs and time referents (e.g. *sometimes*) were recorded from the outset of the study, while modifiers (e.g. *just*) emerged later.

L2 literacy development

Lukas had just arrived in Ireland but he appeared to have some very limited knowledge of English. It was also clear that he had previous literacy experience, and this seemed to aid his engagement with L2 literacy activities. For instance, he could compare English grapho-phonic relations with those of Lithuanian. His knowledge of some of the strategies involved in decoding text also helped him to read familiar words (e.g. on flashcards) and simple storybooks (aimed at 6 to 7-year-old native English-speakers). However, he needed considerable support, particularly with new L2 lexis. From Lesson 3, he was able to copy and write simple words with help from the teacher. In later lessons he could write short sentences but found spelling difficult, commenting in Lesson 8: *it's very hard for me to write . . . all the words*.

Possible influences on L2 development

Individual factors

Lukas was 8 years old by the end of the study and he seemed to progress faster than younger participants who were relatively new to English. However, despite the skills he displayed, particularly in relation to L2 literacy development, the widening gap between mainstream curriculum expectations and the L2 abilities of slightly older EAL pupils was apparent. Evidence of home-language influence emerged in Lukas's engagement with literacy-related tasks. As mentioned above, his literacy in Lithuanian scaffolded his L2 reading and writing. Cross-linguistic influence emerged with regard to phonology and orthography. Lukas appeared to transfer some Lithuanian grapho-phonic relations to his L2 writing (especially his representation of English vowels and diphthongs), while his L2 reading showed similar influence (e.g. reading 'c' as /ts/). Some grammatical issues, such as aspect choice and question syntax, also suggested transfer. Lukas seemed quite an introverted child who was capable of reflecting on his L2 use.

Interaction-related factors

Although he was sometimes reticent, Lukas also had the confidence to take initiatives and elaborate on classroom topics. Turn-types of this nature often exceeded those coded as 'answers', particularly in the second half of the study, as shown in Figure 4.39. Whether this trend was due to greater L2 proficiency (see Figure 4.37) or whether classroom activities in later lessons created opportunities for more active L2 use is less clear. However, some link between discourse patterns and L2 proficiency development cannot be discounted. Maximising peer interaction, which was generally minimal (except in Lesson 7 which involved role-play), may be one way to generate classroom talk that could be optimally conducive to L2 acquisition.

Figure 4.39 Turn-type indicators of interaction patterns for Lukas in selected lessons

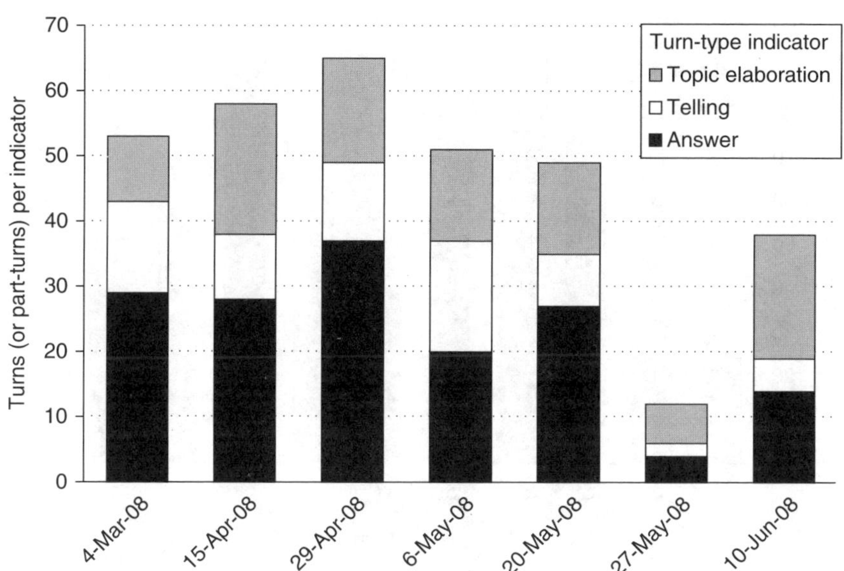

14 Stefan

Table 4.27 presents personal details for Stefan. Figure 4.40 shows that initially most of his analysed spoken turns were associated with *Benchmarks* proficiency level A1, although the proportion of A2-linked turns he produced increased in later lessons. The frequency and accuracy of his use of the quantitatively analysed grammatical indicators is illustrated in Figure 4.41.

Table 4.27 Stefan – personal details

National/cultural background	Polish	**Age at end of study**	8 years
School attended	School 1	**School class**	First Class
English language support commenced	September 2007	**Duration of participation in study**	October 2007 – June 2008
Number of lessons selected for detailed analysis	11 (of total 20)*	**Number of turns-at-talk analysed**	653

** 20 lessons were recorded for Stefan in his regular English language support group; however, one other lesson was recorded in which, due to staff changes, he temporarily participated in another group.*

Figure 4.40 Benchmarks levels recorded for analysed turns produced by Stefan in selected lessons

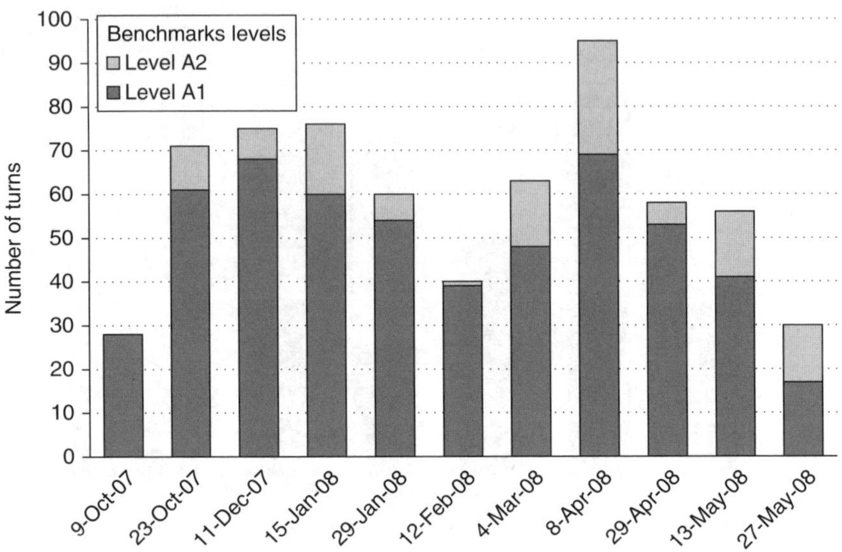

Figure 4.41 Frequency and accuracy of quantitatively analysed grammatical indicators used by Stefan

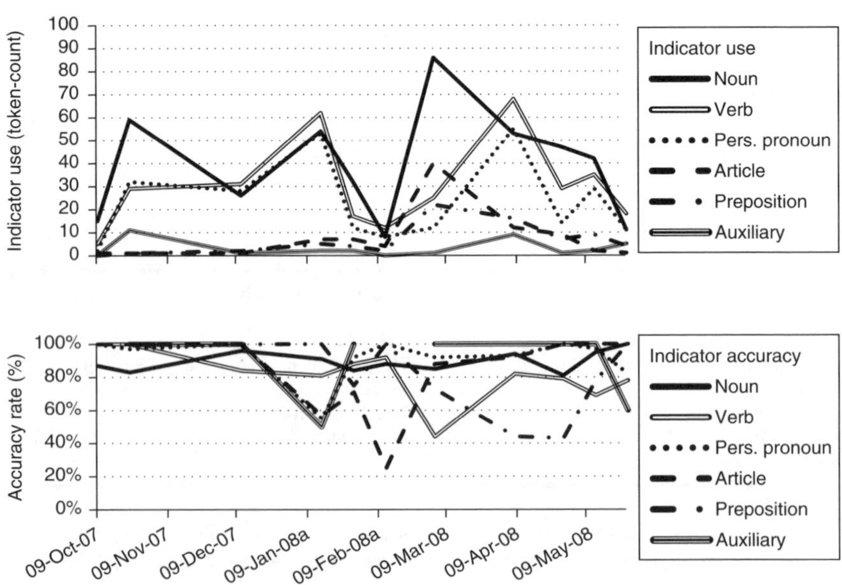

Evidence of L2 acquisition – grammatical indicators

Morphological features

Stefan's production of nouns generally increased over the study period, although actual token-count was influenced by factors such as his level of participation in classroom activities and the extent to which these focused on L2 oral skills (rather than literacy). His accuracy level was more than 80% throughout, but it fluctuated somewhat, particularly in the second half of the study. Most errors were lexical, although some problems were associated with pluralisation. Stefan's verb use was also subject to lesson-related factors, but higher token-counts were recorded later in the study. His verb accuracy varied as the study progressed. Throughout, it generally involved the production of uninflected stem forms and the present tense copula *be*, although progressive verbs (e.g. *bringing*) emerged from Lesson 19. There were no recorded instances of past tense verbs or participles in his analysed oral turns, and the use of present forms for past reference was a major source of error. His pronoun use initially involved only personal pronouns, but demonstratives, substitute and indefinite pronouns emerged as the study progressed. His production of personal pronouns varied in frequency and accuracy, though in later lessons it seemed to become more accurate, with a low level of omission.

Stefan's use of articles was initially infrequent, but production rose in the second half of the study. His accuracy rate fluctuated considerably as production increased, with non-required use of articles accounting for most errors. Omission of articles was very noticeable, often up to five times more frequent than actual article use, although this rate gradually decreased. His production of prepositions increased and diversified during the study. This trend was accompanied by declining accuracy, with errors often involving the over-use of *in* or preposition choice when expressing time (e.g. *at Thursday*). Stefan used auxiliaries only occasionally. However, their production rose across the study, with lesson characteristics (e.g. an activity eliciting the use of *do* in Lesson 4) somewhat affecting this trend. The auxiliary *do* was most frequently used, but *can* was recorded from Lesson 11 and *be* emerged in Lesson 15. Although limited, his auxiliary use was often quite accurate.

Syntactic features

To begin with, Stefan's verb-to-noun ratio was less than 0.2, but by later lessons it was generally in the region of 0.4. His early attempts at negative structures usually involved the inappropriate use of *no*, although *not* (in the contracted form *don't*) emerged from Lesson 4 and *never* was recorded in the final lesson. Instances of double negation were also apparent (e.g. *I don't no like chicken* – Lesson 4). Initially, Stefan just used rising intonation to mark questions. His early attempts at question formation lacked inversion, and although inverted questions developed over the study, they were rarely accurate and sometimes featured verb omission (e.g. *teacher, please can I everything for . . .* – Lesson 11). Stefan generally linked clauses with simple co-ordinating conjunctions. Towards the end of the study, he attempted structures involving the subordinating conjunction *because*.

Evidence of L2 acquisition – lexical indicators

Table 4.28 shows that, while raw scores for 'Wordlist entries' varied (often due to lesson-related factors), evidence of L2 lexical development emerged in Stefan's results for 'Wordlist entries per turn'.

Table 4.28 Stefan – indicators of L2 lexical development

Wordlist results

Lesson	2	4	9	10	11	13	15	17	19	21	23
Wordlist entries per turn per lesson	31	49	60	106	63	36	77	110	76	96	57
Wordlist entries per turn	1.11	0.68	0.80	1.39	1.05	0.9	1.22	1.16	1.31	1.71	1.9
Verb lexemes per lesson	3	3	6	7	5	6	8	17	11	15	7

Semantically, the topics covered by Stefan in the recorded lessons could be linked to the units of work in the *Benchmarks*. However, although the teachers responsible for Stefan's group planned many of their lessons around these themes, they also used mainstream classroom resources to supplement their English language support. While most of Stefan's vocabulary was quite simple, some more specific L2 lexis emerged in his use of nouns (e.g. *chimney*, on the topic 'home'). He generally used basic adjectives (e.g. *easy*), although comparative forms (e.g. *bigger*) and possessive determiners (*my* and *your*) emerged as the study progressed. He produced 42 distinct verb lexemes in the selected lessons. By the end of the study, these included a considerable range of everyday verbs (e.g. *help, draw*). His adverb use also expanded to cover familiar referents to place, time and frequency (e.g. *there, now*) and modifiers (e.g. *very*).

L2 literacy development

Stefan's emerging L2 literacy skills were evident from the outset of the study. In the first lesson he could, with support, attempt a reader aimed at native English-speaking 5–6-year-olds. He also had home-language literary experience, apparent in his comparison of cognate vocabulary and his use of a Polish–English dictionary. This equipped him with decoding strategies which enabled him to access age-appropriate texts despite their challenging L2 lexis. The deep orthography of English (e.g. graphophonic representation of diphthongs) proved difficult but, by the end of the study, Stefan's reading ability seemed ahead of his L2 oral proficiency. He could also competently engage with written activities such as writing short, structured sentences on classroom themes with relatively accurate spelling.

Possible influences on L2 development

Individual factors

Aged 8 years by the end of the study, Stefan was slightly older than some of his mainstream peers. At an early stage of L2 development, he could engage with some age-appropriate activities during the study, but only with considerable support. As noted above, his home-language literacy experience also scaffolded his acquisition of L2 literacy skills. However, like other participating pupils of his age, meeting the linguistic demands of the primary curriculum was difficult. Not surprisingly, he expressed a preference for maths over other school subjects. Polish affected phonological and orthographic features of his English, for instance, his production of the fricative /v/ for the approximant /w/ and his writing of the letter 'w' in place of 'v'. His vowels were often lengthened and he also found English diphthongs challenging (e.g. his use of /æ/ for /eɪ/). Regarding grammar and lexis, some features of L2 use recorded among other children from Slavic language backgrounds also emerged. These typically related to verb aspect, preposition choice and question words (e.g. use of *how* for *what*). Stefan was a rather quiet child but he contributed information on topics of interest. He also proved adept at self-correction.

Interaction-related factors

'Answers' generally predominated over 'telling' or 'topic elaboration' turn-types in Stefan's analysed speech, as shown in Figure 4.42. However, in some of the lessons he seemed to be more actively involved. This was particularly true of Lesson 17, in which his L2 use showed evidence of increasing A2 proficiency (see Figure 4.40). Generally his classroom interaction was teacher directed, although in certain lessons (e.g. Lessons 4 and 9) designated pairwork led to increased peer-directed discourse.

Figure 4.42 Turn-type indicators of interaction patterns for Stefan in selected lessons

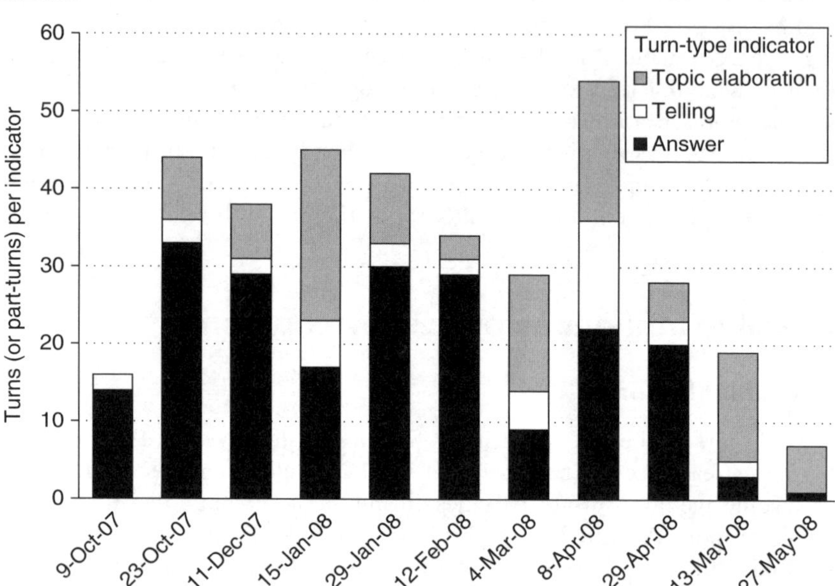

15 Andrei

Andrei's personal details are presented in Table 4.29. The *Benchmarks* proficiency levels associated with his analysed spoken turns are indicated in Figure 4.43. Although much of his L2 use was linked to level A1, he produced an increasing proportion of A2 turns as the study progressed. Frequency and accuracy rates for quantitatively analysed grammatical indicators are shown in Figure 4.44.

Table 4.29 Andrei – personal details

National/cultural background	Romanian	**Age at end of study**	8 years
School attended	School 1	**School class**	First Class
English language support commenced	June 2007	**Duration of participation in study**	October 2007 – May 2008
Number of lessons selected for detailed analysis	11 (of total 21)*	**Number of turns-at-talk analysed**	1,188

** 21 lessons were recorded for Andrei in his regular English language support group; a further three lessons in which, due to staff changes, Andrei joined a group of more proficient EAL pupils, were also recorded.*

Figure 4.43 Benchmarks levels recorded for analysed turns produced by Andrei in selected lessons

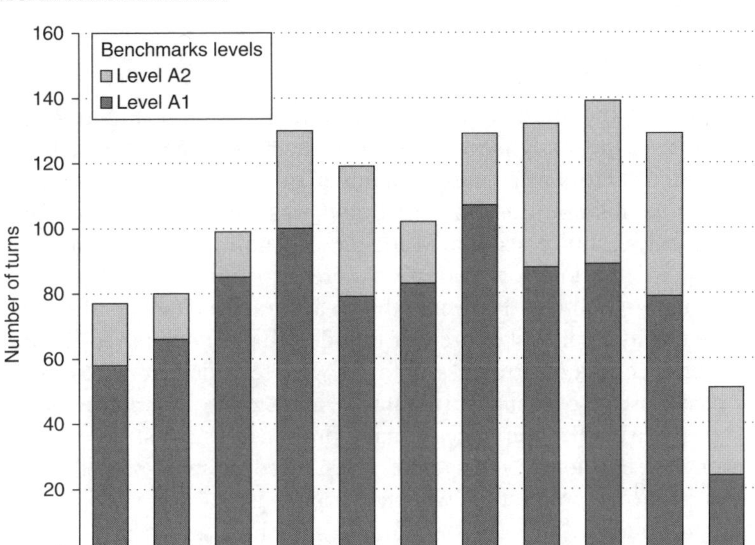

Figure 4.44 Frequency and accuracy of quantitatively analysed grammatical indicators used by Andrei

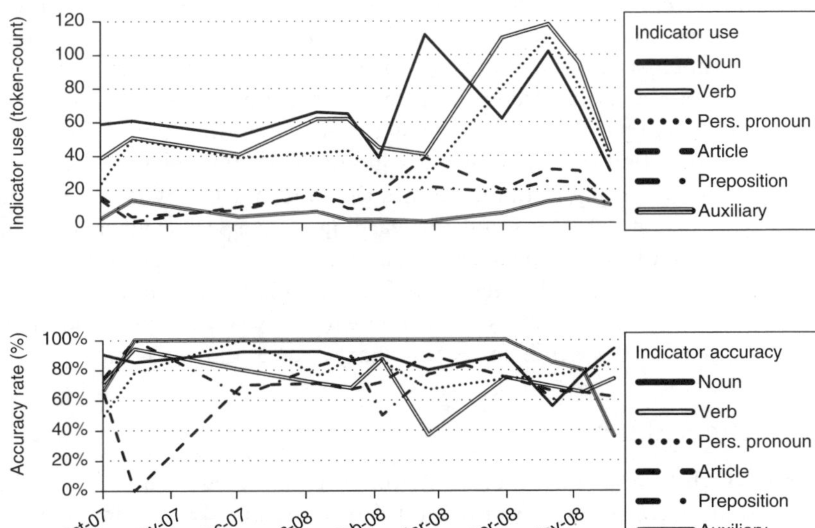

Evidence of L2 acquisition – grammatical indicators

Morphological features

Andrei's use of the grammatical indicators represented in Figure 4.43 generally rose over the study period, although their token-count was subject to lesson-related factors affecting the number of turns available for analysis. On the whole, his noun use increased and was usually over 80% accurate. Incorrect lexical choice accounted for 65% of noun-related errors; pluralisation and the marking of possession were also sources of error. Andrei's verb production fluctuated considerably in accuracy as it diversified. In early lessons, it consisted almost entirely of uninflected present tense forms and the present tense copula *be*. Progressive forms were recorded from Lesson 2. His use of past tense verbs (usually irregular forms, e.g. *forgot*) emerged in Lesson 9, and past participles were occasionally produced as the study progressed. However, present tense verbs were often used in past-related contexts. Andrei's pronoun production widened from basic forms such as demonstrative pronouns to include, for example, indefinite and relative pronouns. Regarding personal pronouns, his accuracy generally increased, although errors of case and gender were noticeable. Omission of personal pronouns was infrequent.

Andrei's use of articles increased throughout the study and was usually more than 60% accurate. Typical errors included: non-required use of articles, confusion of definite/indefinite articles, and the use of *a* before a vowel. His article omission rate fell during the study (to an omission-to-use ratio generally lower than 0.2). Andrei produced an increasing number and range of prepositions across the study period, with fluctuating accuracy. Errors often involved the use of prepositions in non-required contexts or incorrect choice (particularly of *in, on* or *for* in place of *to*). In the first half of the study, Andrei's production of auxiliaries was limited (e.g. present tense forms of *be, do* and occasionally *can*). Sometimes this was affected by lesson-related factors, for instance, in Lesson 4 the learning tasks specifically elicited the use of *do*. From Lesson 9 onwards, his use of auxiliaries diversified to indicate past tense (*did, was*), the present perfect form (*have*), and future reference (*will* and later *going to*). Errors associated with auxiliary use included: non-required use of auxiliaries, incorrect auxiliary choice, and omission.

Syntactic features

Andrei's verb-to-noun ratio increased from less than 0.4 in the first half of the study to more consistently over 0.5 in the second half. The nominal-bias of his production may, however, have been exaggerated by classroom activities requiring short, noun-based answers. Regarding negation, Andrei's inaccurate use of *no* was prominent in earlier lessons, but his use of *not* increased. He formed simple *wh-* questions throughout the study. Inverted questions were recorded from Lesson 4, although his attempts at inversion were not always accurate. Andrei used simple co-ordinating conjunctions from Lesson 1. His use of the subordinating *because* emerged from Lesson 13, with relativisers, such as *who*, produced from Lesson 15. In the final two lessons, clause linkage with *if* was recorded.

Evidence of L2 acquisition – lexical indicators

The results presented in Table 4.30 give an indication of Andrei's L2 lexical range. His 'Wordlist entries per turn' generally increased over the course of the study, accepting the impact of lesson-related variation.

Table 4.30 Andrei – indicators of L2 lexical development

Wordlist results											
Lesson	2	4	9	10	11	13	15	17	19	21	23
Wordlist entries per turn per lesson	82	51	94	131	112	99	97	146	136	152	91
Wordlist entries per turn	1.06	0.63	0.95	1.01	0.93	0.97	0.75	1.10	0.98	1.18	1.78
Verb lexemes per lesson	14	7	16	26	20	16	19	35	28	25	16

The semantic range of lexis used by Andrei in the selected lessons was linked closely to the units of work in the *Benchmarks*. This was not surprising as the teachers responsible for this group planned their lessons around the *Benchmarks* themes. Although Andrei's L2 vocabulary was rather basic, evidence of diversification emerged in his production of nouns such as *fire engine* (in the topic 'modes of transport') and adjectives such as *favourite*. His use of possessive determiners also extended from *my* to include *your* and *his* (by Lesson 17). Verbs used by Andrei in the early lessons included *play* and *like*, but towards the end of the study, verbs such as *allow* and *swap* emerged. In total, he used 62 distinct verb lexemes. He also produced a widening range of adverbs, from basic referents to place, frequency and time to familiar modifiers (e.g. *only*).

L2 literacy development

Andrei found the development of L2 literacy skills challenging throughout the study. His level of English literacy was considerably below what would be expected of his native English-speaking peers. It also lagged behind that of more proficient EAL pupils of his age. There was no indication that he had developed any home-language literacy skills. Early in the study, his attempts to read basic words and phrases relied on visual cues. Reading decontexualised vocabulary at sight proved difficult. From Lesson 11, he engaged with simple readers aimed at younger, native English-speaking children. However, this showed evidence of story-memorisation and guessing. Some recurrent errors were also typical of his contemporaneous L2 oral production (e.g. omission of the third person -*s*). In teacher-created tests towards the end of the study, the accuracy of his word recognition, based on 12 vocabulary items from his reader, varied from 25% to 42% while his identification of letters of the alphabet never exceeded 15 letters. Regarding writing, even in the second half of the study, Andrei still had problems with basic letter formation and copying simple words.

Possible influences on L2 development

Individual factors

Andrei was 8 years old by the end of the study and his development of L2 oral skills was quite extensive. However, he had major difficulty engaging with age-appropriate literacy activities in English which, by the third year of primary education in Ireland (First Class), require considerably more extensive reading and writing skills than the early literacy activities associated with the Infant Classes. It appeared that his home language, Romanian, influenced his L2 phonology in relation to vowel lengthening and the articulation of consonants (particularly plosives). Cognate lexis also exhibited cross-linguistic influence (e.g. the articulation of *giraffe* as /ʒirɑfə/). Andrei was an outgoing child whose extravert personality may have contributed to his competence as an oral communicator. However, his good communication skills sometimes masked other challenges he faced, particularly in relation to L2 literacy.

Interaction-related factors

Analysis of Andrei's turns-at-talk, presented in Figure 4.45, showed that he was capable of taking initiatives and collaborating in classroom talk throughout the study. The proportion of turn-types indicating active participation in classroom discourse ('tellings' and 'topic elaborations') produced by Andrei rose as the study progressed and his L2 proficiency increased. Teacher–pupil talk was prevalent, generally accounting for more than 95% of Andrei's recorded interaction. This often involved IRF sequences in which pupil participation was restricted, rather than creating contexts for more active discourse.

Figure 4.45 Turn-type indicators of interaction patterns for Andrei in selected lessons

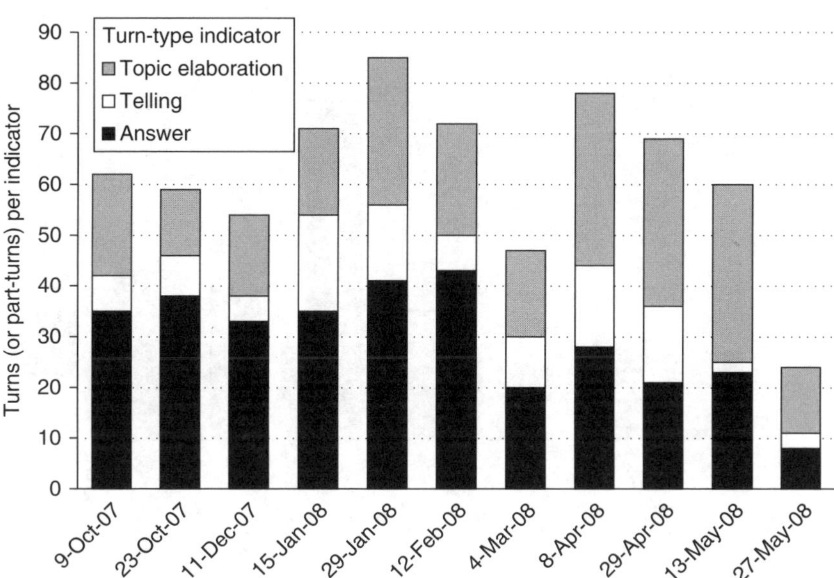

16 Beatriz

Personal details for Beatriz are shown in Table 4.31. Figure 4.46 indicates the *Benchmarks* proficiency levels associated with her analysed spoken turns. In her second year of English language support, Beatriz was capable of B1-linked L2 use from the outset of the study. The proportion of turns at level B1 varied across the selected lessons, but was generally highest in later lessons. Her frequency and accuracy of use of the quantitatively analysed grammatical indicators is displayed in Figure 4.47.

Table 4.31 Beatriz – personal details

National/cultural background	Portuguese	**Age at end of study**	8 years
School attended	School 3	**School class**	First Class
English language support commenced	September 2006	**Duration of participation in study**	October 2007 – February 2008
Number of lessons selected for detailed analysis	8 (of total 15)	**Number of turns-at-talk analysed**	220

Figure 4.46 Benchmarks levels recorded for analysed turns produced by Beatriz in selected lessons

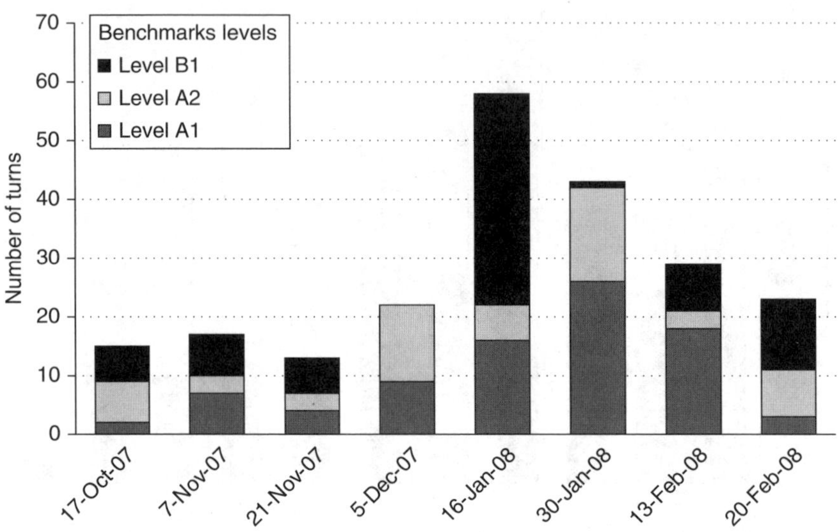

Figure 4.47 Frequency and accuracy of quantitatively analysed grammatical indicators used by Beatriz

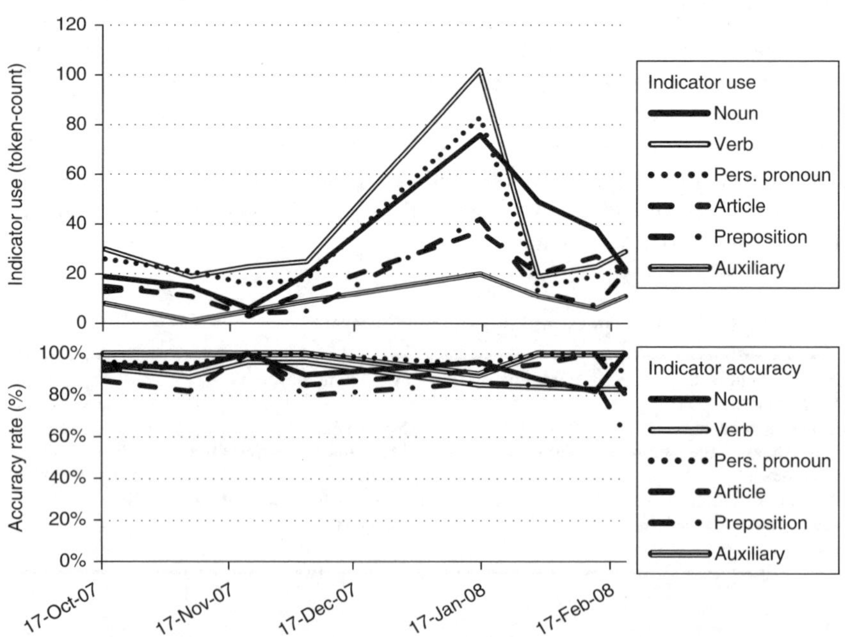

Evidence of L2 acquisition – grammatical indicators

Morphological features

Beatriz's use of the analysed grammatical indicators was affected by the number of turns available for analysis of oral L2 development in each lesson (many of the lessons focused more on literacy). The frequency of her noun production varied, but it was generally more than 90% accurate. Incorrect lexis accounted for most errors, although irregular plurals were sometimes overgeneralised (e.g. *snowmans*). Beatriz's verb use was relatively extensive and accurate throughout the study. She frequently produced past tense forms (both regular and irregular); she also used past participles and progressive forms (in present and past contexts). However, occasional use of present tense verbs for past reference remained a source of error. In the course of the study Beatriz produced a wide range of pronouns, including personal, demonstrative, ordinal, reflexive, quantifying, substitute and reflexive pronouns. The diversity of her pronoun use increased in later lessons. Her production of personal pronouns was more than 90% accurate, with only isolated errors (usually of gender) recorded.

Allowing for lesson-related variance, Beatriz's use of articles seemed to become more extensive and accurate as the study progressed. Errors generally involved non-required article use, but articles were rarely omitted. From the outset of the study, Beatriz could produce a diverse range of prepositions. Her preposition use was usually more than 80% accurate, although this rate fluctuated somewhat. Use of *in* (where *on* or *at* was required) and confusion of *to* and *for* emerged as typical errors. Omission of prepositions was minimal. Diversity was also evident in Beatriz's auxiliary use. From the beginning of the study, she could mark past (both simple past and progressive aspect) and future reference with appropriate auxiliaries (e.g. *did, were* and *will*). She could also express conditionality using *could* and, in later lessons, speak of hypothetical situations by using *might*. She also used modal auxiliaries to express ability and obligation. Her auxiliary use was generally accurate, with only isolated errors (e.g. confusion of *can* and *could*) recorded and occasional cases of omission.

Syntactic features

Beatriz's verb-to-noun ratio was generally in the range 0.6–0.8, which reflected her ability to produce quite complex structures. However, it was also affected by characteristics of each lesson which sometimes favoured short noun-based responses. Regarding negation, Beatriz could competently produce negative structures using *not*, often in contracted form with a range of auxiliaries. However, errors such as double negation occasionally emerged (e.g. *no one can't go in there* – Lesson 10). Beatriz proved capable of forming inverted questions (e.g. *can we bring five cent?* – Lesson 12). She also attempted indirect and reported questions, but these were less accurately constructed. From early lessons Beatriz could link clauses using *because* and relativisers such as *when*. She also used *if* to form conditional sentences from Lesson 6 onwards.

Evidence of L2 acquisition – lexical indicators

Lexical analysis of Beatriz's recorded turns, presented in Table 4.32, showed that her level of lexical diversity was higher throughout the study than many of the pupils who were in their first year of English language support. Variations in results for 'Wordlist entries' and 'Wordlist entries per turn' may be more attributable to features of the lessons: the number of turns they offered for analysis of L2 oral development and the nature of classroom activities.

Table 4.32 Beatriz – indicators of L2 lexical development

Wordlist results								
Lesson	2	4	6	8	10	12	14	15
Wordlist entries per turn per lesson	73	58	54	65	190	92	77	82
Wordlist entries per turn	4.87	3.41	4.15	2.95	3.28	2.14	2.65	2.83
Verb lexemes per lesson	12	10	12	15	31	13	10	13

The semantic fields Beatriz covered reflected many of the units of work in the *Benchmarks*, although the teacher in School 3 did not base her English language support on the *Benchmarks* and only occasionally used resources derived from them in her lessons. Beatriz's L2 vocabulary went considerably beyond core words associated with these themes; for instance, she used nouns such as *needle* (on the topic of 'visiting the doctor') and adjectives such as *spiky*. During the study, her range of possessive determiners expanded to include *my, your, her* and *our*. Increasing lexical diversity emerged in the verbs she used in later lessons (e.g. *celebrate, crash*). She produced 55 distinct verb lexemes. She also used a range of adverbs relating to place, frequency and time, or acting as modifiers (e.g. *sometimes, really*).

L2 literacy development

Beatriz proved consistently capable of engaging with English literacy activities typical of those associated with her mainstream school class. She could read and respond to quite complex readers, although occasionally new L2 lexis proved difficult (e.g. *budgie*). Regarding writing, she could unscramble words to make sentences and write accurate answers to comprehension questions. Generally her syntax and spelling were appropriate, and she could self-correct and assess peers' attempts at writing. She could also engage in less structured writing (e.g. a short paragraph about a postman), although grammatical and orthographic errors were apparent in her extended production. It appeared, however, that she had no home-language literacy skills.

Possible influences on L2 development

Individual factors

Beatriz was 8 years old and in her second year of English language support during the study. She had acquired a level of L2 proficiency that enabled her to engage with activities associated with mainstream education, although she still needed some support. However, it seemed that, due to her early exposure to English, her competence in mainstream First Class activities was greater than that of participating pupils who had just entered the Irish primary school system at this stage of schooling. How long her advantage would hold, as the linguistic demands of the curriculum increased, is impossible to say. Unlike some other participants, she lacked the potential support of home-language literacy. It is difficult to assess the impact of her home language, Portuguese, on Beatriz's L2 acquisition as she was quite accurate in many aspects of L2 production. Phonologically, she had even acquired a local accent in English, but some non-target-like production was still apparent (e.g. lengthening of vowels). Certain grammatical features may also have been transfer related (e.g. double negation). Beatriz was quite a talkative child but her participation in classroom activities varied. She often seemed conscientious, but sometimes her concentration lapsed.

Interaction-related factors

Beatriz relished the chance to tell stories about her own experience; analysis of her L2 oral production indicated this tendency. 'Telling' and 'topic elaboration' turn-types generally exceeded those coded as 'answers' in her analysed speech, as shown in Figure 4.48. In part, this reflected her personality. However, the fact that her L2 proficiency was higher than that of participants in their first year of English language support may have enabled her to take more initiatives in conversation and to contribute more actively to classroom discussion. Nevertheless, interaction patterns in the classroom remained teacher directed, with very few opportunities created for peer-to-peer discourse.

Figure 4.48 Turn-type indicators of interaction patterns for Beatriz in selected lessons

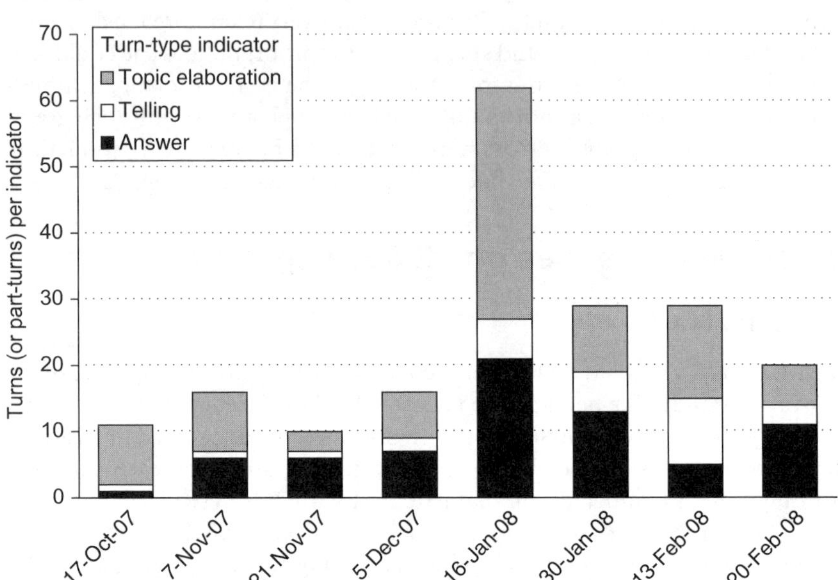

17 Nasreen

Table 4.33 presents personal details for Nasreen. From Figure 4.49 it is evident that she was capable of producing turns associated with *Benchmarks* proficiency level B1 throughout the study. However, the extent of her B1-linked production varied across the selected lessons, due to variation in classroom activities. The frequency and accuracy of Nasreen's use of the quantitatively analysed grammatical indicators is illustrated in Figure 4.50.

Table 4.33 Nasreen – personal details

National/cultural background	Pakistani	Age at end of study	8 years
School attended	School 3	School class	First Class
English language support commenced	February 2006	Duration of participation in study	October 2007 – February 2008
Number of lessons selected for detailed analysis	8 (of total 15)	Number of turns-at-talk analysed	376

Figure 4.49 Benchmarks levels recorded for analysed turns produced by Nasreen in selected lessons

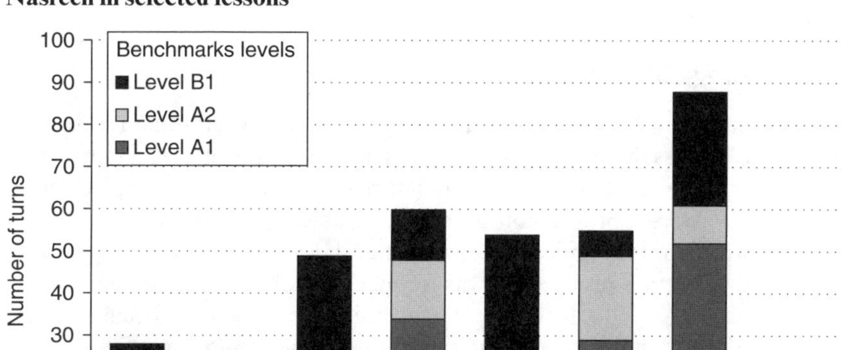

Figure 4.50 Frequency and accuracy of quantitatively analysed grammatical indicators used by Nasreen

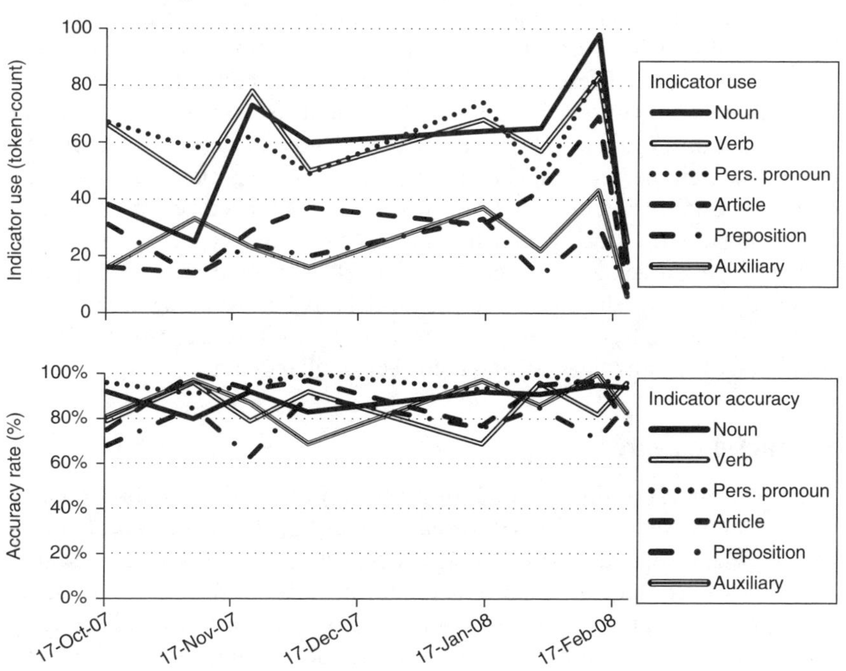

Evidence of L2 acquisition – grammatical indicators

Morphological features

Token-counts for Nasreen's production of the analysed grammatical indicators varied across the study period, due to features of the selected lessons, such as their oral/literacy balance and the nature of classroom activities. Overall, however, Nasreen's production of these variables was more extensive than that of participants in their first year of English language support. Regarding noun use, Nasreen's production was frequent and, by the second half of the study, more than 90% accurate. Her occasional errors were usually lexical but sometimes involved over-generalisation of the *-s* morpheme to irregular plurals (e.g. *peoples*). Her verb use was diverse throughout. From early lessons she could produce progressive forms, simple past tense verbs (regular and irregular), and past participles. Her verb use was usually more than 80% accurate, with a trend towards greater accuracy evident in later lessons. Errors included application of the regular *-ed* ending to irregular past tense forms (e.g. *buyed*) and occasional use of present tense verbs for past reference. Nasreen used a wide range of pronouns including personal, demonstrative, quantifying, indefinite, substitute, ordinal and reflexive pronouns. Her personal pronoun use was more than 90% accurate, with negligible omission.

Nasreen used articles frequently during the study and her accuracy rate was generally high (more than 80%). Some fluctuations in accuracy were, however, recorded. These were mainly due to non-required use of articles and occasional use of *a* before a vowel. She could also use an extensive range of prepositions, again with a relatively high degree of accuracy. Occasional errors tended to be due to a tendency to over-use *in* (especially for time reference) or the confusion of *to* and *for*. Nasreen produced a diversity of auxiliaries during the study, using them (e.g. *be* and *do*) to indicate verb tense, aspect and mood, in present and past contexts, as well as to indicate future reference (*will* and *going to*). She could also use modal auxiliaries. While her auxiliary use was quite accurate, some errors were recorded, typically singular/plural confusion of the auxiliary *be*, and incorrect auxiliary choice.

Syntactic features

The verb-to-noun ratio recorded for Nasreen was relatively stable and consistently in the range 0.4–0.6. However, this may have been due to the nominal bias of classroom activities which elicited short answers (often nouns). Nasreen was competent in her formation of negative structures, using *not* appropriately throughout the study, often in contraction with auxiliaries (e.g. *won't*). From early lessons, she could also produce a range of question forms with accurate inversion as required. She also could use relativisers (e.g. *when, what* and *who*) to link clauses. From the outset of the study she could link clauses using the subordinating conjunctions *because* and *if* (e.g. *because if you fall down if- if then if you didn't have a helmet you fall down . . .* – Lesson 15).

Evidence of L2 acquisition – lexical indicators

As with Beatriz (Profile 16), the lexical diversity exhibited by Nasreen during the study period appeared greater than that associated with participants who were in their first year of English language support. The results for Nasreen's 'Wordlist entries' and 'Wordlist entries per turn' are presented in Table 4.34. While variations in this data are evident, they are probably attributable largely to features of the individual lessons.

Table 4.34 Nasreen – indicators of L2 lexical development

Wordlist results

Lesson	2	4	6	8	10	12	14	15
Wordlist entries per turn per lesson	111	95	150	123	163	126	181	69
Wordlist entries per turn	3.96	3.52	3.06	2.05	3.02	2.29	2.06	4.60
Verb lexemes per lesson	20	18	22	16	27	24	30	10

Nasreen's L2 lexis covered a wide range of semantic fields which were closely related to the units of work in the *Benchmarks*, though the teacher did not consciously structure her lessons around the *Benchmarks* themes. Substantial lexical diversity was apparent in Nasreen's L2 vocabulary; she produced nouns such as *sunflower* (on the topic of 'plants'). She also used adjectives such as *disgusting*, with comparative forms recorded from Lesson 2 (e.g. *brighter*) and superlatives (e.g. *oldest*) in the final lesson. The possessive determiners *my, your, her, our* and *their* also featured in her L2 production. Nasreen's verb lexemes became more diverse as the study progressed, with verbs such as *chew* and *collect* emerging in later lessons. She produced a total of 77 distinct verb lexemes. Her adverb range was extensive, including, for instance: *before, together* and *already*.

L2 literacy development

During the study period, Nasreen was nearing the end of her two years of English language support and appeared able to engage competently with English literacy activities. From early lessons, she could read age-appropriate texts (classroom readers) with fluency, though more complex L2 lexis (e.g. *terrible*) and grapho-phonic relations (such as *-ight*) proved challenging.

Nasreen could also respond to comprehension questions and offer oral definitions for words extracted from these texts (e.g. *litter, fortune-teller*). With support, she could complete gap-fill exercises and rewrite scrambled sentences with correct syntax. In later lessons, her ability to write less structured sentences (e.g. about her daily routine) also emerged. Unlike her older sister, Fatima (see the next profile in this chapter), Nasreen appeared to have little or no home-language literacy experience; she could not read a classroom sign written in Urdu, whereas her sister was already literate in Urdu.

Possible influences on L2 development

Individual factors

Nasreen was 8 years old at the end of the study and it appeared that, after almost two years of English language support, she could participate in many activities typical of her mainstream educational stage (First Class). However, as was apparent in relation to her L2 literacy development, she still required support with new vocabulary and some aspects of L2 syntax and orthography. As pointed out in Chapter 3, the teacher was unsure of Nasreen's home language(s), which may have included Punjabi, Urdu and the extra-curricular learning of Arabic. This makes it impossible to draw conclusions as regards cross-linguistic influence on her L2 development. However, possible transfer was suggested by phonological aspects of her L2 production (e.g. articulation of the fricative /v/ closer to the approximant /ʋ/, the lengthening of vowels, and sentence prosody). Nasreen was an outgoing and talkative child. A motivated learner who contributed eagerly to classroom talk, she could self-correct her L2 production and use communication strategies very effectively.

Interaction-related factors

As is evident in Figure 4.51, Nasreen tended to produce more 'telling' or 'topic elaboration' than 'answer' turn-types. Her ability to play an active role in classroom discourse was probably also enhanced by the fact that her L2 proficiency was considerably greater than that of participating pupils who were in their first year of English language support. However, despite Nasreen's competent contribution to classroom talk, the predominance of pupil–teacher discourse in the selected lessons suggests that her turn-taking opportunities in a group of three children were somewhat limited.

Figure 4.51 Turn-type indicators of interaction patterns for Nasreen in selected lessons

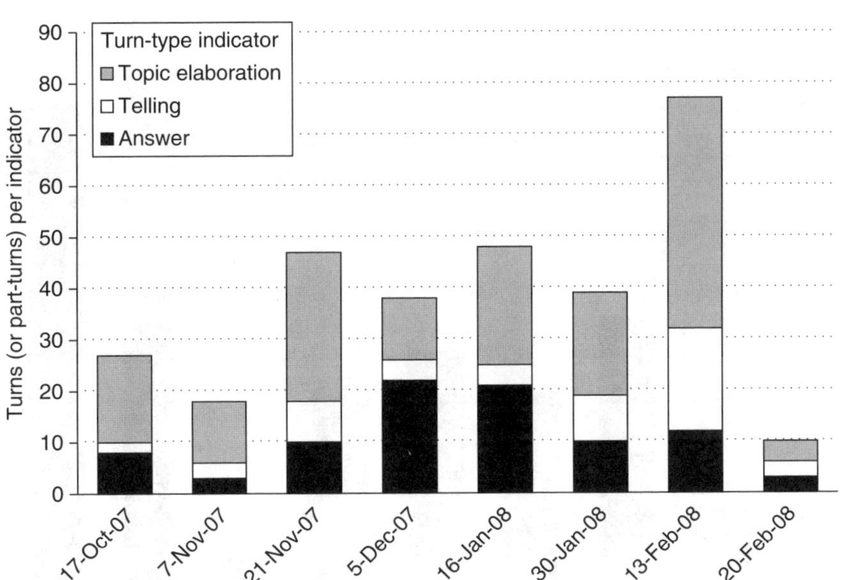

18 Fatima

Personal details for Fatima are summarised in Table 4.35. The *Benchmarks* proficiency levels associated with her analysed spoken turns are presented in Figure 4.52. This shows that, from early in the study, the majority of her turns were linked to level B1; lower-level turns often reflected classroom activities rather than L2 proficiency. Figure 4.53 shows her use of the quantitatively analysed grammatical indicators and the accuracy of this use.

Table 4.35 Fatima – personal details

National/cultural background	Pakistani	**Age at end of study**	10 years
School attended	School 3	**School class**	Third Class
English language support commenced	February 2006	**Duration of participation in study**	October 2007 – February 2008
Number of lessons selected for detailed analysis	8 (of total 13)	**Number of turns-at-talk analysed**	259

Figure 4.52 Benchmarks levels recorded for analysed turns produced by Fatima in selected lessons

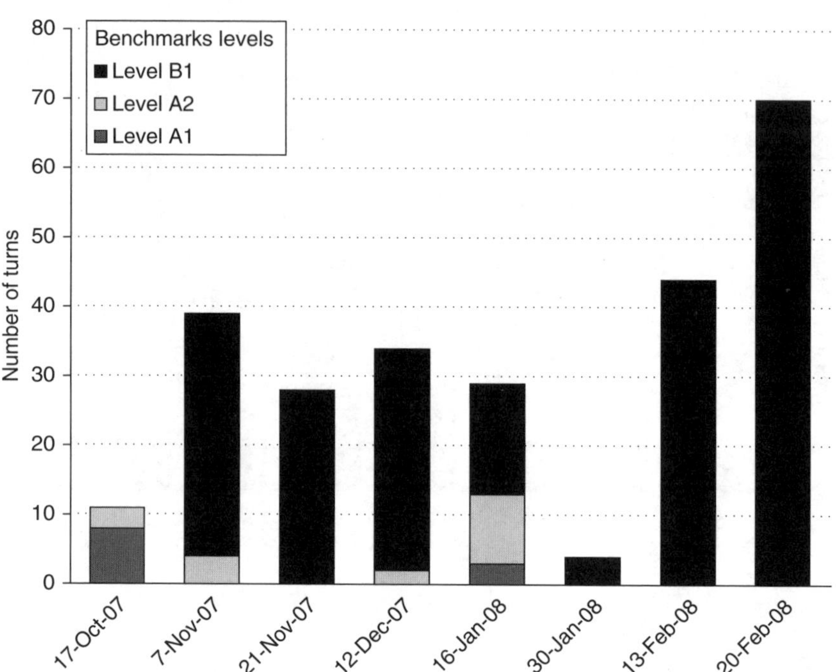

Evidence of L2 acquisition – grammatical indicators

Morphological features

Figure 4.53 shows that Fatima's use of the analysed morphological indicators was generally extensive (reduced token-counts were recorded in Lessons 1 and 11 as these lessons had a text-based literacy focus and offered fewer oral turns for analysis). Throughout the study, the accuracy of her production of these variables was in the region of 90%. Her use of nouns was comprehensive and competent with, for example, well-controlled marking of possession. Errors of lexical choice or over-generalised use of *-s* in irregular plurals (e.g. *childrens*) were noted, but they were infrequent. Fatima's verb production was considerable and generally more than 80% accurate (with accuracy increasing in the second half of the study). Her verb forms included: progressive, simple past (regular and irregular), and past participles. Errors typically involved: the use of present verb-forms in past contexts, some overgeneralisation of the regular *-ed* ending to irregular past forms (e.g. *digged*), and the

Figure 4.53 Frequency and accuracy of quantitatively analysed grammatical indicators used by Fatima

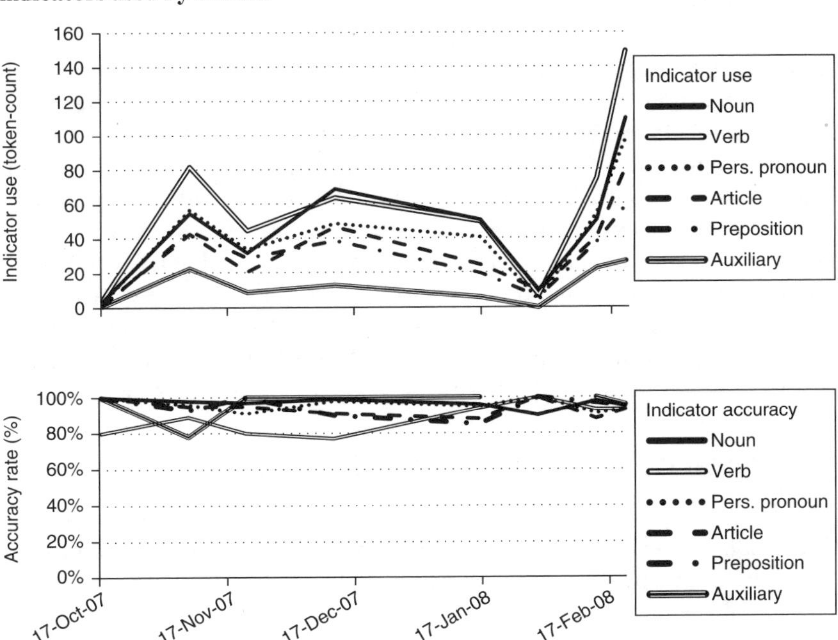

use of simple past rather than past participles with irregular verbs. In the course of the study she used a wide range of pronouns including reflexive, indefinite and relative pronouns. Her use of personal pronouns was very proficient (accuracy rate more than 90% throughout) with only minor errors, usually of number or gender. Omission of personal pronouns was negligible.

Fatima used articles appropriately (accuracy rate usually more than 90%) with few errors, apart from occasional non-required production or use of *a* before a vowel, and minimal omission. Her preposition use was diverse and showed a rising trend across the study (allowing for lesson-related fluctuation). The accuracy of her production was more than 90% throughout; any errors were usually isolated instances of incorrect preposition choice. While the token-count for auxiliaries produced by Fatima varied, due mainly to variations in the number of analysable turns available per lesson, it was highest towards the end of the study. She used a diverse range of auxiliaries to mark tense and aspect (*be, do, will, going to, have*), and to express passive mood (*be, get*). She also used modal auxiliaries to indicate ability (*can, could*), obligation (*have to, must*), and conditionality (*would, could, might*). Her accuracy rate was high for most auxiliaries, although minor errors involving auxiliary choice were evident (e.g. *will/would*).

Syntactic features

In the course of the study, Fatima's verb-to-noun ratio was usually over 0.5, particularly in lessons which afforded her the opportunity for extended narrative. She used *not* appropriately for negation, frequently in contracted form with various auxiliaries, while the negative marker *never* was recorded in Lesson 14. Errors such as inappropriate choice of verb tense following negative contractions occurred (e.g. *he didn't fell*), but these were infrequent. Fatima produced accurate inverted questions from the outset of the study. Indirect questions were also recorded. However sometimes when reporting speech she had a tendency to leave questions in direct, dialogue form. Fatima used co-ordinating conjunctions extensively. From Lesson 3 onwards, it was evident that she could also use relativisers and subordinating conjunctions to link clauses (e.g. *if they sting you might die*). Her use of *that* for clause linkage was recorded from Lesson 13, particularly when reporting speech.

Evidence of L2 acquisition – lexical indicators

The results of the lexical analysis of Fatima's oral turns are shown in Table 4.36. Allowing for the impact of lesson-specific influences, her ratio of 'Wordlist entries per turn' (generally more than 3.0 across the study) suggests considerable L2 lexical proficiency.

Table 4.36 Fatima – indicators of L2 lexical development

Wordlist results								
Lesson	1	3	5	8	9	11	13	14
Wordlist entries per turn per lesson	25	135	104	150	127	31	131	227
Wordlist entries per turn	2.27	3.46	3.71	4.41	4.38	7.75	2.98	3.24
Verb lexemes per lesson	3	25	22	26	27	5	28	45

Although the teacher in School 3 did not base her lessons on the *Benchmarks*, there is considerable correspondence between the semantic fields covered by Fatima in the recorded lessons and the units of work in the *Benchmarks*. Within these fields, Fatima produced quite complex lexis, including nouns such as *junk* and *material* (on the topic of 'environment'). Her adjectives were similarly specific (e.g. *famous*). She could also express the concepts of comparative and superlative (using both inflected forms, e.g. *better, worst*, and the markers *more, most*) and produce a comprehensive range of possessive determiners. Fatima used 90 distinct verb lexemes across the study, including: *measure, explore* and *interview*. Her adverb range was also extensive, featuring modifiers such as *especially* and *greedily*.

L2 literacy development

From the outset of the study Fatima's English literacy abilities were considerable: she was capable of engaging in mainstream literacy-related activities, often outperforming her native English-speaking peers. There was also evidence that she had developed some home-language literacy. She had attended school in Pakistan and presented some examples of writing in Urdu for a project she had completed in School 3. Fatima was a competent reader of age-appropriate fiction (e.g. *Charlie and the Chocolate Factory* by Roald Dahl), even though she admitted that she found this challenging. She had developed aesthetic awareness across different genres, including poetry, and could express opinions in response to written texts. She was able to engage with literacy activities that focused on formal features (e.g. prefixes and suffixes), and adeptly completed word-building tasks. Regarding L2 writing, Fatima showed considerable awareness of orthographic issues such as the spelling of irregular plurals, capitalisation and punctuation. She could also write coherent responses to demonstrate her comprehension of complex texts, and was very competent in creative writing, written argument and summarisation.

Possible influences on L2 development

Individual factors

Fatima was 10 years old at the end of the study. However, her development of extensive L2 skills over the two years following her arrival in Ireland may not be typical of all EAL pupils of her age. She was a highly motivated and cognitively capable child with previous educational experience and home-language literacy skills. She may also have benefited from the fact that School 3 had 'disadvantaged' status and thus smaller class sizes and additional literacy support. Precise information about Fatima's linguistic identity was unobtainable. She had knowledge of Urdu and perhaps also of Punjabi; she was also learning Arabic. It was difficult, therefore, to determine cross-linguistic influence beyond phonological factors such as the lengthening of vowels, articulation of the fricative /v/ (closer to the approximant /ʋ/), and sentence prosody. Fatima appeared to be a reflective child who nonetheless was prepared to take risks when volunteering information or ideas.

Interaction-related factors

The distribution of 'answers', 'tellings' and 'topic elaborations' in Fatima's analysed L2 use, shown in Figure 4.54, corresponded to active participation in classroom discourse. Some of her interaction included extended

Figure 4.54 Turn-type indicators of interaction patterns for Fatima in selected lessons

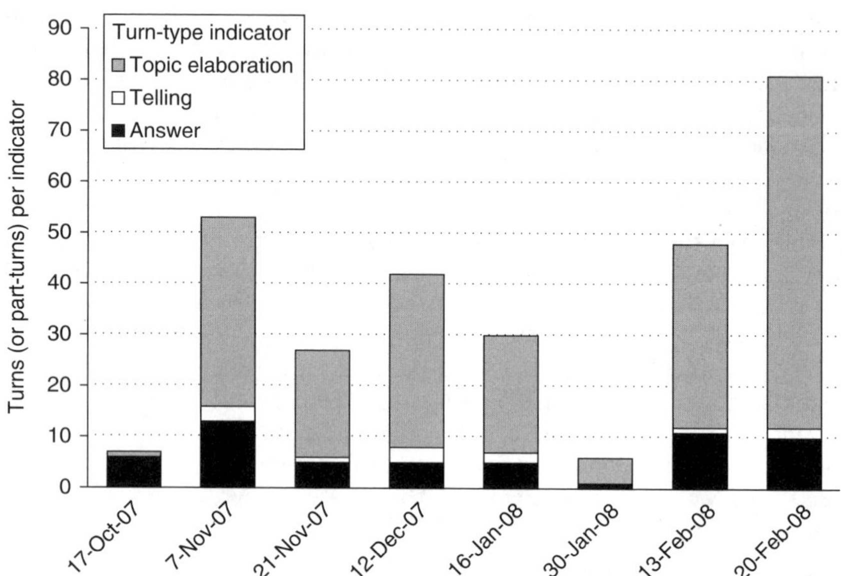

story-telling turns (which could include several instances of the analysed turn-type indicators). However, lesson-specific factors, particularly tasks which required only short responses, also influenced interaction patterns and sometimes limited her contributions. Pupil–teacher interaction predominated in the recorded lessons. This was not surprising as Fatima's group comprised only two pupils and occasionally involved one-to-one lessons. Nevertheless, peer-to-peer discourse accounted for no more than 5% of her L2 production.

Conclusion

The 18 profiles presented in this chapter show progression in the participating pupils' English L2 development over the study period. They also indicate that the *Benchmarks* proficiency levels associated with their analysed spoken turns appear to reflect their acquisition of L2 oral skills. In addition, the summaries of the children's English literacy development offer evidence as to how EAL pupils of different ages and stages of L2 proficiency engage with L2 reading and writing activities. However, the discussion of possible influences on the participants' L2 development suggests that a range of internal and interaction-related factors may have affected these pupils' English L2 acquisition. While many similarities are apparent in the course of their L2 development, individual differences are also evident. Characteristics of the learning environment may have further impacted on these pupils' L2 acquisition. These issues must be taken into consideration in any attempt to compare the findings offered by the 18 case studies. Nevertheless, such comparison is necessary if we are to derive overall evidence of English L2 acquisition among this group of EAL pupils and examine its relation to the trajectory of L2 proficiency development described by the *Benchmarks*. Chapter 5 outlines the processes and outcomes of this comparison.

5

English L2 development among EAL pupils – results from the case studies

The ultimate aim of our research was to derive overall results from the case studies of L2 development compiled for 18 EAL pupils. Following the procedures outlined in Chapter 3, we had to bring together all the data from the individual profiles presented in Chapter 4. We then had to use this database to obtain overall findings in response to the research questions set out in Chapter 1. This cumulative analysis would enable us to determine whether and, if so, to what extent the development of English L2 communicative proficiency among these children reflected the progression described in the *English Language Proficiency Benchmarks*. In addition, the empirical evidence of L2 acquisition gained from this study could provide valuable information as to how the participating EAL pupils developed L2 linguistic competence. It could also highlight, to some extent, how individual variance and external factors may have influenced their English L2 development and help us to identify issues that require further investigation. We could then consider what our analysis of data obtained from the 18 EAL participating pupils allowed us to say about the overall relation between L2 communicative capacity and underlying L2 linguistic competence.

Overview of pupils' English L2 proficiency development

Based on evidence from the 18 pupils' spontaneous oral L2 use in the selected lessons – 7,455 analysable spoken turns – we could examine the relation between EAL pupils' development of L2 communicative proficiency and the learning trajectory described in the *Benchmarks* for the relevant communicative skills (spoken interaction and spoken production). To do this, we had to examine how the *Benchmarks*-linked findings for the 18 EAL pupils' L2 proficiency development related to the duration of their English language support across the study period. This meant we had to bring together evidence of pupils' L2 proficiency at similar points in their English language support allocation and see how this varied over time.

We first grouped the proficiency-linked spoken turns produced by the pupils in the selected lessons according to the month of English language support allocation in which each turn was recorded. This assumed a 10-month-long school year (July and August were excluded as these are the two months of summer holidays in Irish primary schools). Data for 'month 1' was thus produced by pupils in their first month of English language support, turns assigned to months 1–10 were produced by pupils in their first year of English language support, and turns assigned to months 11–20 were produced by pupils in their second year of English language support. Turns for a 21st month were recorded for Nasreen (Profile 17) and Fatima (Profile 18); this was possible because at the time of the study the two-year cap on English language support had been briefly rescinded. The results of this analysis are presented in Figure 5.1.

Before we discuss our findings, we must point out a few minor assumptions made when calculating the duration of English language support. First, for comparative purposes, we assumed that support started at the beginning of the first month of its allocation, since the information regarding its duration was provided by teachers in terms of 'month of commencement'. This could be confirmed for most pupils who had entered the English language support programme at the beginning of the school year 2006–07. In these cases pupils' month of commencement was generally September. For pupils in some groups recorded in Schools 1 and 3, however, English language support started at the beginning of October, either to allow younger children to 'settle in' or simply because of administrative issues affecting the organisation and scheduling of groups. However, the exact date when English language support began could not be obtained for pupils who arrived mid-year and who were often quickly placed into existing lesson groups. Andrei (Profile 15), Ravi (Profile 12), Lukas (Profile 13), Nasreen (Profile 17) and Fatima belonged to this category of 'late-arrival' pupils. For the compilation of Figure 5.1, English language support for these five pupils was dated from the beginning of the month of their enrolment at primary school. Occasionally, this may have led to a very slight over-estimation of an individual pupil's English language support allocation, for example when the child arrived in the middle or towards the end of a calendar month. However, it was not felt likely to distort any overall patterns of English L2 proficiency development emerging from the study.

A potentially more significant issue was that, as pointed out in Chapter 3, the majority (13) of the 18 participating EAL pupils were in their first year of English language support. As a result, we obtained considerably more data relating to English L2 proficiency development in the first 10-month period than in the second. This may mean that our findings provide a somewhat more reliable indication of English L2 proficiency development among pupils in the first year of English language support than among those in their second year.

Figure 5.1 Proficiency levels associated with analysed turns across the recorded duration of pupils' English language support*

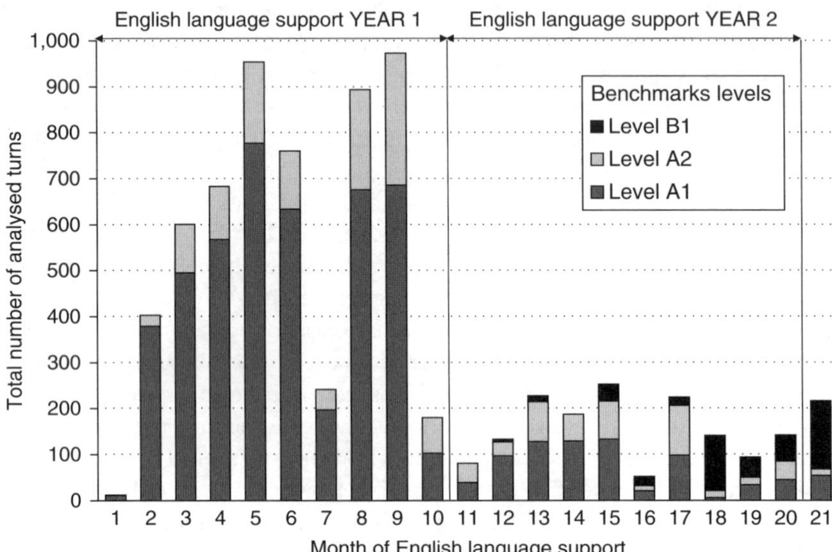

* Duration of English language support as known to the researcher.

From Figure 5.1 it is apparent that, based on the analysed data, turns linked to A1 level *Benchmarks* were dominant during the first year of English language support. However, over this first year, the proportion of A2 level turns produced by pupils increased quite steadily and continued to increase into the second year of English language support. From month 12 onwards, however, evidence of B1 proficiency began to emerge. The proportion of B1 turns generally increased in subsequent months, and B1 became the dominant proficiency level from month 18 onwards – close to the end of the typical two-year allocation of English language support. The proportions of turns associated with the three proficiency levels over the period covered by the analysed data is shown in Table 5.1.

Allowing for some slight fluctuations in the results for participating pupils in their second year of English language support, the trends apparent in Figure 5.1 and Table 5.1 demonstrate an overall increase in English L2 proficiency over time. Also, the variation in the findings for second-year pupils may be primarily due to the reduced quantity of data available for them. This may have rendered our results for the second year of English language support somewhat more susceptible to the influence of lesson-related factors. However, considering Figure 5.1 as a reasonable illustration of developing English L2 proficiency among EAL pupils in Irish primary schools, a clear

Table 5.1 Proportion of turns at proficiency levels A1, A2 and B1 over support duration

Month of support	Total analysed turns	Proportion of A1 turns	Proportion of A2 turns	Proportion of B1 turns
1	12	0.92	0.08	0.00
2	403	0.94	0.06	0.00
3	601	0.82	0.18	0.00
4	683	0.83	0.17	0.00
5	954	0.81	0.19	0.00
6	760	0.83	0.17	0.00
7	242	0.81	0.19	0.00
8	894	0.76	0.24	0.00
9	973	0.71	0.29	0.00
10	180	0.57	0.43	0.00
11	81	0.48	0.52	0.00
12	133	0.73	0.23	0.04
13	228	0.56	0.38	0.06
14	187	0.69	0.31	0.00
15	253	0.52	0.33	0.15
16	52	0.40	0.21	0.39
17	225	0.44	0.48	0.08
18	141	0.04	0.11	0.85
19	94	0.36	0.17	0.47
20	142	0.32	0.28	0.40
21	217	0.25	0.06	0.69

progression in proficiency is evident from A1-dominant to B1-dominant L2 use. This suggests that the *Benchmarks* offer an accurate description of the general trajectory of L2 proficiency development to be expected over a two-year allocation of English language support.

Figure 5.1 also reflects the reality that L2 use frequently involves production which is somewhat below learners' maximum proficiency level at any given point in their learning. This is often due to interactional factors which, in a classroom situation, may be linked to pedagogical practice. For example, in some of the lessons recorded in this study, it appeared that some of the activities with which pupils engaged did not elicit English L2 use to the highest level of their capability. However, despite this potential for distortion, clear evidence of progression in English L2 proficiency emerges from the findings summarised in Figure 5.1. This suggests that the *Benchmarks* offer an appropriate guide to L2 oral proficiency development among EAL pupils; one that accords with actual L2 use in their recorded spoken turns. Furthermore, considering L2 use and learning as inseparable and accepting that the best evidence of learners' L2 acquisition may be found in the development of L2 oral skills, the relation between EAL pupils' acquisition of English L2 and the learning outcomes described by the *Benchmarks* appears to be strong.

Relation between evidence of L2 acquisition and the Benchmarks

Overall findings for analysed indicators of English L2 acquisition

In this section, we examine in greater depth the relation between EAL pupils' oral L2 use and the *Benchmarks* descriptors. To establish whether our initial findings regarding the 18 participating pupils' English L2 proficiency development can be verified by cumulative analysis of L2 grammatical and lexical indicators of L2 acquisition, we investigate evidence derived from a total of 7,455 analysable spoken turns produced by these children. Based on this overall evidence, we then determine whether any emerging patterns are reflected in the trajectory of English L2 proficiency development outlined by the *Benchmarks*.

The outcomes of this analysis are of relevance to core statements regarding progression in L2 development presented in Part I of the *Benchmarks*. These include the description of L2 oral skills development in the global benchmarks of communicative proficiency and the descriptors for grammatical accuracy and vocabulary control in the global scales of underlying linguistic competence (Appendix 2). These statements serve as the basis for the thematic units of work which comprise Part II of the *Benchmarks* (Appendix 2). However, in the interest of maximum thoroughness, our analysis of L2 lexical development also considers the relation between the English lexis produced by the 18 participating pupils and the semantic fields covered by the *Benchmarks'* units of work.

Overall results – L2 grammatical indicators

To derive overall results from the L2 grammatical indicators analysed for each of the 18 participating pupils and to compare these to the *Benchmarks*, it was necessary to group together lessons in which pupils demonstrated similar levels of proficiency. This was done by using the 'proficiency ratio bands' described in Chapter 3 (see pages 60–61). These bands were used to categorise individual pupils' analysed L2 use, in each of the selected lessons, according to the proportion of turns they produced at the highest proficiency level they displayed in any given lesson. This meant that data recorded for each pupil regarding the frequency and accuracy of the quantitatively analysed grammatical indicators used by that pupil in a particular lesson, could be analysed together with data regarding the L2 use of other pupils, for lessons associated with the same proficiency band. Overall findings emerging for these indicators from each 'band' could then be compared with the *Benchmarks* description of English L2 proficiency development. This involved the following steps:

- for each of the selected lessons, the proportion of turns produced at the pupil's highest proficiency level within the lesson was recorded
- the linguistic data available for that pupil, for that lesson, was then classified according to the proficiency band to which it belonged
- for the seven quantitatively analysed L2 acquisition indicators, statistical means for frequency and accuracy of indicator use and mean values for verb-to-noun ratio were calculated, using the SPSS program, within each proficiency band
- for six of these indicators (nouns, verbs, personal pronouns, articles, prepositions and auxiliaries) mean values for frequency and accuracy associated with each proficiency band were illustrated graphically
- for the seventh indicator, verb-to-noun ratio, a separate graphic representation was used to show its variation across the proficiency ratio bands
- for all 10 grammatical indicators (including negative formation, question formation and clause linkage), qualitative features of L2 indicator development were also summarised.

Before we present the results of this final analysis, it is necessary to look at Table 5.2, which shows the distribution of the selected lessons associated with each of the proficiency ratio bands. It is clear from Table 5.2 that more lessons were linked to bands in which pupils' L2 use was associated predominantly with lower proficiency levels (proficiency proportion per lesson <0.5 A2). This meant that less data was likely to be available for bands associated with either a higher proportion of A2 turns or emerging B1 proficiency. As pointed out in our investigation of how pupils' L2 proficiency developed over the two-year allocation of English language support (see Figure 5.1), shortages of data can impact on overall results. This was certainly a risk with regard to the higher level bands, which were sometimes represented by only one pupil or, more occasionally, only one lesson. The data associated with these bands was thus more prone to the influence of additional internal or interactional factors. It should also be noted that no data was available for the three proficiency ratio bands in the range 0.71–1.0 A2. This was possibly due to the limited size of our sample, although some of the interaction-related issues outlined below may also have been a contributory factor.

The proficiency bands used in this part of the final analysis were independent of time. However, both the chronological investigation of English L2 proficiency development illustrated in Figure 5.1 and the lesson-linked proficiency graphs included in the case studies indicate that increasingly proficient L2 use was evident over time among all 18 participating pupils. Any apparent anomalies in Table 5.2 are therefore most likely due to lesson-related factors. For example, Marko's language use could be classified within the band 0.51–0.6 A2 during his third selected lesson, in which he took a very active part,

Table 5.2 Recorded proficiency bands for all analysed turns in all selected lessons

Proportion of turns at highest proficiency level	Number of selected lessons involved	Pupils involved
A1 only	21	Stefan, Tomasz, Patryk, Ravi, Dimitrie, Karina, Zofia
0.01–0.1 A2	26	Stefan, Tomasz, Patryk, Ravi, Lukas, Marko, Dimitrie, Jin, Edyta, Karina
0.11–0.2 A2	22	Andrei, Stefan, Tomasz, Patryk, Ivan, Ravi, Lukas, Marko, Dimitrie, Jin, Vladimir, Edyta
0.21–0.3 A2	21	Andrei, Stefan, Tomasz, Ivan, Ravi, Lukas, Dimitrie, Jin, Edyta, Fatima
0.31–0.4 A2	16	Andrei, Ivan, Lukas, Jin, Vladimir, Edyta
0.41–0.5 A2	6	Stefan, Lukas, Constantin, Vladimir, Edyta
0.51–0.6 A2	7	Andrei, Constantin, Marko, Vladimir, Beatriz
0.61–0.7 A2	1	Vladimir
0.71–0.8 A2	0	
0.81–0.9 A2	0	
0.91–1.0 A2	0	
0.01–0.1 B1	1	Beatriz
0.11–0.2 B1	2	Nasreen
0.21–0.3 B1	1	Beatriz
0.31–0.4 B1	1	Nasreen
0.41–0.5 B1	3	Beatriz
0.51–0.6 B1	4	Beatriz, Nasreen, Fatima
0.61–0.7 B1	2	Beatriz, Nasreen
0.71–0.8 B1	2	Nasreen
0.81–0.9 B1	1	Fatima
0.91–1.0 B1	5	Fatima

but dropped thereafter, not exceeding 0.2 A2 for the remainder of the study (see Profile 6). As pointed out in Chapter 4, this decrease in his A2-linked turns in later lessons may have been, at least partly, the result of his lack of interactional opportunities in what was a rather large lesson group. Likewise, Fatima's analysed spoken turns were classified within band 0.21–0.3 A2 in her first selected lesson (see Profile 18). However, this lesson was primarily focused on literacy; the speaking activities it included were limited and appeared very simple, compared to Fatima's performance in the earlier literacy-related tasks. Throughout subsequent lessons Fatima's L2 use was associated with proficiency bands which indicated a proportion of B1 turns over 0.5. Therefore, her oral L2 use in the first lesson may not have been an adequate reflection of her actual L2 proficiency.

Using the mean values calculated for the frequency and accuracy ratios obtained for each of the quantitatively analysed grammatical indicators within each proficiency band, we were able to compare evidence of pupils' L2 acquisition to the *Benchmarks* proficiency levels associated with their actual L2 use. The results of this comparison are presented graphically in

Figure 5.2 Mean frequency and accuracy of L2 acquisition indicators across L2 proficiency ratios

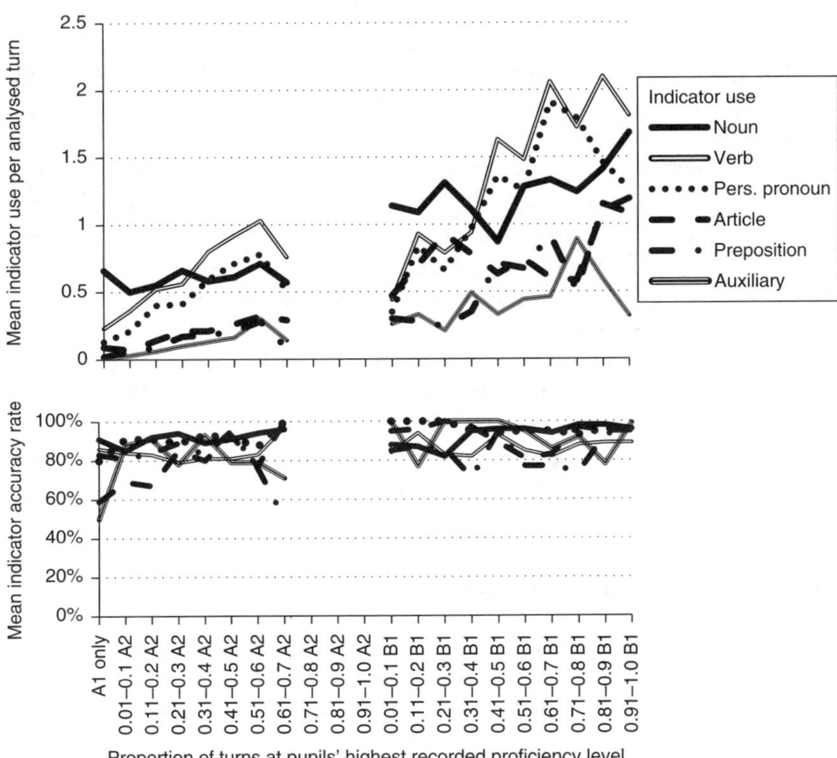

Figures 5.2 and 5.3 (page 172). Following a similar format to that employed in describing the case studies in Chapter 4, we will now look in greater detail at the overall development of the morphological and syntactic features we investigated. The cumulative results of the mixed methods analysis which was undertaken for seven of the grammatical indicators will thus be combined with the outcomes of the qualitative analysis of the remaining three indicators. For each of the seven indicators which were quantitatively analysed, the discussion of statistical results will be further informed by qualitative findings for each variable. Final results for the three syntactic indicators which were analysed by qualitative methods only (negative formation, question formation and clause linkage) will be presented as descriptive overviews.

For each of the 10 analysed variables, more detailed qualitative summaries of L2 indicator development are provided in Appendix 7. These summaries were created by bringing together the descriptions of L2 development from the 18 case studies for each grammatical indicator analysed. This involved grouping descriptions of each indicator's development, for each pupil, using the proficiency ratio bands indicated in Table 5.2. It is worth noting that in all the descriptive overviews included for analysed L2 acquisition indicators, the band-referenced summaries were linked to each pupil's maximum attainment of L2 proficiency evident from the recorded data. For example, Tomasz (Profile 5) reached a maximum proficiency band ratio of 0.21–0.3 A2, while the maximum proficiency band ratio of Beatriz (Profile 6) was 0.61–0.7 B1. Pupils' maximum levels of L2 production at their highest recorded proficiency level were generally associated with lessons later in the study (although, as mentioned above, classroom-related factors also influenced pupils' L2 production in the recorded lessons). Therefore, considering the impact of time on pupils' L2 development, the summaries included in Appendix 7 outline pupils' production of each grammatical feature across the research period with some chronological reference.

This cumulative quantitative analysis of statistical data available for seven of the grammatical indicators and qualitative analysis of all 10 indicators should reveal overall characteristics of the 18 participating pupils' English L2 acquisition during this study. It should also show the relation, if any, of this empirical evidence of their L2 acquisition to the trajectory of L2 proficiency development described by the *Benchmarks*.

Morphological features

Noun development

Figure 5.2 shows an initially gradual but generally consistent rise in mean noun use per analysed turn as English L2 proficiency increases. Nouns were a notable feature in the participating pupils' analysed production from the earliest stages of their L2 development. For lessons associated only with A1-linked L2 use, mean noun use per turn was 0.66, reflecting the tendency towards short noun-based turns evident among pupils at the beginning of their English language support allocation. As pupils' recorded turns became proportionately more associated with A2, the extent of their noun use per turn fluctuated somewhat. This was possibly because, as pupils produced more turns associated with an A2 level of proficiency, their communication became less heavily noun dependent. Overall, however, it would appear that noun production increased with L2 proficiency, from level A1 to A2. When pupils demonstrated a capacity for L2 use which could be linked to B1, their mean noun use per analysed turn rose more dramatically, peaking at a mean of 1.68 nouns per turn when the ratio of their recorded turns classifiable at B1 was between 0.91 and 1.0. This is likely to have been as a result of an expanding L2 lexicon. This was noted in Chapter 4 for Beatriz, Nasreen (Profile 17) and Fatima (Profile 18), whose analysed turns were frequently linked to level B1 *Benchmarks* descriptors and whose noun production was lexically diverse.

Across the proficiency bands, noun use appeared to be relatively accurate (accuracy rate generally over 90% throughout). However, slight dips in mean accuracy were evident in lessons in which pupils' analysed turns were starting to link with *Benchmarks* level B1 (bands 0.01–0.3 B1). While such fluctuations may be more noticeable due to shortage of data for pupils at this stage of English L2 development (see Table 5.2), they may also have been influenced by more proficient pupils' engagement with increasingly specific lexis. This was apparent, for example, in Beatriz's confusion of the names for baby animals (e.g. 'foal' and 'fawn') when her analysed turns could be classified within the proficiency band 0.21–0.3 B1. Noun omission rates (calculated using the SPSS program but not graphically illustrated) were almost negligible, with a mean omission rate of 5% of actual noun production or less recorded across all proficiency ratio bands. A more detailed qualitative summary of pupils' noun production across the proficiency ratio bands, based on the descriptions of noun development included in Chapter 4 is provided in Appendix 7. It should also be noted that pupils' noun use was likely to have been affected by lesson-related factors (e.g. teachers' elicitation of short, often noun-based, responses to 'known answer' questions) as well as to the children's stage of L2 acquisition in any of the selected lessons.

Verb development

Pupils' overall mean verb use per analysed turn also appeared to increase with developing English L2 proficiency (as shown in Figure 5.2). From a mean of 0.23 verbs per analysed turn among pupils whose L2 use was associated only with *Benchmarks* level A1, it rose steadily across lessons in which proportionately more pupil turns could be linked to A2 descriptors, reaching a mean of 1.03 verbs per turn within the proficiency ratio band 0.51–0.6 A2. The slight fall recorded in the subsequent band may be explained by the fact that this band was informed by data from one lesson only (see Table 5.2). Across lessons presenting evidence of English L2 use associated with level B1, mean verb use increased more noticeably (albeit with slight fluctuations possibly due to data availability) to a maximum mean of 2.1 verbs per turn recorded for lessons in which the ratio of turns linked to B1 descriptors was 0.81–0.9. Specific features of pupils' verb development, based on the 18 case studies, are outlined in Appendix 7. These reveal progression from the production of predominantly non-inflected stems to the use of a widening range of verb forms to express tense and aspect as pupils' L2 became increasingly associated with A2 and B1 descriptors.

Overall mean verb accuracy was generally in the region of 80–90%, with minor fluctuations across the proficiency ratio bands. However, higher mean accuracy rates (occasionally over 90%) seemed to be associated with L2 use in lessons in which evidence of increasing English L2 proficiency, particularly level B1-linked production, was recorded. Verb omission rates were considerable (62% of actual verb use) in lessons in which pupils' analysed spoken turns were associated only with A1 *Benchmarks* descriptors. While these rates were probably affected by the fact that actual verb use in these lessons was itself very low, they nevertheless reflect the tendency of pupils in the earliest stages of English L2 development to produce very short, generally noun-based turns, using only a limited range of verbs. However, omission rates fell quickly (to a mean of 5% or less) in lessons in which increasing proportions of A2-linked turns were recorded, and verbs were rarely omitted when pupils displayed a capacity for B1 level production.

Pronoun development

The qualitative descriptions of pronoun development provided in each of the case studies (and summarised in Appendix 7) suggest that pupils' pronoun use diversified with increasing English L2 proficiency. It developed from a very basic range of pronouns (typically personal and demonstrative pronouns, as well as numbers), to more extensive pronoun use (including use of possessive, reflexive, quantifying, substitute, indefinite and relative pronouns). We focused on pupils' production of personal pronouns because they emerged as the most frequently used pronouns within pupils' analysed turns, and also because they represented a linguistic element which was likely to vary in application between English and pupils' home languages (many of which were pro-drop languages).

As Figure 5.2 indicates, personal pronoun use appeared to rise with increasing English L2 proficiency. When pupils' turns within a given lesson were classifiable solely at *Benchmarks* level A1, the mean personal pronoun use per turn was just 0.13. A consistent rise was recorded up to proficiency band ratio 0.51–0.6 A2, when mean personal pronoun use per turn reached 0.78. Across lessons associated with increasing proportions of B1-linked turns, personal pronoun use generally rose, with a maximum mean of 1.91 recorded for lessons in which a ratio of 0.61–0.7 of analysed pupil turns were associated with B1 *Benchmarks* descriptors. While mean personal pronoun use fluctuated somewhat (possibly influenced by a reduced availability of data), it attained and remained at a rate of over 1.25 personal pronouns per analysed turn once the ratio of pupil turns linked to B1 in any specific lesson exceeded 0.4.

In general, the mean accuracy rate of personal pronoun use also increased with apparent proficiency development. It was lowest (80% accurate) when all pupil turns within a given lesson could be linked to level A1. It then rose, with some fluctuation, across lessons in which proportionately more pupil turns could be linked to A2 descriptors. Mean accuracy remained over 90% in lessons in which analysed pupil turns were associated with B1 proficiency.

Regarding pronoun omission, while mean omission rates were generally under 10% of recorded personal pronoun use, they appeared somewhat higher when pupils' analysed L2 use was associated with A1 or A2 level (maximum mean omission rate: 12% of personal pronoun use, within proficiency ratio band 0.41–0.5 A2). In lessons in which at least some analysed turns were linked to level B1 *Benchmarks* descriptors, personal pronoun omission was less frequent (mean omission rate was generally at or below 5% of personal pronoun use). However, it should be remembered that lesson-related factors had the potential to influence pupils' personal pronoun use in the selected lessons. It also appeared (from the case studies) that characteristics of pupils' home languages could affect their acquisition of English pronouns to some extent.

Article development

Pupils' use of articles, as indicated in Figure 5.2, appeared to be very infrequent in lessons in which their analysed turns were linked only to A1 *Benchmarks* descriptors (mean use: 0.09 articles per analysed turn). Article production appeared generally to rise in lessons in which more analysed turns were associated with level A2 proficiency, although overall their use remained quite limited. It was only when pupils proved capable of some degree of B1 proficiency that more sustained increases in mean article use were recorded; up to a maximum mean of 1.18 articles per turn when the ratio of analysed turns classified at level B1 was between 0.91 and 1.0.

The accuracy of article use also increased, subject to some fluctuation, with developing English L2 proficiency. From a mean of just 59% in lessons associated solely with A1 *Benchmarks* descriptors, accuracy rates generally rose across lessons in which an increasing proportion of analysed turns could be linked to A2 level descriptors. In lessons in which some proportion of pupils' L2 production could be associated with proficiency level B1, mean article accuracy rates were usually over 90%.

Article omission rates appeared considerably higher for lessons in which pupils' analysed turns were associated with an A1 or A2 level of proficiency. Mean omission rates (calculated as a ratio of article omission to actual article use) were affected, to an extent, by pupils' rates of article production. However, a downward trend was evident as proficiency increased. The frequency of article omission across the A1 and A2 proficiency ratio bands varied from a minimum mean omission rate of 24% of article use to rates which, in some bands, actually exceeded mean article production. This contrasted with the lower rates of omission (mean ranging from 2% to 14% of article use) recorded among lessons in which some pupil turns could be linked to B1 *Benchmarks* descriptors. Typical features of pupils' article use are summarised in Appendix 7. As discussed in relation to specific pupils in Chapter 4, article production was a variable which appeared to be quite sensitive to characteristics of the children's home languages (in which articles were not always present).

Preposition development

Pupils' production of prepositions appeared to be very limited when their analysed turns were associated only with A1 *Benchmarks* descriptors (mean preposition use per turn: 0.02). As higher proportions of A2-linked turns emerged, mean preposition use increased. It rose more sharply and in general more consistently in lessons which included level B1-linked turns. Maximum preposition use, indicated by a mean of 1.15 prepositions per turn, was recorded within the proficiency ratio band 0.81–0.9 B1.

The results displayed in Figure 5.2 suggest that the accuracy of L2 preposition use fluctuated across all three proficiency levels, with mean accuracy rates generally between 70% and 90%. Mean accuracy of preposition use was only occasionally over 90%, although it was more likely to reach this level in lessons which included a proportion of B1-linked turns. The drop in mean accuracy to 50% associated with proficiency ratio band 0.61–0.7 A2 may, however, be explained by the fact that this band included only one lesson and represented the L2 use of a single participant (Vladimir, whose use of prepositions was often quite inaccurate, possibly due to the influence of features of his home language, as was pointed out (in Profile 9) in Chapter 4). Mean preposition omission rates (up to 25% of preposition use) were perceptibly higher in lessons comprising turns linked solely to either A1 or A2 descriptors. When pupils' analysed turns included English L2 use associated with a B1 level of proficiency, mean omission rates were no higher than 8% of corresponding preposition use (and fell to 0% in several of the B1-linked proficiency bands). A more detailed qualitative description of pupils' preposition use across the study period is included in Appendix 7. As noted in relation to articles, preposition use was one of the L2 grammatical indicators which appeared quite susceptible to cross-linguistic influence, as evident in case studies presented in Chapter 4.

Auxiliary development

Auxiliary use in lessons in which pupils' production could be linked only to A1 *Benchmarks* descriptors was very infrequent (mean auxiliary use per turn: 0.01). It rose gradually as more A2-linked turns emerged in pupils' analysed L2 use. However, it was not until turns associated with level B1 were produced that auxiliary use began to increase considerably. It then rose, though not always consistently, to a maximum mean of 0.89 auxiliaries per turn in lessons in which the B1-linked turns accounted for between 0.71 and 0.8 of analysed production.

Regarding the diversity of pupils' auxiliary use and its relation to developing L2 proficiency, the individual profiles presented in Chapter 4 offer descriptions of pupils' auxiliary production. To summarise, more extensive use of a wider range of auxiliaries was evident in the analysed spoken turns recorded for Beatriz (Profile 16), Nasreen (Profile 17) and Fatima (Profile 18) (turns which were frequently associated with B1 descriptors) in comparison to those produced by pupils whose proficiency linked only to levels A1 and A2. Increasing proficiency also impacted on the accuracy of auxiliary production. Accuracy rates rose, with some fluctuation, from 50% when pupils' analysed turns linked solely to A1 descriptors to a rate generally over 90% when B1-linked turns featured in their L2 oral production. Appendix 7 provides a qualitative overview of pupils' auxiliary use illustrating the emergence and development of specific auxiliaries. Our analysis of each pupil's L2 use in the selected lessons (see Chapter 4), suggests that participants' auxiliary production could also have been subject to the influence of classroom interaction patterns (e.g. the opportunities provided for pupils to ask questions). It may also have been affected by cross-linguistic influence (e.g. due to differences in the expression of tense or aspect between the pupils' home languages and English).

Syntactic features

Structural complexity

As explained in Chapter 3, the ratio of nominal to verbal elements calculated for each pupil for each selected lesson was used as a preliminary guide to the structural complexity of their utterances. The distribution of mean verb-to-noun ratios associated with L2 use across the proficiency level bands is shown in Figure 5.3. This graph suggests that overall the verb-to-noun ratio initially rose as evidence emerged of increasing English L2 proficiency. A sharp rise is apparent between the mean ratios recorded among pupils whose analysed turns were linked only to A1 *Benchmarks* descriptors (mean verb-to-noun ratio 0.12) and those associated with oral production in lessons in which A2-linked turns represented 0.11 to 0.2 of pupils' analysed L2 use (mean verb-to-noun ratio 0.48). This corresponds with the evidence, presented above in the discussion of pupils' noun and verb development, of heavily noun-based production and minimal use of verbs in analysed turns linked solely to level A1. Judging from Figures 5.2 and 5.3, a feature of increasing A2-linked language use was a rise in verb production. This brought the mean verb-to-noun ratios associated with evidence of A2 proficiency to within the range 0.4 to 0.59.

When analysed pupil production showed evidence of B1 proficiency, however, the verb-to-noun ratio fluctuated considerably. This may have been due to reduced availability of data and lesson-related factors. However, it is also likely that the more extensive use of both nouns and verbs per turn in

Figure 5.3 Mean verb-to-noun ratio across pupils' recorded proficiency ratios

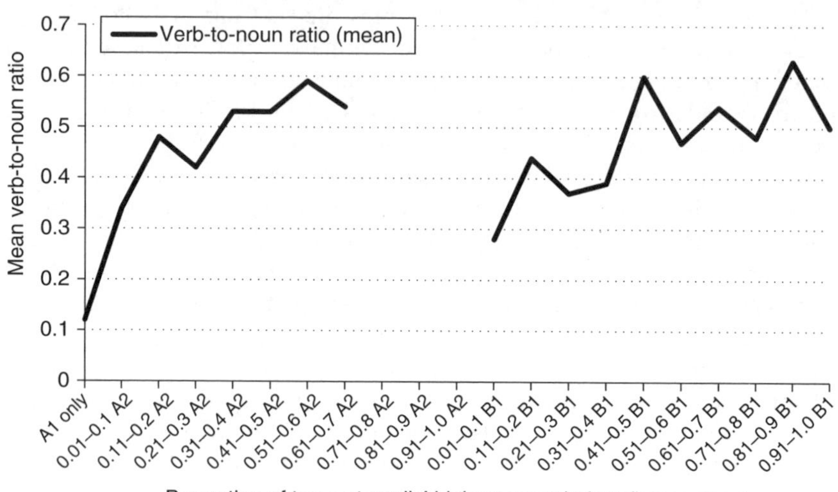

the B1-linked proficiency bands could have balanced each other out to some
extent. The maximum mean verb-to-noun ratio was recorded when 0.81 to 0.9
of all analysed turns were linked to B1 descriptors. However, this finding should
be interpreted alongside the fact that both the mean use of nominals (nouns
and pronouns) and the mean use of verbal elements in bands associated with
evidence of B1 proficiency were generally over 1.0 token per analysed turn. It
would thus appear that the simple calculation of verb-to-noun ratio may have
been less able to capture developments in pupils' L2 structural complexity at
this proficiency level. However, combining results, the ability of pupils whose
turns could be linked to B1 *Benchmarks* descriptors to produce mean values
per turn of >1.0 for nouns, pronouns, and verbs indicated more extensive L2
use. It suggested either that pupils' turns were multi-clausal or that their single-
clause turns were structurally more complex. A summary of pupils' verb-to-
noun ratio across progressive proficiency ratio bands is provided in Appendix
7. Further indicators of structural complexity are evident in the discussion of
negative and question formation and clause linkage, to follow.

Negative formation

Overall results regarding the formation of negative structures were derived
from the qualitative analyses of pupils' individual negation patterns outlined in the case studies. To do this, it was necessary to compare information
regarding the negative forms used by each pupil to that pupil's L2 proficiency
development across the study. It was then possible to group the descriptions of negative formation patterns for each pupil, in accordance with the

proficiency bands outlined in Table 5.2. This meant that features associated with the development of negative structures among all 18 participating pupils could be summarised with reference to their maximum proficiency ratio band, i.e. the band associated with the lesson(s) in which pupils' proportion of turns at their highest recorded level of L2 proficiency was greatest. This final qualitative analysis indicated that pupils' control of L2 negation developed over the course of the study. Evidence from the case studies also suggested that certain features of negative structure development could be linked to particular stages of English L2 proficiency. More detailed findings of this analysis are presented in Appendix 7; its main points are outlined below.

Cumulative analysis of pupils' development of negative structures showed that pupils whose turns were linked solely to A1 level turns tended to rely on the negative marker *no*, often used inaccurately. The marker *not* only began to emerge among pupils who, over the study period, showed some A2-linked English L2 proficiency. As L2 production became more strongly associated with level A2, pupils' use of *not* became more accurate, although over-use of *no* or double negation could lead to inaccuracies. Use of the contracted form of *not* developed (particularly with the auxiliaries *do* and *can*), although auxiliaries were frequently omitted in such structures. As higher proportions of A2-linked turns were recorded in pupils' analysed production, additional negative markers emerged (e.g. *never*). Pupils whose L2 use was becoming more strongly associated with proficiency level B1 could produce *not* in full and contracted form with a wide range of auxiliaries. Increased accuracy was apparent across all negative markers recorded in these pupils' analysed turns.

Question formation

The 18 participating pupils' development of English L2 interrogative structures was analysed using the same approach as that adopted to derive cumulative results for their L2 negative formation. This involved linking the descriptions of question development presented in the case studies to the maximum proficiency ratio band associated with each pupil's analysed L2 use, also taking into account their English L2 development across the study period. The full qualitative summary for L2 question formation is available in Appendix 7.

When pupil production was associated solely with level A1, or to a very limited degree with level A2 (ratio: 0.01–0.1 A2), question structures were usually simple *wh-* questions (e.g. *what is that?*). At this level of English L2 proficiency questioning was otherwise expressed by adding interrogative intonation to declarative statements. Among pupils for whom a higher proportion of turns were linked to A2, attempts at inverted questions began to emerge. These usually involved the copula *be* or auxiliaries, particularly *do* and *can*. For pupils whose maximum proficiency band ratio was in the range

0.11–0.3 A2, these structures were relatively simple (e.g. *do you like X?*). As pupils produced more A2-linked turns, more instances of inversion were recorded. Nevertheless, pupils whose highest proficiency level appeared to be A2 were frequently inaccurate in their attempts to produce inverted questions – omission of required auxiliaries was a typical error. As pupils produced more A2-linked analysed turns, they tended to attempt indirect questions. However, these attempts were often inaccurate and typified by syntactic error. The emergence of question words as relativisers was also noted; particularly as the proportion of A2-linked turns rose among pupils' analysed production.

As pupils' L2 use became more strongly associated with proficiency level B1, their production of inverted and indirect questions became generally accurate, and their use of question words as relativisers was quite frequent. Some issues, however, remained in relation to the formation of more complex questions, for example the conversion of direct speech questions into reported speech forms.

Clause linkage

In a similar manner to that explained above for L2 negative and question formation, a qualitative overview of the 18 participating pupils' linkage of clauses was derived from the individual case studies. Overall results are presented in greater depth in Appendix 7. To summarise these, it appeared from the cumulative analysis that clause linkage emerged as pupils' recorded L2 production began to include a small proportion of turns associated with *Benchmarks* level A2. Initially, it involved the use of simple co-ordinating conjunctions (typically *and*) to link short clauses. As pupils produced more A2-linked turns, the occasional use of the subordinating conjunction *because* and the isolated use of *if* was recorded. The use of relativisers and infrequent, usually unsuccessful, attempts at *that*-clauses also featured among pupils' A2-linked turns, particularly as their L2 use became more predominantly associated with this level of proficiency. Pupils for whom turns associated with B1 were recorded seemed to be quite capable of using subordinating conjunctions and a range of relativisers to construct more complex utterances. More accurate clause linkage using *that* was also recorded towards the end of the study.

Overall relation between grammatical indicators and Benchmarks descriptors

The cumulative analysis of specific features of L2 morpho-syntactic development, outlined above, is summarised in Figure 5.4. It shows clear grammatical progression in the analysed L2 oral production of the participating pupils as their L2 use coincided with higher *Benchmarks* proficiency levels.

Figure 5.4 Summary of quantitative and qualitative results regarding the relation between grammatical indicators of L2 acquisition and the Benchmarks proficiency levels

Increasing use of quantitatively analysed indicators: nouns, verbs, personal pronouns, articles, prepositions, auxiliaries.
Increasing accuracy of indicator use, subject to fluctuation as production rate increases.
Structural complexity developing from noun-based production in the early stages of L2 development.
Development in range and accuracy of syntactic indicators analysed by qualitative methods only: negative and question formation, clause linkage.

Grammatical indicator	A1-linked L2 use (Maximum proficiency ratio band: 1.0 A1)	A2-linked L2 use emerging (Maximum proficiency ratio band in the range: 0.01–0.3 A2)	A2-linked L2 use increasing (Maximum proficiency ratio band in the range: 0.31–0.7 A2)	B1-linked L2 use increasing (Maximum proficiency ratio band in the range: 0.61–1.0 B1)
Noun use	Limited range of nouns, infrequent pluralisation. Typical errors: lexis, non-pluralisation.	Increasing noun production. Some pluralisation, isolated attempts at possessive marking. Typical errors: lexis, pluralisation, non-marking of possession.	Increasing and more accurate noun use. Greater accuracy in pluralisation, occasional marking of possession. Typical errors: lexis, over-generalisation of irregular plurals, non-marking of possession.	Wide range of generally accurate noun use. Generally successful pluralisation and marking of possession. Typical errors (infrequent): lexis, over-generalisation of irregular plurals, non-marking of possession.
Verb use	Limited, often inaccurate verb use – non-inflected stem verbs and copula *be* (present tense). Typical errors: no inflection in required contexts.	Limited but increasing verb use. Generally non-inflected stem verbs and copula *be* in present tense. Attempts at progressive -*ing* form,	Increasing verb use, accuracy increasing subject to fluctuation. Production generally of non-inflected verbs and copula *be*, but	Wide range of more accurate verb use. Generally appropriate production of present and past tense forms (irregular and

Figure 5.4 (continued)

Grammatical indicator	A1-linked L2 use (Maximum proficiency ratio band: 1.0 A1)	A2-linked L2 use emerging (Maximum proficiency ratio band in the range: 0.01–0.3 A2)	A2-linked L2 use increasing (Maximum proficiency ratio band in the range: 0.31–0.7 A2)	B1-linked L2 use increasing (Maximum proficiency ratio band in the range: 0.61–1.0 B1)
Verb use (continued)		and irregular past tense, isolated production of past participle. Typical errors: non-inflection (omission of 3rd person -*s*), tense and aspect choice.	progressive and past forms emerging (usually irregular, some regular). Occasional appropriate use of present and past participles. Typical errors: non-inflection (omission of 3rd person -*s*), tense and aspect choice.	regular). Generally accurate marking of aspect and use of participles. Typical errors (infrequent): occasional over-generalisation of regular -*ed* ending to irregular past forms, slight confusion of past/perfect forms.
Pronoun use	Limited pronoun use. Personal pronouns infrequently but generally accurately used, infrequent omission (although obligatory contexts limited). Typical errors: pluralisation, use of personal pronouns for possession.	Limited range of pronouns, but some diversification across study. Accuracy of personal pronoun use subject to fluctuation, with relatively frequent omission. Typical errors: case, also number and gender.	Increasingly diverse pronoun use. Personal pronoun use becoming more accurate, with infrequent omission. Typical errors: case, number, gender.	Wide range of pronouns used. Personal pronoun use generally accurate with very infrequent omission. Typical errors (infrequent): gender confusion.
Article use	Very limited article use, often inaccurate, with frequent omission. Typical errors: non-required article use, inappropriate article choice.	Limited article use, with fluctuating accuracy and frequent omission. Typical errors: non-required article use, inappropriate article choice, use of *a* before vowel.	Increasing article use, accuracy fluctuating. Considerable omission, although becoming less frequent. Typical errors: non-required article use, inappropriate article choice, use of *a* before vowel.	Substantial, generally accurate article use with low rate of omission. Typical errors (infrequent): non-required article use, inappropriate article choice, use of *a* before vowel.

Preposition use	Very limited preposition use (e.g. within lexical phrase).	Very limited preposition use, generally accurate but with some omission. Typical errors: inappropriate preposition choice (e.g. *in* for *on*).	Increasing and more diverse preposition use. Accuracy increasing, subject to fluctuation, omission generally infrequent. Typical errors: inappropriate preposition choice (e.g. *in* for *on*, *to*, *into*; *for*/*to* confusion).	Frequent use of diverse range of prepositions. Generally accurate use, with infrequent omission. Typical errors (infrequent): inappropriate preposition choice.
Auxiliary use	Very limited and inaccurate auxiliary use. Typical errors: non-required use of auxiliary *be*.	Very limited, often inaccurate auxiliary use – typically: *be, do, can* in present tense contexts – with frequent omission. Typical errors: non-required use of auxiliary *be*, syntactic placement of auxiliaries.	Increasing use of auxiliaries – typically: *be, do* (present and past tense contexts), modals: *can* and *have to*; occasionally tense markers: *will, going to* and *have*; isolated attempts at *could, would*. Accuracy fluctuating, with omission also considerable. Typical errors: non-required use of *be*, inappropriate auxiliary choice (e.g. *be* for *do*; *can* for *could*).	Frequent use of diverse range of auxiliaries: in present and past tense contexts; for future reference; expressing ability, obligation, probability and conditionality (e.g. *must, might, would, could*). Generally accurate use, omission becoming infrequent. Typical errors (infrequent): tense, syntax, choice of conditional modal.
Verb-to-noun ratio	Predominantly nominal-based production.	Predominantly nominal-based production, but increasing use of verbal forms.	Verb-to-noun ratio generally increasing, subject to possible influence of lesson-related factors.	Verb-to-noun ratio reasonably stable, may require more sensitive measure of structural complexity.

Figure 5.4 (continued)

Grammatical indicator	A1-linked L2 use (Maximum proficiency ratio band: 1.0 A1)	A2-linked L2 use emerging (Maximum proficiency ratio band in the range: 0.01–0.3 A2)	A2-linked L2 use increasing (Maximum proficiency ratio band in the range: 0.31–0.7 A2)	B1-linked L2 use increasing (Maximum proficiency ratio band in the range: 0.61–1.0 B1)
Negative formation	Negative marker *no* used in all contexts – often inaccurate.	Negative marker *no* often inaccurately used. *Not* emerging as negative marker, also used in contraction with auxiliaries.	Negative marker *not* increasingly used as appropriate (full and contracted form), less frequent inaccurate use of *no*. Emergence of *never* as negative marker.	Generally accurate use of *not* across wide range of contexts. Negative markers *no* and *never* also accurately used. Infrequent errors (e.g. double negation).
Question formation	Basic *wh-* questions (e.g. *where is X?*), infrequently used.	Basic *wh-* questions, attempts at inversion generally inaccurate. Isolated attempts at indirect questions syntactically inaccurate; isolated use of question-word as relativiser.	Basic *wh-* questions, but more frequent attempts at inversion, although often inaccurate (syntax issues, omission of auxiliaries). Occasional attempts at indirect questions (often inaccurate) and use of question-words as relativisers.	Basic *wh-* questions, but frequent and often successful attempts at inversion. Indirect and reported-speech questions also produced and question-words used as relativisers. Some syntactic errors persist.
Clause linkage	No recorded instances of clause linkage (production confined to simple single-clause structures).	Clause linkage with simple co-ordinating conjunctions. Occasional use of subordinating conjunctions *because* and, less frequently, *if*; isolated attempts at *that* clauses.	Increasing use of sub-ordinating conjunctions (*because* and, occasionally, *if*); emergence of relativisers.	Frequent and generally accurate use of subordinating conjunctions (*because, if*) and a range of relativisers; *that* clauses also used.

The development of the features highlighted, informed by specific aspects of their use emerging from the 18 case studies (as summarised in Appendix 7), seems to correspond to the progression suggested in the *Benchmarks'* global scales of underlying linguistic competence for grammatical accuracy (see Appendix 2).

The evidence of EAL pupils' English L2 acquisition provided by this overall analysis of the 10 grammatical indicators also suggests progression in the type of language functions that pupils could perform as their L2 proficiency increased. The development of functions requiring greater structural complexity (e.g. question formation or clause linkage) appeared to be associated with turns in which pupils' oral L2 use was linked to higher *Benchmarks* proficiency levels (A2 and B1). This functional progression seemed to reflect the one predicted by the global benchmarks of communicative proficiency (Integrate Ireland Language and Training 2003a:6–7; see Appendix 2). This is illustrated in the following examples of pupils' L2 use.

The first two examples show how the L2 proficiency of Andrei (Profile 15) developed both formally and functionally. In Lesson 9, he typically used mere intonation for the purpose of questioning, as in this level A1-linked 'basic request' for clarification regarding whether he should colour a picture:

> *Andrei*: teacher . . . colour this?

Four months later, in Lesson 17, his ability to 'sustain a conversational exchange . . . when carrying out a learning activity' was evident in this more complex request (to do an art activity already completed by another lesson group). While his negative question formation is still inaccurate, these consecutive A2-linked turns show formal and functional progression:

> *Andrei*: I want to do my name.
> *Andrei*: I want my name, why I no write my name in paint.

In the next extract, from Fatima's recollection of the story of *Charlie and the Chocolate Factory*, the formal complexity of this B1-linked turn (e.g. its use of clause linkage) is appropriate to its function – 'to retell the plot of . . . a book he/she has read':

> *Fatima*: and he just em, he just eh now when- when he puts the bar- the chocolate bar into a wooden box and eh he looks at it and look and he looked at it every day and when he couldn't resist to eat it he just eh bite a li-, he just bites a little.

Since our study focused predominantly on the development of EAL pupils' L2 oral skills, the results of this cumulative form-function analysis relate most closely to the global scales provided for spoken interaction and spoken production. The descriptors for spoken interaction accounted for considerably more of the skill-based links in the analysed oral data than those for spoken production, due to the highly interactive nature of classroom communication with young children. However, since spoken interaction involves both listening and speaking skills, results obtained for this skill also related to the development of English L2 listening abilities. Accordingly, our results offer indirect evidence to support the progression of skills suggested in the *Benchmarks'* global scale for listening (see Appendix 2).

Overall results – L2 lexical indicators

It is not an easy task to summarise L2 lexical development across a diverse sample of EAL pupils of different ages, backgrounds and previous cultural and educational experience, attending different schools and belonging to different lesson groups. However, a cursory look at the descriptions of the semantic fields recorded for each of the 18 pupils in Chapter 4 (see also Appendix 6 for summary) reveals similarities in the topics emerging from pupils' analysed spoken turns. In part, this was influenced by the fact that the themes included in the 13 units of work in Part II of the *Benchmarks* were used by some of the teachers in Schools 1 and 2 as a direct guide to their lesson planning. However, even in these schools, teachers applied the *Benchmarks* in a very flexible manner, taking into consideration the individual language learning needs of the children involved in each lesson group and their stage of cognitive development. As noted in Chapter 3, the *Benchmarks* were not the sole resource used to plan the lessons recorded in this study; a wide range of mainstream materials also featured in these English language support classes. Furthermore, in School 3 English language support was not designed with any reference to the *Benchmarks* (although accompanying resources such as *My First English Book* (Integrate Ireland Language and Training 2005) were occasionally used). The fact that the semantic themes covered by the participants in different schools and lesson groups could be identified with the units of work may be due, therefore, to the consistency of these units with the primary curriculum. As pointed out in Chapter 2, the units of work were developed to reflect recurrent curriculum themes with which EAL pupils must engage. The prevalence of topics associated with the units of work in the recorded lessons thus suggests that the *Benchmarks* offer an appropriate guide to the English L2 semantic development of young EAL learners at primary school in Ireland.

That is not to say, however, that these units explicitly cover all the topics emerging from the L2 lexis recorded for the 18 participating pupils. As explained in Chapter 3, Data Analysis Phase I involved the functional coding of pupils' recorded turns. This meant deciding which *Benchmarks* descriptor could most appropriately be linked to each individual turn. This required coding decisions to be made in relation to semantic themes, as well as in relation to language skill and proficiency level. Any turns which, for thematic reasons, could not be associated with a particular *Benchmarks* descriptor were noted. Based on these turns, we compiled a list of suggestions for the possible revision or expansion of the *Benchmarks* topics (see Appendix 5). Further recommendations were also made with regard to turns which could be approximately linked to existing *Benchmarks* descriptors. Often, as shown in Chapter 3, these approximations related to language function. However, in some cases they suggested that more explicit reference to a particular topic might be required (either within one of the current units of work or as part of a new theme). These additional thematic associations were recorded for each lesson group before the more focused investigation of *Benchmarks*-linked turns began in Data Analysis Phase II (details of all suggestions made regarding approximations to specific descriptors can be found in Appendix 5).

Considering all turns analysed for the participating pupils in Data Analysis Phase I, topics identified as possibly deserving more explicit reference in the *Benchmarks* included: body, health and actions; toys, games and leisure activities; home and household items; numbers and mathematical terms; music, songs and rhymes; characters, fantasy and stories; physical features of the natural world and universe. It would be unreasonable and potentially restrictive to expect the *Benchmarks* to describe the entire range of themes with which EAL pupils may wish or be required to engage. Also, many of the topics highlighted above are already implied in the existing units of work (e.g. 'body, health and actions' as part of Unit 1, Myself). However, some extension of the *Benchmarks* to cover these additional areas might further help teachers to plan the delivery of English language support.

An examination of the themes covered by the recorded data indicates that, on the whole, Part II of the *Benchmarks* adequately describes L2 use across most of the thematic areas commonly encountered by EAL pupils at primary school in Ireland. We will now look at pupils' L2 lexical development within these themes. Given the infinite diversity of lexis which may be associated with any particular topic, determining actual L2 lexical development is very challenging and, in a longitudinal study like this one, impossible to quantify fully. However, some indicators outlined in the case studies can at least give an impression of participants' use of L2 lexis over the study period. By deriving these overall findings from the individual data, we can compare features of pupils' L2 lexical development to the learning outcomes associated with relevant *Benchmarks* descriptors for L2 linguistic competence (i.e. vocabulary control, see Appendix 2).

The examples of lexical production included in the 18 case studies provide a preliminary indication of how pupils could communicate meaning in relation to the themes evident in their analysed L2 use. A glance through the profiles at the L2 lexis produced by pupils in the very early stages of English L2 development (e.g. Dimitrie (Profile 3), Karina (Profile 2) and Zofia (Profile 1)) and that produced by pupils nearing the end of their second year of English language support (e.g. Beatriz (Profile 16), Nasreen (Profile 17) and Fatima (Profile 18)) suggests a marked increase in L2 lexical competence as L2 acquisition progresses. However, a more informative comparison of pupils' lexical development may be obtained by cumulatively analysing data relating to the number of individual Wordlist entries recorded for each pupil in each of the selected lessons. As explained in Chapter 3, data obtained using the Wordlist program in Data Analysis Phase II was used as a basic indicator of pupils' lexical range. The results derived for the total number of Wordlist entries offered a useful guide to the number of word-forms to be found in each pupil's analysed turns for each lesson selected. This information could then serve as a basis for overall analysis of L2 lexical development among all 18 participating pupils.

We compared the 18 pupils' Wordlist entry results using an approach similar to the one we devised to compare their production of grammatical indicators of English L2 acquisition. This involved bringing together information associated with lessons in which pupils exhibited an equivalent degree of L2 proficiency, again using the 'proficiency ratio bands' to indicate the proportion of analysed turns at pupils' highest recorded proficiency within any given lesson. For each of these proficiency bands, a mean was calculated for Wordlist entries per analysed turn. This was derived by combining the Wordlist results recorded for individual pupils in lessons in which they demonstrated a similar proportion of turns at their highest proficiency level (e.g. results for all lessons in which, according to the *Benchmarks* associated with their analysed spoken turns, pupils' proficiency ratio was 0.11–0.2 A2). Means across the proficiency bands – from lessons comprising turns linked solely to level A1 to those in which 0.91–1.0 of turns could be associated with B1 – were then plotted to produce the graph shown in Figure 5.5.

Figure 5.5 indicates a clear rise in the mean number of Wordlist entries per analysed turn produced by pupils at successive stages of English L2 proficiency. Fewer than 1.3 Wordlist entries per turn were recorded when the ratio of pupils' analysed spoken turns was 0.3 A2-linked or less. However, as pupils demonstrated evidence of B1 proficiency, this indicator of L2 lexical production increased to a mean which was consistently and often considerably more than 2 Wordlist entries per analysed turn (reaching a maximum of 4.42 when a ratio of between 0.9 and 1.0 of analysed spoken turns were classifiable as B1). This rising trend is all the more striking given the huge potential for distortion in any attempt to analyse naturally occurring L2 lexis. A clear overall relation between L2 lexical development and increasing L2 proficiency emerged, despite the wide range of vocabulary requirements associated with specific classroom topics and tasks, not to mention issues related

Figure 5.5 Mean Wordlist entries per analysed turn across L2 proficiency ratios

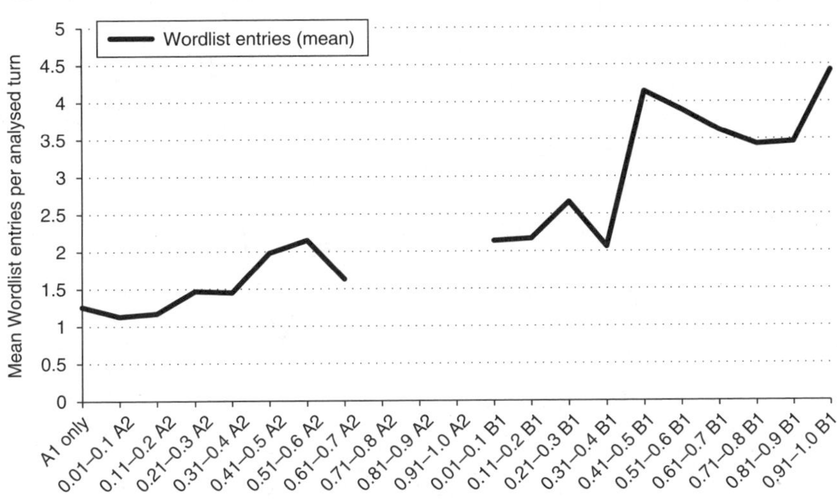

to the relative shortage of data associated with higher proficiency levels. If we take the data obtained regarding the 18 pupils' Wordlist entries to be an appropriate measure of their English L2 lexical range, it seems that the progression of 'vocabulary control' described in the global scales of underlying linguistic competence in Part I of the *Benchmarks* (see Appendix 2) corresponds well with the empirical evidence obtained from our study.

More detailed evidence in relation to a specific aspect of lexical development, the emergence of verb lexemes, could also be gleaned from the case studies. Results for this variable have likewise been compared across the 18 participating pupils. Mean values were calculated for 'verb lexeme per analysed turn' within each selected lesson in order to compensate for differences in lesson length and other classroom factors which could affect individual L2 production (e.g. size of lesson group). These values could then be grouped together for lessons in which the *Benchmarks* links to pupils' analysed spoken turns revealed similar proportions of L2 use at pupils' highest proficiency level in order to obtain overall results. These results are illustrated graphically in Figure 5.6. They give some indication of how L2 lexical diversification generally increased with evidence of rising L2 proficiency.

Mean verb lexemes per analysed turn reached a peak of 0.83 when the proficiency ratio for analysed oral production was in the region 0.91–0.1 B1. Some fluctuations were recorded, for example the slight drops associated with a proficiency ratio band in which a ratio of 0.61–0.7 of analysed turns linked to A2 descriptors, and a band in which 0.21–0.3 of turns were at level B1.

Figure 5.6 Mean verb lexemes per analysed turn across L2 proficiency ratios

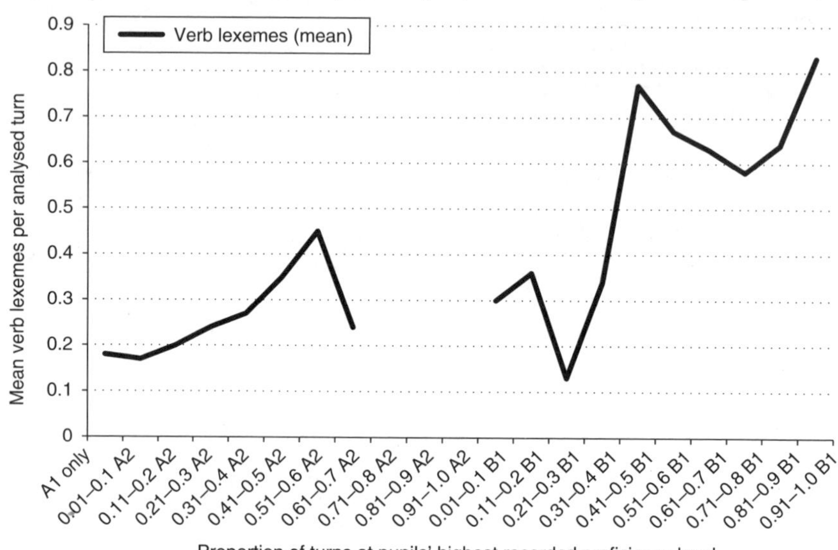

However, these seemed to reflect shortage of data and lesson-related factors rather than any definite pattern of L2 acquisition (both these bands were represented by one pupil and one lesson only).

A closer investigation of the overall number of distinct verb lexemes produced by individual pupils over the study period was then conducted. This allowed evidence of pupils' L2 verb acquisition to be compared as thoroughly as possible with indicators of their highest recorded English L2 proficiency. For each pupil, this was referenced to the maximum proportion of analysed turns produced at their highest recorded proficiency level (e.g. Beatriz reached a maximum of 0.61–0.7 B1). Table 5.3 shows the total number of distinct verb lexemes present in the data.

While it is clear that lesson length and availability of data per pupil influenced verb lexeme records to some extent, it nonetheless seems that pupils' L2 verb lexicon expanded as their English language proficiency increased. Such a trend is apparent both from the raw scores for recorded verb lexemes and from the ratio of verb lexemes to total number of analysed turns. Examples of the actual verb lexis used by pupils can be found in Chapter 4. From the case studies, there is a stark contrast between the very limited repertoire (eight verb lexemes) of a pupil whose proficiency could be linked only to level A1 *Benchmarks* descriptors over the course of the study (Zofia – Profile 1), and that of a pupil whose analysed production was predominantly associated with level B1 descriptors (Fatima – Profile 18), whose recorded range spanned 90 distinct verb lexemes). Thus, it appears that the expansion in lexical diversity

Table 5.3 Overall number of verb lexemes used by pupils across study

Maximum proportion of turns at highest recorded proficiency level	Pupils involved	Total no. verb lexemes	Total no. turns	Overall verb lexemes/turn
A1 only	Zofia	8	111	0.072
0.01–0.1 A2	Karina	22	316	0.070
0.11–0.2 A2	Patryk	33	385	0.086
0.21–0.3 A2	Tomasz	27	217	0.124
	Ravi	45	563	0.080
	Dimitrie	19	155	0.123
0.31–0.4 A2	Ivan	44	466	0.094
	Jin	52	556	0.094
0.41–0.5 A2	Stefan	42	653	0.064
	Lukas	55	628	0.088
	Edyta	56	425	0.132
0.51–0.6 A2	Andrei	77	1,188	0.069
	Constantin	60	434	0.138
	Marko	38	227	0.167
0.61–0.7 A2	Vladimir	53	276	0.192
0.61–0.7 B1	Beatriz	55	220	0.250
0.71–0.8 B1	Nasreen	77	376	0.205
0.91–1.0 B1	Fatima	90	259	0.347

across proficiency levels A1, A2 and B1 envisaged in the *Benchmarks'* global scale for vocabulary control (see Appendix 2) is reflected by the overall results we obtained.

It should be noted that verb lexemes were the focus of this closer investigation into the development of L2 lexical diversity because they could offer the most appropriate empirical evidence in this regard. The reason for this was that, while verbs were relatively numerous in pupils' analysed spoken turns, they appeared to be slightly less influenced by classroom factors (e.g. topic and activity choice within a particular lesson) than nouns, the other main linguistic category of content lexis. Throughout the study, pupils' English L2 verb use often involved lexis that seemed to be quite thoroughly acquired. Their L2 noun use appeared more likely to include early, but possibly isolated and easily forgotten, attempts at new vocabulary, such as words encountered briefly in the course of a specific lesson (e.g. in naming activities). Examples of noun lexis can be found in each of the case studies, along with some of the adjectives that the 18 pupils produced (see also Appendix 6). As with their L2 verbs, increasing lexical complexity is apparent in the nouns and adjectives produced by EAL pupils as their L2 proficiency developed from predominantly A1 production to L2 use associated with level B1.

The Wordlist data files for each pupil, for each selected lesson, also highlighted some further examples of function words – grammatically encoded lexis – within participants' analysed English L2 use. Based on the recorded data, several of these elements which appeared prominently in pupils' L2 use were selected for qualitative analysis. These included: adverb range, use of possessive adjectives (and their lexical diversity), and the production of comparative or superlative adjectives. These features were analysed with respect to the maximum proficiency ratio band attained by specific pupils over the study period (adopting an approach similar to the one we used for the qualitative analysis of the grammatical variables discussed in the previous section). The results of this analysis are summarised in Figure 5.7, with further detail provided in Appendix 7. Evidence emerged to show the development of these additional L2 lexico-grammatical indicators (adverbs, possessive determiners, comparative and superlative forms of adjectives) as pupils' L2 proficiency increased.

These results further suggest that the *Benchmarks* descriptors reflect English L2 development, not only in their outline of the communicative tasks EAL pupils can progressively accomplish through their L2 but 'how well', linguistically, they can perform them. Figure 5.7 provides an overview of the evidence of pupils' L2 lexical development, based on the indicators investigated in this study. In addition to the statistical evidence derived from the quantitative analysis of specific lexical features (see Figures 5.5 and 5.6 and Table 5.3), this summary includes examples of actual L2 lexis from the case studies. It illustrates how the patterns associated with participants' acquisition of L2 lexis correspond with the *Benchmarks* descriptors for vocabulary control presented in Appendix 2.

Relation between evidence of L2 acquisition and the Benchmarks – L2 literacy development

In reporting our overall results, we have thus far concentrated on the relation between the 18 participating pupils' English L2 oral development and aspects of the *Benchmarks* relating to oral communicative skills and underlying linguistic competence. This is in accordance with the primary aim of our study, which was to explore the relation (if any) between EAL pupils' English L2 acquisition and the learning outcomes summarised in the *Benchmarks*, using recordings of participants' L2 oral production as best evidence of their L2 acquisition. It was also important, however, to investigate their L2 literacy development to the extent that our data allowed.

Most of the literacy-related data we obtained came from pupils in Schools 1 and 3; as mentioned in Chapter 4, the recorded lessons for School 2 tended to focus on oral activities. Accordingly, the observations that follow are primarily derived from participants enrolled in Schools 1 and 3, though they seem to be confirmed by evidence of pupils' L2 literacy development collected in School 2. Generally speaking, the literacy activities recorded for participating pupils from the Infant Classes (aged approximately 4–6 years) were very similar to those with which they would engage, alongside native

Figure 5.7 Summary of quantitative and qualitative results regarding the relation between lexical indicators of L2 acquisition and the Benchmarks proficiency levels

Increasing lexical range (based on quantitative analysis of Wordlist entries).
Broadening and deepening of semantic range (themes, specificity of vocabulary).
Diversification of verb lexemes produced.
Lexical diversification of nouns and adjectives.
Widening range of lexico-grammatical features, with lexical development apparent within these emerging categories.

Lexical indicator	A1-linked L2 use (Max ratio 1.0 A1)	A2-linked L2 use emerging (Max ratio 0.01–0.3 A2)	A2-linked L2 use increasing (Max ratio 0.31–0.7 A2)	B1-linked L2 use increasing (Max ratio 0.61–1.0 B1)
Verb lexemes	Verb use across very limited lexical range (e.g. *be, have, look, like*).	Verb use limited in lexical range, although evidence of diversification (e.g. *go, want, eat, run, write*).	Verb use increasing in lexical range, verbs becoming more specific (e.g. *allow, crunch, kick, grow, paint*).	Wide range of verb lexemes used to express specific concepts (e.g. *become, collect, tickle, celebrate, measure*).
Nouns and adjectives	Limited range of very simple nouns (e.g. *pencil, baby*) and adjectives (e.g. *yellow, big*) across semantic themes of immediate relevance.	Increasing range of basic nouns (e.g. *coat, shop*) and adjectives (e.g. *pink, cloudy*), with occasional use of slightly more specific lexis often relating to personal interests (e.g. *dinosaur*), across more diverse semantic fields.	Wide range of basic nouns and adjectives with some more specific lexis also used (e.g. *raspberry, vet, golden, stinky*) across diversity of semantic themes.	Wide range of more specific nouns (e.g. *tornado, snowdrop*) and adjectives (e.g. *disgusting, famous*) used across diversity of semantic themes.

Figure 5.7 (continued)

Lexical indicator	A1-linked L2 use (Max ratio 1.0 A1)	A2-linked L2 use emerging (Max ratio 0.01–0.3 A2)	A2-linked L2 use increasing (Max ratio 0.31–0.7 A2)	B1-linked B2 use increasing (Max ratio 0.61–1.0 B1)
Additional lexico-grammatical indicators	Isolated use of basic adverbs (e.g. *here, there*); occasional use of possessive determiners of immediate relevance (*my, your*).	Limited range of adverbs to mark location, time and frequency or as modifiers (e.g. *again, very*); limited use of possessive determiners of immediate relevance; emergence of comparative adjectives (e.g. *higher*) but use generally inaccurate.	Increasing use of adverbs (e.g. *sometimes, almost*), widening range of possessive determiners (e.g. *his, their*); occasional accurate use of comparative adjectives (e.g. *bigger*).	Frequent use of diverse range of adverbs; wide range of possessive determiners used; comparative and superlative adjectives (e.g. *better, worst*) accurately used.

English-speaking peers, in the mainstream classroom. For pupils who belonged to First and Second Class (aged 7–8 years), recorded literacy activities appeared more linguistically demanding. In terms of complexity, they generally approached the degree of challenge posed by mainstream classroom reading or writing tasks, although they were often simplified versions of such tasks. The oldest of the 18 participating pupils was in mainstream Third Class (aged 10 years at the end the research period), and the literacy activities she took part in were both age-appropriate and considerably more demanding than those with which the younger children engaged. To summarise the specific challenges faced by pupils at different educational stages, we will describe features of the pupils' L2 literacy development on the basis of their age/school class. We will focus first on children who were in the Infant Classes during the study and then consider pupils who were in First, Second or Third Class.

L2 literacy development – pupils in Infant Classes

In all, nine pupils – Tomasz, Patryk, Marko, Dimitrie, Jin, Vladimir, Edyta, Karina and Zofia – were in Junior Infants. Although they generally engaged in oral activities during their English language support lessons, they also showed the capacity to participate in simple emergent literacy tasks in a manner not dissimilar to their mainstream English-speaking peers. Such activities included: identification of basic grapho-phonic relations, recognition of letter names, association of rhyming sounds, recognition of familiar thematically linked words often presented on flashcards, reading of short, familiar phrases (e.g. *Today is . . .*), or sentences from a simple class reader, as well as copying familiar words or short sentences with pictorial support. These activities, which involved the use of very simple vocabulary and structures, were typically associated with level A1 *Benchmarks* descriptors for reading and writing, for example, the Unit 3 (Food and clothes) A1 descriptor for reading: 'Can recognise and understand the names of basic foods' (Integrate Ireland Language and Training 2003a:12). Although they required considerable support from the teacher, even pupils whose oral L2 production was associated predominantly with A1 descriptors showed evidence of participation in such activities. In general, their performance was in keeping with the literacy ability anticipated for native English-speaking children of a similar age.

Only two EAL pupils in Senior Infants were involved in this study: Ivan (Profile 10) and Constantin (Profile 11). Due to scheduling issues and Ivan's departure from Ireland during the study, their participation was somewhat limited (see relevant case studies for details). Both of these pupils were in their second year of English language support, so their introduction to L2 literacy would have begun the previous year, when they were in Junior Infants. While recorded literacy-related activities for these two pupils were not extensive, the reading tasks they engaged in suggested that – like the Junior Infants participants discussed above – they were able to take part in a range of basic literacy-focused tasks.

However, it appeared that Ivan and Constantin both experienced literacy-related difficulties as these tasks became slightly more challenging. This was despite the fact that, judging by the *Benchmarks* descriptors associated with their analysed spoken turns, these pupils were more proficient than most of the Junior Infants pupils in terms of their oral L2 skills (Ivan attained a maximum proficiency ratio of 0.31–0.4 A2; while Constantin's maximum proficiency ratio was 0.51–0.6 A2). The recognition of new content lexis often seemed difficult for these pupils. Their encounters with less common short words used to exemplify rhyming sounds in phonics-based tasks (e.g. *wig* and *mug*) were typical in this regard. Also, the reading of L2 function lexis, which – judging from their L2 oral use – may not have been fully acquired, proved very challenging. Such difficulties were particularly evident in their frequent misreading of basic 'sight vocabulary', either on flashcards or in simple illustrated readers.

Ivan and Constantin were both members of lesson groups which also included pupils of Nigerian background who were not included in the final data analysis for the linguistic reasons given in Chapter 3. However, they clearly found literacy tasks more difficult than the other group members, who had probably had some experience of oral English from infancy. This suggests that although in the early stages of literacy development EAL pupils appear to keep pace with their native English-speaking peers, they may subsequently fall behind. Even by the second year of schooling it appeared that, as literacy-related tasks moved slightly beyond A1 proficiency, EAL pupils required substantial additional support. It was also clear that these two pupils found it difficult to keep up with mainstream literacy targets for the Senior Infants class. This was evident in Constantin's reading from age-appropriate readers (see Chapter 4). For example, his struggling attempt to read a short book about a racing car constituted a less than successful engagement with a task linked to the *Benchmarks* Unit 7 (Transport and travel) A2 descriptor for reading: 'Can read and understand the key points in a short text about travelling or transport' (Integrate Ireland Language and Training 2003a:16).

On the basis of limited evidence for just two pupils, it would be premature to conclude that all EAL pupils of a similar age are likely to face these difficulties – even when developing literacy skills in their native language, individual children experience widely different degrees of challenge. Also, in the present study, Beatriz (Profile 16) and Nasreen (Profile 17) had entered English language support in the Senior Infants class and by the following year had managed to acquire quite extensive English literacy skills. However, it is foreseeable that at least some EAL pupils may require continuing L2 literacy support even when their L2 oral proficiency is sufficient to meet their social and classroom needs.

The challenges faced by Ivan and Constantin highlight the distinction made by Cummins (1979, 2000) *between basic interpersonal communication skills* (BICS), which are often acquired within the first two years of education in an L2-dominant environment, and *cognitive academic language proficiency* (CALP), which may require much longer to develop. Fundamental to ultimate academic success, CALP encompasses 'expertise in understanding and using literacy-related aspects of language' (Cummins 2000:70), so developing L2 CALP is essential for EAL pupils if they are to engage fully with the mainstream primary curriculum. In the early years of primary education, language use may appear to involve a greater use of BICS than CALP, although Cummins cautions against viewing any BICS/CALP distinction as a 'simple dichotomy' (Cummins 2000:73). In any case, the relation between age and cognitive development determines the language required for classroom tasks; 'academic' language for a six-year-old is, among other things, the language associated with simple literacy or numeracy activities. At the same time, evidence from our study showed that even in the Infant Classes, the language used in reading and writing activities is often more specific and/or less contextualised than the language used in everyday oral interaction (e.g. the use of less familiar vocabulary to illustrate phonic patterns). Inevitably, however, as children get older, the CALP component of the language of schooling increases as the primary curriculum poses greater cognitive challenges and becomes more subject specific.

L2 literacy development – pupils from First to Third Class

Not surprisingly, the need for sustained support in relation to L2 literacy emerged even more clearly from the experience of many of the participating pupils who were in mainstream First Class or higher. We will consider the issues facing these remaining participants in two stages, dealing first with the literacy-related challenges evident in the data for pupils in their first year of English language support (Andrei (Profile 15), Stefan (Profile 14), Ravi (Profile 12) and Lukas (Profile 13)), and then focusing on the evidence available for pupils in their second year of support (Beatriz, Nasreen and Fatima (Profile 18)).

Regarding the first group, Andrei, Stefan and Lukas were all in mainstream First Class during the study period, while Ravi was in mainstream Second Class. At the beginning of their participation in the study, all four children were relatively new to English and their ratio of analysed turns at their highest proficiency level ranged from A1 only to 0.51–0.6 A2. Generally, although their L2 oral skills were relatively limited, they could engage with a wider range of literacy-related activities than participants who were in the Infant Classes. Although many of the reading and writing activities they engaged in were still associated with A1 descriptors (e.g. reading words on flashcards, copying or writing words and short phrases), they were able to attempt activities linked to A2 descriptors at quite an early stage. For example, reading short stories about animals could be associated with the *Benchmarks* descriptor included in Unit 12 (Animals and plants) for A2 level reading: 'Can read and understand very short and simple texts about animals, provided they contain a high proportion of familiar words and use appropriate visual support' (Integrate Ireland Language and Training 2003a:21).

Stefan, Ravi and Lukas all seemed to have some previous experience of (home-language) literacy. This sometimes led to minor cases of confusion (see notes in Chapter 4 regarding Lukas's identification of grapho-phonic relationships). However, overall it seemed that these three pupils progressed more quickly in their English L2 literacy development than either younger pupils at a comparable level of L2 oral skills development or Andrei, who did not seem to have any home-language literacy skills. For Stefan, Ravi and Lukas, it also seemed that the development of L2 literacy – possibly supported by experience of reading and writing in their home languages – may have had a positive impact on their acquisition of L2 oral skills, particularly with regard to lexical competence.

Conversely, the case of Andrei (see Chapter 4) highlighted the potential for disadvantage among slightly older pupils. He was aged 8 years by the end of the study but appeared to be without any literacy experience, either in his home language or in English, prior to his enrolment in School 1. Although he received additional L2 literacy support, and accepting that some of his difficulties may have been more reading specific than proficiency related, Andrei's experience reveals how missing out on formative education and trying to meet the 'moving target' of ever-increasing L2 literacy demands in an immersion situation can leave EAL pupils at serious risk of under-achievement (see Cummins 2000:36). Even the other three newly arrived pupils of a similar age (Stefan, Ravi and Lukas), who had some previous schooling and made significant progress in the acquisition of L2 literacy over the study period, found curriculum literacy requirements a formidable challenge. It would have been difficult for any of these pupils to engage in mainstream literacy activities without the considerable level of help they received in the smaller English language support groups. This suggests the need for sustained English language support until EAL pupils are able to meet mainstream literacy requirements without linguistic assistance, rather than imposing a strict time limit on such support. Ongoing support could, however, be provided in the mainstream classroom, with English language support and mainstream teachers working together to ensure that EAL pupils can engage in literacy-related activities alongside their native English-speaking peers.

Finally, we must look at the L2 literacy development of the remaining three older participants – Beatriz, Nasreen and Fatima – who were in their second year of English language support. During the study, all three pupils (Beatriz and Nasreen in First Class, and Fatima in Third Class) were able to engage in age-appropriate L2 literacy activities which generally linked to B1 *Benchmarks* descriptors for reading and writing. However, some factors which may have supported their apparently successful acquisition of L2 literacy skills were noted in the case studies. First, both Beatriz and Nasreen probably benefited from formative literacy activities in the Infant Classes (they enrolled at School 3 in the Senior Infant class). Their L2 literacy abilities had clearly progressed during their initial year of schooling in Ireland to a level that, from the outset of the study, enabled them to engage with the more challenging reading and writing tasks they encountered in mainstream First Class. Secondly, Fatima had developed extensive home-language literacy skills prior to her arrival in Ireland. Thirdly, other factors such as family support, individual learning style and cognitive abilities, and the somewhat smaller class size in School 3 (which had 'disadvantaged' status) may have contributed to the development of these pupils' L2 literacy skills. The L2 literacy experience of these three children across the selected lessons also indicates that, for slightly older pupils, B1 proficiency in both reading and writing is a minimum requirement for effective participation in mainstream English literacy activities from First Class upwards. However, as pointed out above, flexible approaches to the delivery of sustained L2 literacy support should be considered.

L2 literacy development and the Benchmarks – overall findings

We were able to compare evidence from our study with the *Benchmarks* scales for reading and writing, presented in Appendix 2, to determine whether the latter reflected the experience of EAL pupils. It emerged from the links made between the reading and writing descriptors and actual literacy-related activities across the selected lessons that the *Benchmarks* adequately express L2 literacy-related outcomes for children receiving English language support. They also seemed able to take account of age-related variation in the literacy requirements of the curriculum. For example, the descriptors for A1 and A2 reading and writing provided an appropriate description of activities with which pupils in the Infant Classes would have to engage in the mainstream classroom. For children from First Class onwards, the increasing L2 literacy demands of the primary curriculum seem to be adequately expressed in the B1 descriptors for reading and writing. As discussed above (in relation to Beatriz, Nasreen and Fatima), the experience of EAL pupils participating in this study indicated that these descriptors express age-appropriate learning outcomes for these older children. Therefore, the B1 descriptors can be regarded as essential literacy-related targets to be achieved within the English language support allocation of EAL pupils from mainstream First Class upwards, allowing for age-related adaptation of the tasks they entail. Overall, we can conclude that the L2 literacy development of pupils in this study corresponded to the progression in L2 reading and writing summarised in the global benchmarks of communicative proficiency and elaborated in a theme-specific manner in the *Benchmarks* units of work (see Appendix 2).

Possible influences on L2 development – internal factors

In this chapter we have sought to identify overall tendencies in the acquisition of L2 English by a diverse group of EAL pupils, based on evidence of their actual L2 use, in order to compare them with the language learning outcomes described by the *Benchmarks*. However, in reporting the results of our cumulative analysis, we must remember that each pupil's English language development was also subject to a range of internal and external factors. In this section, we draw on observations made during data collection to examine possible individual differences in L2 development, with reference to the potential influences we were able to investigate: age, home language, and factors relating to pupils' learning style and personality.

Age

The impact of age on the development of English L2 literacy emerged as a significant issue in the previous section. However, we must also look at the possible effect of age on pupils' oral L2 development in order to ascertain how this variable may have influenced pupils' L2 acquisition over the course of our study. To do this, we will investigate whether age differences seemed to affect pupils' overall rate of English L2 development, based on the linking of their analysed spoken turns to *Benchmarks* proficiency levels. We will then examine the nature of any apparent age-related influence.

To determine the possible role of age in the 18 participating pupils' L2 acquisition, it was necessary to revisit the data that showed their overall L2 oral development and how this related to the *Benchmarks* levels (see Figure 5.1). We then had to examine this data separately for children of different ages. The distinction between 'early childhood' (from 2 to 7 years) and 'middle childhood' (from 7 to 11 years) proposed by Philp, Mackey and Oliver (2008:5), proved useful in this respect. It also appeared appropriate to the division of school classes in Irish primary education. Accordingly, we divided the participating pupils into two groups: children under 7 years during the study period (pupils in Junior and Senior Infant Classes) and children aged between 7 and 10 years (pupils in First, Second and Third Class); the younger group comprised 11 and the older group seven pupils. It was then possible to examine how the *Benchmarks* proficiency links made for all the analysed spoken turns produced by pupils within each age group varied in terms of their members' stage of English language support. The results for the younger and older groups are presented in Figures 5.8 and 5.9 respectively.

Figures 5.8 and 5.9 show evidence of increasing English L2 proficiency among children in both the younger and older groups. This is indicated by a generally rising proportion of higher-proficiency-linked turns over time and corresponds with the overall findings for the entire sample group (presented in Figure 5.1). However, it appeared that, over the same two-year period of English language support, L2 proficiency among the older pupils developed at a slightly faster rate than among their younger counterparts. Older pupils seemed capable of producing a greater proportion of A2-linked turns during the early months of English language support. In general, over the first year of support, the ratio of turns associated with level A2 proficiency was higher among older than younger pupils. In the second year of English language support, evidence of an increasing proportion of A2-linked turns appeared among the younger group. However, in the older group, we see the emergence of utterances associated with proficiency level B1. In addition, the older pupils, although fewer in number, produced more analysable spoken turns across the study period (3,889 turns; 52% of the turns included in Data Analysis Phase II), than the younger participants (3,566 turns; 48% of the analysed oral data).

It should be noted, however, that Figures 5.8 and 5.9 provide only a rough indication of the way in which age may impact on English L2 development among a limited sample of pupils. As the graphs show, the quantity of data available for pupils, particularly in their second year of English language support, may be an insufficient basis on which to draw firm conclusions. Nevertheless, our results seem to accord with other research findings (see Dimroth 2008, Muñoz 2006) that older children may exhibit a faster rate of L2 development than younger children in a similar learning environment, possibly due to their more developed cognitive skills. However, as pointed out in relation to L2 literacy development, older pupils in L2-dominant immersion education must acquire the language of schooling much more rapidly and to a higher level of proficiency, particularly regarding L2 reading and writing, than younger pupils. Curriculum demands may, therefore, eclipse any apparent age-related advantage for these children. The experience of pupils involved in this study suggests that, in terms of L2 literacy development, the language requirements of mainstream classroom activities prove more challenging, even for slightly older pupils (from First Class onwards) than for younger children (pupils in Infant Classes). Therefore, while research indicates 'evidence of a general long-term advantage for learners whose experience of the target language begins in their childhood years' (Singleton and Ryan 2004:100), curriculum demands must also be considered in the case of immigrant children. In addition, as pointed out by Abrahamsson and Hyltenstam (2009), while biological factors may well be significant,

Figure 5.8 Proficiency levels associated with analysed turns across the recorded duration of English language support for pupils under 7 years old*

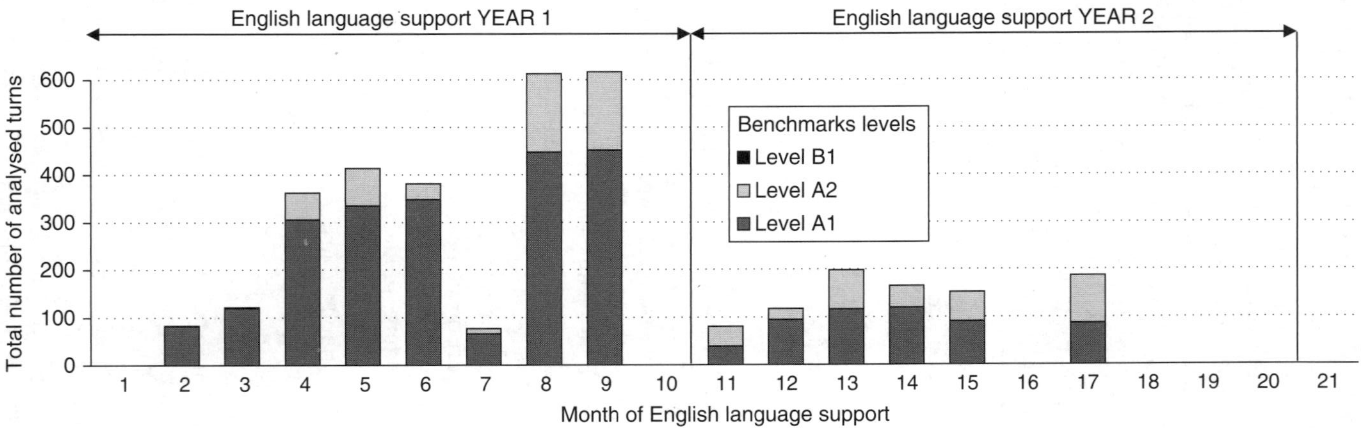

*Duration of English language support as known to the researcher.

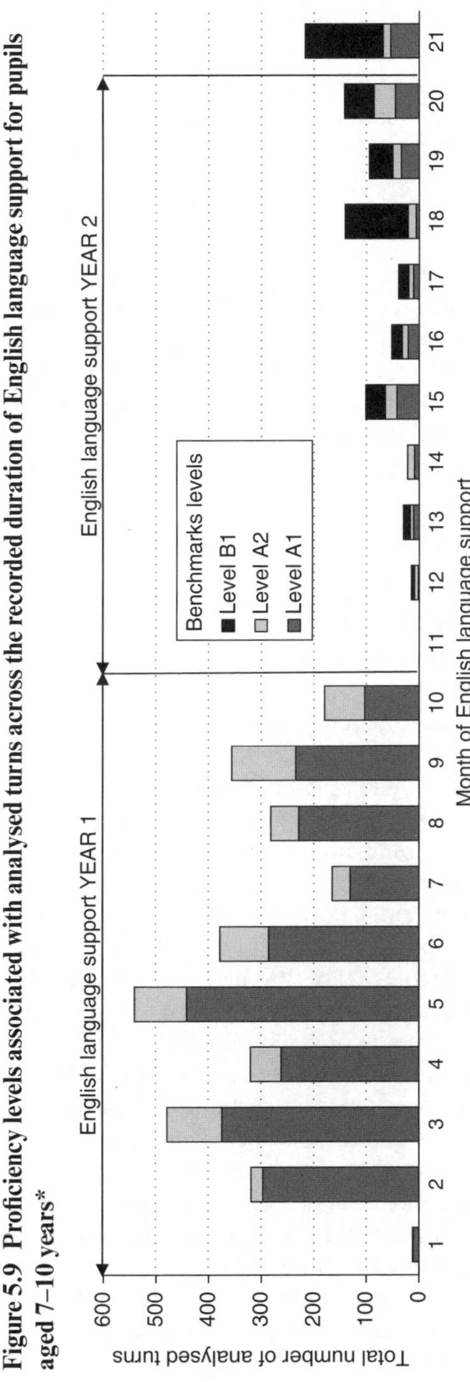

Figure 5.9 Proficiency levels associated with analysed turns across the recorded duration of English language support for pupils aged 7–10 years*

*Duration of English language support as known to the researcher.

environmental and affective issues also impact on L2 acquisition. Less formal, more interactive learning contexts, typical of the early primary years, may be conducive to implicit L2 acquisition, which seems to prevail among children immersed in an L2-dominant environment (see DeKeyser 2003). This may further favour EAL pupils whose L2 development begins in early childhood.

Home language

As emphasised in Chapter 4, it is impossible to draw conclusions regarding the extent of any cross-linguistic influence on the participating pupils' English L2 development without a thorough knowledge of their individual home languages. However, from analysis of the recorded lessons, we can make some general observations about possible home-language influence.

While overall it seemed that there was much similarity between the patterns of L2 development displayed across the sample, some specific aspects of L2 acquisition appeared to be affected by features of pupils' home languages. This was most prominent in relation to L2 phonological development, which was often noticeably influenced by characteristics of L1 phonology. L2 grammatical development also seemed prone to cross-linguistic influence, particularly in relation to syntactic patterns, verb tense and aspect, as well as the use of articles (often not a feature of pupils' home languages) and prepositions. Occasional instances suggest that lexical transfer emerged within the analysed data, but to a much lesser extent than either phonological or grammatical influence. However, this could have been in part due to the nature of the learning environment in which, although home-language use was not excluded, the pedagogical emphasis was on English as the language of instruction (the potential deficiencies of this L2-dominant approach are discussed below). Also, while home-language literacy skills appeared to support older pupils' L2 literacy development to some extent, L1 orthographic conventions and grapho-phonic relationships were sometimes applied to L2 reading and writing. However, L1-literate pupils (for example Stefan (Profile 14) and Lukas (Profile 13)) proved capable of making metalinguistic links between their two languages, and this may have helped them to overcome such potential confusion.

In general, then, although pupils appeared to follow similar overall patterns of English L2 acquisition, cross-linguistic influence contributed to specific features of their L2 development. Further evidence for this conclusion can be drawn from the fact that children from similar L1 backgrounds exhibited similar transfer-linked traits in their analysed L2 use. The case studies in Chapter 4 also suggested that L1 influence was most prominent in the early stages of English L2 development, gradually diminishing as pupils became more L2 proficient. This finding accords with other studies of young L2 learners such as Anderson (2004) and suggests that cross-linguistic influence may be 'developmentally-moderated' in its impact on L2 morpho-syntax (Pienemann 2005:111).

However, it should also be stressed that the parameters of our study allowed only very limited investigation of individual patterns of home-language influence. The study was based solely on data recorded in the EAL pupils' English language support lessons and thus could not account for children's experience of languages in their wider school and social environment – for example, with family members or peers of the same linguistic background. Also, the English language support programme proposed by the DES (for which, as explained in Chapter 1, the *Benchmarks* were developed), is essentially one of monolingual structured immersion. This means that EAL pupils' L2 is accepted as the dominant language of instruction and that little emphasis was placed on the vital role of children's home languages in their learning and development. While the *Benchmarks* and, more specifically, the resources derived from them – particularly the primary ELP (Integrate Ireland Language and Training 2004a) and the intercultural toolkit, *Together Towards Inclusion* (Integrate Ireland Language and Training and Southern Education and Library Board 2007) – support more plurilingual approaches to language education, this potential has been largely under-exploited in Irish primary schools. In general, there has been minimal recognition of children's home languages, despite the introduction of further whole-school guidelines promoting integration and inclusion: *Intercultural Education in the Primary School* and *English as an Additional Language in Irish Primary Schools* (National Council for Curriculum and Assessment 2005, 2006, respectively). As our study shows, teachers may not always be aware of the linguistic background of their pupils. Furthermore, there has been little exploration of pedagogical approaches, such as 'translanguaging', which encourage and respect the use of all languages present in the classroom as media for interaction and knowledge generation – as advocated, for example, by Creese and Blackledge (2010) and Sierens and Van Avermaet (2013).

Therefore, while the findings of this study provide useful information with regard to the 18 participants' English L2 acquisition, it should be remembered that this represents only one aspect of their overall plurilingual development. To derive a full picture of the complex reality of their plurilingualism – including how their various languages influenced each other – would have required further detailed study of the children's language use in a wider range of contexts, both at school and at home.

Learning style and personality

Observations regarding pupils' learning style and personality are included in the case studies presented in Chapter 4. Again, these were limited due to constraints on the study; its focus was on the participating pupils' involvement in English language support classes, recorded at time intervals never more frequent than weekly. However, from these brief observations, it was possible to discern some characteristics which may have influenced pupils' L2 development. The distinction between 'analytical' and 'holistic' styles is often applied to the description of child language acquisition (see Peters 1977), and it seemed that participating pupils tended towards one style or the other. Learning style preferences appeared more pronounced in some cases than in others, which suggests a continuum between analytic and holistic styles (Nelson 1985) and potential variations in style due not only to individual factors but also to features of the learning environment (Dörnyei 2005).

Evidence of an analytic approach to learning was apparent in a tendency towards cautious but relatively accurate speech; quite fluent but often inaccurate production suggested a more holistic style. For example, the contrast between Andrei (Profile 15, a more holistic learner) and Stefan (Profile 14, a more analytic learner) showed how, within the same lesson group, children of similar ages and similar stages of cognitive and English L2 development may exhibit very different learning styles. Although the extent to which children's learning style preferences may have contributed to their overall L2 acquisition lay beyond the scope of our study, observations concerning pupils' general tendencies could be compared with the evidence of L2 development derived from analysis of their actual L2 use. This comparison indicated that pupils whose learning style appeared more analytic may have had slightly more success in relation to L2 literacy than those whose style seemed more holistic.

However, this is only a very tentative suggestion; other factors (e.g. previous literacy experience and general cognitive issues) would have to be investigated more thoroughly to establish any such relation. In any case, age may further influence learning style. It is likely that younger children rely more heavily on memory than older language learners, who depend more on their analytical abilities (Dörnyei and Skehan 2003). Thus, in the early years, L2 acquisition may be largely implicit, which possibly accounts for younger children's apparent capacity for effective L2 learning in the relatively 'unstructured environment' of immersion conditions (DeKeyser 2003:335). However, as they grow older, children may become increasingly capable of more explicit L2 learning, and pedagogical practices should adapt to meet their changing needs in this regard (see McKay 2006). Sensory preferences may also affect children's individual cognitive style and thus impact on their learning of a second language. Preferences for visual, auditory, kinaesthetic and tactile learning have been identified as possible influences on learners' L2 development (Reid 1987), while theories of 'multiple intelligences' proposed by Gardner (1983, 2006) are also worth considering in this regard. Furthermore, as pointed out above, language learning style may vary during the course of the learner's L2 development and thus may be subject to change with increasing L2 proficiency, rather than being an entirely independent variable. In this study, the three most proficient participants, Beatriz, Nasreen (Profile 17) and Fatima (Profile 18), seemed to have a quite analytic approach to their L2 learning.

Links between learning style and personality may also have contributed to a network of internal factors affecting participants' L2 development, for example, confidence in communication. In terms of communicative confidence, participating pupils ranged along a continuum from the extremely talkative to the very quiet. Although this personality trait cannot be automatically associated with any particular patterns of L2 development, it seemed that the more talkative children were quite adept at holding their own in classroom interaction and could secure more opportunities for L2 use than quieter pupils. On the other hand, relatively quiet children frequently exhibited analytical tendencies in their L2 learning. This suggests that L2 use by pupils with a tendency towards introversion may be associated with a greater degree of reflection than that of more extravert, ostensibly communicative, pupils. Consequently, introverts may possess what Dörnyei describes as 'greater ability to consolidate learning, lower distractability and better study habits' (2005:21), although he accepts that 'both extraversion and introversion may have positive features depending on the particular task in question' (Dörnyei 2005:27). This raises the issue of the need for L2 pedagogy to be sufficiently flexible to accommodate learners with a range of different personalities and learning styles.

The observations we have summarised offer no more than a sketchy insight into possible personality-related influence on L2 development. However, the evidence we have presented indicates that the L2 learning experience of these children was distinctly individual. It also suggests that, for pedagogical reasons, such factors deserve further investigation. For instance, cases of deceptive proficiency emerged among skilled communicators whose effective L2 oral skills somewhat masked significant L2 literacy-related problems; this highlights the need for awareness of the possibly hidden challenges which apparently confident EAL pupils may face. On the other hand, quieter pupils could perhaps benefit from alterations in the dynamics of classroom interaction; for example, from a greater emphasis on pair work rather than teacher-led discourse which elicits responses from the whole group and seems to give more confident children greater opportunities to 'take the floor'.

From a pedagogical perspective, these brief observations on learning style and personality factors and the possible links between them, suggest that consideration of individual characteristics is essential if we are to identify and best meet the needs of young EAL learners. Awareness of children's age and educational stage is likewise essential in this respect. Some familiarity with how features of EAL pupils' home language may impact on their L2 development can also help teachers understand the particular challenges these children face in their English L2 development. The existence of this range of possible internal influences highlights the necessity for EAL guidelines which express learning objectives in a manner capable of individual application. The introduction to the *Benchmarks* stresses that they should be used to 'identify individual pathways of learning' (Integrate Ireland Language and Training 2003a:3). Their focus on skill-specific descriptors most relevant to the learning needs of any given EAL pupil facilitates an individualised approach and supports a language pedagogy which accepts and reflects the diversity of young learners.

Possible influences on L2 development – interaction-related factors

In Chapter 3 we acknowledged that the possible impact of external influences relating to the context of learning must also be considered when investigating L2 acquisition. Regarding English L2 development in Irish primary schools, such influences range from factors associated with the L2 learning environment created in pupils' English language support lesson groups, to features of the mainstream classroom, to wider social issues affecting the overall integration of these children in the host society as determined by a network of home, school and community influences. However, as we have already pointed out, practical constraints meant that our study was restricted to the context of participating pupils' English language support lessons. Accordingly, our examination of possible external factors influencing these children's English L2 acquisition is limited to the potential effect of classroom interaction patterns in the recorded lessons. We cannot take account of broader social variables such as socio-economic status, cultural background and the opportunities for integration afforded by the local community, which may have a profound bearing on immigrant children's experience within an L2-dominant education system. At the same time, investigating classroom talk may be pedagogically significant, since managing the interaction dynamic of the language learning environment is one of the few controllable factors likely to influence L2 acquisition. Any evidence that relates features of interaction to developing L2 proficiency should be useful to teachers seeking to create optimally beneficial classroom environments. We will also consider the role of the *Benchmarks* in this regard, looking at the extent to which the guidelines they provide for English language support can account for possible interaction-linked influences on EAL pupils' English L2 acquisition. We will identify the types of classroom interaction promoted by the *Benchmarks* and examine whether and how these patterns of discourse may support L2 development.

Both in the case studies and in our observations on the possible influence of personality-related factors on participating pupils' L2 development, it appeared that interactional factors could affect certain features of pupils' analysed L2 use. If we view L2 learning as a variety of L2 use, in accordance with the CEFR's 'action-oriented' approach (Council of Europe 2001:9), we shall expect that learners' L2 development depends in part on the opportunities for L2 use/learning that arise in classroom interaction. Given the limitations of our research (scope of study and time constraints), it was not feasible to conduct an exhaustive analysis of all interactional patterns emerging within the recorded data and to examine their likely impact on pupils' L2 acquisition. However, as explained in Chapter 3, by coding each transcribed turn in terms of criteria derived from CA, we could describe pupils' classroom talk in some depth and thus derive a clear impression of the interactional dynamic in each lesson.

In addition, we conducted a more detailed analysis of some specific patterns of interaction, in order to examine more closely the likely influence of classroom talk on participating pupils' L2 acquisition over the course of the study. In doing so, we concentrated on the distribution of three turn-type indicators – coded as 'answers', 'tellings' and 'topic elaborations' – which were readily identifiable in the data and were associated with a considerable proportion of the spontaneous L2 use examined in Data Analysis Phase II. In Chapter 3 we gave examples of these three turn-types, showing how they provided indications of pupils' response-based talk ('answers'), their initiation of new topics ('telling'), and their ability to contribute to classroom discussion on a self-initiated or other-initiated theme ('topic elaborations'). The distribution of each of these turn-types in pupils' analysed L2 production was then recorded. The results of this analysis were presented for each of the 18 participating pupils in Chapter 4. The patterns of interaction emerging from the analysis raise two interesting questions. To what extent did pupils' English L2 proficiency enable them to engage in classroom talk? And, conversely, did the interactional patterns apparent within a given lesson influence pupils' L2 use within that lesson?

From the case studies, it seemed that recorded L2 use which linked to higher-level *Benchmarks* descriptors was often associated with lessons in which the pupil produced more 'tellings' and 'topic elaborations' than 'answers'. However, it seemed that the relationship between L2 proficiency and interactional engagement was likely to be more complex than simply one of cause and effect. The distribution of the three analysed turn-types suggested that classroom factors, particularly choice of activities, could affect the nature of the interaction required of the participating pupils. Lessons in which L2 learning tasks seemed to involve more opportunities for active classroom talk ('telling' and 'topic elaboration') rather than interaction in a predominantly responding role ('answers'), were frequently those in which a greater proportion of participants' L2 use was associated with their highest recorded proficiency levels. While this did not preclude the possibility that pupils would become more active as their overall English L2 development progressed, it did indicate that learning activities which promoted the initiation and sustaining of discussion may encourage pupils to use their L2 to their maximum ability, rather than simply providing minimal responses.

This suggests that the most beneficial pedagogical tasks are likely to be those that require L2 use associated with the upper reaches of learners' achieved proficiency level. Certainly the findings presented in the case studies, though only a rough guide to possible interactional influence on L2 acquisition, appear to correspond with the theory that L2 development is likely to occur when learners are able to use their L2 to their maximum capacity in a supportive learning environment. Such findings accord with the idea that socially mediated learning can occur within the learner's 'zone of proximal development' (Vygotsky 1978:86) when appropriate interactional conditions exist. They also point to the need to provide rich opportunities for output, to encourage learners to use language actively and to their highest proficiency level instead of confining them to responding roles that require minimal production. Swain emphasises that output operates as 'a socially-constructed cognitive tool' (2000:112), and highlights the pedagogical significance of creating conditions for active discourse which may thus be conducive to L2 learning.

In order to arrive at a more detailed impression of the possible relationship between patterns of classroom interaction and English L2 proficiency development, it was necessary to bring together the results from the individual case studies. By analysing these, we could discover whether any general patterns emerged. The results of this cumulative analysis are presented in Figure 5.10. It illustrates the overall distribution of the three analysed indicators ('tellings', 'topic elaborations' and 'answers'), based on the mean values for each of these turn-types calculated across lessons associated with similar proficiency ratio bands (using the bands defined for the cumulative analysis of the linguistic indicators of L2 development; see Table 5.2). The purpose of Figure 5.10 is to show the mean distribution of each indicator as a proportion of the total mean occurrence of the three analysed turn-types within each proficiency band. Highlighting the occurrence of the three turn-types across the bands allows these features of the 18 participating pupils' classroom interaction to be compared with evidence of their L2 proficiency development. Using mean values mitigated the risk of distortion due, for example, to variations in lesson length. Although shortages in the available data may render the means calculated for the more proficient pupils more susceptible to lesson-specific influences, Figure 5.10 provides a useful overall comparison of typical turn-types noted in the participants' recorded L2 use.

Figure 5.10 shows that, while the proportion of more active turn-types – 'telling' and 'topic elaboration' – rose with evidence of increasing proficiency in English, L2 use beyond solely response-based discourse was apparent from the earliest stages of participating pupils' English L2 acquisition. Conversely, although the proportion of 'answers' was generally highest when L2 proficiency levels appeared to be low, 'answer' type responses still featured among the analysed production of even the most proficient pupils. Table 5.4 shows the proportion of 'answers' compared to the combined proportion

Figure 5.10 Mean distribution of analysed turn-type indicators across L2 proficiency ratios

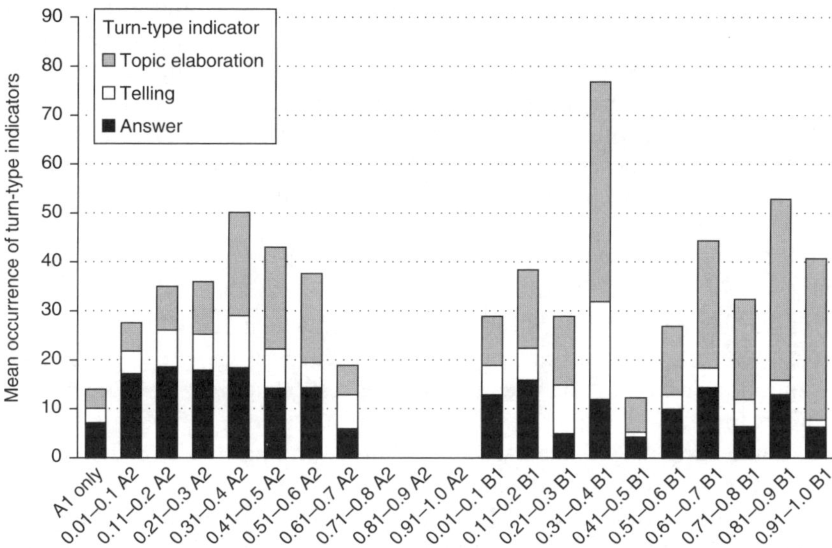

Table 5.4 Overall ratios of response-based and active turn-types among analysed indicators

Maximum proportion of turns at highest recorded proficiency level	Total no. 'answers'	Total no. 'tellings'	Total no. topic 'elabora-tions'	Ratio of 'answers' among three analysed turn-type indicators	Ratio of 'tellings' and 'topic elaborations' among three analysed turn-type indicators
A1 ONLY	151	62	83	0.51	0.49
0.01–0.1 A2	449	120	150	0.62	0.38
0.11–0.2 A2	411	165	196	0.53	0.47
0.21–0.3 A2	378	154	225	0.50	0.50
0.31–0.4 A2	296	170	338	0.37	0.63
0.41–0.5 A2	86	48	125	0.33	0.67
0.51–0.6 A2	101	36	127	0.38	0.62
0.61–0.7 A2	6	7	6	0.32	0.68
0.01–0.1 B1	13	6	10	0.45	0.55
0.11–0.2 B1	32	13	32	0.42	0.58
0.21–0.3 B1	5	10	14	0.17	0.83
0.31–0.4 B1	12	20	45	0.16	0.84
0.41–0.5 B1	13	3	21	0.35	0.65
0.51–0.6 B1	40	12	56	0.37	0.63
0.61–0.7 B1	29	8	52	0.33	0.67
0.71–0.8 B1	13	11	41	0.20	0.80
0.81–0.9 B1	13	3	37	0.25	0.75
0.91–1.0 B1	32	7	165	0.16	0.84

of 'tellings' and 'topic elaborations' for each stage of English L2 proficiency development identified in the data.

In terms of L2 pedagogy, our data shows that, as with infants developing their first language(s), young EAL learners are capable of active communication from the very beginning of their L2 development. Facilitating this kind of communication may also be advantageous in terms of L2 acquisition, as shown in the following example. Tomasz (Profile 5), at an early stage of his English language development (recorded in Lesson 5) was able to produce this 'telling' turn on a topic of interest – his dog in Poland:

Tomasz: My dog can't see really well

This was his only A2-linked turn in a lesson in which 22 of his 27 analysed turns were 'answers' – short, often single-word, responses (e.g. *cat* or *fish*) to questions asked by the teacher. This suggests that creating more opportunities for 'telling' might have allowed Tomasz to risk using his L2 to his maximum level of proficiency, rather than confining him to the safer but more restrictive role of producing basic 'answers'.

From our study, however, it did not appear that this potential for language learning inherent in active communication was recognised by the teachers. On the other hand, the fluctuating but relatively substantial ratio of 'answers' across the proficiency levels raises pedagogical concerns, particularly as the detailed codes applied to the analysed turns showed that these were predominantly responses to teacher-posed, 'known answer' questions. Even pupils who were very capable of producing B1-linked turns were sometimes restricted in this way due to the nature of classroom activities. This was noted earlier in relation to Fatima's first selected lesson in which over half (six out of 11) of her analysed spoken turns were 'answers' to simple questions asked by the teacher (see also Profile 18).

This raises the question whether the patterns of classroom interaction evident in this study are those most apt to facilitate effective L2 learning. It seems likely that these patterns are typical of discourse in EAL instruction at primary level in Ireland generally, since they emerge from lessons recorded in 10 English language support groups in three different schools.

Our findings suggest that interactional patterns are likely to be linked to more than L2 proficiency alone. They indicate that classroom management and task characteristics can play an important role in creating opportunities for increased and enriched L2 use, which in turn may lead to enhanced L2 learning. In this regard, it is worth considering an additional variable likely to impact on classroom interaction patterns. The extent to which each of the 18 participants' analysed spoken turns were addressed to the teacher or to another pupil in the group was recorded across the lessons selected in Data Analysis Phase II (see Chapter 3 for an outline of this process). From the case studies, it is evident that pupil–teacher discourse predominated over pupil–pupil discourse, in all 10 lesson groups in the three participating schools. These individual findings were cumulatively analysed, with the results shown in Figure 5.11. This shows clearly that a very low ratio of peer-directed to teacher-directed discourse was recorded among the turns (or part-turns) for which the participants' interlocutor was clearly identifiable (i.e. the vast majority of analysed turns, excluding infrequent ambiguously directed turns or instances of self-talk). Irrespective of evidence of English L2 proficiency, it seemed that participants' rate of peer-directed discourse was usually under 10% of their rate of teacher-directed talk, and often substantially lower.

Figure 5.11 Overall ratio of pupil–pupil discourse to pupil–teacher discourse

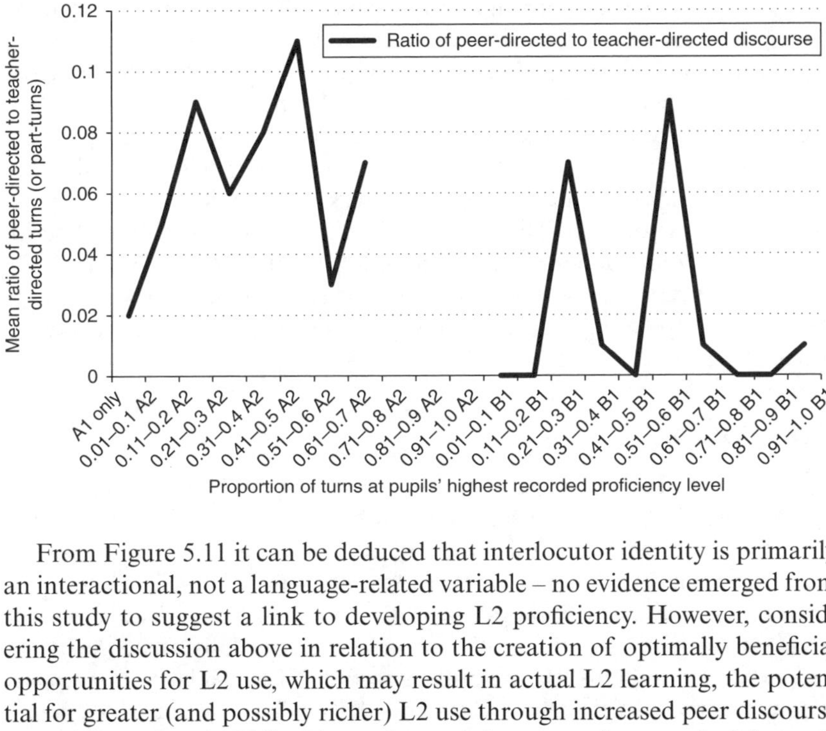

From Figure 5.11 it can be deduced that interlocutor identity is primarily an interactional, not a language-related variable – no evidence emerged from this study to suggest a link to developing L2 proficiency. However, considering the discussion above in relation to the creation of optimally beneficial opportunities for L2 use, which may result in actual L2 learning, the potential for greater (and possibly richer) L2 use through increased peer discourse should be explored. While this was beyond the scope of our study, it is worth noting that classroom tasks (e.g. role-play activities) which were associated with higher levels of pupil–pupil discourse seemed to result in more extensive L2 output and, possibly, evidence of higher L2 proficiency. For example, in the role-play extract included in Chapter 3 (Figure 3.2), Ravi (Profile 12) and Lukas (Profile 13) both produced level A2 turns at a point in their English language proficiency development more associated with level A1 production. Therefore, the potential advantages of increased peer-directed talk in terms of L2 learning opportunities seem worth considering. This applies not only in the small group environment of the English language support classroom but also in the wider context of mainstream primary education, in which the pupil–teacher ratio is much higher and opportunities for the EAL pupil to secure turn-taking slots in teacher-directed discourse are significantly reduced.

The overall indications emerging from this study, then, suggest that interaction patterns may impact on EAL pupils' L2 acquisition. However, more research would be required for any firmer conclusions to be drawn regarding the nature and complexity of any such relationship. The pedagogical implications of these findings, highlighted above, nevertheless deserve consideration. Our findings support an interactive approach to L2 learning and teaching which emphasises active communication and the possible benefits of maximising peer discourse. This would seem to accord with the communicative approach to language teaching implied by the *Benchmarks*. The activities suggested by the descriptors in both the global benchmarks of communicative proficiency and the thematic units of work emphasise, for example: peer interaction, initiating and sustaining conversational exchanges, and active L2 use to the maximum extent of the pupil's L2 proficiency in a supportive learning environment. This is apparent in the following A2 level descriptor for spoken interaction included in Unit 2, 'Our school': 'Can generally sustain a conversation with another pupil when working collaboratively in the classroom (painting a picture, making a model, playing with puppets etc.)' (Integrate Ireland Language and Training 2003a:11).

Conclusion

The results presented in this chapter show how English L2 proficiency developed progressively among a sample of 18 EAL pupils at primary school in Ireland. They confirm that this progression reflects the trajectory of English L2 development described by the *Benchmarks* – from proficiency level A1 through A2 to B1. The findings of our functional analysis indicate that the *Benchmarks* descriptors for both oral and literacy skills relate clearly to the participating pupils' L2 use in their recorded English language support lessons. Overall formal analysis also shows that evidence of English L2 acquisition among these 18 pupils, obtained from a data-driven range of grammatical and lexical indicators, is in accordance with the *Benchmarks* scales for the development of communicative language competence. Moreover, the case studies reveal specific features of the grammatical and lexical progression from level A1 to B1, from the basic forms and lexis used when pupils' spoken turns linked mainly to A1 descriptors to the much wider lexical and grammatical range evident when pupils' L2 oral production was associated with level B1 descriptors. Thus, the 18 profiles (presented in Chapter 4) and the summary of their qualitative aspects provided by the overview of the analysed indicators of pupils' L2 acquisition (Appendix 7), offer a detailed illustration of how the *Benchmarks'* global scales of underlying linguistic competence for vocabulary control and grammatical accuracy are realised in pupils' actual L2 use.

However, as well as illustrating common aspects of English L2 acquisition at particular *Benchmarks* proficiency levels, our study also highlights considerable individual differences in the L2 development of the 18 participating pupils. Our observations regarding possible internal influences on their English L2 acquisition identify likely sources of this variation. Our analysis of the pupils' patterns of classroom interaction further reveals how pedagogical approaches may also have impacted on their English L2 development. Consequently, the capacity of the *Benchmarks* to accommodate individual language learning needs and to promote a pedagogy that encourages active L2 learning is significant. In Chapter 6, we briefly discuss the implications of these findings, in terms of what they tell us about English L2 development among immigrant pupils in Irish primary schools and regarding the wider relevance of our research.

 **Conclusion**

Aims of the research

In the school year 2007–08 a substantial bank of data was collected from English language support classrooms in three primary schools in the northeast of Ireland. The data was transcribed, coded and analysed following procedures explained in Chapter 3 in order to yield the 18 developmental profiles of participating EAL pupils presented in Chapter 4, and re-analysed to obtain the overall results reported in Chapter 5. The purpose of the research was to:

- determine the extent to which the development of the participating EAL pupils' communicative proficiency in English corresponded to the trajectory hypothesised in the *English Language Proficiency Benchmarks* (see Appendix 2)
- explore the development of individual pupils' underlying linguistic competence in English and the degree to which that development was marked by back-sliding, variance, etc.
- consider what the analysis of data obtained from a selection of individual pupils allowed us to say about the overall relation between communicative capacity in English and underlying linguistic competence.

Participating pupils' acquisition of English L2 – summary of findings

The participating pupils' proficiency in English L2 developed over the period of their English language support both functionally, in terms of the range and complexity of the activities they could perform, and linguistically, in terms of grammatical and lexical indicators of L2 acquisition. The general trajectory of L2 development that emerged from the sample as a whole suggested a considerable degree of consistency, with similar functional abilities and similar evidence of L2 acquisition apparent among pupils at equivalent stages of English language support.

At the same time, internal factors seem to have impacted on specific features of individual pupils' English L2 acquisition. Age, for example, may have affected the rate of L2 development to some extent: there was some evidence that oral L2 skills developed slightly faster among pupils aged 7 years and older than among those under 7. Also, pupils' acquisition of English seemed to be influenced by their home language, particularly as regards phonology and syntax. Personality and individual learning style may also have played a role. Further research is needed to assess fully the extent of these potential influences on EAL pupils' acquisition of English. Such research would usefully take account of pupils' language use outside as well as inside school, treating their acquisition of English as one element in their expanding plurilingual repertoire – home language(s), other languages acquired in the community, Irish and foreign languages learned at school. The findings of such research could be used to inform an explicitly plurilingual approach to the education of children from immigrant backgrounds, even in an apparently L2-dominant context.

If L2 use plays an essential role in L2 learning, it seems likely that interaction-related factors have the potential, over time, to influence EAL pupils' overall acquisition of English in terms of both rate and diversity of development. Patterns of classroom interaction certainly appeared to affect the quality and quantity of participating pupils' use of English in the lessons selected for analysis. In particular, there was some evidence to support the view that allowing learners to occupy active roles in classroom discourse is likely to support their L2 learning. Further research is necessary to investigate the nature of the relation between the interactional characteristics of classroom talk and EAL pupils' L2 development.

The main focus of our study was on participating pupils' oral development, partly because we could most easily collect oral data and partly on the ground that their use of spoken English was the best available indicator of acquisition. Our data nevertheless contained some evidence regarding pupils' L2 literacy development. In general, they made progress in reading and writing English during their period of English language support. Individual pupils' L2 literacy development seemed, however, to be affected by age and the literacy requirements of the mainstream curriculum. There was also evidence to suggest that previous educational experience, including L1 literacy, could support the acquisition of L2 reading and writing skills. The gradually expanding literacy-related demands of the mainstream curriculum in L2-dominant education emerged, however, as a significant challenge, particularly for pupils aged 7 years and over.

Implications of the research findings for the English Language Proficiency Benchmarks

In terms of the communicative functions they were able to perform at successive stages of English L2 development, the evidence emerging from participating pupils' analysed spoken turns corresponded closely to the learning outcomes for oral skills summarised in the global benchmarks of communicative proficiency and the thematic units of work (see Appendix 2). And although evidence of L2 literacy development was more limited, pupils' developing proficiency in performing reading and writing tasks also appeared to reflect the learning outcomes hypothesised by the literacy-related descriptors in the global benchmarks of communicative proficiency and the units of work (again, see Appendix 2). These descriptors also proved sufficiently sensitive to the gradual increase in mainstream classroom literacy requirements across the primary school years, and thus capable of reflecting the developmental trajectories of individual EAL pupils of different ages and at different stages of cognitive development. Perhaps not surprisingly, none of the participating pupils performed at level A2 before first performing at level A1, or at level B1 before first performing at level A2.

Thorough investigation of grammatical and lexical indicators of English L2 acquisition established a clear link to the descriptors for vocabulary control and grammatical accuracy included in the global scales of underlying linguistic competence. Evidence based on observation of the phonological characteristics of pupils' oral L2 use and the analysis of recorded literacy-related activities also suggested that the scales for phonological and orthographic control are an accurate reflection of these aspects of L2 linguistic development at successive stages of English L2 proficiency, although more specific research focusing on these features would be welcome.

The themes covered in the 13 units of work recurred throughout our data, whatever the age of the pupils, their school and their lesson group, and regardless of whether or not teachers drew on the *Benchmarks* to plan their lessons. Extensive linkage between pupils' L2 use and these thematic descriptors was recorded for almost all the units of work. Our analysis nevertheless leads us to recommend the inclusion of some additional themes or sub-themes in future versions of the *Benchmarks* in order to consolidate their relation to the primary curriculum; for example, a more explicit focus on language associated with numbers and mathematics seems called for (all our suggestions are recorded in Appendix 5). Although tools derived from the *Benchmarks*, like the primary ELP (Integrate Ireland Language and Training 2004a) and *Together Towards Inclusion* (Integrate Ireland Language and Training and Southern Education and Library Board 2007), acknowledge EAL pupils' plurilingual repertoires, the plurilingual dimension might also be dealt with more directly and in greater detail in an updated version of the *Benchmarks*.

Our analysis of individual participants' use of English L2 confirmed that the *Benchmarks* can be applied to individual learners, notwithstanding the fact that individual factors (L1, age, personality and learning style) may impact on particular features of their L2 acquisition. It would be useful, either in a revised version of the *Benchmarks* or in a separate handbook for teachers, to indicate the existence of these individual factors and suggest ways of taking them into account in English language and mainstream classrooms. This pedagogical guidance might also include: advice on how to incorporate children's home languages into their classroom learning in a plurilingual approach to education; how to adjust teaching practices to cater for younger and older EAL pupils; how best to respond to pupils who may be going through a 'silent period' of L2 acquisition; and how to ensure that apparent competence in BICS-related aspects of L2 proficiency does not mask problems in the development of L2 CALP (the handbook *Up and Away* (Integrate Ireland Language and Training 2006b) already provides some guidance on these issues).

As regards the possible influence of classroom interaction patterns on learners' L2 acquisition, our results suggest that communication-rich tasks such as those captured by the *Benchmarks* descriptors offer optimal opportunities for L2 use and potential L2 learning. This seems to be the case especially when EAL pupils are enabled to engage in tasks that demand their highest level of proficiency at a given point in their L2 learning. Forms of interaction that emerged from our study as having the capacity to maximise quantity and quality of L2 use are also centrally present in the *Benchmarks*. They include: peer-to-peer interaction, communication involving various initiating discourse roles across different genres, and sustained L2 use at the maximum level of the pupil's achieved proficiency, supported by scaffolding appropriate to their L2 proficiency level.

In sum, our study confirms the usefulness of the *Benchmarks* for the purposes they were designed to serve: initial diagnostic assessment; designing an individually appropriate course of learning; planning lessons and choosing activities; formative and summative assessment based on classroom observation; communicating progress and concerns to mainstream teachers and parents.

In the Introduction we described our research as a first step towards transforming the *English Language Proficiency Benchmarks* from a framework into domain-specific and age-appropriate RLDs. When we first embarked on the research, in 2006, IILT's future seemed secure and the DES was in the process of increasing its investment in support for EAL pupils and students. We expected that in due course we would apply our findings in two ways: by revising the *Benchmarks* while ensuring that they remained compact and usable on a day-to-day basis; and by writing an accompanying handbook for teachers in which our empirical findings, including those relative to pupils' acquisition of formal features of English L2, would play a central role. And we assumed that this work would provide a basis for further research, which would progressively associate itself with other relevant research, including the EPP. Unfortunately, just as we came to the end of data collection, in the summer of 2008, Ireland faced an unprecedented economic crisis, IILT was closed down, and the DES's investment in English language support quickly began to shrink. Since then there has been neither an organisational framework in which to undertake further research nor the funding to support it.

Broader implications of the study

Our findings have implications that go some way beyond the Irish context. By confirming the robustness of the *Benchmarks* as a framework to guide the design and delivery of support for EAL pupils, they confirm the value of the CEFR as a descriptive resource that maintains a fruitful interaction between the social and cognitive dimensions of L2 learning. Like the CEFR (Council of Europe 2001:9), the *Benchmarks* are founded on the belief that language learning is a variety of language use. The descriptors summarise EAL pupils' ability to participate in classroom communication at three levels of proficiency and, in very general terms, key features of the underlying linguistic competence on which that ability rests. Our analysis of a large database of naturally occurring L2 use by a sample of 18 EAL pupils produced consistent and comparable information that linked likely indicators of L2 acquisition (emerging from formal analysis) to successive stages of English L2 proficiency (identified through functional analysis), thus confirming the essential inseparability of language learning and language use. This result suggests that the approach we adopted in the *Benchmarks* – identifying individual and domain-specific learning needs and describing learning outcomes in terms of the communicative activities associated with successive stages of L2 proficiency – could serve as a model for developing L2 curricula for other target groups and other languages, taking account of differences in age, learning environment and L2 learning requirements or goals.

Although the *Benchmarks* are primarily functional in orientation, the descriptors carry obvious grammatical and lexical implications: clearly, the communicative and linguistic dimensions support and depend on each other (as is also the case in the CEFR). Our study shows the same interdependence of functional capacity and linguistic resources in the English L2 development of the participating pupils, and thus confirms that functional criteria supplemented by formal analysis can serve to outline developing L2 proficiency in a way that closely reflects the 'naturalistic' L2 development typically associated with children growing up in an L2-dominant society. Some applied linguists have complained that the CEFR is not based on research into the nature of L2 acquisition (e.g. Hulstijn 2007); our research suggests, however, that there is a close relation between the CEFR's functional progression and the growth of learners' linguistic resources.

Finding an adequate response to the language learning needs of children from immigrant backgrounds is more than a pedagogical matter: it has to do with making the most of society's human capital, fostering social cohesion, and respecting basic human rights. Unless they become fully proficient in the language of schooling, children from immigrant families cannot be fully integrated into the school and wider community, neither can they fulfil their academic potential. Bilingual programmes which foster both L1 and L2 development may appear to be the most desirable option, but they are often not feasible, especially when immigrant populations are drawn from a wide variety of language backgrounds. In view of the large numbers of children and adolescents from immigrant backgrounds in L2-immersion education not only in Ireland but worldwide, there is a need for detailed and individually sensitive guidelines that respond to these learners' educational needs and L2 acquisition sequences. Our study indicates that the *Benchmarks* provide a robust instance of such guidelines, with their focus on skills associated with both social and academic language, their ability to accommodate differences of age, linguistic and cultural background, personality and learning style, and to promote interactional practices likely to be maximally beneficial to L2 learning.

Areas for future research

At various points in the book we have acknowledged the limitations of our study. Here we bring together some of the obvious focuses for further research. Some of them are specific to the Irish context, while others have more general relevance.

1. It is well established that many immigrant children have difficulty surmounting the challenge posed by the acquisition of L2 literacy, whereas our own research has been concerned mostly with participating pupils' development of English L2 oral skills. There is a need for longitudinal studies of the development of EAL pupils' literacy skills in English, which would necessarily involve pupils older than the majority of our 18 participants. Such studies could investigate English L2 literacy development from the perspective of the *Benchmarks*, the relation between L2 oral and L2 literacy development, and the role of L1 literacy in the development of reading and writing skills in English. Findings could be compared to the findings of international research, especially research carried out in other English-speaking countries.

2. Our study is based on data collected in English language support lessons. It is also desirable to investigate EAL pupils' mainstream classroom experience during their first two years of English L2 immersion, partly in order to complement our own findings and partly with a view to exploring the relation between English language support

and mainstream classrooms. It would also be worth investigating the contribution that whole-school approaches to EAL teaching can make to language learning and integration, as part of a strategy of intercultural education.

3. It is necessary to investigate EAL pupils' English L2 development after their allocation of English language support has expired, considering how best to enable them to reach their full academic potential in the longer term and taking wider social factors into account.

4. It is also necessary to explore, more thoroughly than we were able to, the impact of such internal factors as age, home language (including home-language maintenance), and personality or learning style on the English L2 acquisition of EAL pupils.

5. We excluded 11 Nigerian pupils from our study because for at least 10 of them Nigerian English was (at least one of) the language(s) of the home. A future study could usefully investigate the linguistic development of pupils from immigrant backgrounds who are speakers of a variety of English other than that of their indigenous peers, to ascertain how the linguistic identity of these children may be appropriately recognised and respected.

6. There is a need for research into the impact of different patterns of classroom interaction on EAL pupils' English L2 acquisition, with particular reference to the ways in which the interactional dynamic may best facilitate their L2 learning.

7. There are good reasons to suspect that EAL students in Irish post-primary schools fare much less well than their peers at primary level (see, for example, Lyons and Little 2009). There is thus a need for research that replicates the present study in its focus and methods, but with reference to post-primary EAL learners. All the follow-up research recommended for primary level is also necessary at post-primary level.

8. More generally, there is a need for greater exploitation of mixed methods research in the study of L2 acquisition among young learners, both as a means of achieving optimally informative analysis, particularly in multiple-subject longitudinal studies, and as a tool for effective comparison of emerging research findings in this field.

9. Finally, more research is needed into the linguistic development of primary school children from immigrant backgrounds in L2-immersion contexts in countries other than Ireland, involving other educational systems, other approaches to L2 support, and languages of schooling other than English. Comparison of findings would be greatly facilitated if such research were supported by CEFR-derived frameworks like the *English Language Proficiency Benchmarks*.

Final comments

As we have explained, the *English Language Proficiency Benchmarks* were developed and implemented at a time when the DES was in a position to invest significantly in the linguistic and educational integration of children and adolescents from immigrant backgrounds. Since Ireland's economic collapse in 2008, however, English language support has suffered serious setbacks due to reduced funding (see Lyons and Little 2009:84). It would be a disservice to EAL pupils, and could contribute to their long-term disadvantage, if these recent changes impact negatively on the delivery of English language support. Considering the challenges faced by children from immigrant backgrounds in L2-immersion education (highlighted, for example, by Cummins 2000, 2001), it is essential that the curricular and pedagogical practices associated with the *Benchmarks* continue to be implemented with proper resourcing and training. Otherwise, much of the progress made over the last decade in responding to the needs of EAL pupils in Irish primary schools is likely to be lost.

On a more positive note, the conclusion of this study that the *Benchmarks* map the L2 proficiency development of young learners in an L2-immersion context in a manner that clearly correlates with their patterns of L2 acquisition has considerable potential in relation to the education of children from immigrant backgrounds. The results of our research show that a framework derived from the CEFR can serve as an appropriate basis for learning, teaching and assessment for children whose home language is not the language of schooling. It is to be hoped that the model provided by the *Benchmarks* will be refined, expanded on and applied beyond the Irish context to enable young L2 learners to learn more effectively *through* their second language in the context of L2-dominant education.

Appendix 1: CEFR self-assessment grid

		A1	A2	B1	B2	C1	C2
U N D E R S T A N D I N G	Listening	I can understand familiar words and very basic phrases concerning myself, my family and immediate concrete surroundings when people speak slowly and clearly.	I can understand phrases and the highest frequency vocabulary related to areas of most immediate personal relevance (e.g., very basic personal and family information, shopping, local area, employment). I can catch the main point in short, clear, simple messages and announcements.	I can understand the main points of clear standard speech on familiar matters regularly encountered in work, school, leisure, etc. I can understand the main point of many radio or TV programmes on current affairs or topics of personal or professional interest when the delivery is relatively slow and clear.	I can understand extended speech and lectures and follow even complex lines of argument provided the topic is reasonably familiar. I can understand most TV news and current affairs programmes. I can understand the majority of films in standard dialect.	I can understand extended speech even when it is not clearly structured and when relationships are only implied and not signalled explicitly. I can understand television programmes and films without too much effort.	I have no difficulty in understanding any kind of spoken language, whether live or broadcast, even when delivered at fast native speed, provided I have some time to get familiar with the accent.

UNDERSTANDING						
Reading	I can understand familiar names, words and very simple sentences, for example on notices and posters or in catalogues.	I can read very short, simple texts. I can find specific, predictable information in simple everyday material such as advertisements, prospectuses, menus and timetables and I can understand short, simple personal letters.	I can understand texts that consist mainly of high-frequency everyday or job-related language. I can understand the description of events, feelings and wishes in personal letters.	I can read articles and reports concerned with contemporary problems in which the writers adopt particular attitudes or viewpoints. I can understand contemporary literary prose.	I can understand long and complex factual and literary texts, appreciating distinctions of style. I can understand specialised articles and longer technical instructions, even when they do not relate to my field.	I can read with ease virtually all forms of the written language, including abstract, structurally or linguistically complex texts such as manuals, specialised articles and literary works.

SPEAKING						
Spoken Interaction	I can interact in a simple way provided the other person is prepared to repeat or rephrase things at a slower rate of speech and help me formulate what I'm trying to say. I can ask and answer simple questions in areas of immediate need or on very familiar topics.	I can communicate in simple and routine tasks requiring a simple and direct exchange of information on familiar topics and activities. I can handle very short social exchanges, even though I can't usually understand enough to keep the conversation going myself.	I can deal with most situations likely to arise whilst travelling in an area where the language is spoken. I can enter unprepared into conversation on topics that are familiar, of personal interest or pertinent to everyday life (e.g., family, hobbies, work, travel and current events).	I can interact with a degree of fluency and spontaneity that makes regular interaction with native speakers quite possible. I can take an active part in discussion in familiar contexts, accounting for and sustaining my views.	I can express myself fluently and spontaneously without much obvious searching for expressions. I can use language flexibly and effectively for social and professional purposes. I can formulate ideas and opinions with precision and relate my contribution skilfully to those of other speakers.	I can take part effortlessly in any conversation or discussion and have a good familiarity with idiomatic expressions and colloquialisms. I can express myself fluently and convey finer shades of meaning precisely. If I do have a problem I can backtrack and restructure around the difficulty so smoothly that other people are hardly aware of it.

	A1	A2	B1	B2	C1	C2
Spoken Production	I can use simple phrases and sentences to describe where I live and people I know.	I can use a series of phrases and sentences to describe in simple terms my family and other people, living conditions, my educational background and my present or most recent job.	I can connect phrases in a simple way in order to describe experiences and events, my dreams, hopes and ambitions. I can briefly give reasons and explanations for opinions and plans. I can narrate a story or relate the plot of a book or film and describe my reactions.	I can present clear, detailed descriptions on a wide range of subjects related to my field of interest. I can explain a viewpoint on a topical issue giving the advantages and disadvantages of various options.	I can present clear, detailed descriptions of complex subjects integrating sub-themes, developing particular points and rounding off with an appropriate conclusion.	I can present a clear, smoothly flowing description or argument in a style appropriate to the context and with an effective logical structure which helps the recipient to notice and remember significant points.
Writing	I can write a short, simple postcard, for example sending holiday greetings. I can fill in forms with personal details, for example entering my name, nationality and address on a hotel registration form.	I can write short, simple notes and messages. I can write a very simple personal letter, for example thanking someone for something.	I can write simple connected text on topics which are familiar or of personal interest. I can write personal letters describing experiences and impressions.	I can write clear, detailed text on a wide range of subjects related to my interests. I can write an essay or report, passing on information or giving reasons in support of or against a particular point of view. I can write letters highlighting the personal significance of events and experiences.	I can express myself in clear, well-structured text, expressing points of view at some length. I can write about complex subjects in a letter, an essay or a report, underlining what I consider to be the salient issues. I can select a style appropriate to the reader in mind.	I can write clear, smoothly flowing text in an appropriate style. I can write complex letters, reports or articles which present a case with an effective logical structure which helps the recipient to notice and remember significant points. I can write summaries and reviews of professional or literary works.

Source: Council of Europe (2001: 26–27)

Appendix 2: English Language Proficiency Benchmarks

Global benchmarks of communicative proficiency

		A1 BREAKTHROUGH	A2 WAYSTAGE	B1 THRESHOLD
UNDERSTANDING	Listening	Can recognise and understand basic words and phrases concerning him/herself, family and school. Can understand simple questions and instructions when teachers and other pupils speak very slowly and clearly.	Can recognise and understand frequently used words relating to him/herself and family, classroom activities and routines, school instructions and procedures, friends and play. Can understand a routine instruction given outside school (e.g., by a traffic warden). Can understand what is said in a familiar context such as buying something in a shop (e.g., price). Can follow at a general level topics covered in the mainstream class provided key concepts and vocabulary have been studied in advance and there is appropriate visual support.	Can understand the main points of topics that are presented clearly in the mainstream classroom. Can understand the main points of stories that are read aloud in the mainstream classroom. Can understand a large part of a short film on a familiar topic provided that it is age-appropriate. Can understand detailed instructions given in all school contexts (classroom, gym, playground, etc.). Can follow classroom talk between two or more native speakers, only occasionally needing to request clarification.

		A1 BREAKTHROUGH	A2 WAYSTAGE	B1 THRESHOLD
U N D E R S T A N D I N G			Can follow and understand a story if it is read slowly and clearly with visual support such as facial expression, gesture and pictures.	
	Reading (if appropriate to the age of the pupil)	Can recognise the letters of the alphabet. Can recognise and understand basic signs and simple notices in the school and on the way to school. Can recognise and understand basic words on labels or posters in the classroom. Can identify basic words and phrases in a new piece of text.	Can read and understand very short and simple texts that contain a high proportion of previously learnt vocabulary on familiar subjects (e.g., class texts, familiar stories). Can use the alphabet to find particular items in lists (e.g., a name in a telephone book).	Can read and understand the main points in texts encountered in the mainstream class, provided the thematic area and key vocabulary are already familiar. Can read and understand descriptions of events, feelings and wishes. Can use comprehension questions to find specific answers in a piece of text. Can use key words, diagrams and illustrations to support reading comprehension. Can follow clearly written instructions (for carrying out a classroom task, assembling or using an object, following directions, etc.).
S P E A K I N G	**Spoken Interaction**	Can greet, say *please* and *thank you*, and ask for directions to another place in the school. Can respond non-verbally to basic directions to a place in the school when the other person supplements speech with signs or gestures. Can give simple answers to basic questions when given time to reply and the other person is prepared to help.	Can ask for attention in class. Can greet, take leave, request and thank appropriately. Can respond with confidence to familiar questions clearly expressed about family, friends, school work, hobbies, holidays, etc., but is not always able to keep the conversation going.	Can speak with fluency about familiar topics such as school, family, daily routine, likes and dislikes. Can engage with other pupils in discussing a topic of common interest (songs, football, pop stars, etc.) or in preparing a collaborative classroom activity. Can keep a conversation going, though he/she may have some difficulty making him/herself understood from time to time.

S P E A K I N G		Can make basic requests in the classroom or playground (e.g., for the loan of a pencil) and respond appropriately to the basic requests of others.	Can generally sustain a conversational exchange with a peer in the classroom when carrying out a collaborative learning activity (making or drawing something, preparing a role-play, presenting a puppet show, etc.). Can express personal feelings in a simple way.	Can repeat what has been said and convey the information to another person.
	Spoken Production	Can use simple phrases and sentences to describe where he/she lives and people he/she knows, especially family members.	Can use a series of phrases and sentences to describe in simple terms his/her family, daily routines and activities, and plans for the immediate or more distant future (e.g., out-of-school activities, holiday plans).	Can retell a story that has been read in class. Can retell the plot of a film he/she has seen or a book he/she has read and describe his/her reactions. Can describe a special event/celebration in the family (religious festival, birthday, new baby, etc.). Can give an account of an experience or event (travel, an accident, an incident that occurred, etc.). Can briefly give explanations and reasons for opinions and plans.
W R I T I N G	**Writing (if appropriate to the age of the pupil)**	Can copy or write his/her name. Can copy or write words and short phrases that are being learned in class. Can copy or write labels on a picture. Can copy short sentences from the board. Can spell his/her name and address, and the name of the school.	Can enter newly learnt terms in a personal or topic-based dictionary, possibly including sample sentences. Can write short texts on specific or familiar topics (e.g., what I like to do when I'm at home). Can write a short message (e.g., a postcard) to a friend.	Can write a diary or news account with accuracy and coherence. Can write a short letter describing an event or a situation. Can write a brief summary of a book or film. Can write an account of his/her feelings or reactions to an event or situation. Can write a short dialogue to be performed by puppets.

Global scales of underlying linguistic competence

	A1 BREAKTHROUGH	A2 WAYSTAGE	B1 THRESHOLD
Vocabulary control	Can recognise, understand and use a limited range of basic vocabulary which has been used repeatedly in class or has been specifically taught.	Can recognise, understand and use a range of vocabulary associated with concrete everyday needs or learning experiences (e.g., topics or routines that have been introduced and practised in class).	Can recognise, understand and use a range of vocabulary related to familiar classroom themes, school routines and activities. Errors still occur when the pupil attempts to express more complex ideas or handle unfamiliar topics.
Grammatical accuracy	Can use a very limited number of grammatical structures and simple sentence patterns that he/she has learned by repeated use (e.g., *My name is . . .*)	Can use simple grammatical structures that have been learned and practised in class. Makes frequent basic mistakes with tenses, prepositions and personal pronouns, though when he/she is speaking or writing about a familiar topic the meaning is generally clear.	Can communicate with reasonable accuracy on familiar topics (those being studied or occurring frequently during the school day). Meaning is clear despite errors. Unfamiliar situations or topics present a challenge, however, particularly when the connection to familiar patterns is not obvious.
Phonological control	Can pronounce a very limited repertoire of learned and familiar words and phrases. Native speakers who are aware of what the pupil has been learning and familiar with the pronunciation patterns of pupils from different language backgrounds can understand his/her pronunciation, but sometimes with difficulty.	Can pronounce familiar words (those being learned in class or used in the school generally) in a reasonably clear manner, though with a noticeable foreign accent. It is sometimes necessary to ask the pupil to repeat what he/she has said.	Can pronounce words with confidence in a clearly intelligible way. Some mispronunciations still occur, but in general he/she is closely familiar with the sounds of English.
Orthographic control (if appropriate to the age of the pupil)	Can copy keywords from the board, flashcards or posters. Can copy or write his/her name, address and the name of the school.	Can copy or write short sentences or phrases related to what is being studied in class. Sentence breaks are generally accurate. Words that he/she uses orally may be written with phonetic accuracy but inaccurate spelling.	Can produce short pieces of continuous writing that are generally intelligible throughout. Spelling, punctuation and layout are accurate enough to be followed most of the time.

Unit 1: Myself

		A1 BREAKTHROUGH	A2 WAYSTAGE	B1 THRESHOLD
UNDERSTAND	Listening	Can recognise his/her name when it is spoken by another person. Can understand basic questions asked by the teacher or another pupil (e.g., *What is your name? How old are you?*). Can understand simple instructions when they are spoken slowly and accompanied by appropriate gestures.	Can follow conversations between peers during play. Can follow the important points in instructions or advice (e.g., *Stay safe*).	Can understand what is said by teachers and peers without the need for frequent repetition or supporting gestures.
READING	Reading (if appropriate to the age of the pupil)	Can find his/her name on a list.	Can read very short and simple texts with a high frequency of familiar words on topics such as children, families and school. Can use the alphabet to find his/her name in a list.	Can read and understand age-appropriate stories about children and their lives, including life in different environments (e.g., country, city, abroad).
SPEAKING	Spoken Interaction	Can answer basic questions about his/her name, age, family when supported by prompts. Can respond non-verbally (e.g., with a nod or shake of the head) or with single-word or very brief answers to basic questions about his/her likes or dislikes (e.g., *Do you like ice-cream?*). Can greet the teacher and other pupils and say goodbye. Can indicate personal needs (e.g., to go to the toilet).	Can reply with confidence to familiar questions about his/her name, age, number of brothers and sisters, etc. Can initiate conversation on a familiar topic (e.g., why he/she was late for school). Can use greetings naturally and appropriately. Can say how he/she feels (tired, upset, ill, etc.). Can tell parents about what he/she did in school. Can ask for clarification when necessary.	Can ask and respond to questions on a wide range of familiar topics (family, home, interests, etc.). Can express worries or concerns to the teacher or some other responsible person. Can give parents a detailed account of what has taken place in school and describe his/her successes and achievements.

Unit 1: Myself (continued)

		A1 BREAKTHROUGH	A2 WAYSTAGE	B1 THRESHOLD
S P E A K I N G	Spoken Production	Can make a short, incomplete statement about him/herself (e.g., *name is . . .*).	Can describe his/her own appearance, including eye and hair colour, size, height. Can describe his/her family, daily routines, plans (e.g., for holidays), likes and dislikes.	Can explain his/her attitudes in an age-appropriate way (e.g., family values, ethnic or religious difference). Can relate an event in sequence, using descriptive language (especially appropriate adjectives).
W R I T I N G	Writing (if appropriate to the age of the pupil)	Can copy or write his/her name, address, name of school. Can copy words about him/herself from the board (e.g., *my name is . . .* , *I live in . . .*).	Can write short texts describing his/her family, daily routines, etc. Can write short texts describing personal interests, likes and dislikes (food, TV programmes, etc.).	Can write age-appropriate descriptions of important events or personal experiences (a new baby in the family, travelling to Ireland, etc.). Can write a brief comparison of his/her life now and in the past (e.g., before attending school, in another country). Can write about personal likes and dislikes, hobbies, interests, etc.

Unit 2: Our school

		A1 BREAKTHROUGH	A2 WAYSTAGE	B1 THRESHOLD
U N D E R S T A N D I N G	Listening	Can understand basic school and classroom rules when they are explained very simply and with appropriate gestures. Can recognise and understand the names of school equipment, resources, etc., when they occur in instructions. Can understand and follow basic instructions from peers for playing games in the playground.	Can understand instructions given in the classroom, gym, playground, etc. Can understand basic information about half days, school closures, doctor's visits, etc. Can understand at a general level topics dealt with in the mainstream class when they are introduced and explained clearly.	Can understand detailed instructions in the classroom, gym, etc. Can understand a presentation given by another pupil on a familiar topic (*My interests, My family*, etc.).
	Reading (if appropriate to the age of the pupil)	Can recognise and understand labels on doors in different parts of the school (*Hall, Secretary, Staff Room*, etc.). Can recognise and understand signs in the school (*Fire Exit, No running*, etc.). Can recognise and understand words and numbers on posters and drawings in the classroom (days of the week, months of the year, etc.) Can find his/her name on a list.	Can read and understand texts about school that use a high frequency of words already familiar or recently learned.	Can read and understand texts on school subjects provided that difficult key words and/or concepts are introduced beforehand.

Unit 2: Our school (continued)

	A1 BREAKTHROUGH	A2 WAYSTAGE	B1 THRESHOLD
Spoken Interaction S P E A K I N G	Can ask permission to go to the toilet. Can respond non-verbally (e.g., with a nod or shake of the head) or with single-word or very brief answers to basic questions on classroom topics. Can use *please* and *thank you* appropriately. Can ask for familiar classroom objects and materials (book, crayons, paper, etc.).	Can ask for attention in class. Can pass on a simple message from one teacher to another. Can generally sustain a conversation with another pupil when working collaboratively in the classroom (painting a picture, making a model, playing with puppets, etc.). With appropriate support from the teacher, can explain a situation that has arisen (e.g. a dispute with another pupil).	Can interact spontaneously in the playground, engaging with other pupils in games and activities. Can give parents a detailed account of what happens at school. Can ask and answer questions about specific classroom topics or in general discussion.
Spoken Production	Can use key words and simple phrases/sentences to describe a playground game.	Can use a series of phrases and sentences to describe what he/she watches on television, how he/she likes to do homework after school, and what he/she does at home.	Can give a simple talk about the school. Can explain to other pupils about going to school in another country.
Writing (if appropriate to the age of the pupil) W R I T I N G	Can copy letters and key words from the board, including phrases or simple sentences related to a classroom topic.	Can write short texts describing the classroom or other pupils in the class. Can write short texts based on a topic recently studied in class.	Can write an account of the daily routine in the school. Can write about his/her friends in school and what they like to do together.

Unit 3: Food and clothes

		A1 BREAKTHROUGH	A2 WAYSTAGE	B1 THRESHOLD
UNDERSTANDING	**Listening**	Can recognise and understand the words for key items of clothing (coat, shoes, etc.). Can recognise and understand the words for the key items of a school uniform. Can recognise and understand the words for key items of food typically brought to school by pupils (e.g., sandwich, apple, biscuit). Can understand routine classroom instructions about food or clothing (e.g., *Put on your apron for painting*).	Can understand instructions given about clothing for a particular purpose (e.g., going on a school trip). Can understand rules about bringing particular foods to school (e.g., chewing gum, crisps, etc.) and the reason for the rules.	Can understand classroom talk, including stories, containing a wide range of vocabulary related to food/clothing.
	Reading (if appropriate to the age of the pupil)	Can recognise and understand the names of basic foods. Can recognise and understand the names of the principal items of clothing.	Can read and understand the menu from a café or fast-food outlet. Can read and understand the names of foods typically seen in the supermarket. Can read and understand simple descriptions of food or clothing that occur in a story.	Can read and understand about healthy eating, using the food pyramid for illustration.
SPEAKING	**Spoken Interaction**	Can request basic items of food/drink in a shop. Can ask how much an item costs. Can respond non-verbally (e.g., with a nod or shake of the head) or with single-word or very brief answers to questions about the food/drink and clothes he/she likes or dislikes.	Can ask and answer basic questions about the food/drink he/she likes or dislikes and briefly report the likes and dislikes of others. Can discuss a menu and select what he/she would like. Can answer questions about items and types of clothing, e.g., what is suitable for different kinds of weather.	Can repeat an instruction given by the teacher regarding food or clothing. Can engage in discussion about clothing/fashion and food/drink, expressing personal preferences.

Unit 3: Food and clothes (continued)

		A1 BREAKTHROUGH	A2 WAYSTAGE	B1 THRESHOLD
S P E A K I N G	**Spoken Production**	Can use key words and simple phrases/sentences to describe likes and dislikes (e.g., *I do not like green apples, I like my new coat*).	Can use a series of phrases and sentences to describe the type of meal that he/she likes best. Can use a series of phrases and sentences to describe the events surrounding a meal of particular importance in the family (e.g., a religious festival, New Year, etc.).	Can describe his/her favourite items of clothing and explain why he/she likes them. Can explain the importance of particular foods in his/her family or culture. Can explain the importance of particular items of clothing in his/her family or culture.
W R I T I N G	**Writing (if appropriate to the age of the pupil)**	Can copy or write lists of different foods (fruits, vegetables, meats, etc.). Can copy or write lists of clothing according to contexts of use (e.g., outdoor, indoor, school, sports).	Can write a short text describing an event in which food plays a central role (e.g., a family celebration). Can write short texts describing his/her favourite items of clothing.	Can write in an age-appropriate way about clothes/fashion and food/drink. Can write instructions for making a dish/meal that he/she likes.

Unit 4: Colours, shapes and opposites

		A1 BREAKTHROUGH	A2 WAYSTAGE	B1 THRESHOLD
UNDERSTANDING	Listening	Can identify basic colours, shapes and opposites when they are called out by the teacher. Can find basic colours, shapes and opposites when they are called out by the teacher, e.g. in a classroom game. Can point to objects in the room on the basis of description by colour or shape.	Can follow instructions that are based on or include reference to the colour, shape or size of objects.	Can understand with ease references to colours, shapes and sizes that occur in classroom talk, including stories read aloud by the teacher, and in instructions given in the classroom or playground.
	Reading (if appropriate to the age of the pupil)	Can recognise and understand the words for basic colours. Can recognise and understand the words for basic shapes.	Can read and understand references to colour, shape or size in a simple text.	Can identify differences between objects, animals or people when they are described in terms of their colour, shape or size.
SPEAKING	Spoken Interaction	Can answer basic questions about the colours he/she likes best. Can answer basic questions about the colours of the clothes he/she is wearing.	Can ask and answer questions related to colours, shapes, size and opposites in discussion of familiar items such as clothing, food, classroom objects, etc.	Can discuss, e.g., items of clothing, food or locations in the school with reference to colour, size or shape.

Unit 4: Colours, shapes and opposites (continued)

		A1 BREAKTHROUGH	A2 WAYSTAGE	B1 THRESHOLD
S P E A K I N G	**Spoken Production**	Can name basic colours and shapes.	Can use a series of phrases and sentences to explain what colours he/she likes and why.	Can explain in an age-appropriate way the importance we attach to colours and the effect they have on us (a grey day, red for danger, etc.).
W R I T I N G	**Writing (if appropriate to the age of the pupil)**	Can copy or write the words for basic colours and shapes.	Can write a short description that includes reference to colours, size, shapes and opposites (e.g., *On the beach*).	Can write a postcard or short letter describing an object or a place with detailed reference to colour, size and shape. Can include reference to colour, size or shape in a written dialogue (e.g., for a puppet show). Can write a description of his/her favourite clothing, food, place, etc. with detailed reference to colours, sizes and shapes.

Unit 5: People who help us

		A1 BREAKTHROUGH	A2 WAYSTAGE	B1 THRESHOLD
U N D E R S T A N D I N G	**Listening**	Can recognise and understand basic words for people who help (e.g., teacher, guard, doctor, nurse) when they are spoken or read aloud.	Can understand the main points of classroom talk, including stories about people with particular responsibilities in the community, provided the vocabulary used is familiar. Can understand what is said by people who help in familiar situations (the school traffic warden, shop assistants, etc.).	Can listen to a talk given by a person from the community and understand most of what is said. Can watch a video (e.g., news or documentary) about a typical incident in the community and understand most of the commentary.
	Reading (if appropriate to the age of the pupil)	Can recognise and understand the words for people who help (e.g., teacher, guard, doctor, nurse) when they appear on flashcards and posters or in simple text.	Can read and understand short texts describing the work done by people who help (doctor, dentist, shop assistant, fireman, bus driver, etc.), provided the texts contain a high frequency of familiar words.	Can read and understand a variety of texts about different jobs and responsibilities.
S P E A K I N G	**Spoken Interaction**	Can use gestures, key words and simple phrases/sentences to ask for help (e.g., in *Stay Safe* role-plays). Can reply using key words and simple phrases/sentences to basic questions about the jobs of people who can help (e.g., *Where do we find a . . .? What does he/she do?*).	Can ask and answer questions about what people in familiar roles do in their jobs. Can talk with the teacher or another pupil about personal experiences with people in roles of responsibility (e.g., visit to doctor, parent is a nurse/doctor, school traffic warden, postman).	Can ask and answer questions about different jobs and responsibilities. Can ask questions of a speaker who has been invited to the school to talk about his/her job. Can answer typical questions that may be asked by a person in responsibility (e.g. in role-plays involving emergencies, danger, etc.).

Unit 5: People who help us (continued)

		A1 BREAKTHROUGH	A2 WAYSTAGE	B1 THRESHOLD
S P E A K I N G	**Spoken Production**	Can give his/her name, address and school to a person in authority.	Can use a series of phrases and sentences to give a brief oral description of a visit to a particular place and the people who work there (e.g., hospital, library, fire station).	Can talk about the responsibilities of people who help, using an age-appropriate range of descriptive vocabulary.
W R I T I N G	**Writing (if appropriate to the age of the pupil)**	Can copy or write the words for people in roles of responsibility. Can label pictures of people in roles of responsibility and performing familiar jobs in the community. Can copy short sentences describing the jobs that people do.	Can write short texts using familiar vocabulary to describe what people who help (e.g., shop assistant, postman, park attendant) do during their working day.	Can write briefly about a day in the life of a person with responsibility in the community, organising the text in a logical sequence and using an age-appropriate range of vocabulary. Can write a brief letter of thanks to someone who has given help (e.g., in the library, at the swimming pool).

Unit 6: Weather

		A1 BREAKTHROUGH	A2 WAYSTAGE	B1 THRESHOLD
UNDERSTANDING	**Listening**	Can recognise and understand basic words related to weather (e.g., *sun, rain, snow, hot, cold*) when they are spoken or read aloud.	Can follow at a general level weather-related topics covered in the mainstream class provided key vocabulary and concepts have been studied in advance and there is appropriate visual support.	Can watch a weather forecast on television and understand the main points. Can understand the key vocabulary used by the teacher to explain a unit in the textbook relating to weather.
	Reading (if appropriate to the age of the pupil)	Can recognise and understand basic words related to weather when they appear on a weather chart or flash-cards or in a simple text.	Can use the pictures in a textbook to identify and understand key information about weather (*rain, wind, temperature*, etc.). Can identify and understand words to do with weather in stories and other texts.	Can identify and understand the key words in, e.g., a geography text relating to weather and can use them to categorise further information in the text (e.g., the effects of wind).
SPEAKING	**Spoken Interaction**	Can respond non-verbally (e.g., with a nod or shake of the head) or with single-word or very brief answers to basic questions about the weather (e.g., *Is it cold outside?*) and the kind of weather he/she likes and dislikes.	Can respond to questions about the weather he/she likes. Can take part in discussion about the weather in Ireland and about the clothing necessary for different types of weather.	Can ask and answer questions about types of weather and the effects of weather on lifestyle.

Unit 6: Weather (continued)

S P E A K I N G	**Spoken Production**	Can use simple phrases and sentences to make a short, possibly incomplete, statement about the weather.	Can use a series of phrases and sentences, with appropriate adjectives, to describe in simple terms the weather outside the classroom.	Can compare the weather in Ireland with weather in other parts of the world.
W R I T I N G	**Writing (if appropriate to the age of the pupil)**	Can copy or write basic words to do with the weather. Can copy from the board short sentences about the weather (e.g., when writing 'news').	Can write sentences about the clothes that are necessary for different types of weather. Can write a short text about 'a perfect day'.	Can write a short letter describing the weather in Ireland and the types of clothing and other items that are necessary for different kinds of weather. Can write a short text describing the influence of weather on people in different parts of the world.

Unit 7: Transport and travel

		A1 BREAKTHROUGH	A2 WAYSTAGE	B1 THRESHOLD
U N D E R S T A N D I N G	**Listening**	Can recognise and understand basic words that refer to different modes of transport (*train*, *car*, *plane*, etc.) when they are spoken or read aloud.	Can understand references to different modes of transport that occur in classroom talk and in stories and other texts read aloud in class.	Can understand the main points in an oral account of a journey. Can understand the main points of topics related to travel and transport presented in the mainstream classroom. Can recognise and understand all frequently occurring words to do with travel and transport.
	Reading (if appropriate to the age of the pupil)	Can recognise and understand labels on pictures and posters depicting modes of transport. Can identify and understand basic words to do with transport in a simple text.	Can read and understand the key points in a short text about travelling or transport.	Can use key words and pictures/ diagrams to access text about travelling and transport. Can use key words to categorise information contained in a text (e.g., *Where did it happen?*, *Who was there?*).

Unit 7: Transport and travel (continued)

S P E A K I N G	**Spoken Interaction**	Can respond briefly, using gesture if necessary, when asked '*How did you come to school today?*' When prompted by the teacher and supported by pictures, can use basic words (including the vocabulary of colour, size and shape) and simple phrases to describe different forms of transport.	Can respond with confidence to questions about how he/she likes to travel. Can discuss experiences he/she has had in travelling. Can ask other pupils about their experience of travel.	Can participate in discussions of different modes of travel and express personal preferences. Can use illustrations in a textbook to discuss, e.g., similarities and differences between travelling now and travelling in the past. Can find out what other pupils think about different modes of transport.
	Spoken Production	Can use key words and simple phrases to name different modes of transport depicted in posters and pictures.	Can use a series of phrases and sentences to describe how he/she comes to school every day. Can name and describe briefly the different types of transport that can be seen outside the school (cars, lorries, buses, bicycles, etc.).	Can give a short talk about the types of transport seen outside the school. Can talk in an age-appropriate way about his/her experiences when travelling a long distance.
W R I T I N G	**Writing (if appropriate to the age of the pupil)**	Can copy or write key words relating to transport. Can label a picture or poster that depicts different modes of transport. Can copy from the board short sentences to do with transport (e.g., *I come to school each day by bus*).	Can write short texts about different forms of transport, using a textbook for support if necessary. Can write sentences that describe a familiar journey (e.g., from home to school).	Can write a short letter describing to another person how he/she travels to school. Can write 'news' about an incident that occurred when travelling to school.

Unit 8: Seasons, holidays and festivals

		A1 BREAKTHROUGH	A2 WAYSTAGE	B1 THRESHOLD
U N D E R S T A N D I N G	**Listening**	Can recognise and understand the words for seasons, holidays and festivals when they are spoken or read aloud. Can follow spoken instructions to find pictures or objects in the classroom that are related to different seasons or festivals.	Can recognise and understand common words related to seasons and festivals when the teacher introduces the topic in class. Can follow at a general level stories and classroom talk about seasons or festivals.	Can understand the main points of classroom talk about seasons and festivals, using visual supports (e.g., illustrations in text book) to check the teacher's explanation. Can understand the main points of a video that shows typical activities during a festival.
	Reading (if appropriate to the age of the pupil)	Can recognise and understand the words for seasons, holidays and festivals on posters or flashcards and in very simple texts.	Can read and understand a simple description of a season or the events surrounding a festival, using pictures for support. Can read and understand simple stories that contain a high proportion of familiar vocabulary about typical seasonal or festival activities (e.g., the countryside in spring, going to the beach in summer, preparing for a religious festival).	Can read and understand the main points of texts about seasons, holidays and festivals encountered in the mainstream class. Can use key words and pictures/diagrams to access texts about seasons and festivals (e.g., in a geography textbook) and to categorise the information they contain.

Unit 8: Seasons, holidays and festivals (continued)

S P E A K I N G	**Spoken Interaction**	Can respond with key words or simple phrases/sentences to questions about when the different seasons fall, what weather is typical of the different seasons, and when the major festivals occur.	Can respond in simple terms to questions about a festival or occasion that is important to his/her family or community. Can ask simple questions about seasonal matters or festivals that are unfamiliar. Can talk with other pupils about how particular festivals are celebrated in their homes.	Can describe and respond to questions about what takes place during a festival or celebration in his/her family or community. Can discuss and compare family/religious celebrations with other pupils. Can talk and ask questions about typical Irish festivals.
	Spoken Production	Can name the seasons and the principal festivals of the year.	Can use a series of phrases and sentences to give a simple description of the school holidays or a holiday taken abroad with the family. Can use a series of phrases and sentences to describe a special celebration at home.	Can describe to the rest of the class a special event/celebration in the family (religious festival, birthday, new baby, etc.).
W R I T I N G	**Writing (if appropriate to the age of the pupil)**	Can copy or write the names of the seasons and principal festivals. Can copy from the board short sentences about the seasons and festivals.	Can write simple sentences describing an event in the family (e.g., in 'news'). Can write simple sentences describing a party held to celebrate a festival (e.g., Halloween – games, food, etc.).	Can write a short text describing a festival or celebration, with comments about his/her reaction (e.g., excited, nervous, happy, tired).

Unit 9: The local and wider community

		A1 BREAKTHROUGH	A2 WAYSTAGE	B1 THRESHOLD
U N D E R S T A N D I N G	Listening	Can recognise and understand the names for people who live and work in the local community when they are spoken or read aloud. Can listen and point to pictures or a map showing where different people work (e.g., library, chemist, supermarket, police station, swimming pool).	Can understand the main points of classroom talk, including stories read aloud by the teacher, about persons working in a particular situation (e.g., station master). Can use familiar words to access the teacher's introduction to work on a theme based on the local environment.	Can use familiar vocabulary and concepts to understand the teacher's introductions to themes related to the local community. Can use familiar vocabulary and concepts to understand a video about local history, typical occupations, etc.
	Reading (if appropriate to the age of the pupil)	Can recognise and understand the names on important buildings, signs, or shops in the area. Can recognise and understand the names of buildings/places on a map of the area.	Can read and understand simple texts that provide public information (e.g., about the swimming pool), identifying essential information – what place is referred to, what happens there, etc.	Can use familiar vocabulary to understand a local information leaflet (e.g., outlining the history of a place).

Unit 9: The local and wider community (continued)

S P E A K I N G	**Spoken Interaction**	Can respond to simple questions by giving the names of buildings and places where people live and work in the area. Can use key words and simple phrases/sentences to answer basic questions about places he/she has visited in the area. Can participate in classroom discussion by naming his/her favourite place in the area (e.g., football field, park, shop).	Can ask and answer simple questions about what happens in the main public buildings in the area. Can ask and answer simple questions about what people do in those buildings.	Can discuss places that he/she has visited in the area and explain why he/she would/would not like to visit them again. Can ask and answer questions about the activities that take place in different buildings. Can ask and answer questions about the importance to the community of different buildings and activities.
	Spoken Production	Can use key words and simple phrases/sentences to describe his/her favourite place.	Can use a series of phrases and sentences to explain why he/she likes or dislikes a particular place or area.	Can talk about a place that he/she has visited. Can talk about what people do in particular places in the area (e.g., people working in library, shops, health centre, bank).
W R I T I N G	**Writing (if appropriate to the age of the pupil)**	Can copy or write the names of places in the area. Can copy from the board short sentences describing the activities associated with different places in the area.	Can write simple sentences describing his/her favourite place in the area and explaining why he/she likes it. Can write 'news' about a place in the area he/she has visited.	Can write a short description of a favourite place and what takes place there. Can write a short text describing where a particular building is located and why it is important. Can write a postcard briefly describing a place in the area.

Unit 10: Time

		A1 BREAKTHROUGH	A2 WAYSTAGE	B1 THRESHOLD
U N D E R S T A N D I N G	**Listening**	Can recognise and understand days of the week and clock times when they are spoken or read aloud (e.g., in information given by the teacher – *There will be a half day next Wednesday*).	Can understand at a general level information about the recent past or near future presented in school announcements, TV news or a documentary. Can understand the general context (past time) when the teacher introduces a historical theme in class. Can recognise the connections between past and present in stories told or read aloud in class (e.g., *Cinderella*).	Can understand the main points when the teacher introduces a historical topic in the mainstream classroom. Can understand the main points of a video film on a historical topic, using visual support. Can understand the concept of the future in fantasy stories (e.g., space and time travel).
	Reading (if appropriate to the age of the pupil)	Can recognise and understand the day and month when they are written on the board. Can recognise and understand a timetable organised according to the days of the week.	Can recognise and understand references to days, months and years in written text. Can understand a simple school notice about a forthcoming event (e.g., when it will occur, how long it will last).	Can recognise when a text refers to the past (e.g., through use of past tenses, the information provided, pictures depicting the past). Can read and understand text that refers to a time in the past (e.g., in the history textbook), using pictures/ diagrams for support.

Unit 10: Time (continued)

Spoken Interaction S P E A K I N G	Can use single words and simple phrases to answer basic questions about what he/she does every day, or what he/she did yesterday or last week.	Can discuss with other pupils how he/she knows that time has passed (e.g., children grow bigger, hair grows longer, plants grow and change, seasons follow one another). Can ask and answer simple questions about his/her recent past, previous school, etc.	Can answer questions about what he/she hopes to do in the future (e.g., after school, at the weekend, during school holidays). Can ask other pupils about their past experiences and future plans. Can explain to a new pupil about the school week/term/year.
Spoken Production S P E A K I N G	Can name the days of the week and months of the year. Can name the days when school takes place.	Can use a series of phrases and sentences to describe what happens in the course of a typical day in school. Can use a series of phrases and sentences to explain simply but clearly how the school year matches the calendar year.	Can talk about the changes in his/her life from past to present. Can talk about the changes in a plant/animal, etc. over time.
Writing (if appropriate to the age of the pupil) W R I T I N G	Can copy or write the days of the week and months of the year.	Can write sentences about his/her favourite day of the week or time of the year. Can write sentences comparing last year, last birthday, etc. with this year, this birthday, etc.	Can write a short text for a historical project describing past situations or events or comparing past and present. Can write a short imaginative text about the future.

Unit 11: People and places in other areas

		A1 BREAKTHROUGH	A2 WAYSTAGE	B1 THRESHOLD
U N D E R S T A N D I N G	**Listening**	Can recognise and understand the names of countries and nationalities represented in the school when they are spoken or read aloud. Can recognise when a simple story is located in another country.	Can understand at a general level classroom talk, including stories read aloud, about another country. Can understand the main points when the teacher introduces a topic about another country (e.g., in geography).	Can understand a video about life in another country, using visual support to aid comprehension. Can understand the main points in an oral account of an event in another country/society.
	Reading (if appropriate to the age of the pupil)	Can use pictures to identify references to different parts of the world in stories and textbooks.	Can read short simple texts, with a high proportion of familiar words, which describe features of life in other countries, using pictures for support.	Can read and understand texts about other countries, using familiar words and key concepts to aid comprehension and organise information.

Unit 11: People and places in other areas (continued)

S P E A K I N G	**Spoken Interaction**	Can use key words and simple phrases/sentences to answer basic questions about where his/her family came from. Can ask other pupils basic questions about their nationality and where they came from.	Can talk with other pupils about people in other countries in order to prepare poster projects, role-plays, etc.	Can discuss how children live in different parts of the world. Can talk with other pupils about the countries that they go to for holidays. Can talk about where he/she would like to live in the future.
	Spoken Production	Can say which country he/she came from and his/her nationality.	Can use a series of phrases and sentences to describe his/her parents' country of origin.	Can compare the principal features of life in another country with the principal features of life in Ireland. Can describe the particular features of life in his/her parents' country of origin.
W R I T I N G	**Writing (if appropriate to the age of the pupil)**	Can copy from a poster or map the names of countries and other places relevant to the class (e.g., countries of origin of other pupils). Can copy or write the name of his/her country of origin. Can draw a map of another country and copy or write the names of the country and its principal cities, etc.	Can write brief notes about life in another country after reading or hearing about that country in class.	Can draw and label maps of other countries. Can write a short 'news' account of daily life in another country. Can write a letter describing the main features of daily life in Ireland. Can write a brief summary of a story about another country.

Unit 12: Animals and plants

		A1 BREAKTHROUGH	A2 WAYSTAGE	B1 THRESHOLD
U N D E R S T A N D I N G	Listening	Can recognise and understand basic words relating to animals and plants when they are spoken or read aloud, especially when supported by pictures, mime, etc. Can recognise and understand the names of familiar animals and plants when they are read aloud in stories and other texts.	Can understand the main points in classroom talk about animals or plants, including stories and other texts read aloud by the teacher. Can understand at a general level when the teacher introduces a topic that includes references to animals or plants (e.g., Environmental Studies), provided key vocabulary has been prepared in advance.	Can understand the main points in a video about the natural world. Can understand the main points when the teacher introduces a topic about the natural world.
	Reading (if appropriate to the age of the pupil)	Can use pictorial support to recognise and understand the names of animals and plants when they are written down (e.g., in a picture dictionary). Can recognise and understand the names of animals on flashcards or posters.	Can read and understand very short and simple texts about animals, provided they contain a high proportion of familiar words and use appropriate visual support.	Can understand the main points in a text about the natural world, using familiar key words and pictures/ diagrams to support comprehension and organise information.

Unit 12: Animals and plants (continued)

S P E A K I N G	**Spoken Interaction**	Can use key words and simple phrases/sentences to answer basic questions about keeping a pet, liking animals, etc. Can use key words and simple phrases/sentences to answer basic questions about changes in plants that are kept in the classroom.	Can answer questions about which animals or plants he/she likes and dislikes. Can ask and answer questions about keeping a pet.	Can discuss with other pupils how to include animals/plants in a project, role-play, poster project, etc. Can pass on information about taking care of animals or plants.
	Spoken Production	Can name the animals that he/she is familiar with. Can say the names of the objects on the nature table.	Can use a series of phrases and sentences to talk about keeping a pet. Can use a series of phrases and sentences to talk about wild animals and where they may be found. Can use a series of phrases and sentences to explain the purpose of the objects on the nature table.	Can explain in some detail how to look after a pet. Can retell a story about animals.
W R I T I N G	**Writing (if appropriate to the age of the pupil)**	Can draw animal outlines, copying or writing appropriate labels.	Can write simple sentences about a pet or wild animal, using familiar vocabulary.	Can write an account of an incident involving an animal (e.g., a dog saves a child from drowning, a wild animal survives against the odds). Can write a summary of a story involving animals.

Unit 13: Caring for my locality

		A1 BREAKTHROUGH	A2 WAYSTAGE	B1 THRESHOLD
UNDERSTANDING	**Listening**	Can recognise and understand basic words for the main places in the area and for what happens there (e.g., shops – buy food, park – play football) when they are spoken or read aloud.	Can understand the main points in classroom talk about environmental topics, including texts read aloud by the teacher. Can understand the main points when the teacher introduces an environmental theme, provided key vocabulary has been prepared in advance.	Can understand the main points in a talk or presentation about the local environment (e.g., given by a visiting speaker from the local library). Can understand the main points when the teacher introduces an environmental topic or one related to local activities (beach clean-up, collecting litter in the park, etc.).
	Reading (if appropriate to the age of the pupil)	Can recognise basic words for buildings or places in the area (e.g., bank, shop, park, playground) on labels, maps, flashcards, etc.	Can read and understand a leaflet about a place in the locality (e.g., the local park and its wildlife), identifying key words/information, using a dictionary if necessary. Can read and understand the main points of public information leaflets about litter and other environmental dangers, using pictorial support and a dictionary if necessary.	Can read and understand a text (e.g., ENFO information sheet) about the natural world, local geographical features, care for the environment, etc., using familiar words and accompanying pictures/diagrams to aid comprehension.

Unit 13: Caring for my locality (continued)

S P E A K I N G	**Spoken Interaction**	Can use key words and simple phrases/sentences to answer basic questions about where he/she has been in the area. Can use key words and simple phrases/sentences to answer basic questions about where he/she likes to go in the area.	Can ask and answer basic questions about activities that take place in different places in the locality, including whether and for whom these activities are important. Can ask other pupils where they have been in the locality.	Can exchange ideas with other pupils on local environmental matters (e.g., when designing a project to care for a local feature).
	Spoken Production	Can say the names of the principal places in the area, using a map for support.	Can use a series of phrases and sentences to talk about a favourite place in the area.	Can give a short age-appropriate talk on a project about local community or environmental matters.
W R I T I N G	**Writing (if appropriate to the age of the pupil)**	Can copy or write onto a local map the names of buildings and locations in the area. Can copy or write basic words related to different buildings and locations (*swimming, books, money, stamps*, etc.).	Can write sentences about important places in the area, including information about the responsibilities of people living in the locality.	Can write a brief account of a local project, activity day or festival. Can write notes following a talk given by a visiting speaker on some aspect of the local environment or community.

Appendix 3
Transcription conventions

.	Falling intonation followed by noticeable pause (as at end of declarative sentence).
?	Rising intonation followed by noticeable pause (as at end of interrogative sentence).
,	Continuing intonation: may be slight rise or fall in contour (less than [.] or [?]); may be followed by a pause (shorter than [.] or [?])
!	Animated pause.
. . .	Noticeable pause or break in rhythm without falling intonation (each half-second pause is marked).
–	Self-interruption.
(talk)	Production is somewhat unclear but is capable of transcription.
xxx	Production cannot be transcribed (unintelligible, or produced by non-participant).
"a"	Letter name (e.g. 'ay') produced, rather than phoneme (e.g. /a/).
emph	Underlining used to indicate emphatic stress.
CAPS	Used to indicate named reference e.g. (PUPIL 1); see notes below regarding role markers.
Italics	Used to provide contextual information associated with production (may include some indication of its phonological characteristics).

Role markers used in transcripts:

P2	Pupil – e.g. Pupil 2. For ethical reasons, participating pupils were numerically coded (codes later changed to pseudonyms).
T	Teacher.
R	Researcher.
NPP	Non-participating pupil.

Source: adapted from Schiffrin (1994)

Appendix 4
Coding scheme

Strand 1: Functional analysis (Coding with respect to the *English Language Proficiency Benchmarks*)		
Example codes	**Signification**	**Comments**
U3/A1/SpInt/1	Transcribed pupil turn links to *Benchmarks* Unit 3/Proficiency level A1/Skill spoken Interaction/1st descriptor: 'Can request basic items of food/drink in a shop' (Integrate Ireland Language and Training 2003a:12).	Where multiple descriptors are associated with specific skills and proficiencies within the *Benchmarks* units of work, individual descriptors are identified numerically – e.g. in Unit 3, for the skill of spoken interaction at proficiency level A1 there are three descriptors, numbered accordingly: 1st=/1, 2nd=/2, 3rd=/3.
List	Listening	
Read	Reading	
SpInt	Spoken Interaction	
SpProd	Spoken Production	
Write	Writing	
%	Transcibed pupil turn links, by approximation, to a *Benchmarks* descriptor: e.g. U3/A1/SpInt/1%, an approximate link to the descriptor cited above – would be appropriate if a pupil *responds* in a simple manner to a request for basic items of food/drink in a shop.	*Benchmarks* associated with such approximations may need some minor adjustment, e.g. U3/A1/SpInt/1 may require expansion to cover both simple requests and simple responses to requests. *(All suggestions resulting from these approximations have been noted and are presented in Appendix 5.)*
$	Difficult to link transcribed pupil turn to a specific *Benchmarks* descriptor.	A new *Benchmarks* descriptor may be required to cover e.g. a slightly wider range of topic areas within an existing thematic unit or a new theme. *(All suggestions resulting from such unlinkable turns have been noted and are presented in Appendix 5.)*
>	Link to another *Benchmarks* descriptor / Link to another thematic unit, e.g. if a pupil's transcribed turn: 'yeah it's red and white' focusses on	Pupils' transcribed turns are coded with respect to the *Benchmarks* by considering the functional focus of each turn in its particular context. However, given the semantic

Strand 1: Functional analysis (Coding with respect to the *English Language Proficiency Benchmarks*) (continued)		
Example codes	**Signification**	**Comments**
	the colour of a car it may be coded as U4/A2/SpInt/1/(>U7) to indicate that it links to a descriptor from Unit 4 (Colours, shapes and opposites), but also connects to Unit 7 (Transport and travel).	connections between different themes and the functional connections between descriptors, information regarding any secondary thematic/descriptor links is included where appropriate.
#	Uncertainty	Uncertainty in coding due either to ambiguous, fragmented or indistinct production, may be associated with 'borderline' cases in deciding between *Benchmarks* associated with different proficiency levels.
X	Pupil's transcribed turn is not coded with respect to *Benchmarks* as it is either indecipherable or lacks sufficient context to determine meaning.	Includes e.g. single-word turns comprising expressives such as 'oh!' for which it may be difficult to establish actual reference or meaning from the recording.

Strand 2: Formal analysis (Basic linguistic coding)		
Code	**Signification**	**Comments**
N	Noun – singular	Common noun, singular form, includes compound nouns e.g. schoolbag, pencil-case, break-time etc.
Npl	Noun – plural	Common noun, plural form.
PN	Proper noun	Personal names of pupils, teachers, or other individuals such as family members or friends (these are anonymously referenced in the transcripts e.g. PUPIL 7), well-known character names e.g. Spider-Man (transcribed), place names (local place names are anonymously referenced in transcript – more 'globalised' place names are transcribed e.g. McDonald's), and product names (transcribed e.g. Coca-Cola).
Nposs / PNposs	Noun with possessive marker	Common or proper noun modified to indicate possession ('-s or -s').
Nln	Letter name	Alphabetical 'name' of letter e.g. 'a', 'b', 'c' etc.
Ph	Phonic sound	Phonic sounds associated with letters or beginnings of words e.g. ssss.
PROpers	Personal pronoun	Pronoun – personal (singular/plural) I, you, she, they, me, him, us etc.

Strand 2: Formal analysis (Basic linguistic coding) (continued)		
Code	**Signification**	**Comments**
PROposs	Possessive pronoun	Mine/yours/his/hers etc.
PROrefl	Reflexive pronoun	Myself/yourself etc.
PROdem	Demonstrative pronoun	This/that/these/those.
PROindef	Indefinite pronoun	Somebody/anybody/nothing/everything etc.
PROsubst	Substitute pronoun	One/ones e.g. this one.
PROnum	Numeral	Exact quantitatives – 'names' of numbers e.g. two/ten etc.
PROquant	Quantifier	Inexact quantitatives e.g. all, both, many, half, some, few, none, much, several, each, a lot, a great deal etc.
PROord	Ordinatives	Exact ordinatives e.g. the first/second etc. or inexact ordinatives e.g. the following.
PROrel	Relative pronoun	Pronouns binding a relative subordinate clause to (an element of) the main clause e.g. who/whom/which/that. 'Question words' used as PROrel marked as PROrelQ (to investigate in greater depth emerging features of L2 acquisition).
DETart	Article	Definite: the. Indefinite: a/an; some (plural).
DETposs	Possessive determiner	My/your/his/her etc.
DETdem	Demonstrative determiner	This/that/these/those (+ noun).
DETnum	Numeral as determiner	e.g. five cars/three houses.
DETquant	Quantifier (as determiner)	Includes e.g. all children/all the children (both/many/much/some/many/much/some/few/several # noun) also distributives (each/every + noun), fractions/multipliers e.g. half/double the size.
DETord	Ordinative determiner	e.g. his first jump.
Q	Question word	'Wh' question words: who, whom, whose, which, what, where, why, when, how. May be used as a single code or added as code to other elements. For purposes of analysis, # use of 'question words' as direct questions is coded: /Q/; their use as relativisers is coded e.g. /PROrelQ/ or /ADVrelQ/; their use as indirect questions is coded: /IQ/. Question formation by inversion is coded e.g. AUX+Q or VcopQ.

Strand 2: Formal analysis (Basic linguistic coding) (continued)		
Code	**Signification**	**Comments**
A	Adjective	Adjective (non-comparative /non-superlative form).
Acomp	Comparative adjective	Adjective morphologically marked to indicate comparative e.g. bigger.
Asup	Superlative adjective	Adjective morphologically marked to indicate superlative e.g. biggest.
AMcomp / AMsup	Adjective modifier	Modifier used with adjective to indicate comparative (more)/superlative (most). Applies to use of more/most only in cases of adjective modification.
V	Verb	Verb in infinitive stem or present form (includes morphological marking 3p '-s' and imperative use).
Ving	Present participle form of verb, marked by '-ing' ending	Used to indicate aspect e.g. verb in present progressive form marked by '-ing'.
Vpast	Verb in simple past tense with marking '-ed' or irregular past verb	Verbs in past tense form marked by '-ed' or irregular past tense forms (e.g. walked/went).
Vpp	Past participle form of verb ('-en'/'-ed'/ irregular past participle)	Verb form used to indicate aspect in present, past and future perfect tenses e.g. broken/ walked / gone – also used to indicate passive voice.
Vcop	Copular verb 'to be'	Verb 'to be' linking subject with predicate (focus only on copular verb 'be' in this study as it is frequently used as an indicator of L2 acquisition), use within past context e.g. 'was'/'were' coded as VcopPast, use within question context coded as VcopQ, or VcopPastQ.
VN	Verbal noun	Participle of verb functioning as a noun e.g. learning English is easy (in this study, also applied to the use of '-ing' endings within the formation of compound noun phrases e.g. swimming pool, involving some modification of verbs which pupils are in the process of acquiring).
VApp	Verbal adjective	Adjective formed using past participle of verb e.g. a broken pencil (in this study generally only used in relation to verbs which appear to be concurrently in the process of acquisition, i.e. some evidence of modification, verb-derived adjectives which appear to be used only in an adjectival sense within the transcripts are usually coded, based on context /A/).

Code	Signification	Comments
Strand 2: Formal analysis (Basic linguistic coding) (continued)		
AUX	Auxiliary verb	Auxiliary verbs used to indicate tense/aspect/ mood/voice (auxiliaries are coded to indicate verbal origin, interrogative and negative mood, tense): e.g. AUXbePastNeg.
AUXbe	Verb 'to be' used as auxiliary	Aspect markers e.g. present progressive: is/are making/past progressive: was/were making (also in conjunction with other auxiliaries e.g. future progressive, future form 'going to' and perfect forms) also passive markers e.g. is made/was made.
AUXdo	Verb 'to do' used as auxiliary	Present or past tense use of do/did in negatives and questions – e.g. he doesn't walk/did she walk?
AUXhave	Verb 'to have' used as auxiliary	Use of has/have/had to indicate aspect in perfect tenses.
AUXwill	Verb form 'will' to indicate future	Positive and negative use of 'will' to indicate future reference (this is really just a specific instance of use of modals for prediction, however for research purposes it is interesting to examine when learners develop ability to express future reference).
AUXgoto	Form 'going to' indicate future (e.g. plans)	Form 'going to' used with AUXbe to indicate future reference (e.g. plans), may also appear in transcripts as 'gonna', to indicate phonetic contraction.
AUXmod	Verb form used as modifier to indicate ability, possibility, obligation etc.	Forms such as can/could/would/may/might/ must/should etc. also includes units which may be considered 'phrasal' or 'semi' auxiliaries e.g. 'have to'.
ADV	Adverb	Adverb modifying verb/circumstantial adverbs (modifying degree of adjective, noun phrase or prepositional phrase – e.g. really/just/only etc.; conjunctive adverbs (e.g. so); deictic references e.g. here/there/now/then etc. (Prepositional adverbs are considered in notes for PREP below).
ADVrel	Relative adverb	Relative adverbs e.g. when/why/where, functioning as a clause marker e.g. 'the time when . . .', generally require use of 'question word' – coded as /ADVrelQ/.
PREP	Preposition	Preposition indicating location/time/relationship/ means/causality, connected to a phrase or clause, prepositions as particles in phrasal verbs/ prepositional adverbs (generally coded as/PREP/ considering early stage of participants' L2 development).

Strand 2: Formal analysis (Basic linguistic coding) (continued)		
Code	Signification	Comments
INF	Infinitive particle	The use of 'to' to indicate the infinitive form of the verb.
NEG/Neg	Negative particle	Negative particle 'not' used independently or, often in contracted form, with auxiliaries – e.g. do not/do+n't). In this study, may be added to pronouns and adverbs may indicate negativity, e.g. never: ADVNeg/nobody PROindefNeg, in order to examine more fully the development of negative expression in participants' L2 use.
CON	Co-ordinating conjunction	Conjunctions linking units of equal grammatical status: e.g. and/but/or.
SUB	Subordinating conjunction	Conjunctions binding clauses of unequal grammatical status (main to subordinate/ hierarchical series of subordinate clauses) e.g.: because/if etc.
TC	Subordinator marking 'that-clause'	Subordinator 'that' functioning as a complementizer, e.g. You know that I don't want to read the book.
IQ	Indirect question	Nominal subordinate clause introduced by a 'question word' – wh-binding elements, wh-adverbs (how/why/when/where) or wh-pronouns (what/who/which/whose) e.g. I don't know where the pencil is.
EXP	Expressives	Includes interjections e.g. oh!/ah!/aha!/ wow!/ouch!/oops!/cool! Also expletives – swear words etc., phrases e.g. Oh my God! Also animal noises e.g. baa etc. – coded EXPnoise.
INTmin	Minimal interactives	Interactives functioning primarily to maintain interaction e.g. yes/yeah/no/OK/oh/ah
INTsoc	Social interactives	Interactives with an identifiable social purpose e.g. hi/bye/hello/please/thank you/excuse me/ sorry etc.
*	Non-target-like use	* Indicates that element is produced in non-target-like manner (in terms of grammar OR lexis) e.g. I go to school yesterday – PROpers/V*/N/ADV//, also includes omissions of elements, marked /*/ e.g. I want book – PROpers/V/*/N//. Can also indicate semantic inappropriateness. (See page 268 for further coding of non-target-like production as part of Data Analysis Phase II).
~	Hesitation in production of language element	Can come before element (e.g. false start) or after (e.g. incomplete utterance).

Strand 2: Formal analysis (Basic linguistic coding) (continued)		
Code	**Signification**	**Comments**
#	Uncertainty re language element	May depend on context, e.g. is the pupil using the word 'sleep' as a verb or a noun? Can also indicate any phonological uncertainty noted in the transcripts.
X	Non-analysable element	Element cannot be analysed, generally due to indecipherability.

Coding was generally applied at word-level (sensitive to morphological markings); however, a single code may cover a multi-word unit performing a single grammatical function e.g. Santa Claus – /PN/.

Strand 3: Conversation analysis (coding of interactional features)			
Codes indicating basic adjacency pairs			
First pair part (FPP)		**Second pair part (SPP)**	
QUESTION	**Q**	ANSWER	**Ans**
Information-seeking question – elicits information not known to speaker.	**Q(IS)**	Provide 'acceptable' (sufficient/anticipated) response information/ opinion).	**Ans(Iprov)** **Ans(Oprov)**
Elicit information known to questioner.	**Q(IK)**	Provide 'partial' response – may require expansion/ repair.	**Ans(Ipart)** **Ans(Opart)**
Opinion seeking question.	**Q(OS)**	Provide response which	**Ans(Iprov)***
Elicit response from selection of known information.	**Q(SEL)**	is not acceptable to questioner – requires further work/repair.	**Ans(Oprov)***
Knowledge-checking question (e.g. do you know X?)	**Q(EK)**	Respond with: Suggestion. Partial suggestion. Unacceptable suggestion. (SUG also be used as FPP – see below.)	**SUG** **SUGpart** **SUG***
		Minimal response indicating knowledge.	**Ans(K)**
		Minimal response indicating lack of knowledge.	**Ans(NK)**
		N.B.: after SPP, responses may be accepted or rejected by questioner.	**Ac(Ans)** **Rej(Ans)**

Strand 3: Conversation analysis (coding of interactional features) (continued)			
Codes indicating basic adjacency pairs			
First pair part (FPP)		**Second pair part (SPP)**	
TOPIC PROFFER Provide information/ opinion on new aspect of topic/'news-marker' indicating shift of focus, e.g. by elaborating on FPP/SPP/asking a topic-related question (often a yes/no or tag question) aligns with speaker, may extend sequence (see *Post* sequences below).	**TOP** **TOP(EL)** **TOPQ** **TOPQtag**	RESPONSE TO TOPIC Align with speaker – accept and elaborate on topic – generally additional information, but possibly adding opinion. Accept topic (e.g. following tag question) without expansion. Deny alignment with speaker (reject topic).	**TOP(EL)** **TOP(EL-Oprov)** **Ac(TOP)&NEL** Minimal alignment (without elaboration, see also *Post* sequences below) **Rej(TOP)** Non-alignment.
TELLING Initiation providing information (e.g. explanation etc.) or opinion. Story telling: telling sequence negotiated so as to allow extended multi-unit turns.	**TEL** **TEL(Iprov)** **TEL(Oprov)** **TEL(Story)**	RESPONSE: Provide information/opinion. Reaction to information/ opinion: Aligning with speaker (accepting information/ opinion). Denying alignment (rejecting information/ opinion).	**Ac(TEL)** **Rej(TEL)** Telling may be responded to by elaboration **R(TEL)&EL**
Request for item/action to be performed/ permission/practical or language-related help. Request for clarification (relates to *Repair* sequences, see below).	**REQ** **REQclar**	Accept/Reject (decline) request. Request acceptance may be in form of e.g. offer. Request may be challenged. Accept request for clarification by providing clarification.	**Ac(REQ)** **Rej(REQ)** **OFF** **Chall(REQ)** **CLAR**
OFFER	**OFF**	Accept/Reject (decline) offer.	**Ac(OFF)** **Rej(OFF)**
INVITATION	**INV**	Accept/Reject (decline) invitation.	**Ac(INV)** **Rej(INV)**

Strand 3: Conversation analysis (coding of interactional features) (continued)			
Codes indicating basic adjacency pairs			
First pair part (FPP)		**Second pair part (SPP)**	
SUGGESTION Making a suggestion (may be topic or sequence related). In pedagogical context, may include partial suggestion to be completed.	**SUG** **SUGpart**	Accept/Reject (decline) suggestion. Complete partial suggestion with acceptable information.	**Ac(SUG)** **Rej(SUG)** **SUGcomp**
INSTRUCTIONS May also include instructions to focus (see below). Also, within L2 classroom, teacher may give 'instruction to repeat' – (see Repair sequences).	**INST** **INST(Rp)**	Respond to instructions. May include non-verbal response. Respond by repeating in accordance with instruction.	**R(INST)** **NVR** **Rp**
SUMMONS Orients recipients' attention by 'calling on' recipient.	**SUM**	Respond to summons (could also reject/ challenge summons in manner similar to requests – see above).	**R(SUM)**
FOCUS Focus marker – functions to orient attention (cf. summons).	**FOC**	Respond to focus of attention (e.g. request) which generally follows.	**R(FOC)**
ANNOUNCEMENT Generally indicating orientation within interaction e.g. 'I'm finished' etc. If content based, treat as TEL(Iprov).	**ANN**	Respond to announcement (could also challenge).	**R(ANN)**
COMPLAINT Also includes reprimands.	**CMP**	Accept and remedy complaint. Reject/deny complaint. Challenge (e.g. with counter complaint).	**Ac(CMP)** **(CMP)** **Chall(CMP)**
ACCUSATION	**ACC**	Respond to accusation. Reject accusation. Challenge accusation (could also make a complaint).	**R(ACC)** **Rej(ACC)** **Chall(ACC)**

Strand 3: Conversation analysis (coding of interactional features) (continued)			
Codes indicating basic adjacency pairs			
First pair part (FPP)		**Second pair part (SPP)**	
APOLOGY	**APOL**	Accept apology. Reject apology.	**Ac(APOL)** **Rej(APOL)**
EXCLAMATION	**EXCL**	Respond to exclamation.	**R(EXCL)**
GREETING	**GRT**	Greeting response.	**GRT**
SOCIAL ENQUIRY Generally follows on from greeting: 'How are you?' etc.	**ENQsoc**	Respond to social enquiry (with conventional/anticipated response). Respond to social enquiry with (more meaningful) elaboration.	**R(ENQ)** **R(ENQ)&EL**
LEAVE-TAKING (See also *Closing* sequences below)	**LT**	Leave-taking response.	**LT**
READING Turn involving reading (aloud). Request to read. Partial reading	**READ** **REQ(READ)** **READpart**	Respond to reading (accept or reject). Respond to request to read by reading. Complete reading.	**Ac(READ)** **Rej(READ)** **READ** **READcomp**
SPELLING Spelling aloud	**SPELL**	Respond to spelling (accept or reject). Sequences may also comprise requests to spell/completion of spellings etc. (see 'reading' above).	**Ac(SPELL)** **Rej(SPELL)**
RECITATION In primary school context e.g. nursery rhymes, poems etc.	**RECIT**	Respond to recitation (accept or reject). Sequences may also comprise requests to recite/completion of recitation etc. (see 'reading' above).	**Ac(RECIT)** **Rej(RECIT)**
SINGING	**SING**	Respond to singing (cf. 'reading' for further sequence options).	**R(SING)**
NOISE Non-verbal but 'meaningful' noise e.g. making animal or vehicle sounds.	**NOISE**	Respond to noise.	**R(NOISE)**

Strand 3: Conversation analysis (Coding of interactional features) (continued)			
Sequence expansion/Completion/Repair/General codes			
INDICATION OF MAIN ADJACENCY PAIRS	**F** **S**	Highlight main pairs within sequence: FPP base SPP base	**Fb:** **Sb:**
PRE-EXPANSION	**Pre:**	Pre-sequences may be identifiable as: Pre-request Pre-telling Pre-question Pre-offer Pre-summons Pre-announcement Prefacing story	For example: **Pre:REQ** Pre-pre-sequences may also occur (adjacency pairs in pre-sequences are not separately coded as F/S).
INSERT EXPANSION	**Ins:**	Insertion of sub-sequence after FPP but before SPP.	Insert expansion may include its own distinct adjacency pairs – e.g. **Ins:Q(IS)// Ins:Ans(Iprov)** These are not separately coded (as F/S).
POST-EXPANSION	**Post:**	Expansion following SPP. May also involve repair (if so, coded as **REP:** – see below	Post expansion may include its own distinct adjacency pairs – not separately coded (as F/S).
EXTENDED TURN EXPANSION	**EXT:**	One speaker allowed extended turns due to the nature of the sequence e.g. story-telling, reading aloud.	Also **Fbext: / Sbext:** where the base FPP (or SPP) in the extended sequence comprises several units.

Strand 3: Conversation analysis (Coding of interactional features) (continued)			
Sequence expansion/Completion/Repair/General codes			
SEQUENCE CLOSING THIRDS Turns designed to achieve sequence closure (N.B.: may still be followed by further expansion, see e.g. **PCM** below)	**SCT:**	Following *Fb/Sb* or *Fb/Sb/Post* sequence. Marked for repair sequences. SCT may be minimal e.g. Oh/OK (previous turn received/ accepted). May comprise social phrases – thanks etc. May include assessment e.g. 'Good'. Or SCT may be composite: e.g. Oh. OK./Oh, good (including element of assessment).	**SCT** **SCTrep** **SCT: Ac(X)** **SCT: SOC** **SCT:AS** **SCT:Ac(X)&AS**
SOCIAL EXPRESSIONS	**SOC**	Generally featuring in closing sequences e.g. 'enjoy your meal'/thank you etc. (see also 'social enquiry' *Fb/Sb* pairs above).	**SOC**
ASSESSMENT	**AS**	Assessment – # evaluation (generally positive, possibly with upgrading) resulting in alignment as a means of sequence closure e.g. 'good', 'great' etc. N.B. negative assessments may require further expansion.	**Ac(AS)** **Rej(AS)**
POST COMPLETION MUSING	**PCM**	Additional turn relating to completed sequence.	
POST-EXPANSION AFTER DISPREFERRED SPP	**Rej / Chall**	Rejection of/challenge to SPP – disagreement-based expansion required – may involve reworking of original SPP until disagreement is resolved. May also involve accounting for non-alignment following Rej/Chall etc.	**R(Rej)** **Rej(Chall)** **ACO**

Strand 3: Conversation analysis (Coding of interactional features) (continued)			
Sequence expansion/Completion/Repair/General codes			
ELABORATION OF SPP	**EL**	Elaboration resulting from SPP, may involve conveying of new information or opinions (cf. 'topicalisation' above). Could be expanded to involve assessment or qualification (negative evaluation). In *Post* sequence, opportunity to elaborate need not be taken up, resulting in non-elaboration. Also consider request for elaboration.	**R(EL) & TOP(EL)** **R(EL)&AS** **R(EL)&NEL** **TOP(EL)**
	REQ(EL)	Response – elaboration on topic requested. (In L2 classroom context, such sequences may have a more linguistic focus.)	
COUNTER	**COU**	Projects the FPP back upon the original speaker.	
PAUSE	**Pau**	May indicate topic break or need for repair.	
HESITATION	**H**	Hesitation – may be due to interactional or language factors – marked by use of non-verbals (e.g. 'em'/'eh'). N.B. – incomplete or hesitant attempts at verbal production may be classified within Repair sequences.	
LAUGH	**Lau**	Laughter as part of turn.	
WORD-PLAY	**wp**	Ludic use of language, generally added as a sub-code.	

Strand 3: Conversation analysis (Coding of interactional features) (continued)			
Sequence expansion/Completion/Repair/General codes			
REPAIR Particularly in L2 classroom interaction, repair initiation and actual repair may occur across a (lengthy) sequence of turns by different speakers – i.e. *Repair* sequence. May occur as either Insert expansion or Post expansion.	**REP:**	May be: Self-initiated self-repair (Speaker indicates & solves prob). Self-initiated other-repair (Speaker indicates prob – other solves). Other-initiated self-repair (Other indicates prob, Speaker solves). Other-initiated other repair (Other indicates and solves prob).	**CORself** Indicates self-initiated self-repair within own turn. Instances of other (initiated) repair are identifiable from the overall repair sequence – N.B. codes e.g. **REC / COR** etc. (explained below).
RECAST	**REC**	Recasting (some or all) of problem source turn (generally for linguistic reasons). May recast (elements of) own turn of or other's turn. Other-initiated recasts (e.g. by the teacher) may or may not be incorporated by the subsequent speaker (e.g. pupil). Recasting also relates to the more general concept of 'reworking' e.g. of FPP.	**RECself** Self-recast within own turn. Recast of other marked as sub code: 'rec' e.g. **Ac(EL)rec** **Ac(Ans)rec** **R(SUG)rec** **Fb(1) / Fb(2)** Before any definite repair sequence emerges, a problematic or unclear **Fb1** may be recast (by the same speaker) to make it more accessible to the recipient **(Fb2)**.
REPEAT	**Rp** **Irp**	Repeat production (own or another's) – could be delayed. Immediate repetition of some/all or another speaker's turn – direct repetition. May also feature as a sub-code.	For example: **Ans(Iprov)irp**
CORRECTION	**COR**	Correction, may be direct or embedded. May also involve providing 'missing info' e.g. after a pause (no response).	**COR(Iprov)**

Strand 3: Conversation analysis (Coding of interactional features) (continued)			
Sequence expansion/Completion/Repair/General codes			
RESPONSE TO CORRECTION	**Ac(COR)** **Rej(COR)** **Chall(COR)**	Correction may be accepted e.g. direct repetition of **COR** item, or it may be incorporated into the recipient's turn. Correction may also be declined (rejected/ignored/challenged). Acceptance of **COR** by immediate repetition. **COR** in response to prompt (assisted, but not full correction). **COR** partially successful, some incorporation of **COR** but needs further repair. In some cases **COR** may not be incorporated.	**CORirp** **CORprom** **CORpart** **CORninc**
PROMPT	**PROM**	Prompting suggesting target response without providing full correction – includes part of target response (otherwise classify as e.g. **SUGpart**). Prompt may result in correction (see above), or may not be incorporated.	**PROMninc**
REQUEST FOR CLARIFICATION	**REQ(CLAR)**	Clarification provided as means of repair (see 'requests' above). Correction may require clarification.	**CLAR**
EXPRESSION OF NEED FOR REPAIR	**TEL(NK)**	Turn indicating a problem exists e.g. 'I don't know' (may be language or cognition related).	**R(TEL) &** **TEL(Iprov)**

Strand 3: Conversation analysis (Coding of interactional features) (continued)			
Sequence expansion/Completion/Repair/General codes			
PRE-REPAIR PROBLEM SOURCE	(!)	Indicates that turn may lead to a repair sequence (e.g. turn contains linguistic error) – depends on context as to whether this will be addressed). N.B. original speaker's turn may not appear problematic (e.g. teacher's turn), however it may cause issues for the recipient (e.g. pupil), possibly due to comprehension difficulties.	
CHECK	**CH**	Could be related to language/cognition/ listening abilities/ concentration/ environmental factors. May involve: Minimal check – may be non-verbal e.g. 'hmh?' or 'yes?'/'no?' Check (e.g. answer) by immediate repetition. Check with new question (tag questions may also act as 'checks'). May appear in *Repair* sequences or precipitate repair.	**CH(Ans)irp** **CH(Q)**
CONFIRM	**Cf**	Confirmation of a response e.g. 'yeah' (minimal acceptance), or confirmation with immediate repetition, may follow a 'check'. Generally appear in *Post* or *Repair* sequences.	**Cf(Ac)**
TURN MANAGEMENT In classroom interaction, some short turns may function solely to manage the turn-taking sequence (cf. SUM / FOC etc. above).	**TM**	Possible turn management: Move on Go ahead Giving other speaker right to take turn. TM may be responded to with further TM.	**R(TM)**

Strand 3: Conversation analysis (Coding of interactional features) (continued)			
Sequence expansion/Completion/Repair/General codes			
INTERLOCUTOR IDENTITY	**p–p (p–ps)** **p–t** **p–self** **t–p (t–ps)**	For each turn, the identity of speakers is marked: pupil to other pupil(s) pupil to teacher pupil self-talk teacher to pupil(s)	
UNCERTAINTY	#	Uncertainty as to how the turn element should be coded (due to ambiguities in context).	
UNFINISHED	~	Turn or turn element appears to be unfinished (due either to interruption or to language issues).	
INTERRUPTION	^	Interruption by other speaker or due to two or more speakers speaking together.	
BREAK IN CODING	<	Break where a non-participating pupil's turn (non-transcribed, marked xxx) intervenes in sequence involving participating pupils.	
SEQUENCE UNCLEAR	(seq?)	Break due to gap in transcription due to interruption of lesson, indecipherability or non-transcribed (lengthy) teacher turn.	
NON-ANALYSABLE	X	Turn or turn element is not analysable, generally due to indecipherable production.	
SEQUENCE MARKERS	{ }	Marking the beginning and end of identifiable interactional sequences	

Data Analysis Phase II: Additional linguistic sub-codes

The coding system presented below shows how linguistic errors and omissions were further described in Data Analysis Phase II. This system is based on the L2 production of EAL pupils participating in our study and has been used to provide a detailed, data-driven illustration of their L2 use. Due to the diversity of this L2 use, it was necessary to devise an extensive range of linguistic sub-codes. We present a sample of these codes, particularly those relating to the six grammatical indicators of L2 acquisition which were analysed both quantitatively and qualitatively as explained in Chapter 3. The sample below is not an exhaustive list of these codes. However, additional sub-codes for these six grammatical indicators, and elements which do not feature in this sample (e.g. adjectives, possessive determiners) were devised in a similar fashion. In each case, the nature of the error/omission involved and the likely production of a native-English-speaking child in an equivalent context was considered.

Sample of additional linguistic sub-codes used in Data Analysis Phase II	
#phon	Phonological ambiguity.
#ambig	Semantic ambiguity may relate to lexical choice or to child's idiosyncratic interpretation of talk topic.
#nob	Omission of element in non-obligatory context (e.g. omission of article in context of a guessing or naming activity in which a native-English-speaking child may not necessarily include articles).
#frag	Fragmented or unfinished turn – often due to interruption.
#play	Ambiguity possibly due to word play.
IC	Incorrect choice – refers to incorrect choice of lexis or, in combination with other sub-codes, to incorrect choice of grammatical element.
N*NoSR	Noun with incorrect number – singular required.
N*NoPLR	Noun with incorrect number – plural required.
N*PossR	Noun form incorrect – possessive form required.
V*NoSR	Verb with incorrect number – singular required.
V*NoPLR	Verb with incorrect number – plural required.
V*TPastR	Verb in incorrect tense – past required.
V*TPresR	Verb in incorrect tense – present required.
V*TVppR	Verb in incorrect tense – past participle required.
V*AProgR	Verb with incorrect aspect – progressive required.
Ving*AVstemR	Verb with incorrect aspect – simple required.

Sample of additional linguistic sub-codes used in Data Analysis Phase II (continued)	
V*VInfR	Incorrect verb form – infinitive required.
Vcop*NoSR	Copular verb 'to be' with incorrect number – singular required.
Vcop*NoPLR	Copular verb 'to be' with incorrect number – plural required.
PROpers*CSubjR	Personal pronoun with incorrect case – subject pronoun required.
PROpers*CObjR	Personal pronoun with incorrect case – object pronoun required.
PROpers*GenMR	Personal pronoun with incorrect gender – masculine required.
PROpers*GenFR	Personal pronoun with incorrect gender – feminine required.
PROpers*NoSR	Personal pronoun with incorrect number – singular required.
PROpers*NoPR	Personal pronoun with incorrect number – plural required.
PROpers*ICpossR	Incorrect choice of personal pronoun – possessive marker required.
DETart*ICaR	Incorrect choice of article – 'a' required.
DETart*ICthe R	Incorrect choice of article – 'the' required.
DETart*ICanR	Incorrect choice of article – 'an' required.
DETart*ICpossR	Incorrect use of article – possessive marker required.
DETart*NR	Article used when not required.
PREP*IC	Incorrect choice of personal pronoun, generally sub-coded to indicate nature of error (e.g. PREP*ICinRon: 'in' used incorrectly in context requiring 'on').
PREP*NR	Preposition used when not required
AUXbe*IC	Incorrect choice of auxiliary, generally sub-coded to indicate nature of error (e.g. AUXbe*ICdoR – auxiliary 'be' used incorrectly in context requiring auxiliary 'do').
AUXbe*NoPLR	Auxiliary used with incorrect number – plural required.
AUXbe*TPastR	Auxiliary used with incorrect tense – past form required.
O*N	Omission of noun.
O*V	Omission of verb, generally sub-coded to indicate nature of omission (e.g. O*Vcop, O*Vpast etc.).
O*PROpers	Omission of personal pronoun, generally sub-coded to indicate nature of omission (e.g. O*PROpersSubj, O*PROpersObj).
O*DETart	Omission of article.
O*PREP	Omission of preposition.
O*AUXbe	Omission of auxiliary e.g. 'be'.
O*Mult	Omission of multiple elements (ambiguity may arise if elements individually specified).
O*X	Omission of element, ambiguous.

Appendix 5
Suggested adjustments to the Benchmarks

Table A5.1 shows the frequency with which *Benchmarks* descriptors were directly activated in the lessons selected for Data Analysis Phase II. Table A5.2 lists the approximations involved in linking participants' L2 production to the *Benchmarks* descriptors across the selected lessons. Occasionally, in some lessons, only approximations (and direct links) could be made to certain descriptors. Most of these approximations were relatively minor and often influenced by the interactional context of pupils' L2 use; for example, they may have produced response turns related to questions specified by the *Benchmarks* descriptors. Such approximations do not necessitate any adjustment of the *Benchmarks*. However, any topics which may require further elaboration were highlighted. Evidence from the study suggests that it would be worth creating new descriptors for these topics, possibly within the existing *Benchmarks* themes. Some suggestions for the adjustment of existing descriptors (expansion or combination) are also provided. In addition, any links apparent between existing descriptors were noted. This most frequently involved links between descriptors for spoken interaction (recorded in the selected lessons) and those for spoken production at levels A1 and A2. Generally, this was due to the interactional context of the recorded lessons, in which group discussion rather than extended pupil-initiated production was the norm. Obviously, not all *Benchmarks* descriptors were covered in these lessons, and further research would be required in order to assess the remaining descriptors. Nevertheless, the information provided in Table A5.2 could be used to guide further adjustments.

Table A5.1 Frequency of occurrence of Benchmarks descriptors in the selected lessons

Benchmarks Unit	Skill	A1 *Benchmarks* descriptors	School 1	School 2	School 3	A2 *Benchmarks* descriptors	School 1	School 2	School 3	B1 *Benchmarks* descriptors	School 1	School 2	School 3
Global benchmarks of communic- ative proficiency	Listening												
	Reading	GB/A1/Read/1	16	4	6								
						GB/A2/Read/2			1				
		GB/A1/Read/4	10	4									
	Spoken Interaction												
	Spoken Production												
	Writing												
Unit 1: Myself	Listening	U1/A1/List/3	2		2								
	Reading					U1/A2/Read/1	5		5	U1/B1/Read/1			14
	Spoken Interaction	U1/A1/SpInt/1	20	8	7	U1/A2/SpInt/1	5	2	2	U1/B1/SpInt/1			4
		U1/A1/SpInt/2	9	3	2	U1/A2/SpInt/2	19	4	5				
		U1/A1/SpInt/3	1	4									
		U1/A1/SpInt/4	10		1	U1/A2/SpInt/4	2						
						U1/A2/SpInt/6	20	5	5				
	Spoken Production	U1/A1/SpProd/1	1							U1/B1/SpProd/1			1
										U1/B1/SpProd/2			7
	Writing	U1/A1/Write/1	7	2	1	U1/A2/Write/1	1						
		U1/A1/Write/2	1										

Table A5.1 (continued)

Benchmarks Unit	Skill	A1 *Benchmarks* descriptors	School 1	School 2	School 3	A2 *Benchmarks* descriptors	School 1	School 2	School 3	B1 *Benchmarks* descriptors	School 1	School 2	School 3
Unit 2: Our school	Listening												
	Reading					U2/A2/Read/1	1			U2/B1/Read/1			7
		U2/A1/Read/3	5	1	3								
	Spoken Interaction					U2/A2/SpInt/1	2	1		U2/B1/SpInt/1			2
		U2/A1/SpInt/2	39	14	18	U2/A2/SpInt/2	1						
		U2/A1/SpInt/3	6	4	6	U2/A2/SpInt/3	37	14	14	U2/B1/SpInt/3			13
		U2/A1/SpInt/4	19	6	4	U2/A2/SpInt/4	7	4					
	Spoken Production												
	Writing	U2/A1/Write/1	5		1								
						U2/A2/Write/2	1		2				
Unit 3: Food and clothes	Listening	U3/A1/List/3	1										
		U3/A1/List/4	1										
	Reading	U3/A1/Read/1	5	1		U3/A2/Read/1	1						
		U3/A1/Read/2	2										
						U3/A2/Read/3	3						
	Spoken Interaction	U3/A1/SpInt/1		2		U3/A2/SpInt/1	8	5	3	U3/B1/SpInt/1			1
		U3/A1/SpInt/2		2		U3/A2/SpInt/2	1	3		U3/B1/SpInt/2			5
		U3/A1/SpInt/3	27	11	9	U3/A2/SpInt/3	1	5	3				

Unit	Skill												
	Spoken Production	U3/A1/SpProd/1	2			U3/A2/SpProd/1		1					
	Writing	U3/A1/Write/1	1		1	U3/A2/Write/1			1				
Unit 4: Colours, shapes and opposites	Listening	U4/A1/List/1	4	1									
		U4/A1/List/2	1										
	Reading	U4/A1/Read/1	1	1		U4/A2/Read/1			2				
	Spoken Interaction	U4/A1/SpInt/1	21	9	12	U4/A2/SpInt/1	8	5	2				
		U4/A1/SpInt/2		1	2								
	Spoken Production	U4/A1/SpProd/1	7										
	Writing												
Unit 5: People who help us	Listening												
	Reading	U5/A1/Read/1	1		1	U5/A2/Read/1	2						
	Spoken Interaction					U5/A2/SpInt/1	5		2	U5/B1/SpInt/1			2
		U5/A1/SpInt/2	6	2	3	U5/A2/SpInt/2	1	1	2				
	Spoken Production									U5/B1/SpProd/1			1
	Writing	U5/A1/Write/3	2										
Unit 6: Weather	Listening												
	Reading	U6/A1/Read/1	1	1	1	U6/A2/Read/1	1						
						U6/A2/Read/2	1						
	Spoken Interaction	U6/A1/SpInt/1	9	8	7	U6/A2/SpInt/1		1	3	U6/B1/SpInt/1			3

Immigrant Pupils Learn English

Table A5.1 (continued)

Benchmarks Unit	Skill	A1 Benchmarks descriptors	School 1	School 2	School 3	A2 Benchmarks descriptors	School 1	School 2	School 3	B1 Benchmarks descriptors	School 1	School 2	School 3
						U6/A2/SpInt/2	2						
	Spoken Production	U6/A1/SpProd/1	1										
	Writing												
Unit 7: Transport and travel	Listening												
	Reading	U7/A1/Read/1	1		2	U7/A2/Read/1	1						
	Spoken Interaction	U7/A1/SpInt/1	6		4	U7/A2/SpInt/1	1		1	U7/B1/SpInt/1			1
		U7/A1/SpInt/2	11	4	4	U7/A2/SpInt/2	8		4				
										U7/B1/SpInt/3			2
	Spoken Production					U7/A2/SpProd/2	2						
	Writing												
Unit 8: Seasons, holidays and festivals	Listening												
	Reading												
	Spoken Interaction	U8/A1/SpInt/1	1	7	8	U8/A2/SpInt/1			1	U8/B1/SpInt/1			3
						U8/A2/SpInt/2	3	3	7				
										U8/B1/SpInt/3			5
	Spoken Production	U8/A1/SpProd/1		1						U8/B1/SpProd/1			1
	Writing												

Unit	Skill												
Unit 9: **The local and wider community**	Listening	U9/A1/List/2	2										
	Reading	U9/A1/Read/1		1		U9/A2/Read/1			1				
		U9/A1/Read/2	1										
	Spoken Interaction	U9/A1/SpInt/1	9	2	1	U9/A2/SpInt/1	4						
		U9/A1/SpInt/2	5	2	1	U9/A2/SpInt/2	2	1					
	Spoken Production												
	Writing					U9/A2/Write/1			1				
Unit 10: **Time**	Listening												
	Reading	U10/A1/Read/1		2	1	U10/A2/Read/1			1				
	Spoken Interaction	U10/A1/SpInt/1		7	8	U10/A2/SpInt/1			3				
						U10/A2/SpInt/2		1	1	U10/B1/SpInt/2			1
	Spoken Production	U10/A1/SpProd/1	1		1								
	Writing	U10/A1/Write/1		1		U10/A2/Write/1			1				
Unit 11: **People and places in other areas**	Listening												
	Reading					U11/A2/Read/1	1						
	Spoken Interaction	U11/A1/SpInt/1	6			U11/A2/SpInt/1	6		2				
		U11/A1/SpInt/2			1								
	Spoken Production												
	Writing												

Table A5.1 (continued)

Benchmarks Unit	Skill	A1 *Benchmarks* descriptors	School 1	School 2	School 3	A2 *Benchmarks* descriptors	School 1	School 2	School 3	B1 *Benchmarks* descriptors	School 1	School 2	School 3
Unit 12: Animals and plants	Listening	U12/A1/List/1	1	1		U12/A2/List/1	1		1				
	Reading	U12/A1/Read/1	4	1	2	U12/A2/Read/1	12	1	5	U12/B1/Read/1			3
		U12/A1/Read/2	1	1	1								
	Spoken Interaction	U12/A1/SpInt/1	21	12	13	U12/A2/SpInt/1	11	9	7	U12/B1/SpInt/1			3
		U12/A1/SpInt/2	2	2	3	U12/A2/SpInt/2	6	1		U12/B1/SpInt/2			1
	Spoken Production	U12/A1/SpProd/1	1	1	1								
										U12/B1/SpProd/2			2
	Writing	U12/A1/Write/1	1	1	2								
Unit 13: Caring for my locality	Listening												
	Reading												
	Spoken Interaction	U13/A1/SpInt/1	1			U13/A2/SpInt/1	1						
	Spoken Production												
	Writing	U13/A1/Write/1	1										

Table A5.2 Approximations to Benchmarks descriptors and suggested amendments

Based solely on the production of participating pupils in the selected lessons. Suggested adjustments to existing descriptors are underlined and deletions enclosed in square brackets; suggestions for new descriptors are marked with an asterisk (*); and suggestions highlighting links between existing descriptors (including possible combinations) are marked with an ampersand (&).

NEW	Additional topics covered in the selected lessons	School 1	School 2	School 3
*	Maths *(links to Unit 2/Unit 4?)*	16	6	7
*	Seeking attention *(at A1 level – links to Unit 2?)*	9	6	9
*	Body/health *(links to Unit 1?)*	9	5	5
*	Natural world *(links to Unit 6/Unit 11?)*	5		2
*	Home/household items *(links to Unit 1?)*	9	1	9
*	Toys/games/activities *(links to Unit 1/Unit 2?)*	10	1	3
*	Feelings/opinions *(at A1 level – links to Unit 1?)*	7		1
*	Actions *(links to Unit 1?)*	1	2	1
*	Nursery rhymes/songs *(links to Unit 2?)*	3	4	9
*	Characters/fantasy *(links to Unit 1/Unit 10?)*	3	5	3
*	Music *(e.g. instruments – links to Unit 1/Unit 2?)*	2		1
*	Religion *(links to Unit 1/Unit 8?)*	1		
UNIT	Approximations to the existing *Benchmarks* descriptors in the selected lessons	School 1	School 2	School 3
Global BM	GB/A1/Read/1% Can recognise the letters of the alphabet <u>and understand basic grapho-phonic relations</u>.	11	3	2
	GB/A1/Read/4% Can identify basic words and phrases in a new piece of text <u>or in sets of related words e.g. phonics-based wordlists or lists of 'sight vocabulary'</u>.	8	3	

Table A5.2 (continued)

UNIT	Approximations to the existing Benchmarks descriptors in the selected lessons	School 1	School 2	School 3
UNIT 1	U1/A2/Read/1% Can read very short and simple texts with a high frequency of familiar words on topics such as children, families and school, or words relating to home and household items.	1		
	U1/B1/Read/1% Can read and understand age-appropriate stories about children and their lives, including life in different environments (e.g., country, city, abroad), can also read extracts from these texts included in comprehension activities.			1
	U1/A1/SpInt/1% Can answer basic questions about him/herself: e.g about his/her name, age, family, possessions (toys etc.), and routines when supported by prompts.	15	5	7
	U1/A1/SpInt/2% Can respond non-verbally (e.g., with a nod or shake of the head) or with single-word or very brief answers to basic questions about his/her likes or dislikes (e.g., *Do you like ice-cream?*), and express very basic reactions/opinions.	4	1	
	U1/A1/SpInt/3% Can greet the teacher and other pupils and say goodbye, or respond to basic questions about how he/she feels e.g. 'how are you?'	1		
	U1/A1/SpInt/4% Can indicate personal needs (e.g., to go to the toilet) and feelings (e.g., hunger, illness), or the needs of others.	8		1
	U1/A2/SpInt/1% Can reply with confidence to familiar questions about his/her name, age, number of brothers and sisters, etc., and ask or answer similar questions in relation to other pupils.	3	1	2

	U1/A2/SpInt/2% Can initiate conversation on a familiar topic (e.g., why he/she was late for school), <u>or comment on a familiar home-related issue involving him/herself or a familiar person.</u>	2		
	U1/A2/Write/1% Can write short texts describing his/her family, daily routines etc. <u>(texts may be structured, may require support)</u>.	1		
UNIT 2	U2/A1/Read/3% Can recognise and understand words and numbers <u>and short captions</u> on posters and drawings in the classroom, <u>or in books</u> (days of the week, months of the year, task instructions etc.).	4	1	3
*	U2/A1/SpInt/2% Can respond non-verbally (e.g., with a nod or shake of the head) or with single-word or very brief answers to basic questions on classroom topics. <u>Can take part in classroom activities, using basic words and phrases to indicate participation, e.g. responses to instructions, announcements</u> such as 'finished'. • *May need an additional descriptor?*	37	14	16
	U2/A1/SpInt/3% Can use <u>basic polite expressions, e.g.</u> *please* and *thank you* appropriately.	2		
	U2/A1/SpInt/4% Can <u>make very simple requests, e.g. asking</u> for familiar classroom objects and materials (book, crayons, paper, etc.). <u>Can respond to basic requests with simple offers.</u>	6	3	
	U2/A2/SpInt/2% Can pass a simple message from one teacher to another <u>or pass information about a topic learned in the mainstream class to another teacher.</u>	1		
*	U2/A2/SpInt/3% Can generally sustain a conversation with another pupil when working collaboratively in the classroom (painting a picture, making a model, playing with puppets, etc). <u>Can participate in classroom talk about a familiar activity or topic with other pupils and/or the teacher (e.g. organising activities, giving ideas and reasons etc.).</u> • *May need additional descriptor?*	34	14	14

Table A5.2 (continued)

UNIT	Approximations to the existing Benchmarks descriptors in the selected lessons	School 1	School 2	School 3
	U2/A2/SpInt/4% With appropriate support from the teacher, can explain a situation that has arisen (e.g., a dispute with another pupil, a complaint when working together on class activity, or a hypothetical problem, e.g. being 'lost').	9	4	
	U2/B1/SpInt/1% Can interact spontaneously in the playground, engaging with other pupils in games and activities, or can report or comment about these games etc.			1
	U2/B1/SpInt/3% Can ask and answer questions or offer information about specific classroom topics or in general discussion.			1
	U2/A2/Write/2% Can write or complete in an age-appropriate manner short texts based on a topic recently studied in class.			1
UNIT 3	U3/A1/List/3% Can recognize and understand the words for key items of food such as those typically brought to school by pupils (e.g. sandwich, apple, biscuit) and indicate (e.g. by drawing, marking) their preferences in relation to these.	1		
	U3/A1/List/4% Can understand routine classroom instructions about food or clothing (e.g., *Put on your apron for painting*), or identify food/clothes in picture-recognition activities.	1		
	U3/A2/Read/1% Can read and understand the menu from a café or fast-food outlet, or short texts including references to food and places to eat.			1

	U3/A2/Read/3% Can read and understand simple descriptions of food or clothing that occur in a story <u>or classroom text about clothes (and e.g. weather)</u>.	1		1
	U3/A1/SpInt/1% Can request basic items of food/drink in a shop <u>and respond to such requests</u>.	1	2	
	U3/A1/SpInt/2% Can ask <u>and answer basic questions about</u> how much an item costs.	1	2	
&	U3/A1/SpInt/3% Can respond non-verbally (e.g., with a nod or shake of the head) or with single-word or very brief answers to questions about [the] food/drink and clothes [he/she likes] <u>for example about his/her likes and dislikes</u>. • *Links to: U3/A1/SpProd/1*	25	10	8
	U3/A2/SpInt/1% Can ask and answer basic questions about the food/drink he/she likes or dislikes and briefly report the likes and dislikes of others, <u>can comment about familiar meals and cooking</u>.	8	5	4
	U3/A2/SpInt/2% Can discuss a menu and select what he/she would like, <u>or use phrases and sentences to indicate preferences in a shop or restaurant</u>.	1	2	
	U3/A2/SpInt/3% Can answer questions <u>and offer information</u> about items and types of clothing, e.g. what is suitable for different kinds of weather.	1	1	
	U3/A2/SpProd/1% Can use a series of phrases and sentences to describe <u>a familiar meal or food, e.g.</u> the type of meal that he/she likes best.		1	
	U3/B1/SpInt/1% Can repeat an instruction given by the teacher regarding food and clothing, <u>or can give</u> instructions, e.g. regarding the preparation of food or the production of food/clothes.			1

Table A5.2 (continued)

UNIT	Approximations to the existing Benchmarks descriptors in the selected lessons	School 1	School 2	School 3
	U3/B1/SpInt/2% Can engage in discussion about clothing/fashion and food/drink, expressing personal preferences or talking about own experiences.			3
	U3/A2/Write/1% Can write or complete a short text about food (e.g. describing an event in which food plays a central role such as a family celebration).			1
UNIT 4	U4/A1/List/1% Can identify and respond to (e.g. by drawing, actions) basic colours, shapes and opposites when they are called out by the teacher.	2	1	
	U4/A1/Read/1% Can recognise and understand the words for basic colours, e.g. on flashcards, posters or in short labels.	1		
	U4/A1/Read/2% Can recognise and understand the words for basic shapes and opposites.		1	
&	U4/A1/SpInt/1% Can answer basic questions, e.g. identifying colours and shapes and opposites and about the colours he/she likes best. • *Links to U4/A1/SpProd/1*	20	10	12
&	U4/A1/SpInt/2% Can answer basic questions or offer basic information about the colours of the clothes he/she is wearing (or clothes in picture). • *Could be combined with U4/A1/SpInt/1?*	2		1
	U4/A2/SpInt/1% Can ask and answer questions or offer information about colours, shapes, size and opposites in discussion of familiar items such as clothing, food, classroom objects, etc.	1	2	1

UNIT 5	U5/A1/Read/1% Can recognise and understand the words for people who help (e.g., teacher, guard, doctor, nurse) or basic words relating to them when they appear on flashcards and posters or in simple text.	1		1
	U5/A1/SpInt/2% Can reply using key words and simple phrases/sentences to basic questions identifying and talking about the jobs of people who can help (e.g., *Where do we find a . . .?, What does he/she do?*).	5	2	2
	U5/A2/SpInt/1% Can ask and answer questions, or offer information in discussion, about what people in familiar roles do in their jobs.	5		1
	U5/A2/SpInt/2% Can talk with the teacher or another pupil about personal experiences with people in roles of responsibility (e.g. visit to doctor, parent is a nurse/doctor, school traffic warden, postman) or about jobs he/she likes; can also respond to other pupils' experiences.	2	2	2
	U5/B1/SpInt/1% Can ask and answer questions about different jobs and responsibilities, including e.g. information based on their own experience.			2
	U5/B1/SpProd/1% Can talk about the responsibilities of people who help, possibly based on their own experience, using an age-appropriate range of descriptive vocabulary.			1
UNIT 6 &	U6/A1/SpInt/1% Can respond non-verbally (e.g., with a nod or shake of the head) or with single-word or very brief answers to basic questions about the weather (e.g. *Is it cold outside?*) or weather/sky-related items (e.g. sun, moon, stars). ● *Links to U6/A1/SpProd/1*	8		6
&	U6/A2/SpInt/1% Can respond to questions about the weather he/she likes or comment on the weather conditions outside the classroom or those shown in a picture. ● *Links to U6/A2/SpProd/1*	2	1	3

Table A5.2 (continued)

UNIT	Approximations to the existing Benchmarks descriptors in the selected lessons	School 1	School 2	School 3
	U6/B1/SpInt/1% Can ask and answer questions about types of weather and the effects of weather on lifestyle, including questions about present weather conditions, or personal experience of severe weather.			2
7	U7/A1/SpInt/1% Can respond briefly, using gesture if necessary, when asked *How did you come to school today?* and respond to basic questions about his/her everyday travel or own transport e.g. own bike.	6		1
&	U7/A1/SpInt/2% When prompted by the teacher and supported by pictures, can use basic words (including the vocabulary of colour, size and shape) and simple phrases to identify and describe different forms of transport. ● *Links to U7/A1/SpProd/1*	9	1	3
&	U7/A2/SpInt/1% Can respond with confidence to questions about how he/she likes to travel or types of transport he/she or another pupil likes, or the uses of different forms of transport. ● *Links to U7/A1/SpProd/1 and U7/A2/SpProd/2*	1		2
&	U7/A2/SpInt/2% Can discuss experiences he/she has had in travelling, and talk about personal knowledge and experience of transport ● *Links to U7/A1/SpProd/1 and U7/A2/SpProd/2*	7	4	3
	U7/A2/SpProd/2% Can name and describe briefly the different types of transport that can be seen outside the school (cars, lorries, buses, bicycles, etc.), or in a picture, e.g. own drawing.	2		
	U7/B1/SpInt/1% Can participate in discussions of different modes of travel and express personal preferences, or explain his/her own experiences.			1

	U7/B1/SpInt/3% Can find out what other pupils think about different modes of transport and discuss his/her own experience of these.			2
UNIT 8	U8/A1/SpInt/1% Can respond with key words or simple/phrases to questions, e.g. about when the different seasons fall, what weather is typical of the different seasons, when the major festivals occur, and basic items associated with these.	1	1	8
	U8/A2/SpInt/2% Can ask and answer simple questions about seasonal matters or festivals that may be unfamiliar.	3	2	5
	U8/B1/SpInt/1% Can describe and respond to questions about what takes place during a festival or celebration in his/her family or community, or activities associated with a particular season.			1
	U8/B1/SpInt/3% Can talk and ask questions about typical Irish festivals, explaining his/her experience of these.			2
UNIT 9	U9/A1/SpInt/1% Can respond to simple questions [by giving] relating to [the names of] buildings and places where people live and work in the area.	6	1	1
	U9/A1/SpInt/2% Can use key words and simple phrases/sentences to answer basic questions about places he/she has visited in the area, or which are known to his/her family (e.g. parents' workplaces).	4	2	1
&	U9/A2/SpInt/1% Can ask and answer simple questions about [what happens] in the main public buildings in the area, e.g. what happens in them. ● *Could combine with U9/A2/SpInt/2?*	4	1	
	U9/A2/SpInt/2% Can ask and answer simple questions about what people do in those buildings or public places, e.g. park	1		

Table A5.2 (continued)

UNIT	Approximations to the existing Benchmarks descriptors in the selected lessons	School 1	School 2	School 3
UNIT 10	U10/A1/Read/1% Can recognise and understand the day and month when they are written on the board, and simple references to these, e.g. today is Monday.		1	
&	U10/A1/SpInt/1% Can use single words and simple phrases to answer basic questions, e.g. about what he/she does every day, or what he/she did yesterday or last week, or naming the day of the week or month of the year. • *Links to U10/A1/SpProd/1*		6	7
	U10/A2/SpInt/1% Can discuss with other pupils or the teacher how he/she knows that time has passed (e.g. children grow bigger, hair grows longer, plants grow and change, seasons follow one another).			3
	U10 /B1/SpInt/1% Can answer questions or offer information about what he/she hopes to do in the future (e.g. after school, at the weekend, during the holidays or through the school year).			1
	U10/B1/SpInt/2% Can ask other pupils about their past experiences and future plans, or explain his/her own.			1
	U10/A2/Write/1% Can write sentences about his/her favourite day of the week or time of year or routine activities associated with different days/times.			1
UNIT 11	U11/A1/SpInt/1% Can use key words and simple phrases/sentences to answer basic questions, e.g. where his/her family is from, names of countries and places.	5		
	U11/A1/SpInt/2% Can ask other pupils basic questions about their nationality, and/or say where they come from.			1

*	U11/A2/SpInt/1% Can talk with other pupils about people in other countries, or personal experience of other countries, or can talk about e.g. natural environments, or places in Ireland in order to prepare poster projects, role-plays etc. • *May need new descriptor?*	5		2
UNIT 12	U12/A1/List/1% Can recognise and understand basic words relating to animals and plants when they are spoken or read aloud, especially when supported by pictures, mime, etc. and follow simple instructions regarding these (e.g. by drawing).	2		
	U12/A1/Read/1% Can use pictorial support to recognise and understand the names of animals and plants, and basic words relating to them, when they are written down (e.g. in a picture dictionary or simple book).	1	1	
	U12/B1/Read/1% Can understand the main points in a text about the natural world, using familiar key words and pictures/diagrams to support comprehension, or can respond to text with own opinions.			1
&	U12/A1/SpInt/1% Can use key words and simple phrases/sentences to answer basic questions or suggest basic information about animals, e.g. keeping a pet, liking animals etc. • *Links to U12/A1/SpProd/1*	21	12	11
&	U12/A1/SpInt/2% Can use key words and simple phrases/sentences to answer basic questions, e.g, identifying plants or about changes in the plants that are kept in the classroom. • *Links to U12/A1/SpProd/2*	2	2	3
&	U12/A2/SpInt/1% Can ask and answer questions about animals and plants, e.g. which animal or plants he/she likes and dislikes or his/her experience of seeing animals. • *Links to U12/A2/SpProd/2*	8	9	4

Table A5.2 (continued)

UNIT	Approximations to the existing Benchmarks descriptors in the selected lessons	School 1	School 2	School 3
&	U12/A2/SpInt/2% Can ask and answer questions, or offer information about keeping a pet. • *Links to U12/A2/SpProd/1*	3		
	U12/B1/SpInt/1% Can discuss with other pupils how to include animals/plants in a project, role-play, poster, project etc., or can answer questions or offer information or opinions about animals.			2
	U12/B1/SpInt/2% Can pass on information about taking care of, or own experience of, animals and plants.			1
	U12/A1/Write/1% Can [draw animal outlines] copy or write animal names, e.g. adding appropriate labels to drawings of animal outlines.			2
UNIT 13 &	U13/A1/SpInt/1% Can use key words and simple phrases/sentences to answer basic questions about where he/she has been in the area (or e.g. near a relative's house). • *Could combine with U9/A1/SpInt/2?*	1		
&	U13/A2/SpInt/1% Can ask and answer basic questions about activities that take place in different places in the locality, including whether and for whom these activities are important, or the location of places, e.g. in relation to his/her home. • *Could combine with U9/A2/SpInt/1?*	1		

Appendix 6: Examples of L2 lexis produced by EAL pupils, showing relation between their semantic fields and units of work*

SEMANTIC FIELD / EAL PUPIL	Body parts	Personal/ family	Actions	Home/ household	Toys/play/ entertain-ment	School	Numbers	Food/drink	Clothing/ accessories	Colours/ shapes	Size/other attributes
Zofia	nose	baby	look	house	jigsaw	pencil	up to 14	carrot	gloves	yellow	big
Karina	mouth	mammy	clap	toothbrush	ball	scissors	up to 30	apple	trousers	red	short
Dimitrie	eye	name	smell	freezer		book	up to 4	ice-cream		blue	hot
Patryk	teeth	grandma	swim	kitchen	computer	rubber	up to 10	banana	shoe	orange	good
Tomasz	hair	daddy	carry	window	teddy	pencil	up to 5	bread		black	long
Marko	feet	mum	jumping		swing	sentence, correct	up to 7	potato, milk	uniform	pink, circle	heavy
Jin	finger	people	kicking	television	sandcastle	marker, paper	60 euro	broccoli	socks	grey	delicious, stupid
Edyta	brain	brother	howl	shelf	film	yard	fifth, thousands	sweet-corn	shorts	golden	cosy
Vladimir	head	sister	throw	chimney	DVD	letters	millions, cent	coconuts	scarf	purple	giant, angry
Ivan	ears	grandfather	reach	cup	skateboard, movie	crayons	up to 8	straw-berries	helmet	yellow	stinky
Constantin	face	mammy	climb	candles	PlayStation	letters, numbers	up to 8, half	chocolate	jumper	purple	different
Related units of work in *Benchmarks*	Unit 1: Myself					Unit 2: Our school		Unit 3: Food and clothes		Unit 4: Colours, shapes and opposites	

** Lexical forms presented as used by the 18 participating pupils in the selected lessons. As far as possible a variety of lexis is presented for each semantic field, although not all pupils produced L2 lexis for all of the themes covered. For some themes (e.g. colours/shapes) lexical diversity was more limited than for others, due to the English L2 proficiency of the children but also to their stage of cognitive development and their context of learning.*

SEMANTIC FIELD / EAL PUPIL	Body parts	Personal/ family	Actions	Home/ household	Toys/play/ entertain-ment	School	Numbers	Food/drink	Clothing/ accessories	Colours/ shapes	Size/other attributes
Ravi	chin	friend	running	spoon	cricket, basketball	principal, P.E.	thousand	rice	coat	white, diamond	plain
Lukas	elbow	grandmother	reach	card	laptop	class	hundred times, euro	sausages	jacket, buttons	green	naughty
Stefan	mouth	dad	catch	saucepan	football, goalkeeper	homework	up to 10, equals	raspberry, orange juice	t-shirt	rectangle, brown	easy
Andrei	hands	girlfriend	fix	garden	trampoline	sharpener, schoolbag	up to 9	pizza, popcorn	umbrella	triangle, black	favourite
Beatriz	knee	aunty	bite, cook	cushions	bingo, binoculars	class, ruler	five cent	pancakes	tracksuit, sunglasses	green, round	little, spiky
Nasreen	shoulder, gums	sister	fly, tickle	fork	diary	jumbled up words	11 years old	custard, whiskey	basket, dress	grey	curly, disgusting
Fatima	blood	neighbour, uncle	mopping, squawks	mattress, sofa	spade, seashells	chapter, detention	10 rupees, coin	chewing gum	pockets	yellow	famous, wooden
Related units of work in *Benchmarks*	**Unit 1:** Myself					**Unit 2:** Our school		**Unit 3:** Food and clothes		**Unit 4:** Colours, shapes and opposites	

SEMANTIC FIELD / EAL PUPIL	Jobs/ aspects of work	Weather	Modes of transport	Seasons	Festivals/ occasions	Buildings/ familiar places	Time	Countries/ far-away places	Animals	Plants	Environment
Zofia	teacher	snowman			stocking, present		names of days		cat		
Karina	teacher	sun	bike			shop	names of days		owl		
Dimitrie	teacher	sun	tractor	autumn	presents			Romania	dinosaur		
Patryk	dentist	cloudy	helicopter			hospital	tomorrow	Poland	snake	grass	
Tomasz	teacher		bus		birthday	hospital			crocodile		
Marko	teacher	wet	car	spring	Christmas	sea, zoo			lamb	flowers	
Jin	farmer	rainbow	ship	winter	Easter	super-market	names of days	jungle	piglet	flower	
Edyta	mechanic, vet	melt	tractor	summer	decorations	swimming pool	names of days/ months	Polish	squirrels	daffodils	
Vladimir	policeman	wind		autumn	Santy	pool, shop	names of days/ months		ladybird, tadpole	leaves	
Ivan	pilot	snow	motorbike, wheels			library, park		moon	hamster	grass	
Constantin	armies	sun	tanks, helicopter		holiday, witch	shop		Romania	wolf, butterfly	flower	
Related Units of work in *Benchmarks*	Unit 5: People who help us	Unit 6: Weather	Unit 7: Transport and travel	Unit 8: Seasons, holidays and festivals		Unit 9: The local and wider community	Unit 10: Time	Unit 11: People and places in other areas	Unit 12: Animals and plants		Unit 13: Caring for my locality

SEMANTIC FIELD / EAL PUPIL	Jobs/ aspects of work	Weather	Modes of transport	Seasons	Festivals/ occasions	Buildings/ familiar places	Time	Countries/ far-away places	Animals	Plants	Environment
Ravi	doctor, operation		van			restaurant	names of days	India, Australia	bee		bin, waste
Lukas	fireman	mild	truck			church	names of days	Lithuania, Russia	spider		rubbish
Stefan	policeman	warm	boat			jail, station	names of days	Poland	kangaroo, monkey		
Andrei	fireman, policeman	sunny, snowman	fire engine, train		Christmas, Santa	farmhouse	half, yesterday	Romania	gorilla, elephant	grass	
Beatriz	doctor, needle	windy	ambulance	summer	Valentine's, crackers	beach	names of months	Portugal	donkey, foal		
Nasreen	doctor, plaster	rainy	bicycle, pedal		Halloween, vampire	factory	names of days/ months	Pakistan	humming-bird	sunflower	
Fatima	police woman	tornado, storm	ambulance digger			factory, mountain	nineteen eighties	Pakistan, Connacht	parrot	snowdrop	junk, iron, material
Related units of work in *Benchmarks*	Unit 5: People who help us	Unit 6: Weather	Unit 7: Transport and travel	Unit 8: Seasons, holidays and festivals		Unit 9: The local and wider community	Unit 10: Time	Unit 11: People and places in other areas	Unit 12: Animals and plants		Unit 13: Caring for my locality

Appendix 7
Qualitative overview of analysed indicators of EAL pupils' L2 acquisition

Overview of noun use

Maximum proportion of turns at highest recorded proficiency level	Pupil(s)	Features of noun use
A1 only	Zofia	Noun production with very limited lexical range, but increasing across study period. Accuracy rate generally over 80%, dipping slightly in later lessons in which more nouns attempted. Infrequent successful attempts at pluralisation. Errors generally of lexical choice, but some use of singular forms in plural contexts.
0.01–0.1A2	Karina	Noun production increasing over study period although lexical range limited throughout. Accuracy rate generally over 80%. Some successful attempts at pluralisation from outset of study although, overall, plural forms infrequent. Errors generally of lexical choice, occasional use of singular forms in plural contexts.
0.11–0.2 A2	Patryk	Noun production across widening lexical range (extent influenced by lesson-related factors). Accuracy rate generally over 80%. Some successful attempts at pluralisation. Errors generally of lexical choice; use of singular forms in plural contexts and omission of possessive markers also recorded.
0.21–0.3 A2	Tomasz, Ravi, Dimitrie	Noun production across widening lexical range (influenced by lesson-related factors). Accuracy rate generally between 80% and 90%, with evidence of increasing accuracy towards end of study. Some successful attempts at pluralisation, isolated instance of possessive marking. Errors (#), generally of lexical choice, but use of singular forms in plural contexts, over-generalisation of *-s* ending to irregular plurals (e.g. *peoples*) and omission of possessive markers also recorded.

Maximum proportion of turns at highest recorded proficiency level	Pupil(s)	Features of noun use
0.31–0.4 A2	Ivan, Jin	Increasing noun use across range of lexical fields. Accuracy rate generally over 80%, often over 90%. Some successful pluralisation although persistent errors involving use of singular forms in plural context and overgeneralisation of -*s* for irregular plurals. Lexical choice generally main error source, omission of possessive marker also recorded.
0.41–0.5 A2	Stefan, Lukas, Edyta	Increasing noun use across range of lexical fields. Accuracy rate over 80%, often over 90%. Increasing proportion of accurately pluralised nouns. Isolated, but generally accurate attempts at marking possession. Errors generally of lexical choice although pluralisation issues persist, including overgeneralised irregular plurals.
0.51–0.6 A2	Andrei, Constantin, Marko	Increasing noun use across range of lexical fields. Accuracy rate generally 80–90%, new lexis accounting for most inaccuracies. Pluralisation often accurate, but inappropriate use of singular nouns in plural contexts still apparent. Isolated, but successful attempts at possessive marking recorded.
0.61–0.7 A2	Vladimir	Noun use across range of lexical fields (subject to lesson-related factors). Accuracy rate generally over 90%, errors usually due to lexical choice. Pluralisation generally appropriate to context.
0.61–0.7 B1	Beatriz	Noun use across wide range of lexical fields (subject to lesson-related factors). Accuracy rate generally over 90%. Pluralisation almost always successful, appropriate marking of possession also recorded. Most errors lexical.
0.71–0.8 B1	Nasreen	Noun use across wide range of lexical fields (subject to lesson-related factors). Accuracy rate over 80% throughout, rising to over 90% towards end of study. Pluralisation generally successful, appropriate marking of possession also recorded. Errors generally lexical, occasional overgeneralisation of irregular plurals and omission of possessive markers.
0.91–1.0 B1	Fatima	Noun use across wide range of lexical fields. Accuracy rates over 95% throughout. Generally successful pluralisation and marking of possession. Infrequent errors, mostly lexical or due to overgeneralisation of irregular plurals.

Overview of verb use

Maximum proportion of turns at highest recorded proficiency level	Pupil(s)	Features of verb use
A1 only	Zofia	Very limited verb use, increasing slightly towards end of study. Accuracy rate generally over 70%. Verbs generally in uninflected stem form, use of 3rd person form of copula *be* also recorded. No apparent generative attempts at marking tense or aspect (although some inflected forms, e.g. *finished*, used in set phrases). Errors generally involving application of uninflected stem where inflection required.
0.01–0.1 A2	Karina	Very limited verb use, increasing towards end of study. Accuracy rate generally over 80%. Non-inflected stem verb and 3rd person form of copula *be* accounting for most verb production. Very occasional, not always accurate use of progressive forms (e.g. *eating*) and irregular past tense (e.g. *made*). Errors generally omission of 3rd person *-s* ending in present tense. Verbs often lexically incorrect or omitted.
0.11–0.2 A2	Patryk	Very limited verb use, but increasing towards end of study. Accuracy rate initially high, falling to under 70% in later lessons as more verbs produced. Initially verb production involved uninflected stem verbs and copula *be* (generally *is*). In second half of study, occasional attempts at progressive verb forms (e.g. *taking*) and irregular past (e.g. *went, saw, broke*). Such attempts not always successful, widespread errors, particularly in the over-use of non-inflected verbs recorded.
0.21–0.3 A2	Tomasz, Ravi, Dimitrie	Initially limited but increasing verb use. Accuracy rates fluctuating, often in the region 70–80%. Verb use diversifying over study period from uninflected stem and copula *be* in present tense contexts, to include progressive and, generally later, past forms (usually irregular), isolated constructive use of past participles (e.g. *broken*) recorded. Widespread errors involving over-use of uninflected forms or inappropriate inflection.
0.31–0.4 A2	Ivan, Jin	Widening range of verb use. Accuracy level fluctuating from 50% to over 90%. Majority of verbs uninflected stem forms or copula *be* in present tense contexts. Attempts at progressive forms and, generally later, past tense verbs (usually irregular, occasionally regular, e.g. *pushed*). Occasional production of past participles and use of present participles as verbal nouns. Errors include omission of *-s* ending in present tense and inappropriate use of progressive or past forms.

Maximum proportion of turns at highest recorded proficiency level	Pupil(s)	Features of verb use
0.41–0.5 A2	Stefan, Lukas, Edyta	Widening range of verb use. Accuracy rate generally over 80%, although subject to fluctuation. Uninflected stem verbs and copula *be* dominant in verb production although diversification evident across study to include appropriately used progressive forms and, generally later, past verb forms (irregular and, less frequently, regular), occasional use of past participles (sometimes to express passive mood). Errors include omission of 3rd person *-s* in present tense, use of present tense verb forms in past tense contexts, confusion of simple and progressive aspect.
0.51–0.6 A2	Andrei, Constantin, Marko	Widening range of verb use. Accuracy rate fluctuating from 50% to over 80%, some evidence of increasing accuracy towards end of study. Verb use still commonly involving uninflected stem forms and copula *be* in present tense contexts. Verb diversification apparent, however, in use of progressive and, generally later, past tense forms (generally irregular, although also regular), with past participles and verbal nouns also produced. Errors include omission of 3rd person *-s* in present tense, use of present tense verb forms in past tense contexts, confusion of simple and progressive aspect.
0.61–0.7 A2	Vladimir	Widening range of verb use. Accuracy rate generally over 80%, with some fluctuation. Verb use still predominantly involving present simple forms, but with more accurate inflection (in 3rd person forms). Verb use also including progressive and past tense forms (generally irregular), past participles and verbal nouns. Errors generally involving use of present tense verb forms in past tense contexts, occasional confusion of simple and progressive aspect also recorded.
0.61–0.7 B1	Beatriz	Considerable and diverse range of verb use. Accuracy rates generally over 80%, although with some fluctuation. Verb use including present tense forms (generally uninflected stem verbs and copula *be*), progressive forms and past tense verbs (irregular and regular), and past participles. Errors such as omission of 3rd person *-s* in present tense, over-generalisation of *-ed* ending to irregular past tense verbs (e.g. *hided*) and aspect confusion also recorded.
0.71–0.8 B1	Nasreen	Considerable and increasing verb use. Accuracy rate generally over 80%, with some fluctuation. Diverse range of verb forms produced: simple present tense verbs, including copula *be*, progressive

Maximum proportion of turns at highest recorded proficiency level	Pupil(s)	Features of verb use
		forms, past tense (irregular and regular), past participles and verbal nouns. Errors including omission of 3rd person -*s* in present tense, over-generalisation of past tense -*ed* ending to irregular verbs (e.g. *buyed*), some confusion of simple past and past participle contexts.
0.91–1.0 B1	Fatima	Considerable and diverse verb use. Accuracy rate generally over 80% rising to over 90% towards end of study. Wide range of verbs appropriately produced including: simple present, progressive aspect, and simple past forms, past participles and verbal nouns. Infrequent errors (e.g. present forms in past contexts or over-generalisation of -*ed* ending in past tense).

Overview of pronoun use

Maximum proportion of turns at highest recorded proficiency level	Pupil(s)	Features of pronoun use
A1 only	Zofia	Pronoun use only beginning to emerge in first half of study. Early pronoun use limited to occasional production of personal pronouns, followed by demonstratives and the substitute pronoun *one*. Accuracy of personal pronoun use generally over 80%, although errors involving use of singular pronouns in plural contexts or to indicate possession. Occasional omission of personal pronouns (within context of infrequent use).
0.01–0.1 A2	Karina	Limited pronoun use – personal and demonstrative pronouns, numbers; isolated instances of possessive (*mine*), substitute pronoun and quantifiers (e.g. *all*). Accuracy of personal pronoun use fluctuating considerably (20–100%) throughout selected lessons; errors often involving the use of object pronouns in subject-requiring contexts (e.g. *me* for *I*). Some omission of personal pronouns, generally subject pronouns.
0.11–0.2 A2	Patryk	Initially pronoun use limited to personal and demonstrative pronouns, later diversifying to include numbers, substitute *one*, quantifiers and possessives (*mine*). Accuracy of personal pronoun

Maximum proportion of turns at highest recorded proficiency level	Pupil(s)	Features of pronoun use
		use generally over 90%, although occasional subject/object confusion. Some omission of personal pronouns, generally subject pronouns.
0.21–0.3 A2	Tomasz, Ravi, Dimitrie	Initially pronoun use limited to personal and demonstrative pronouns, later diversifying to include numbers, substitute *one*, indefinites (e.g. *everybody*), and isolated instances of reflexives (*myself*) and the relative pronoun *who*. Accuracy of personal pronoun use varying, although generally over 80%. Errors generally of subject/object confusion, although inaccurate use of singular rather than plural form also recorded. Rate of personal pronoun omission fluctuating, often quite high – subject pronouns generally omitted.
0.31–0.4 A2	Ivan, Jin	Widening range of pronouns used: personal pronouns, demonstratives, quantifiers, numbers; diversifying later to include: substitute pronoun, indefinites, and possessives (*mine*). Accuracy of personal pronoun use often over 90%, although some errors of case and gender recorded. Omission of personal pronouns relatively infrequent, subject pronouns generally omitted.
0.41–0.5 A2	Stefan, Lukas, Edyta	Widening range of pronouns used: personal pronouns, demonstratives, quantifiers, numbers; diversifying later to include: substitute pronoun, indefinites, reflexives (*myself*) and relativising pronouns. Accuracy of personal pronoun use generally over 80%, often over 90%. Some errors recorded such as singular/plural confusion and non-required personal pronoun use. Omission of personal pronouns relatively infrequent, omission rate falling over course of study; generally subject pronouns omitted.
0.51–0.6 A2	Andrei, Constantin, Marko	Widening range of pronouns used: personal pronouns, demonstratives, quantifiers, numbers; diversifying later to include: substitute pronoun, indefinites, possessives, reflexives and relativising pronouns. Accuracy rate for personal pronoun use generally over 80%, sometimes over 90%, although fluctuations also recorded. Errors of case and gender apparent, occasional over-use of personal pronouns. Omission of personal pronouns generally infrequent (omission rates higher towards beginning of study), subject pronouns more likely to be omitted than object pronouns.
0.61–0.7 A2	Vladimir	Widening range of pronouns used: personal pronouns, demonstratives, quantifiers, numbers, indefinites; diversifying later to include: substitute

Maximum proportion of turns at highest recorded proficiency level	Pupil(s)	Features of pronoun use
		pronoun and possessives (e.g. *yours*). Accuracy rate for personal pronouns generally over 90%, with occasional fluctuation. Errors generally of gender choice. Omission of personal pronouns infrequent (either subject or object pronouns).
0.61–0.7 B1	Beatriz	Wide and diversifying range of pronouns used throughout study: personal pronouns, demonstratives, quantifiers, numbers, substitute pronoun, indefinites, possessives, and reflexives. Accuracy rate over 90% throughout. Very occasional error, e.g. gender confusion. Omission of personal pronouns infrequent (either subject or object pronouns).
0.71–0.8 B1	Nasreen	Wide range of pronouns used throughout study: personal pronouns, demonstratives, quantifiers, numbers, substitute pronoun, indefinites, possessives, reflexives and relative pronouns. Accuracy rate over 90% throughout. Omission of personal pronouns very infrequent.
0.91–1.0 B1	Fatima	Wide range of pronouns used throughout study including: personal pronouns, demonstratives, quantifiers, numbers, substitute pronoun, indefinites, reflexives and relative pronouns. Accuracy rate over 90% throughout. Omission of personal pronouns very infrequent.

Overview of article use

Maximum proportion of turns at highest recorded proficiency level	Pupil(s)	Features of article use
A1 only	Zofia	Initially no articles used. Very limited, often inaccurate article use later in study. Articles frequently omitted.
0.01–0.1 A2	Karina	Very limited article use, increasing slightly towards end of study. Accuracy rate generally under 50%, errors generally involving non-required article use, also *a/an* confusion. Article omission rate high, often exceeding rate of article use.
0.11–0.2 A2	Patryk	Very limited article use. Accuracy rate fluctuating (0–100%), although slightly more accurate towards end of study. Errors include use of *the* for *a* and non-required article use. Article omission rate high, often exceeding rate of article use.

Maximum proportion of turns at highest recorded proficiency level	Pupil(s)	Features of article use
0.21–0.3 A2	Tomasz, Ravi, Dimitrie	Very limited article use, increasing somewhat towards end of study. Fluctuating accuracy rate (0–100%), generally over 60% accurate. Errors generally of non-required use or over-use of the definite article. Article omission rate high, although possibly influenced by L1 background of pupil.
0.31–0.4 A2	Ivan, Jin	Increasing article use. Accuracy fluctuating (60–100%), rising towards end of study. Errors generally of non-required use; over-use of the definite article, and use of *a* before vowels also recorded. Article omission rate high, declining slightly towards end of study.
0.41–0.5 A2	Stefan, Lukas, Edyta	Increasing article use. Accuracy generally over 70%, with substantial fluctuation, rising towards end of study. Errors generally of non-required use; over-use of the definite article (also in place of possessive determiner), and use of *a* before vowels recorded. Article omission rate high among most pupils, although lower towards end of study.
0.51–0.6 A2	Andrei, Constantin, Marko	Increasing article use (among most pupils). Accuracy generally over 60%, with fluctuation, rising towards end of study. Errors generally of non-required use; over-use of the definite article (also in place of possessive determiner), and use of *a* before vowels recorded. Articles frequently omitted (particularly by pupil for whom articles were not a feature of L1), but omission rates falling over study period.
0.61–0.7 A2	Vladimir	Increasing article use. Accuracy generally increasing up to and over 80%, but subject to substantial fluctuation (0–100% accurate). Errors generally of non-required use. Omission rates initially very high, dropping considerably across study period.
0.61–0.7 B1	Beatriz	Substantial and increasing article use. Accuracy generally over 80%. Errors generally of non-required use; over-use of the definite article and use of *a* before vowels also recorded. Very low omission rate.
0.71–0.8 B1	Nasreen	Substantial and increasing article use. Accuracy generally over 90%. Errors generally of non-required use; over-use of the definite article and use of *a* before vowels also recorded. Generally, very low omission rate.
0.91–1.0 B1	Fatima	Substantial and increasing article use. Accuracy generally over 90%. Errors generally of non-required use; over-use of the definite article and use of *a* before vowels also recorded. Very low omission rate.

Overview of preposition use

Maximum proportion of turns at highest recorded proficiency level	Pupil(s)	Features of preposition use
A1 only	Zofia	Single instance of preposition use: *at* in final lesson, within phrase: *look at*.
0.01–0.1 A2	Karina	Very limited preposition use, initially in set phrases (e.g. *tidy up*), generally to indicate place or motion (e.g. *in, out*). Generally accurate, although some omission of prepositions.
0.11–0.2 A2	Patryk	Very limited preposition use (emerging prepositions, e.g. *in, with, to, on, for*). Generally accurate although some errors in use of *in* and *on*. Occasional omission of prepositions.
0.21–0.3 A2	Tomasz, Ravi, Dimitrie	Very limited preposition use (emerging prepositions, e.g. *in, on, with, of, for, to*). Accuracy rates generally over 70%, although some fluctuation. Errors generally involving confusion of prepositions, particularly *in* and *on*. Some omission of prepositions.
0.31–0.4 A2	Ivan, Jin	Increasing and more diverse preposition use (e.g. *behind, over, from*). Accuracy rates variable, generally over 60%, rising over course of study. Errors generally of preposition choice, particularly use of *in* rather than *on, to, into* or at. Omission infrequent.
0.41–0.5 A2	Stefan, Lukas, Edyta	Increasing and more diverse preposition use (e.g. *beside, under*). Accuracy rate fluctuating, often over 80%, although occasionally much lower. Errors generally of preposition choice, particularly the inappropriate use of *in* and the over-use of *at* and *for*. Omission infrequent.
0.51–0.6 A2	Andrei, Constantin, Marko	Increasing and more diverse preposition use. Accuracy rate often over 80%, although fluctuating considerably. Errors generally of preposition choice, particularly inappropriate use of *in* and *on* with verbs of motion, and confusion of *for* and *to*. Some omission of prepositions.
0.61–0.7 A2	Vladimir	Increasing and more diverse preposition use. Accuracy rate fluctuating (under 40–100%), although rising towards end of study. Errors generally of preposition choice, particularly the inappropriate use of *in* (for *on, to* or *into*), possibly L1 influenced. Omission infrequent.
0.61–0.7 B1	Beatriz	Diverse and frequent use of prepositions. Accuracy rate generally over 80%, with some fluctuation. Errors generally of preposition choice, particularly the inappropriate use of *in* (for *on* and *at*). Omission very infrequent.

Maximum proportion of turns at highest recorded proficiency level	Pupil(s)	Features of preposition use
0.71–0.8 B1	Nasreen	Diverse and frequent use of prepositions. Accuracy rate generally over 80%, with some fluctuation. Errors generally of preposition choice, particularly the inappropriate use of *in* (for *on, to* or *at*), and *to/for* confusion. Omission very infrequent.
0.91–1.0 B1	Fatima	Diverse and frequent use of prepositions. Accuracy rate generally over 90%, with some fluctuation. Occasional errors in preposition choice, particularly the inappropriate use of *in* and *on*. Omission very infrequent.

Overview of auxiliary use

Maximum proportion of turns at highest recorded proficiency level	Pupil(s)	Features of auxiliary use
A1 only	Zofia	Single instance of auxiliary use recorded – inaccurate use of progressive *be* in context requiring simple present tense.
0.01–0.1 A2	Karina	Very infrequent, generally inaccurate auxiliary use. Single instance of appropriate use of progressive *be*. Errors include syntactically inappropriate *do* and non-required *be*.
0.11–0.2 A2	Patryk	Very limited auxiliary use, often inaccurate. Appropriate auxiliaries used: progressive *be*, modal can, with very isolated attempts at *have* and *going to*. Frequent omission of auxiliaries.
0.21–0.3 A2	Tomasz, Ravi, Dimitrie	Limited auxiliary use, increasing over study period, but often inaccurate. Appropriately used auxiliaries include: *be* (occasional use of past form emerging later), *do* (occasional use of past form emerging later), modal *can*; isolated instances of auxiliaries *have, will* and *going to* emerging towards the end of the study. Errors generally involving non-required use of auxiliary *be*. Omission frequent.
0.31–0.4 A2	Ivan, Jin	Increasing auxiliary use, although often inaccurate. Appropriately used auxiliaries include: *be, do* (occasional use past form emerging later), modals *can* and *have to*; isolated instances of auxiliaries *have, will* and *going to* emerging later in study. Errors involving use of present tense auxiliaries in past tense contexts, use of auxiliary *do* in contexts requiring the perfect tense marker *have*, and inaccurate syntactic placement. Omission frequent.

Maximum proportion of turns at highest recorded proficiency level	Pupil(s)	Features of auxiliary use
0.41–0.5 A2	Stefan, Lukas, Edyta	Increasing auxiliary use, with fluctuating accuracy. Appropriately used auxiliaries include: *be* (occasional use of past form emerging later), *do* (occasional use past form emerging later), modals *can* and *have to*; isolated instances of auxiliaries *have, will, going to*, and the modals *would* and *could* emerging later in study. Errors generally involve non-required use of *be*, and use of present auxiliaries in past tense contexts. Considerable omission, although rate decreasing towards end of study.
0.51–0.6 A2	Andrei, Constantin, Marko	Increasing auxiliary use, with fluctuating accuracy. Appropriately used auxiliaries include: *be* (occasional use of past form emerging later), *do* (occasional use past form emerging later), modals *can* and *have to*; isolated instances of auxiliaries *have, will, going to* emerging later in study. Errors generally involve non-required use of *be*, use of *be* in contexts requiring *do*; non-inflection of *do* in 3rd person present form also recorded. Considerable omission.
0.61–0.7 A2	Vladimir	Generally increasing auxiliary use, with fluctuating accuracy. Appropriately used auxiliaries include: *be, do* (occasional use past form emerging later), modal *can*; isolated instances of auxiliaries *will* and *going to* emerging later in study. Errors generally involve non-required use of *be*; use of *can* in contexts requiring *could* also recorded. Considerable omission.
0.61–0.7 B1	Beatriz	Frequent and diverse use of auxiliaries, generally accurate. Appropriately used auxiliaries include: *be* (present and past forms), *do* (present and past forms), the future referents *will* and *going to*, modals *can, have to*, and *could*; occasional use of the modal *might* and the present perfect tense indicator *have* also recorded. Errors infrequent, generally relating to tense or choice of conditionality marker. Occasional omission.
0.71–0.8 B1	Nasreen	Frequent and diverse use of auxiliaries, generally accurate. Appropriately used auxiliaries include: *be* (present and past forms), *do* (present and past forms), the future referents *will* and *going to*, modals *can, have to*, and *could*. Errors infrequent, generally relating to tense, syntax or choice of conditionality marker. Occasional omission.

Maximum proportion of turns at highest recorded proficiency level	Pupil(s)	Features of auxiliary use
0.91–1.0 B1	Fatima	Frequent and diverse use of auxiliaries, generally accurate. Appropriately used auxiliaries include: *be* (present and past forms), *do* (present and past forms), the future referents *will* and *going to*, modals *can, have to, could* and *would*; occasional use of the modals *must* and *might* and the present perfect tense indicator *have* also recorded. Errors infrequent, generally relating to tense or choice of conditionality marker. Infrequent omission.

Overview of verb-to-noun ratio

Maximum proportion of turns at highest recorded proficiency level	Pupil(s)	Features of verb-to-noun ratio
A1 only	Zofia	Predominantly nominal-based production, verb-to-noun ratio increasing towards end of study.
0.01–0.1 A2	Karina	Predominantly nominal-based production, verb-to-noun ratio increasing towards end of study.
0.11–0.2 A2	Patryk	Predominantly nominal-based production, verb-to-noun ratio increasing towards end of study.
0.21–0.3 A2	Tomasz, Ravi, Dimitrie	Predominantly nominal-based production, verb-to-noun ratio increasing towards end of study. Ratio may be influenced by lesson-related factors (opportunities to create turns more complex than simple noun phrase responses).
0.31–0.4 A2	Ivan, Jin	Verb-to-noun ratio generally in the range 0.4–0.6, fluctuating, with some evidence of gradual increase, across study. Ratio may be influenced by lesson-related factors.
0.41–0.5 A2	Stefan, Lukas, Edyta	Verb-to-noun ratio generally in the range 0.4–0.6, fluctuating, with some evidence of gradual increase, across study. Ratio may be influenced by lesson-related factors.
0.51–0.6 A2	Andrei, Constantin, Marko	Verb-to-noun ratio generally in the range 0.4–0.6, fluctuating, with some evidence of gradual increase, across study. Ratio may be influenced by lesson-related factors.
0.61–0.7 A2	Vladimir	Verb-to-noun ratio generally in the range 0.4–0.6, fluctuating, with some evidence of gradual increase, across study. Ratio may be influenced by lesson-related factors.

Maximum proportion of turns at highest recorded proficiency level	Pupil(s)	Features of verb-to-noun ratio
0.61–0.7 B1	Beatriz	Verb-to-noun ratio reasonably stable (generally in the range 0.4–0.6). Turns becoming structurally more diverse, may require more sensitive indicator of complexity. Lesson-related factors may still impact on ratio.
0.71–0.8 B1	Nasreen	Verb-to-noun ratio reasonably stable (generally in the range 0.4–0.6). Turns becoming structurally more diverse, may require more sensitive indicator of complexity. Lesson-related factors may still impact on ratio.
0.91–1.0 B1	Fatima	Verb-to-noun ratio reasonably stable (generally in the range 0.4–0.6). Turns becoming structurally more diverse, may require more sensitive indicator of complexity. Lesson-related factors may still impact on ratio.

Overview of negative formation

Maximum proportion of turns at highest proficiency level	Pupil(s)	Features of negative formation
A1 only	Zofia	Negative marker *no* predominates, often inaccurately used.
0.01–0.1 A2	Karina	Negative marker *no* predominates, often inaccurately used, single instance of appropriately used *not*.
0.11–0.2 A2	Patryk	Initially negative marker *no* predominates. *Not* beginning to emerge although inaccurate use of *no* persisting throughout.
0.21–0.3 A2	Tomasz, Ravi, Dimitrie	Initially use of *no* as negative marker, *not* emerging later, contractions e.g. *don't* and *can't* developing although auxiliaries may be omitted in structures requiring *not*.
0.31–0.4 A2	Ivan, Jin	Use of *not* generally accurate (some inaccurate use of *no* early in study period), wider range of contractions, e.g. *didn't*, some omission of auxiliaries in negative structures.
0.41–0.5 A2	Stefan, Lukas, Edyta	Use of *not* generally accurate (occasional inaccurate use of *no* and double negation early in study period), contractions produced but auxiliaries sometimes omitted, use of *never* as negative marker.

Maximum proportion of turns at highest proficiency level	Pupil(s)	Features of negative formation
0.51–0.6 A2	Andrei, Constantin, Marko	Use of *not* as negative marker generally accurate (although some inaccurate use of *no* early in study period), range of contractions but auxiliaries sometimes omitted.
0.61–0.7 A2	Vladimir	Accurate use of *not* in full and contracted form.
0.61–0.7 B1	Beatriz	Accurate use of *not* in full form and across a wide range of contractions.
0.71–0.8 B1	Nasreen	Accurate use of *not* in full form and across a wide range of contractions.
0.91–1.0 B1	Fatima	Accurate use of *not* in full form and across a wide range of contractions, accurate use of *never*. Some minor tense-related issues still apparent in negative structures (e.g. *didn't fell*).

Overview of question formation

Maximum proportion of turns at highest proficiency level	Pupil(s)	Features of question formation
A1 only	Zofia	Basic *wh-* questions.
0.01–0.1 A2	Karina	Basic *wh-* questions, phonologically inflected statements, no inversion.
0.11–0.2 A2	Patryk	Initially basic *wh-* questions, attempts at inversion emerging later but infrequent and inaccurate, attempts at indirect questions generally syntactically inaccurate.
0.21–0.3 A2	Tomasz, Ravi, Dimitrie	Initially basic *wh-* questions and phonologically inflected statements, attempts at inversion emerging later, but infrequent and inaccurate, attempts at indirect questions often syntactically inaccurate, very isolated attempts at using a question word as a relativiser.
0.31–0.4 A2	Ivan, Jin	Basic *wh-* questions and attempts at inversion throughout, often inaccurate, however, with omission of auxiliaries after question word, attempts at indirect questions throughout although often syntactically inaccurate, emergence of question-word relativisers.
0.41–0.5 A2	Stefan, Lukas, Edyta	Basic *wh-* questions and attempts at inversion throughout, although frequent omission of required auxiliaries, attempts at indirect questions

Maximum proportion of turns at highest proficiency level	Pupil(s)	Features of question formation
		throughout but often syntactically inaccurate, use of question-word relativisers recorded.
0.51–0.6 A2	Andrei, Constantin, Marko	Basic *wh-* questions and attempts at inversion throughout, although frequent omission of required auxiliaries, attempts at indirect questions throughout but often syntactically inaccurate, wider range of question-word relativisers.
0.61–0.7 A2	Vladimir	Basic *wh-* questions and attempts at inversion throughout, quite accurate, attempts at indirect questions often syntactically inaccurate, use of question-word relativisers.
0.61–0.7 B1	Beatriz	Basic *wh-* and inverted questions generally accurate throughout, indirect questions used but with some syntactic inaccuracy, attempts at question formation in reported speech but some inaccuracies, wider range of question-word relativisers.
0.71–0.8 B1	Nasreen	Basic *wh-* and inverted questions generally accurate throughout, indirect questions used but with some syntactic inaccuracy, wider range of question-word relativisers.
0.91–1.0 B1	Fatima	Basic *wh-* and inverted questions generally accurate throughout, indirect questions used but with some syntactic inaccuracy, attempts at question formation in reported speech although generally articulated as direct speech dialogue, wider range of question-word relativisers.

Overview of clause linkage

Maximum proportion of turns at highest recorded proficiency level	Pupil(s)	Features of clause linkage
A1 only	Zofia	No recorded attempts at clause linkage.
0.01–0.1 A2	Karina	Words linked using conjunction *and*, no recorded attempts at clause linkage.
0.11–0.2 A2	Patryk	Use of simple co-ordinating conjunctions (*and*, occasionally *but*) for clause linkage, isolated use of subordinating conjunction *because*.

Maximum proportion of turns at highest recorded proficiency level	Pupil(s)	Features of clause linkage
0.21–0.3 A2	Tomasz, Ravi, Dimitrie	Use of simple co-ordinating conjunctions (*and*, later attempts at *but* and *or*), occasional use of subordinating conjunctions (generally *because*, but isolated use of *if*), relativisers for clause linkage and attempt at *that* clause, towards end of study.
0.31–0.4 A2	Ivan, Jin	Use of simple co-ordinating conjunctions (*and*, sometimes *but*), occasional use of subordinating conjunctions (*because, if*) and relativisers, generally towards end of study.
0.41–0.5 A2	Stefan, Lukas, Edyta	Use of simple co-ordinating conjunctions (*and*, less frequently *but* and *or*), use of *because* and occasional use of relativisers throughout, use of *if* emerging towards end of study.
0.51–0.6 A2	Andrei, Constantin, Marko	Effective use of co-ordinating conjunctions, use of *because* and some relativisers throughout, *if* emerging towards end of study, isolated attempt at *that* clause.
0.61–0.7 A2	Vladimir	Effective use of co-ordinating conjunctions, use of *because* and relativisers, *if* emerging towards end of study.
0.61–0.7 B1	Beatriz	Effective use of co-ordinating conjunctions, use of subordinating conjunctions (*because, if*) and frequent use of range of relativisers throughout.
0.71–0.8 B1	Nasreen	Effective use of co-ordinating conjunctions, use of subordinating conjunctions (*because, if*) and frequent use of range of relativisers throughout.
0.91–1.0 B1	Fatima	Effective use of co-ordinating conjunctions, use of subordinating conjunctions (*because, if*) and frequent use of range of relativisers throughout, accurate use of *that* clause towards end of study.

Overview of additional lexico-grammatical features revealed in Wordlist data

Maximum proportion of turns at highest recorded proficiency level	Pupil(s)	Lexico-grammatical indicators
A1 only	Zofia	Isolated use of adverbs, basic location markers (e.g. *here*); occasional possessive determiners towards end of study (e.g. *my, your*).

Maximum proportion of turns at highest recorded proficiency level	Pupil(s)	Lexico-grammatical indicators
0.01–0.1 A2	Karina	Use of basic adverbs as location markers (e.g. *here, there*); occasional use of possessive determiners (e.g. *my*).
0.11–0.2 A2	Patryk	Use of basic adverbs as location markers, later to mark frequency (e.g. *again*) or as modifiers (e.g. *very*); isolated, inaccurate use of comparative adjectives.
0.21–0.3 A2	Tomasz, Ravi, Dimitrie	Use of growing range of adverbs to mark location, time or for modification (e.g. *somewhere, now, really*); use of personally relevant possessive determiners (e.g. *my, your*).
0.31–0.4 A2	Ivan, Jin	Use of increasing range of adverbs (e.g. *nearly, altogether*); use of wider range of possessive determiners (e.g. *his*) towards end of study.
0.41–0.5 A2	Stefan, Lukas, Edyta	Use of range of adverbs (e.g. *always, already almost*); use of wider range of possessive determiners (e.g. *their*).
0.51–0.6 A2	Andrei, Constantin, Marko	Use of range of adverbs (e.g. *only, just*); range of possessive determiners; comparative adjectives (e.g. *bigger*) used appropriately.
0.61–0.7 A2	Vladimir	Use of range of adverbs (e.g. *sometimes*); range of possessive determiners (as above).
0.61–0.7 B1	Beatriz	Frequent use of wide range of adverbs throughout; use of wide range of possessive determiners (e.g. *our*); use of comparative and superlative adjectives (e.g. *older, biggest*).
0.71–0.8 B1	Nasreen	Frequent use of wide range of adverbs throughout; use of wide range of possessive determiners (e.g. *our, their*); use of comparative and superlative adjectives (e.g. *brighter, oldest*).
0.91–1.0 B1	Fatima	Frequent use of wide range of adverbs throughout, including more specific modifiers (e.g. *especially, greedily*); use of wide range of possessive determiners; use of comparative and superlative adjectives (e.g. *better, worst*).

References

Abrahamsson, N and Hyltenstam, K (2009) Age of onset and nativelikeness in a second language: Listener perception versus linguistic scrutiny, *Language Learning* 59 (2), 249–306.

Anderson, R (2004) Phonological acquisition in pre-schoolers learning a second language via immersion: A longitudinal study, *Clinical Linguistics and Phonetics* 18, 183–210.

Baker, C L (1997) *English Syntax*, 2nd edition, Cambridge: Massachusetts Institute of Technology Press.

Cambridge Assessment (2007) *Cambridge Assessment Annual Review 2005–2006*, available online: www.cambridgeassessment.org.uk

Central Statistics Office (2012) *This Is Ireland: Highlights from Census 2011, Part 1*, Dublin: Stationery Office.

Christensen, G and Segeritz, M (2008) An international perspective on student achievement, in Bertelsmann Stiftung (Ed), *Immigrant Students Can Succeed: Lessons from Around the Globe*, Gütersloh: Bertelsmann Stiftung, 11–33.

Council of Europe (2001) *Common European Framework of Reference for Languages: Learning, Teaching, Assessment*, Cambridge: Cambridge University Press.

Council of Europe (2005) *Reference Level Descriptions for National and Regional Languages (RLD): Draft Guide*, Strasbourg: Council of Europe, available online: http://www.coe.int/t/dg4/linguistic/Source/DNR_Guide_EN.pdf

Creese, A and Blackledge, A (2010) Translanguaging in the bilingual classroom: A pedagogy for learning and teaching?, *The Modern Language Journal* 94 (1), 103–115.

Cummins, J (1979) Linguistic interdependence and the educational development of bilingual children, *Review of Educational Research* 49, 222–251.

Cummins, J (2000) *Language, Power and Pedagogy: Bilingual Children in the Crossfire*, Clevedon: Multilingual Matters.

Cummins, J (2001) The entry and exit fallacy in bilingual education, in Baker, C and Hornberger, N (Eds) *An Introductory Reader to the Writings of Jim Cummins*, Clevedon: Multilingual Matters, 110–138.

Cummins, J (2013) Language and identity in multilingual schools: Constructing evidence-based instructional policies, in Little, D, Leung, C and Van Avermaet, P (Eds) *Managing Diversity in Education: Languages, Policies, Pedagogies*, Bristol: Multilingual Matters, 3–26.

DeKeyser, R (2003) Implicit and explicit learning, in Doughty, C J and Long, M H (Eds) *The Handbook of Second Language Acquisition*, Oxford: Blackwell, 313–348.

Department of Education and Skills and Office of the Minister for Integration (2010) *Intercultural Education Strategy*, Dublin: Department of Education and Skills and Office of the Minister for Integration.

Dimroth, C (2008) Perspectives on second language acquisition at different ages, in Philp, J, Oliver, R and Mackey, A (Eds) *Second Language Acquisition and the Younger Learner: Child's Play?*, Amsterdam: John Benjamins, 53–79.

Dörnyei, Z (2005) *The Psychology of the Language Learner: Individual Differences in Second Language Acquisition*, Mahwah: Lawrence Erlbaum Associates.

Dörnyei, Z (2007) *Research Methods in Applied Linguistics*, Oxford: Oxford University Press.

Dörnyei, Z and Skehan, P (2003) Individual differences and second language learning, in Doughty, C J and Long, M H (Eds) *The Handbook of Second Language Acquisition*, Oxford: Blackwell, 589–630.

Ellis, R M and Barkhuizen, G (2005) *Analysing Learner Language*, Oxford: Oxford University Press.

Gardner, H (1983) *Frames of Mind. The Theory of Multiple Intelligences*, New York: Basic Books.

Gardner, H (2006) *Multiple Intelligences: New Horizons*, New York: Basic Books.

Gass, S M (2003) Input and interaction, in Doughty, C J and Long, M H (Eds) *The Handbook of Second Language Acquisition*, Oxford: Blackwell, 224–255.

Gass, S and Selinker, L (2008) *Second Language Acquisition: An Introductory Course*, 3rd edition, New York: Routledge.

Green, A (2012) *Language Functions Revisited: Theoretical and Empirical Bases for Language Construct Definition Across the Ability Range*, English Profile Studies volume 2, Cambridge: UCLES/Cambridge University Press.

Hawkins, J A and Filipović, L (2012) *Criterial Features in L2 English: Specifying the Reference Levels of the Common European Framework*, English Profile Studies volume 1, Cambridge: UCLES/Cambridge University Press.

Hellerman, J (2008) *Social Actions for Classroom Language Learning*, Clevedon: Multilingual Matters.

Hulstijn, J H (2007) The shaky ground beneath the CEFR: Quantitative and qualitative dimensions of language proficiency, *Modern Language Journal* 91 (4), 663–667.

Hyltenstam, K and Abrahamsson, N (2003) Maturational constraints in SLA, in Doughty, C J and Long, M H (Eds) *The Handbook of Second Language Acquisition*, Oxford: Blackwell, 539–588.

Integrate Ireland Language and Training (2003a) *English Language Proficiency Benchmarks for Non-English-speaking Pupils at Primary Level*, Version 2.0, Dublin: Integrate Ireland Language and Training, available online: www.ncca. ie/iilt

Integrate Ireland Language and Training (2003b) *English Language Proficiency Benchmarks for Non-English-speaking Students at Post-primary Level*, Version 2.0, Dublin: Integrate Ireland Language and Training, available online: www. ncca.ie/iilt

Integrate Ireland Language and Training (2004a) *European Language Portfolio (Primary): Learning the Language of the Host Community*, Dublin: Integrate Ireland Language and Training, available online: www.ncca.ie/iilt

Integrate Ireland Language and Training (2004b) *European Language Portfolio (Post-primary): Learning the Language of the Host Community*, Dublin: Integrate Ireland Language and Training, available online: www.ncca.ie/iilt

Integrate Ireland Language and Training (2005) *My First English Book*, Dublin: Integrate Ireland Language and Training, available online: www.ncca.ie/iilt

Integrate Ireland Language and Training (2006a) *Integrate Ireland Language and Training: Annual Activities Report 2005*, Dublin: Integrate Ireland Language and Training.

Integrate Ireland Language and Training (2006b) *Up and Away: A Resource Book for English Language Support in Primary Schools*, Dublin: Integrate Ireland Language and Training, available online: www.ncca.ie/iilt

Integrate Ireland Language and Training and Southern Education and Library Board (2007) *Together Towards Inclusion: Toolkit for Diversity in the Primary School*, Dublin/Armagh: Integrate Ireland Language and Training/Southern Education and Library Board, available online: www.ncca.ie/iilt

Johnson, L and Newport, E (1989) Critical period effects in second language learning: The influence of maturational state on the acquisition of English as a second language, *Cognitive Psychology* 21, 60–99.

Kirwan, D (2013) From English language support to plurilingual awareness, in Little, D, Leung, C and Van Avermaet, P (Eds), *Managing Diversity in Education*, Bristol: Multilingual Matters, 191–205.

Klammer, T, Schultz, M R and Della Volpe, A (2006) *Analysing English Grammar*, 5th edition, New York: Pearson Education.

Lakshmanan, U (2009) Child second language acquisition, in Bhatia, T and Ritchie, W (Eds) *A New Handbook of Second Language Acquisition*, Bingley: Emerald Group, 377–399.

Levinson, S (1983) *Pragmatics*, Cambridge: Cambridge University Press.

Liddicoat, A (2007) *An Introduction to Conversation Analysis*, London: Continuum.

Little, D (2006) The Common European Framework of Reference for Languages: Content, purpose, origin, reception and impact, *Language Teaching* 39 (3), 167–190.

Little, D (2009) *The European Language Portfolio: Where pedagogy and assessment meet*, paper presented at the 8th International Seminar on the European Language Portfolio, Graz, 29 September–1 October 2009, available online: www.coe.int/t/dg4/education/elp/elp-reg/Publications_EN.asp

Little, D (2010) *The Linguistic and Educational Integration of Children and Adolescents from Migrant Backgrounds*, Strasbourg: Council of Europe, available online: www.coe.int/t/dg4/linguistic/ListDocs_Geneva2010.asp

Little, D (2011) The Common European Framework of Reference for Languages: a research agenda, *Language Teaching* 44 (3), 381–393.

Little, D, Lazenby Simpson, B and Finnegan Ćatibušić, B (2007) *Primary School Assessment Kit*, Dublin: Department of Education and Science, available online: www.ncca.ie/iilt

Lyons, Z and Little, D (2009) *English Language Support in Irish Post-primary Schools: Policy, Challenges and Deficits*, Dublin: Trinity College, available online: www.elsp.ie/theReport.shtml

McGorman, E and Sugrue, S (2007) *Intercultural Education: Primary Challenges in Dublin 15*, Dublin: Stationery Office.

McKay, P (2006) *Assessing Young Language Learners*, Cambridge: Cambridge University Press.

Morley, G D (2004) *Explorations in Functional Syntax: A New Framework for Lexicogrammatical Analysis*, London: Equinox.

Muñoz, C (2006) Effects of age on foreign language learning: The BAF Project, in Muñoz, C (Ed) *Age and the Rate of Foreign Language Learning*, Clevedon: Multilingual Matters, 1–40.

National Council for Curriculum and Assessment (1999) *Primary School Curriculum*, Dublin: National Council for Curriculum and Assessment, available online: www.ncca.ie/en/Curriculum_and_Assessment/

Early_Childhood_and_Primary_Education/Primary_School_Curriculum/
Assessment/Assessment_Guidelines/

National Council for Curriculum and Assessment (2005) *Intercultural Education in the Primary School: Guidelines for Teachers,* Dublin: National Council for Curriculum and Assessment, available online: www.ncca.ie/uploadedfiles/publications/Intercultural.pdf

National Council for Curriculum and Assessment (2006) *English as an Additional Language in Irish Primary Schools: Guidelines for Teachers*, Dublin: National Council for Curriculum and Assessment, available online: www.ncca.ie/uploadedfiles/publications/EALangIPS(1).pdf

Nelson, K (1985) *Making Sense: The Acquisition of Shared Meaning*, New York: Academic Press.

Nicholas, H and Lightbown, P M (2008) Defining child second language acquisition, defining roles for L2 instruction, in Philp, J, Oliver, R and Mackey, A (Eds) *Second Language Acquisition and the Younger Learner: Child's Play?,* Amsterdam: John Benjamins, 27–51.

Odlin, T (2003) Cross-linguistic influence, in Doughty, C J and Long, M H (Eds) *The Handbook of Second Language Acquisition*, Oxford: Blackwell, 436–486.

Organisation for Economic Co-operation and Development (2004) *Messages from PISA 2000*, Paris: Organisation for Economic Co-operation and Development.

Organisation for Economic Co-operation and Development (2006) *Where immigrant students succeed: A comparative review of performance and engagement in PISA 2003*, OECD briefing note for Germany, Paris: Organisation for Economic Co-operation and Development, available online: www.oecd.org/pisa/pisaproducts/pisa2003/36701527.doc

Organisation for Economic Co-operation and Development (2010) *PISA 2009 Results: Overcoming Social Background – Equity in Learning Opportunities and Outcomes (Volume II)*, Paris: Organisation for Economic Co-operation and Development, available online: dx.doi.org/10.1787/9789264091504-en

Peters, A (1977) Language learning strategies: Does the whole equal the sum of the parts?, *Language* 53 (3), 560–573.

Philp, J, Mackey, A and Oliver, R (2008) Child's play? Second language acquisition and the younger learner in context, in Philp, J, Oliver, R and Mackey, A (Eds) *Second Language Acquisition and the Younger Learner: Child's Play?*, Amsterdam: John Benjamins, 3–23.

Pienemann, M (2005) *Cross-linguistic Aspects of Processability Theory*, Amsterdam: John Benjamins.

Reid, J (1987) The learning style preferences of ESL students, *TESOL Quarterly* 21, 87–111.

Richards, K and Seedhouse, P (2005) *Applying Conversation Analysis*, Basingstoke: Palgrave Macmillan.

Romaine, S (2003) Variation, in Doughty, C J and Long M H (Eds) *The Handbook of Second Language Acquisition*, Oxford: Blackwell, 409–435.

Schegloff, E (2007) *Sequence Organization in Interaction: A Primer in Conversation Analysis*, Volume 1, Cambridge: Cambridge University Press.

Schiffrin, D (1994) *Approaches to Discourse*, Oxford: Blackwell.

Sidnell, J (2009) Comparative perspectives in conversation analysis, in Sidnell, J (Ed) *Conversation Analysis: Comparative Perspectives*, Cambridge: Cambridge University Press, 3–27.

Sierens, S and Van Avermaet, P (2013) Language diversity in education: Evolving from multilingual education to functional multilingual learning, in Little,

D, Leung, C and Van Avermaet, P (Eds) *Managing Diversity in Education: Languages, Policies, Pedagogies*, Bristol: Multilingual Matters, 206–224.

Singleton, D and Ryan, L (2004) *Language Acquisition: The Age Factor*, 2nd edition, Clevedon: Multilingual Matters.

Smyth, E, Darmody, M, McGinnity, F and Byrne, D (2009) *Adapting to Diversity: Irish Schools and Newcomer Students*, Dublin: Economic and Social Research Institute.

Swain, M (2000) The output hypothesis and beyond: Mediating acquisition through collaborative dialogue, in Lantolf, J P (Ed) *Sociocultural Theory and Second Language Learning*, Oxford: Oxford University Press, 97–114.

ten Have, P (2007) *Doing Conversation Analysis*, London: Sage.

Vygotsky, L S (1978) *Mind in Society: The Development of Higher Psychological Processes*, Cambridge: Harvard University Press.

Watson-Gegeo, K A and Nielsen, S (2003) Language socialization in SLA, in Doughty, C J and Long, M H (Eds) *The Handbook of Second Language Acquisition*, Oxford: Blackwell, 155–177.

Young, R F (2007) Language learning and teaching as discursive practice, in Hua, Z, Seedhouse, P, Wei, L and Cook, V (Eds) *Language Learning and Teaching as Social Interaction*, Houndmills: Palgrave Macmillan, 251–271.

Author index

Subject index